ECONOMIC AND SOCIAL SURVEY OF ASIA AND THE PACIFIC 2006

Energizing the global economy

ECONOMIC AND SOCIAL COMMISSION FOR ASIA AND THE PACIFIC

The work is published for
and on behalf of the United Nations

ACADEMIC FOUNDATION

The secretariat of the Economic and Social Commission for Asia and the Pacific (ESCAP) is the regional development arm of the United Nations and serves as the main economic and social development centre for the United Nations in Asia and the Pacific. Its mandate is to foster cooperation between its 53 members and 9 associate members. It provides the strategic link between global and country-level programmes and issues. It supports Governments of countries in the region in consolidating regional positions and advocates regional approaches to meeting the region's unique socio-economic challenges in a globalizing world. The ESCAP secretariat is located in Bangkok, Thailand. Please visit the ESCAP website at <www.unescap.org> for further information.

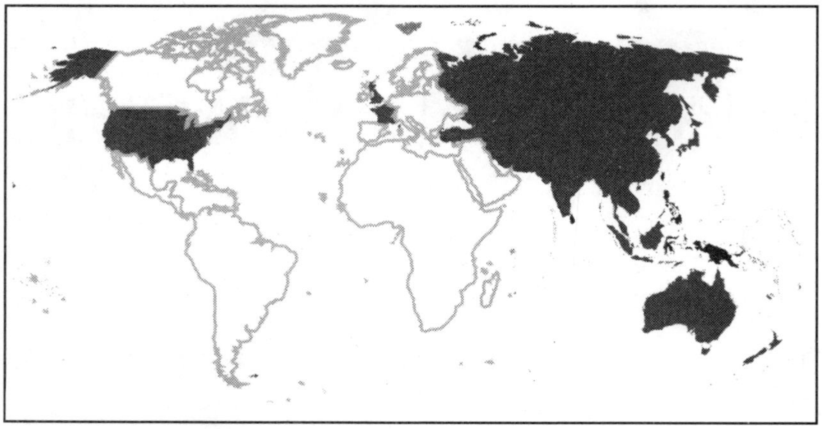

The shaded areas of the map indicate ESCAP members and associate members.

Cover design by Bryan Joseph Granados Sabroso

UNITED NATIONS PUBLICATION

The work is published for and
on behalf of the United Nations
by

ACADEMIC FOUNDATION

4772 / 23, Bharat Ram Road, (23 Ansari Road),
Darya Ganj, New Delhi - 110 002.

Tel : +91-11-23245001 / 02 / 03 / 04
Fax : +91-11-23245005
e-mail : academic@vsnl.com
www.academicfoundation.com

ISBN 81-7188-569-1

This edition is printed in India in 2006

FOREWORD

Many economies in the ESCAP region continue to perform impressively, and the region as a whole is now a major contributor to global growth. In 2005, growth in gross domestic product slowed only slightly, and inflation remained mild by historical standards despite high energy prices. The risks associated with global imbalances and the danger that avian influenza could develop into a pandemic loom in the background. But the broad consensus of opinion among experts is that such risks are unlikely to affect the region's progress in 2006.

Still, the region continues to face serious and urgent demands. In many countries, economic growth is not generating enough well-paying jobs or even enough to absorb new entrants to the workforce. Inequality within countries appears to be on the rise. The environment continues to deteriorate, with deforestation, biodiversity loss, soil degradation, and air and water pollution constantly on the rise. Across the region, the least developed and Pacific island countries remain marginalized, unable to participate fully in the region's dynamism. South Asia, where GDP growth rates have risen dramatically in the last two years, must sustain that growth and translate it into a better quality of life for the poor. Central Asian economies are making good progress, but integration into the wider global economy remains a daunting challenge. In East and South-East Asia, pockets of poverty continue to exist.

Thus there is no room for complacency. Governments must continue to strive for development through a combination of macroeconomic prudence and strong investment in the future – in physical, social and human assets – so that the pace of progress can be maintained and its fruits shared more equitably.

As a document of record, and one which has sought to encapsulate and analyse the changing panorama of this vast and diverse part of the world over many years, the *Economic and Social Survey of Asia and the Pacific* performs a valuable service for readers both in the ESCAP region and elsewhere. The 2006 *Survey* also provides Governments in the region with a range of policy options for dealing with the challenges facing them in the years ahead. I commend it to a wide global audience.

Kofi A. Annan
Secretary-General

March 2006

ACKNOWLEDGEMENTS

The *Economic and Social Survey of Asia and the Pacific 2006* was prepared primarily by the Poverty and Development Division of the ESCAP secretariat with important contributions made by the Least Developed Countries Coordination Unit, Office of the Executive Secretary, the Trade and Investment Division and the Emerging Social Issues Division.

Ravi Ratnayake, Chief, Poverty and Development Division, was responsible for overall production and led a team of experts from within and outside the ESCAP secretariat with the assistance of Shamika Sirimanne, Shahid Ahmed, Amarakoon Bandara and Eugene Gherman. The staff members of the Poverty and Development Division who prepared the *Survey 2006* included: Shahid Ahmed, Amarakoon Bandara, Shuvojit Banerjee, Pradip Bhatnagar, Eugene Gherman, Nobuko Kajiura, Muhammad H. Malik, Syed Nuruzzaman, Hiren Sarkar, Seok-Dong Wang and Juthathip Jongwanich. Inputs for the *Survey 2006* also came from Aynul Hasan, Hirohito Toda and Marin Yari of the Least Developed Countries Coordination Unit. Staff analysis was based on data and information available up to the end of February 2006. Research assistance was provided by Somchai Congtavinsutti, Kiatkanid Pongpanich and Amornrut Supornsinchai. All graphics work was done by Somchai Congtavinsutti. The logistics of processing and administrative action were handled by Dusdeemala Kanittanon and Woranut Sompitayanurak.

Major inputs for the *Survey 2006* were received from the following external consultants: Mushtaq Ahmad, Tarun Das, Ron Duncan, Muhammad Allah Malik Kazemi, Yuba Raj Khatiwada, Mohammad Korbache, Panom Lathouly, George Manzano, Hang Chuon Naron, Penjore, and Vo Tri Thanh.

The substantive editing of the manuscript was provided by Communications Development Incorporated headed by Bruce Ross-Larson. The support, comments and contributions from the Statistics Division, the Editorial Unit, and other Divisions in the ESCAP are noted with appreciation.

EXECUTIVE SUMMARY

The global economy grew by 3.2 per cent in 2005, down from growth of 4.0 per cent in 2004. Notwithstanding the slight deceleration, performance in 2005 was remarkable in view of an increasingly adverse economic environment, led by high and volatile oil prices, widening current account imbalances and a softening of global trade. Economic growth in 2005 was driven essentially by the strong performance of China and the United States of America. The growth rate of ESCAP developing countries decelerated moderately, by about 1 percentage point, in 2005 owing largely to high oil and commodity prices and the global slowdown in trade.

The rise in oil and other commodity prices did, however, increase inflation in 2005 relative to 2004, although the increase in prices throughout the region remained mild by historical standards. Economies adjusted well to the higher oil and commodity prices, some attenuating the effects of those prices by continuing to subsidize petroleum products and others by pre-emptively tightening monetary policy, and these measures served to dampen inflationary expectations. Prospects for the ESCAP region for 2006 indicate that output growth should maintain its current momentum while price pressures are likely to abate somewhat despite continuing high energy and commodity prices.

The principal policy issues and challenges facing the region over the next 12 months are concerned with the course of oil prices, the threat of global external payment imbalances unwinding precipitously, the impact of higher interest rates and the potential for the avian influenza to develop into a human pandemic. Longer-term issues relate to the ongoing challenge of poverty reduction, utilizing the benefits of home remittances to simultaneously improve social indicators and macroeconomic fundamentals, and re-energizing the trade liberalization agenda following the Sixth World Trade Organization Ministerial Conference, held in Hong Kong, China, in December 2005.

Oil prices

Oil prices have doubled since the beginning of 2004 and have trebled since 2002 as global demand has exceeded limited supplies, especially of petroleum products. Despite the high prices of oil there has been no sign yet of a major global economic slowdown. Notwithstanding these factors, the Asian and Pacific region, which is highly dependent on oil, remains vulnerable to any significant increase in oil prices in 2006. ESCAP forecasts assume that oil prices in 2006 will be similar to those prevailing in 2005, i.e., in the $50-$55 range. However, net oil-importing countries need to take steps to prepare for the risk of a large increase in oil prices both to mitigate the adverse social impact of such prices as well as to counter their negative macroeconomic effects.

In this regard, streamlining the existing system of subsidies is clearly warranted, particularly when the subsidies do not reach the intended groups. In view of the fiscal burden on Governments, subsidies on fuel types that are not widely used by the poor could be phased out. Within the region, the least developed countries in particular face significant vulnerabilities as a result of rising oil prices. These countries have little access to alternative sources of financing to cushion a temporary increase in balance of payments deficits caused by high oil prices. Therefore, international financial institutions need to provide, or arrange, financial assistance for these countries as was done in the 1970s through the oil facility of the International Monetary Fund. Net oil exporters of the region, for example in Central Asia, also need to adjust to rising income from oil. The focus should be on efficiently managing the oil windfalls without jeopardizing short-term macroeconomic stability, as there is likely to be pressure on real exchange rates to appreciate.

Both oil-importing and -exporting countries should take steps to develop a longer-term policy response to reduce their dependency on oil, improve energy efficiency and promote energy conservation. Rationalization of energy pricing, greater public awareness of alternative energy options, improved regulations to ensure a minimum level of energy efficiency and fiscal incentives to reduce energy consumption are some of the measures that have already proven to be effective in various settings. Their wider application should be promoted as a matter of priority in the region.

External payment imbalances

The widening imbalances in the external accounts of major economies in the world pose a major risk for the economy of the Asian and Pacific region in 2006. A rapid unwinding of these imbalances could create large upheavals in the international financial markets and cause significant exchange rate instability not merely involving the dollar but perhaps several currencies in the region. Such a phenomenon would, in turn, have a negative impact on the regional economy by making consumers and investors more risk averse, tempting them to divert more savings into real estate and precious metals than is currently the case. However, there is only limited scope for action to address this problem at the national level.

An appropriate policy approach would be to view current account imbalances as a reflection of a structural mismatch between domestic savings and investment. Those countries with excess savings over investments tend to run current account surpluses. The opposite is true for low-saving countries. Remedying the imbalances therefore would require higher investment in the surplus countries and higher savings in deficit countries, the United States in particular.

In view of the widespread negative implications that an abrupt and large-scale unwinding of global current account imbalances would have if Governments depend on financial markets alone, a concerted multilateral response is certainly needed. Rather than trying to correct imbalances that may lead to sharp contractions in the wider global or regional economies, a more effective solution would be to strive for a balanced, medium-term approach, with exchange rate adjustments effected over a period, within an agreed regional framework, for example.

Impact of higher interest rates

An important issue with which economies in the region would have to deal in 2006 is the potentially adverse impact on growth of tighter fiscal and monetary policies. For a number of years, many countries have been following a policy of fiscal consolidation, with a view to reducing the growing burden of public debt and providing more opportunities for private investment activity. Inflationary pressures induced by higher oil prices have resulted in a tightening of monetary policy, with interest rates generally rising across countries in the region, although some countries are notable exceptions.

Reinforcing the effects of long-term fiscal consolidation, especially in countries where it is being brought about through cuts in government expenditure rather than through improved tax revenues, are higher interest rates. They are bound to adversely affect the pace of economic activity. A particular danger exists in those economies where low interest rates have fuelled strong growth in debt-financed private consumption and have created asset bubbles in real estate and in stock markets.

In this regard, higher interest rates should prove less deleterious for economic growth than cuts in government spending, especially in the poorer developing countries where government development expenditure is often the key to the pace of development. However, in the richer developing countries where real interest rates are already high, a further significant increase could trigger a hard landing of the economy through a sharp decline in asset prices. Thus, the policy challenge is to mix fiscal and monetary policies judiciously so as to ensure steady growth in output over the next 12 to 18 months. Most investors value policy predictability; Governments should therefore develop medium-term scenarios for GDP growth, inflation and budgetary and balance-of-payments outcomes through a process of consultation with all relevant stakeholders.

Avian influenza

From December 2003 to the beginning of February 2006, 161 people in the region have been infected with avian influenza and 86 of them died. No vaccine is currently available to protect humans from avian influenza. The number of people who might die in a possible global pandemic if the highly pathogenic avian influenza becomes transmissible between humans range from an estimated 5 million to 150 million people worldwide. Should such a pandemic occur, it would inevitably cause massive disruptions to everyday life through overloaded health-care systems, widespread quarantines and travel restrictions, among others. As a conservative estimate, the loss in GDP globally from such a pandemic could amount to $200 billion in a single quarter and in the worst case scenario could plunge the global economy into recession.

Given these risks, there is an urgent need for collective preparedness in the region involving the stockpiling of medical supplies and the taking of joint action on possible control measures, such as travel restrictions, to prevent the spread of the disease if a pandemic occurs. It is also important from the standpoint of cost-effectiveness to concentrate resources and action on controlling the disease at its source before it develops into a more rapidly spreading contagion.

The ongoing challenges of poverty and inequality

Although the Asian and Pacific region has been growing faster than most regions of the world for two decades or more, the eradication of extreme poverty remains its most important challenge. In tackling the problem of poverty it is important to remember that rapid growth remains the surest route to reducing both income poverty and non-income poverty. Rapid economic growth provides opportunities for employment in both the formal and informal sectors of an economy. It also generates resources for the public sector whereby issues of non-income poverty, such as insufficient or poor-quality public goods (education, health, transport and housing), can be meaningfully addressed.

However, rapid economic growth alone may not be enough. In countries where poverty is widespread, jobs and income growth alone do not seem to make a positive impact on non-income poverty. In such cases, the Governments concerned need to intervene in order to make the growth process more equitable by significantly expanding the provision of, and access to, public goods, particularly for and by the poor.

Remittances

Remittances sent to their families by migrants and temporary workers on contract abroad have greatly helped to raise the standard of living of some of the poorest sections of society in countries in South Asia, South-East Asia and the Pacific. Governments in these and other countries with high levels of underemployment and with limited opportunities for employment in the formal sector could follow the example set by the Philippines and systematically promote the temporary export of workers as a part of their national development and poverty-reduction strategies.

Countries facing general labour shortages or lacking workers with specific skills should consider allowing migrants to work legally in their economies. Such a policy approach would have a positive impact on the unemployment problem in many countries of the region and lead to a better utilization of skills across different subregions.

The WTO agenda

The previously mentioned Sixth WTO Ministerial Conference concluded with the adoption of a wide-ranging ministerial declaration. While the declaration puts the Doha round back on track, an issue of fundamental importance is whether it holds the promise that the Doha round will ultimately correct the development deficit of the Uruguay round. A key challenge facing ESCAP members and associate members over the next year will be finding ways to reinvigorate the Doha development agenda.

ESCAP developing countries are likely to be challenged in the months ahead to make concessions of a commercial value so that developed countries will remain committed to the development process. Thus, the trade-dependent countries of the region need to determine ways to harness the traditional reciprocity dynamics of WTO to move forward on their market access expectations. At the same time, a jump-start will be needed to open up the service sector. Efforts to do so by some increasingly dynamic service exporters in this region would be worthy of further support by other developing countries in Asia and the Pacific.

Emerging issues of unemployment in the region: rising to the challenges

The number of people unemployed in East Asia increased from 4 million in 1992 to 9 million in 2002, while the number in South-East Asia and the Pacific increased from 5.5 million to 14.6 million in the same period. Total unemployment in South Asia increased by 7 million over the same period. Unemployment is highly concentrated among youth throughout the region. However, among children between the ages of 5 and 14, sadly too many are employed. The region harbours an estimated 127 million or 52 per cent of the world's 246 million working children. As for underemployment, the problem is even more widespread than unemployment, particularly in rural areas.

Jobless growth

There are two major reasons for high unemployment and underemployment. First, the rate of growth of the labour force is high. Second, the pace of job creation has not kept up with that growth. In addition demand for labour has been declining owing to technological changes and the considerable downsizing that has occurred in public sector employment following privatization in some countries. There is widespread concern that many countries in the region are achieving high output growth at the expense of employment creation. The charge of jobless growth is being made, particularly in rapidly growing economies where the rate of unemployment has recently tended to rise.

Working poor

A large number of those employed in countries in the region earn paltry wages. The share of the working poor measured in terms of those earning less than $2 a day (defined in terms of purchasing power parity) in total employment in 2003 was 88 per cent in South Asia, 59 per cent in South-East Asia and 49 per cent in East Asia. Data indicate that the vast majority of such people earn wages that are just above the $1 a day poverty line. As a result, the likelihood of the working poor sliding into extreme poverty because of internal or external shocks is very high.

Improving the functioning of labour markets is of vital importance in tackling the problem of unemployment. In the formal sector, the region's labour markets are excessively rigid. The low level of education among workers and the mismatch of educational attainment and the skills demanded by the private sector are major causes of unemployment.

Youth unemployment

Compulsory education up to a reasonable age could help to address the complex problem of child labour. Educational reforms in countries where female unemployment is high or the female participation rate is low may break this vicious circle by providing a more conducive socio-cultural environment in which women could receive an education. This would improve their productivity and help in eliminating wage and employment discrimination against women. Enhancing the employability of youth, but not children, should be a key component of labour-market policies and educational reforms.

Policy responses

Striking the right balance between high growth and employment creation requires measures to improve the productivity of workers in niche industries while focusing on sectors where the majority of labour is concentrated, giving particular emphasis to capacity-building. In agriculture, land reform, extension services, the provision of credit, crop diversification and rural infrastructural development would obviously play a critical role in this respect. Improved marketing facilities and cooperative organizations could also be effective instruments in advancing rural employment.

In both rural and urban areas the development of micro- and small- and medium-sized enterprises has the greatest potential for generating employment and this process needs to be facilitated by providing business with a conducive environment, in particular by reducing entry costs, by providing institutional support, by building capacity and by implementing the principles of good governance.

In this regard, employers also need to display better corporate responsibility by providing opportunities for the training and retraining of workers, collaborating with the public sector in enabling unemployed youth to obtain training and by ensuring workplace safety and the welfare of employees.

International migration could play a valuable supporting role in stabilizing the labour markets of both labour-importing and -exporting countries. In this respect, the organized flow of persons under a global framework such as Mode 4 of the WTO General Agreement on Trade in Services could create tangible benefits for all the countries concerned.

CONTENTS

CONTENTS *(continued)*

BOXES

TABLES

FIGURES

FIGURES *(continued)*

Page

FIGURES *(continued)*

FIGURES *(continued)*

Page

EXPLANATORY NOTES

The term "ESCAP region" is used in the present issue of the *Survey* to include Afghanistan; American Samoa; Armenia; Australia; Azerbaijan; Bangladesh; Bhutan; Brunei Darussalam; Cambodia; China; Cook Islands; Democratic People's Republic of Korea; Fiji; French Polynesia; Georgia; Guam; Hong Kong, China; India; Indonesia; Iran (Islamic Republic of); Japan; Kazakhstan; Kiribati; Kyrgyzstan; Lao People's Democratic Republic; Macao, China; Malaysia; Maldives; Marshall Islands; Micronesia (Federated States of); Mongolia; Myanmar; Nauru; Nepal; New Caledonia; New Zealand; Niue; Northern Mariana Islands; Pakistan; Palau; Papua New Guinea; Philippines; Republic of Korea; Russian Federation; Samoa; Singapore; Solomon Islands; Sri Lanka; Tajikistan; Thailand; Timor-Leste; Tonga; Turkey; Turkmenistan; Tuvalu; Uzbekistan; Vanuatu; and Viet Nam. The term "developing ESCAP region" excludes Australia, Japan and New Zealand. Non-regional members of ESCAP are France, the Netherlands, the United Kingdom of Great Britain and Northern Ireland and the United States of America.

The term "Central Asian countries" in this issue of the *Survey* refers to Armenia, Azerbaijan, Georgia, Kazakhstan, Kyrgyzstan, Tajikistan, Turkmenistan and Uzbekistan.

The term "East and North-East Asia" in this issue of the *Survey* refers to China; Hong Kong, China; Mongolia; and the Republic of Korea.

The designations employed and the presentation of the material in this publication do not imply the expression of any opinion whatsoever on the part of the Secretariat of the United Nations concerning the legal status of any country, territory, city or area, or of its authorities, or concerning the delimitation of its frontiers or boundaries.

Mention of firm names and commercial products does not imply the endorsement of the United Nations.

The abbreviated title *Survey* in footnotes refers to the *Economic and Social Survey of Asia and the Pacific* for the year indicated.

Many figures used in the *Survey* are on a fiscal year basis and are assigned to the calendar year which covers the major part or second half of the fiscal year.

Growth rates are on an annual basis, except where indicated otherwise.

Reference to "tons" indicates metric tons.

Values are in United States dollars unless specified otherwise.

The term "billion" signifies a thousand million. The term "trillion" signifies a million million.

In the tables, two dots (..) indicate that data are not available or are not separately reported, a dash (–) indicates that the amount is nil or negligible, and a blank indicates that the item is not applicable.

In dates, a hyphen (-) is used to signify the full period involved, including the beginning and end years, and a stroke (/) indicates a crop year, fiscal year or plan year. The fiscal years, currencies and 2005 exchange rates of the economies in the ESCAP region are listed in the following table:

Country or area in the ESCAP region	*Fiscal year*	*Currency and abbreviation*	*Rate of exchange for $1 as at November 2005*
Afghanistan	21 March to 20 March	afghani (Af)	3 000.00
American Samoa	..	United States dollar ($)	1.00
Armenia	1 January to 31 December	dram	449.35
Australia	1 July to 30 June	Australian dollar ($A)	1.34
Azerbaijan	1 January to 31 December	Azeri manat (AZM)	4 593.00[a]
Bangladesh	1 July to 30 June	taka (Tk)	65.85
Bhutan	1 July to 30 June	ngultrum (Nu)	45.94
Brunei Darussalam	1 January to 31 December	Brunei dollar (B$)	1.69
Cambodia	1 January to 31 December	riel (CR)	4 166.00
China	1 January to 31 December	yuan renminbi (Y)	8.08
Cook Islands	1 April to 31 March	New Zealand dollar ($NZ)	1.43
Democratic People's Republic of Korea	..	won (W)	141.50
Fiji	1 January to 31 December	Fiji dollar (F$)	1.73
French Polynesia	..	French Pacific Community franc (FCFP)	94.70[b]

Country or area in the ESCAP region	*Fiscal year*	*Currency and abbreviation*	*Rate of exchange for $1 as at November 2005*
Georgia	1 January to 31 December	lari (L)	1.79
Guam	1 October to 30 September	United States dollar ($)	1.00
Hong Kong, China	1 April to 31 March	Hong Kong dollar (HK$)	7.75
India	1 April to 31 March	Indian rupee (Rs)	45.94
Indonesia	1 April to 31 March	Indonesian rupiah (Rp)	10 035.00
Iran (Islamic Republic of)	21 March to 20 March	Iranian rial (Rls)	9 077.00
Japan	1 April to 31 March	yen (¥)	119.63
Kazakhstan	1 January to 31 December	tenge (T)	134.07
Kiribati	1 January to 31 December	Australian dollar ($A)	1.34
Kyrgyzstan	1 January to 31 December	som (som)	41.19
Lao People's Democratic Republic	1 October to 30 September	new kip (NK)	10 855.00[c]
Macao, China	1 July to 30 June	pataca (P)	8.00
Malaysia	1 January to 31 December	ringgit (M$)	3.77[d]
Maldives	1 January to 31 December	rufiyaa (Rf)	12.80
Marshall Islands	1 October to 30 September	United States dollar ($)	1.00
Micronesia (Federated States of)	1 October to 30 September	United States dollar ($)	1.00
Mongolia	1 January to 31 December	tugrik (Tug)	1 221.00[d]
Myanmar	1 April to 31 March	kyat (K)	5.96
Nauru	1 July to 30 June	Australian dollar ($A)	1.33
Nepal	16 July to 15 July	Nepalese rupee (NRs)	74.10
New Caledonia	..	French Pacific Community franc (FCFP)	94.70[b]
New Zealand	1 April to 31 March	New Zealand dollar ($NZ)	1.43
Niue	1 April to 31 March	New Zealand dollar ($NZ)	1.43
Northern Mariana Islands	1 October to 30 September	United States dollar ($)	1.00
Pakistan	1 July to 30 June	Pakistan rupee (PRs)	59.78
Palau	1 October to 30 September	United States dollar ($)	1.00
Papua New Guinea	1 January to 31 December	kina (K)	3.09
Philippines	1 January to 31 December	Philippine peso (P)	54.00
Republic of Korea	1 January to 31 December	won (W)	1 033.50
Russian Federation	1 January to 31 December	ruble (R)	28.73
Samoa	1 July to 30 June	tala (WS$)	2.74
Singapore	1 April to 31 March	Singapore dollar (S$)	1.69
Solomon Islands	1 January to 31 December	Solomon Islands dollar (SI$)	7.58[d]
Sri Lanka	1 January to 31 December	Sri Lanka rupee (SL Rs)	102.00
Tajikistan	1 January to 31 December	somoni	3.20
Thailand	1 October to 30 September	baht (B)	41.17
Timor-Leste	1 July to 30 June	United States dollar ($)	1.00
Tonga	1 July to 30 June	pa'anga (T$)	1.97[d]
Turkey	1 January to 31 December	Turkish lira (LT)	1.35
Turkmenistan	1 January to 31 December	Turkmen manat (M)	5 200.00
Tuvalu	1 January to 31 December	Australian dollar ($A)	1.33
Uzbekistan	1 January to 31 December	som (som)	1 152.00
Vanuatu	1 January to 31 December	vatu (VT)	109.88[d]
Viet Nam	1 January to 31 December	dong (D)	15 878.00[c]

Sources: United Nations, *Monthly Bulletin of Statistics*, available at <http://esa.un.org/unsd/mbs/mbssearch.asp>, accessed on 2 February 2006; and EIU, *Country Reports*, available at <http://db.eiu.com/countries.asp>, accessed on 2 February 2006.

[a] September 2005.
[b] Average 2005.
[c] August 2005.
[d] October 2005.

ABBREVIATIONS

ADB	Asian Development Bank
AFTA	ASEAN Free Trade Area
ASEAN	Association of Southeast Asian Nations
BIS	Bank for International Settlements
c.i.f.	cost, insurance, freight
CD-ROM	compact disk read-only memory
CIS	Commonwealth of Independent States
CPI	consumer price index
ECE	Economic Commission for Europe
ECO	Economic Cooperation Organization
EIU	Economist Intelligence Unit
EU	European Union
FAO	Food and Agriculture Organization of the United Nations
FDI	foreign direct investment
f.o.b.	free on board
FTAs	free trade agreements
GATS	General Agreement on Trade Services
GATT	General Agreement on Tariff and Trade
GDP	gross domestic product
GSP	generalized system of preferences
HIPC	heavily indebted poor countries
ICT	information and communication technology
ILO	International Labour Organization
IMF	International Monetary Fund
IT	information technology
M1	currency in circulation

ABBREVIATIONS *(continued)*

M2	broad money supply
M3	total money supply
MFA	Multifibre Arrangement
NGO	non-governmental organization
NPL	non-performing loan
ODA	official development assistance
OECD	Organisation for Economic Co-operation and Development
OPEC	Organization of the Petroleum Exporting Countries
PRSP	Poverty Reduction Strategy Paper
PPP	purchasing power parity
R&D	research and development
RTA	regional trade agreement
SAARC	South Asian Association for Regional Cooperation
SAFTA	South Asian Free Trade Area
SME	small and medium-sized enterprise
SOE	State-owned enterprise
SPARTECA	South Pacific Regional Trade and Economic Cooperation Agreement
UNCTAD	United Nations Conference on Trade and Development
UNESCO	United Nations Educational, Scientific and Cultural Organization
UNICEF	United Nations Children's Fund
VAT	value added tax
WTO	World Trade Organization

I. GLOBAL AND REGIONAL ECONOMIC DEVELOPMENTS AND PROSPECTS: IMPLICATIONS FOR THE ESCAP REGION

OVERVIEW

The economy of the Asian and Pacific region grew strongly in 2005, aided by a buoyant global economy, and the region should maintain its growth momentum in 2006, barring any unfavourable external events. Despite high energy prices globally, price pressures rose only moderately in 2005 and are expected to remain muted, or even ease slightly, in 2006. The region's notable performance in 2005 is all the more impressive considering several exogenous developments that might at first glance appear to impinge negatively on the region. These range from the unsustainably large global imbalances, the unwinding of which would almost certainly involve exchange rate realignments of the major currencies in the region, to the weak outcome of the World Trade Organization (WTO) ministerial meeting in Hong Kong, China, in December 2005, the threat of avian influenza becoming a human pandemic and the development of a firmer interest rate environment. However, the consensus is that the region can sustain growth in an environment of continuing low inflation in 2006 despite the significant risks.

These and other matters, such as output and macroeconomic trends in the global economy, the overall trade and financial market environment, developments in the housing markets in the region, the need for greater equity in development outcomes, the increasing economic and social significance of workers' remittances and the associated policy trade-offs and challenges that the Governments of countries in the region may need to address in 2006, are discussed later in this chapter. The performance, medium-term prospects and principal policy issues of the subregions, the least developed countries and the developed countries in the Asian and Pacific region are discussed in detail in chapter II.

THE INTERNATIONAL ENVIRONMENT

The United States of America and China drive global growth

The global economy grew at an average annual rate of 3.2 per cent in 2005, down from growth of 4.0 per cent in 2004 (table I.1). Notwithstanding the slight deceleration, the performance in 2005 was impressive as oil prices rose 28 per cent in 2005, reaching nearly $71 a barrel, following a rise of 35 per cent in 2004, thus effectively doubling over a period of two years. Natural gas prices rose more than 25 per cent in 2005; they have trebled since 2002. Higher energy costs also exerted upward pressure on electricity prices. Non-oil commodity prices (in dollar terms) rose more than 14 per cent in 2005, including a 26 per cent rise in the price of metals, adding to overall cost pressures in manufacturing. Alongside rising oil and commodity prices, global imbalances reached unprecedented levels in 2005, revolving around the current account deficit of the United States.

Although compared with earlier episodes, the impact of the current phase of higher energy and commodity prices on output growth and inflation has been relatively mild so far, monetary authorities virtually across the globe began tightening monetary policy in 2005. The rationale was that inflationary pressures tend to become self-perpetuating when action to counter them is delayed. Accordingly, with inflationary pressures low by historical standards, the raison d'être for the current policy tightening has been largely pre-emptive. In addition, policy tightening in the United States, where the federal funds rate rose from 1 per cent in mid-2003 to 4.50 per cent in early 2006, has reduced the spread between interest rates in the Asian and Pacific region and rates in the United States, leading to a degree of exchange rate volatility for Asian currencies. Meanwhile, low inflation has enabled many Governments in the region to begin the politically sensitive task of reducing or eliminating subsidies on petroleum product prices in view of the growing fiscal burden.

A closer examination of global growth in 2005 shows that it was driven essentially by the United States and China, in a repeat of what had occurred in 2004. Together, these two economies account for more than a third of global output (in purchasing power parity terms) and nearly a fifth of global trade. They have provided strong momentum to both global and regional growth in the last three years. Growth in the United States economy slowed somewhat in 2005 relative to 2004 but remained around the long-term trend. The economy of China grew even faster than in 2004 and, based on the revision of its GDP announced by the National Bureau of Statistics in December 2005, is the sixth largest economy in the world at market exchange rates. Other economies, notably Japan, which is the largest in the Asian and Pacific region, and the members of the euro area experienced a moderate loss of growth momentum relative to that of 2004 but nevertheless continued to match or exceed their performance in the two years prior to 2004 (see table I.1).

From a regional perspective, growth, though lower, was well distributed across subregions and groups of countries. In addition, it is satisfying to note that growth has been shared in the last few years by both the devel-

Table I.1. Selected indicators of global economic conditions, 2002-2006

(Percentage)

		2002	*2003*	*2004*[a]	*2005*[b]	*2006*[b]
Economic growth (percentage change of GDP)						
World						
At market exchange rates		1.7	2.6	4.0	3.2	3.3
At purchasing power parity exchange rates		3.0	3.9	5.1	4.4	4.3
Developed economies		1.2	1.9	3.3	2.5	2.7
Japan		0.1	1.8	2.3	2.5	2.0
United States		1.6	2.7	4.2	3.6	3.3
Euro area		0.9	0.7	2.0	1.2	1.8
Developing economies		4.8	6.5	7.3	6.4	6.1
Developing countries in the Asian and Pacific region		6.1	6.5	7.4	6.6	6.5
Trade in goods and services (percentage)						
World		3.3	5.4	10.3	7.0	7.4
Developed economies	Exports	2.2	3.1	8.3	5.0	6.3
	Imports	2.6	4.1	8.8	5.4	5.8
Developing economies	Exports	6.6	10.8	14.5	10.4	10.3
	Imports	6.0	11.1	16.4	13.5	11.9
Inflation rate (percentage)[c]						
Developed economies		1.5	1.8	2.0	2.2	2.0
Developing economies		6.0	6.0	5.8	5.9	5.7

Sources: United Nations, *World Economic Situation and Prospects 2006* (United Nations publication, Sales No. E.06.II.C.2); International Monetary Fund, *World Economic Outlook, September 2005: Building Institutions* (Washington, D.C., IMF, 2005); and *The Economist* (London, 4 February 2006).

[a] Estimate.
[b] Forecast.
[c] Consumer price index; developed and developing economies, ratios weighted at purchasing power parity.

oping and transition economies of the region, with the transition economies now having grown for seven consecutive years. The number of countries in which output per capita increased by more than 3 per cent doubled between 2002 and 2004. Of 32 countries monitored in East, West and South Asia, 22 exceeded the 3 per cent level in 2004. This broad-based growth is expected to continue over the next 12 months.

Despite China's rapid rise and its growing contribution to growth and trade flows in the Asian and Pacific region, the fortunes of the developing economies in the region are still closely linked to the economies of the United States, Japan and the European Union. Together, these economies are the destination for more than 50 per cent of exports from the region. Among the three, the United States economy, as mentioned, slowed in the second half of 2005, with GDP growth likely to be 3.6 per cent or lower for 2005 as a whole, down from 4.2 per cent in 2004. However, even at this rate, United States growth would still be above its long-term potential and the highest among the Group of Seven (G-7) economies.

In addition to robust productivity growth, there is relatively strong domestic demand, with retail sales growing by close to 4.5 per cent over the 12 months prior to November 2005. Retail sales growth was driven by continuing strong consumer demand, the wealth effect of rising house prices, the easy availability of consumer credit and the decline in unemployment. However, by mid-2005, with private consumption adversely affected by steadily rising petrol prices and the continuing upward trend in interest rates set by the Board of Governors of the Federal Reserve System, growth started to lose momentum. In the second half of the year, hurricanes Katrina and Rita caused considerable human and property losses, but their impact was confined to the states around the Gulf of Mexico.

Will growth slow in the United States?

It is important to emphasize that, although the United States economy has given the rest of the world a significant boost over the last few years, its current account deficit has worsened steadily. By the third quarter of 2005, the deficit had reached $780 billion, equivalent to 6.5 per cent of GDP, double its level as a percentage of GDP as recently as 1999 and three times the 2 per cent of GDP average it had been over the past two decades. The rapid widening of the deficit has contributed significantly to the global current account imbalances, the overall size of which poses a major risk to the near-term global outlook. With the household savings rate in the United States having fallen to zero and the emergence of a significant fiscal deficit after 2001, only large inflows of foreign savings are financing the current account deficit, a state of affairs that is clearly unsustainable beyond the short term.

A new uncertainty that emerged towards the end of 2005 was the inversion in the yield curve for United States bonds (yields on long-term bonds fell below those on short-term bonds). In the past, such inversions have predicted slower future output growth as the authorities first raise interest rates to counter inflationary pressure and then lower them as the pace of activity slows in response. The significance of such an inversion now, when interest rates are still only marginally positive in real terms and the future course of inflation is not clear, has reinforced doubts about the future strength of the United States economy.

In contrast to the United States, the 12 European Union members of the euro area recorded lacklustre growth of 1.2 per cent in 2005, down from 2 per cent in 2004. The slow recovery of domestic demand and low consumer and investor confidence, especially after rejection of the European Union constitution and failure to agree on the European Union budget, had a major effect on this outcome. Growth was the result of higher net exports that were enhanced by the robust global economy, aided by a moderate depreciation of the euro during the year. However, the relative importance of these factors varied across the euro area. For example, Germany and Italy were affected by lethargic domestic demand while exports performed well; the opposite was true for France and Spain.

Continuing weakness in domestic demand in the euro area, however, kept inflation low at 2 per cent in 2005 notwithstanding the pressure from rising energy prices. Despite the persistently weak economic environment, the monetary stance remained tight as the European Central Bank made attempts to pre-empt the danger of higher inflation in the months ahead. On the fiscal side, the average budget deficit for the euro area is estimated to be about the 3 per cent of GDP upper limit prescribed in the Growth and Stability Pact, although France, Germany and Italy, the three largest economies of the euro area, are expected to exceed this rate by a wide margin.

Prospects for strengthening the persistently weak economic enviroment remain uncertain, despite impressive profit growth by German corporations in 2005, as weak internal demand and structural rigidities in the product and labour markets continue to undermine productivity-enhancing investments in the wider European Union economy. Furthermore, even though the euro area trades primarily within the European Union, the internal structural weaknesses of the European Union make it vulnerable to external developments, such as a sharp slowdown in the global economy, euro appreciation or still higher energy prices.

In the United Kingdom of Great Britain and Northern Ireland, the largest European Union economy outside the euro area, growth slowed sharply in 2005 to 1.9 per cent from 3.2 per cent in the previous year. The main reasons were the slower growth of private consumption, higher oil prices and the cooling of the housing market, offset to some extent by continuing fiscal stimulus. Inflation rose slightly above the Bank of England target ceiling of 2 per cent and the fiscal deficit is expected to reach 3.2 per cent of GDP in 2005 to support higher spending on health and education. Against this environment, the Bank of England attempted to maintain a cautious monetary policy stance balancing the risks of higher inflation against the probability of weaker output growth towards the later part of 2005. Accordingly, interest rates have been on hold since August 2004, apart from a quarter-point increase in August 2005, and are not expected to rise in the near term.

Japan will maintain steady growth

After GDP growth of 2.3 per cent in 2004, the Japanese economy registered growth of 2.5 per cent in 2005, a relatively strong performance compared with the virtual stagnation it experienced between 1997 and 2003. Growth was driven by a recovery in consumer demand and investment, and not by exports as in other recent episodes of recovery. Growth in private consumption was helped by rising wages and new employment opportunities, while strong profit growth and improved investor confidence helped corporate investment to pick up. Contributing to the recovery of domestic demand have been some key structural reforms undertaken to address long-standing weaknesses in the banking and corporate sectors. Private sector reform and corporate restructuring to improve productivity and profitability, primarily by streamlining operations and closing down loss-making operations, finally appear to be bearing fruit.

Monetary policy in Japan has been kept loose for a number of years, with interest rates close to zero, as the authorities struggled to overcome the persistent deflation that has lasted seven years. That phase is drawing to a close, with deflation expected to end in 2006. Attention accordingly is being focused on the fiscal situation and on Japan's massive public debt. While efforts at fiscal consolidation have resulted in a lower fiscal deficit of 6.7 per cent of GDP in 2005 compared with 7.2 per cent in 2004, more ambitious fiscal tightening may be required to attain a more sustainable level of public debt by 2010, as previously envisaged. Looking ahead, several downside risks to growth remain. A further rise in energy prices, upward pressure on the yen and a simultaneous slowdown in the United States and Chinese economies may affect the export sector, which is still an important driver of growth.

Prospects for 2006: growth momentum will be maintained

There is consensus that, as the world economy successfully coped with high oil and energy prices in 2004 and 2005, prospects for 2006 are broadly for a continuation of current trends with oil prices fluctuating between $50 and $55 a barrel, and the balance of risks possibly weighted slightly on the downside. For instance, growth could slow significantly in the United States if the recent inversion of the yield curve proves an accurate predictor of the future. It could also slow as firmer interest rates more strongly affect the housing market and private consumption by reducing the wealth effect of buoyant house prices and by reducing the demand for credit. In the wider global economy, growth could ease as businesses readjust corporate budgets and consumers readjust household spending to absorb the higher energy prices. Moreover, a significant oil supply shock, such as from further difficulties in Iraq or in any other major oil-producing country, cannot be ruled out. The persistent current account imbalances, with their implications for exchange rates, also overhang investor perceptions about the future, creating a degree of risk aversion.

More positively, growth could speed up in the European Union, remain at its current level in Japan and strengthen in the developing countries of the Asian and Pacific region. As a result, world trade in goods and services would pick up modestly in 2006 compared with 2005 but remain below the growth rate of 2004; however, trade in goods and services, both exports and imports, of developing countries is likely to ease slightly in 2006 relative to 2005.

TRADE

Oil and commodity prices remain high

World trade volume grew by more than 10 per cent in 2004 but the rate of growth eased to 7 per cent in 2005. The main reason was the slower pace of growth in the United States, Japan and the European Union. Alongside the rising price of energy, other commodity prices also strengthened considerably (table I.2). For instance, non-oil commodity prices rose by 18.5 per cent (in dollar terms) overall, with metals up 28.5 per cent, non-food agricultural raw materials up 15.6 per cent and industrial raw materials up 24.4 per cent. Part of the increase can be explained by the depreciation of the dollar, with dollar prices for commodities adjusting upwards to reflect the lower exchange rate of the dollar. Even so, the increase in overall commodity prices has been significant and has reinforced the upward pressure on overall prices caused by higher energy prices.

Trade has been central to the rapid growth achieved by the region both historically and in the last decade as the forces of globalization have gathered speed. By and large, the region has outpaced the rest of the world in the rate at which its trade has grown, both trade with the rest of the world and increasingly within the region. The recent contributions of China to global and regional trade growth have been re-

Table I.2. Price trends of major commodities, 2001-2005

(Current prices in United States dollars)

	2001	*2002*	*2003*	*2004*	*2005*[a]
Cotton (per pound)	0.48	0.46	0.63	0.62	0.55
DRAM chip (all types) (per average selling price)	2.90	3.80	3.80	4.40	3.70
Flash memory (per average selling price)	5.20	4.30	4.70	4.70	4.50
Integrated circuits (per average selling price)	1.70	1.50	1.50	1.70	1.70
Microprocessor (per average selling price)	79.50	75.70	85.20	103.60	105.80
Oil: Brent (per barrel)	24.50	25.00	28.80	38.50	55.00
Palm kernel oil (per ton)	308.50	416.00	458.50	647.50	633.30
Palm oil (per ton)	285.80	390.00	443.30	471.30	407.30
Rice (per ton)	177.50	197.30	201.00	244.80	291.30
Rubber (per ton)	746.80	906.80	1 230.00	1 479.50	1 672.30
Soybean oil (per ton)	353.80	449.00	556.50	615.80	532.50
Soybeans (per ton)	193.00	209.30	257.80	301.50	264.00
Steel (per ton)	205.80	256.30	297.90	534.20	503.80
Sugar (per pound)	0.09	0.07	0.07	0.07	0.10
Tea (per kilogramme)	1.60	1.50	1.50	1.70	1.60

Sources: Derived from various sources including World Bank, International Monetary Fund and *Asian Wall Street Journal*.

[a] Estimate.

markable. Between 2002 and 2004, the value of imports by China from the rest of the world increased by more than $250 billion, compared with the United States ($320 billion) and Japan ($117 billion). In the same period, China increased its imports from the Asian and Pacific region by more than $100 billion, almost keeping pace with the United States ($106 billion) but outpacing Japan significantly ($60 billion).

China's massive and growing role in international and regional trade has meant that China heavily influences the prices of many manufactured goods (for example, steel) and commodities (for example, oil, coal and copper) and trade in these items plus the services associated with their movement across borders, such as shipping, logistics and insurance. Several suppliers of these goods and services have enjoyed huge gains in revenues and earnings in the last two years. This situation may not last long, however.

In addition to China's contribution to global and regional trade, the Asian and Pacific region, especially the East and North-East and South-East Asian subregions, is the most significant participant in the trade in high-technology goods, particularly in the information and communication technology industry. For example, the Republic of Korea's exports of digital electronic goods exceeded $100 billion in 2005, with semiconductors accounting for about $30 billion, and China overtook the United States in the export of high-technology products in 2004. Despite its rapid growth in the last decade, the global information and communication technology industry has distinct cyclical characteristics. There was a downturn in late 2004 and early 2005 and the beginning of an upturn in the second half of 2005, with global semiconductor demand growing by 6.6 per cent in 2005 as a whole, a trend that should last well into 2006.

The cyclicality in the global high-technology industry is almost certainly driven by the rapid development of new technology, especially in semiconductors, that characterizes the industry. Technological obsolescence is an inherent characteristic of an industry in which new products and applications are constantly being created and old ones become obsolete at a pace unknown in other manufacturing sectors. There is thus an ongoing risk of overcapacity being created in the industry and of significant price weakness. Countries that are major participants in this industry, for instance some of the economies of East and North-East and South-East Asia, are consequently prone to greater cyclical fluctuations in trade than others, a feature that would then feed backwards into domestic production. However, the impact of such fluctuations is becoming less acute for various reasons.

Although economies in the Asian and Pacific region are known primarily for their manufacturing prowess across virtually the full spectrum of technologies, the region as a whole and several individual economies within it are also major producers and exporters of a number of agricultural commodities and industrial raw materials that play an important part in the economic life of these countries. They include cotton, palm oil, rice, rubber, tea, coal and iron ore. Some of these commodities and raw materials are more subject to cyclicality than others.

It is noteworthy that even when the quantities of these commodities traded internationally are relatively small, the region now exercises a strong influence on their prices. In this context, major price increases occurred in 2004. Since then, prices have tended to remain relatively flat, although with notable exceptions such as those of rice and rubber, but have not displayed any pronounced weakness because demand has remained strong. The expectation among commodity traders is that these trends are likely to continue into 2006: prices will remain firm and the quantities traded will grow but at a somewhat slower pace than in 2003 and 2004, when concerns about a potential shortage led to a spike in demand and a sharp increase in commodity and raw material prices, especially for steel.

Textiles and clothing trade: after the WTO Agreement on Textiles and Clothing

An industry of wide significance to the region is textiles and clothing, the development of which has been affected by the complex application of country quotas by major importing countries over the years. At the beginning of 2005 these quotas came to an end with the expiration of the Multifibre Arrangement, although some residual bilateral safeguard measures continued to operate, particularly for the export of textiles and clothing from China. The phase-out of quotas has had a substantial impact on international markets. The import by the United States of textiles and clothing from China increased by 64 per cent (about $6 billion) in the first eight months of 2005 and China's share of United States imports increased from 17 to 26 per cent. European Union imports of these items from China went up by 67 per cent in the first six months of 2005.

However, contrary to initial fears, other producers from the region also performed well. For example, United States imports from Bangladesh and India increased by 20 per cent in the first eight months of 2005, while imports from Cambodia and Indonesia rose by 15 per cent. At the same time United States imports from Hong Kong, China; Macao, China; Singapore; and Taiwan Province of China fell by 20 per cent. Similar developments were evident in the European Union. Both the United States and the European Union responded to the surge in exports from China by invoking safeguard measures on selected textile and clothing imports from that country. Chinese exports of several textile and clothing items to the United States and the European Union were subject to new restraints for a transitional period.

It is too early to predict how the implementation of the WTO Agreement on Textiles and Clothing will ultimately affect the region as a whole. Most industry experts predict that global buyers will not risk placing all their orders with China, preferring a diversified set of suppliers. Furthermore, it is unlikely that China can, or would aim to, dominate every market segment in this industry. The global textiles and clothing market is vast and has several niche segments that China may not be able to satisfy. Moreover, China is likely to be aware of the sensitivities if its industry were to dominate others in the region. (Trade policy issues following the Sixth WTO Ministerial Conference, which was held in Hong Kong, China in December 2005, are discussed later in the chapter.)

In summary, while the region is integrated into global trade and will inevitably be influenced by global developments, it has simultaneously developed considerable autonomy over the last few years. Economies in the Asian and Pacific region not only figure increasingly in trading volumes and the size of trading links but also influence the prices of many of the goods and commodities. The phenomenon of "componentization" that began in the information and communication technology industry is a case in point. The growing role of domestic demand in driving growth in the region is another factor that is increasing the autonomy of the region and is making it less dependent on global developments for sustaining its growth.

CAPITAL FLOWS

International capital serves to bridge the gap between domestic saving and investment for countries with balance of payments deficits, financing varying shares of domestic investment depending upon the country concerned. Where such gaps or deficits do not exist, as in much of the Asian and Pacific region, the surplus savings usually go into reserves. Capital inflows are also playing more of an indirect, developmental role than savings and investments in the transfer of new technology, management know-how and skills and wider marketing links. The pattern of capital outflows, on the other hand, provides a picture of how surplus domestic savings are being deployed in other countries, and of the outlets and the instruments chosen (whether finance alone, as in placements with banks or the purchase of government or private sector securities, or direct investment in enterprises). The pattern indicates the degree of risk aversion by investors, the institutions chosen for intermediation and their maturity preferences. Capital outflows do not originate just in countries with current account surpluses. Countries with current account deficits may also have considerable capital outflows. United States financial markets, for example, intermediate between unrelated third-country savers and investors.

Global savings currently amount to about 25 per cent of global GDP, about 2 percentage points higher than in the 1990s, an increase accounted for largely by higher savings in developing countries.[1] The major contributor has

---

[1] Bank for International Settlements, *BIS 75th Annual Report* (Basel, BIS, 2005).

been the Asian and Pacific region, especially China, the national saving rate of which has risen to more than 45 per cent of GDP. On the other side of the balance sheet, global investment levels have risen more moderately, from an average of 24 per cent of GDP in the 1990s to 24.6 per cent in 2004, again with much of the increase occurring in the Asian and Pacific region.

The higher global savings relative to unchanged investment levels have almost certainly contributed to the low interest rates on the global financial scene for the last two to three years. Low inflation rates have also helped. Low interest rates have meant that savers have been forced to seek alternative means for deploying their assets. They have invested the bulk of their savings in real estate, mainly housing. Prices of residential property have risen to unprecedented levels in the last few years. As not all the investment in real estate has been financed through equity, households have built up high levels of debt. Again, low interest rates have played a part in this development. In 2005, however, short-term interest rates globally and in the region began to firm, although surprisingly they eased in China and in the Philippines.

There is a perception, however, that while aggregate savings have risen worldwide that rise conceals wide variations across countries. Savings have fallen in the United States, for instance, and have become increasingly locked in relatively illiquid investments, such as housing, leaving less available for other investments. The rather slow recovery in corporate investment activity in the Asian and Pacific region has been due, in part, to the diversion of investment into housing and real estate and the higher returns available there, as suggested by the huge increase in property prices (discussed more fully later) almost everywhere in the world. In view of this, the volume and pattern of international capital flows in the near term may become constrained, favouring particular locations and activities. In this context, there is no evidence that low interest rates have made investors less risk averse; with interest rates widely expected to rise, households may be keener to consolidate their balance sheets than to seek new outlets for their assets.

Capital flows to the region fall sharply

The latest data indicate that net capital flows to the region fell fairly sharply in 2005 following huge increases in 2004 (table I.3). The decline was almost entirely due to both portfolio and private capital flows dropping close to zero, indeed, portfolio flows on a net basis were negative in 2005 despite the region's buoyant stock markets. The experience of individual economies is more relevant. Thus, significant net inflows occurred in both 2004 and 2005 in India, Malaysia, the Philippines and Thailand, whereas net outflows occurred in Indonesia and the Republic of Korea. Singapore and Hong Kong, China, have traditionally been responsible for large net outflows, but only in their role as financial centres. While portfolio inflows can boost stock markets and lower the cost of capital for enterprises, such flows tend to be volatile and can be instrumental in creating asset bubbles. Indeed, buoyant stock markets in the region might attract even larger inflows in 2006, creating difficult trade-offs for the conduct of monetary policy for the countries concerned. One feature of the foreign direct investment (FDI) flows in 2005 is the growing importance of mergers and acquisitions. FDI flows in the form of mergers and acquisitions do not add to the stock of capital. They should, however, generate improvements in the use of capital by creating economies of scale and by increasing the efficiency of capital by facilitating consolidation in different sectors of the economy.

Stock markets globally and within the region showed mixed trends: the indices for the major United States stock markets, that is, the Dow Jones Industrial Average and the NASDAQ Composite Index, were generally flat, while those for other developed country markets showed considerable buoyancy. The Japanese stock market indices (Nikkei and Topix) reached their highest levels in five years. However, elsewhere within the region, China's stock markets declined as did Malaysia's, while most other markets rose strongly. Stock markets in India, Pakistan, the Republic of Korea, the Russian Federation and Turkey were among the best performing in the world. These mixed trends in the region suggest that country-specific influences, such as corporate profits, were at work, more so than systemic influences governing capital flows in the region as a whole.

Table I.3. Net capital flows of developing countries and of all Asian developing countries, 1995-2005

(Billions of United States dollars)

	1995	*1996*	*1997*	*1998*	*1999*	*2000*	*2001*	*2002*	*2003*	*2004*	*2005*
Total											
Net private capital flows[a]	211.5	496.7	191.7	76.2	86.0	74.3	66.2	68.2	158.2	232.0	132.9
Net private direct investment	98.2	116.0	146.2	158.6	173.2	167.0	178.6	142.7	153.4	189.1	209.2
Net private portfolio investment	42.7	86.3	60.8	42.6	69.5	21.0	−83.6	−87.6	−7.3	64.0	−28.6
Net other private capital flows	70.5	−5.6	−15.3	−125.0	−156.7	−113.7	−28.8	13.0	12.1	−21.1	−47.7
Net official flows	26.5	−6.8	28.4	56.0	18.3	−52.1	−0.6	10.6	−61.7	−81.0	−137.1
Changes in reserves[b]	−118.2	−90.3	−105.2	−34.8	−93.4	−113.2	−115.9	−185.7	−364.6	−517.4	−510.5
Developing Asia[c]											
Net private capital flows[a]	96.9	119.4	36.6	−49.9	11.8	7.5	14.7	21.0	62.0	132.9	84.6
Net private direct investment	52.6	53.4	55.7	56.6	67.1	59.8	48.6	47.5	67.1	81.6	84.2
Net private portfolio investment	22.7	32.5	6.8	8.7	55.8	20.1	−54.7	−60.2	4.9	25.8	−3.3
Net other private capital flows[d]	21.6	33.5	−26.0	−115.2	−111.1	−72.4	20.7	33.7	−10.0	25.4	3.8
Net official flows	4.5	−14.5	22.7	15.4	−0.3	−11.7	−11.3	5.2	−16.6	5.8	13.1
Changes in reserves[b]	−43.3	−46.3	−36.0	−52.9	−87.5	−52.5	−90.9	−149.9	−227.8	−342.7	−291.6

Source: International Monetary Fund, *World Economic Outlook, September 2005: Building Institutions* (Washington, D.C., 2005).

Note: Net capital flows comprise net direct investment, net portfolio investment, and other long- and short-term net investment flows, including official and private borrowing.

[a] Because of data limitations, figures may include some official flows.

[b] A minus sign indicates an increase.

[c] Consists of Asian developing countries and the newly industrializing Asian economies (Hong Kong, China; Republic of Korea; Singapore; and Taiwan Province of China).

[d] Excluding the effects of the recapitalization of two large commercial banks in China with foreign reserves of the Bank of China ($45 billion), net private capital flows to emerging economies in Asia in 2003 were $101.1 billion while other net capital flows to Asia amounted to $28.0 billion.

Foreign direct investment flows increase

In contrast to portfolio flows, net FDI flows rose in 2005 and reached their highest level since 1994. Economies attracting higher FDI were China; Hong Kong, China; India; Indonesia; Malaysia; and Turkey. Economies experiencing outflows were China; Hong Kong, China; India; the Republic of Korea; Malaysia; and Singapore. The increase in net FDI inflows is of major significance considering the rapid increase in FDI outflows from the region. It also belies the fear that FDI into China may be crowding out FDI to other economies in the region. It is worth emphasizing that the amount of FDI is not fixed: more for one country does not necessarily mean less for others. FDI in one country may well stimulate FDI in others when the production process can be broken down into segments. This phenomenon has already occurred in textiles and clothing, in shoes, in many information and communication technology investments, and is happening increasingly in automobiles and could happen in other production lines. Moreover, the size of FDI flowing into China is not disproportionate to the size of that country's economy.

One of the puzzles of 2005, however, is why the large and growing global current account imbalances, a potential source of instability in financial markets and hence in cross-border financial flows, did not emerge as a major policy issue in the region during the year. Exchange rates and financial markets, by and large, remained stable in 2005. The dollar depreciated by about 10 per cent on a trade-weighted basis, with the euro and the yen bearing most of the burden of adjustment. Among the developing countries of the Asian and Pacific region, the Chinese yuan, Malaysian ringgit, Philippine peso and Republic of Korea won appreciated against the dollar, while the Indian rupee, Indonesian rupiah and Thai baht depreciated slightly during 2005. The relative exchange rate stability in 2005 should not be taken to signify that it will continue into 2006 and beyond, however.

Reserves in the region increased in 2005

The low level of real interest rates in the region mirrors the low level of global real interest rates and, more specifically, United States interest rates. These phenomena have been reflected, as previously mentioned, in the buoyant housing and real estate markets during the last few years and, more recently, in the price of gold. However, Governments of countries in the region seeking to resist appreciation of their currencies have accumulated very large reserves. Reserves in the region (excluding Japan) increased by 26 per cent in 2003 and 30 per cent in 2004. The pace of reserve accumulation slackened somewhat in 2005, particularly in the second half, but reserves rose by nearly 28 per cent up to September 2005, reaching more than $1.8 trillion. In 2005, the pace of reserve accumulation was driven more by China's current account surplus, which rose from $46 billion in 2004 to $128.5 billion in 2005, than by short-term capital inflows. Such inflows have been important for India and the Republic of Korea, which have seen large portfolio flows into their stock markets. Reserve holdings are typically held in low-yielding government securities and are heavily weighted in dollar-denominated instruments. They are now a massive resource and countries of the region are incurring considerable opportunity costs by eschewing alternative, though somewhat riskier, investments in the region, such as in infrastructure.

Against the background of the principal trends and prospects for the global economy outlined above, a number of issues need elucidation. Some of the issues are challenges that Governments of countries in the region may have to confront during 2006, such as even higher oil prices, global current account imbalances and the impact of higher interest rates. There is also a degree of uncertainty about the multilateral trade liberalization agenda following the previously mentioned WTO ministerial meeting in Hong Kong, China in December 2005 and the growing fear that avian influenza might develop into a human pandemic in the near future. Other issues embody longer-term problems and opportunities for the countries of the region, such as the unequal sharing of the fruits of development in the region and the steadily rising economic and social importance of home remittances. Both these issues, discussed later, will need policy attention over the medium term.

OIL PRICES: A NEW OIL SHOCK?

Oil prices reach record levels

Oil prices have doubled since the beginning of 2004 and have trebled since 2002. These increases are similar in scale to the price increases of 1973-1974, 1979-1980 and 1990-1991, each of which was followed by rising inflation and global recession. The current real price adjusted for global export prices, the appropriate measure for oil-importing countries, is also above the peaks it reached in 1974 and 1980.

While both demand and supply factors have contributed to the recent rise in oil prices, demand seems to be the more dominant factor. Demand for oil grew by 3.2 per cent in 2004 and 2.1 per cent in 2005, compared with 1.4 per cent between 2000 and 2003 (table I.4). This was the highest growth rate since 1976. The growing demand for oil is set to continue, rising from 84.2 million barrels per day in 2005 to 86 million barrels per day in 2006 as vehicle ownership increases rapidly in many developing countries.

The low global spare capacity, the result of inadequate investments in both upstream and downstream activities, especially refineries, has also contributed to the rise in prices. The hostilities in Iraq and other geopolitical developments have also contributed to volatility in the oil markets. In addition, the volume of trading in financial instruments linked to oil- and energy-related commodities, especially among non-commercial traders, has increased sharply in recent months, indicating that speculation is also contributing to rising prices.

Table I.4. Global oil consumption

	Millions of barrels per day						Annual percentage change			
	1980-1989	1990-1999	2000-2003	2004	2005[a]	2006[a]	2000-2003	2004	2005[a]	2006[a]
United States	16.3	17.9	19.8	20.7	20.8	21.2	0.7	3.3	0.5	1.9
Europe	14.1	15.4	16.0	16.3	16.3	16.4	0.0	1.2	0.0	0.6
Japan	4.7	5.6	5.5	5.4	5.4	5.4	−0.5	−3.2	0.0	0.0
China	1.9	3.3	5.1	6.5	7.0	7.5	6.2	17.1	7.7	7.1
India	0.9	1.5	2.2	2.3	2.4	2.4	3.4	4.5	4.1	4.1
Other Asia	2.9	5.9	7.6	8.2	8.5	8.7	2.6	3.6	3.7	2.4
Middle East	2.7	4.1	5.0	5.6	5.9	6.2	3.1	6.3	5.2	5.1
Africa	1.8	2.2	2.6	2.8	2.9	3.0	2.6	2.5	3.2	3.1
Latin America	2.6	3.5	4.1	4.2	4.3	4.4	−0.2	4.7	2.6	2.5
OECD[b]	39.1	44.6	48.1	49.5	49.9	50.4	0.4	1.7	0.8	1.0
Global demand	**61.8**	**70.3**	**78.3**	**82.5**	**84.2**	**86.0**	**1.4**	**3.2**	**2.1**	**2.1**

Source: Energy Information Administration, International Energy Agency and United Nations Economic and Social Commission for Asia and the Pacific calculations.

[a] Expected value, from Energy Information Administration.
[b] Organisation for Economic Co-operation and Development.

Although the recent oil price increase is similar in scale to that of the oil shocks of the 1970s and 1980s, there has been no sign thus far of an impending global economic slowdown as a result of the latest episode. There are three reasons for the continuing growth in the face of rising oil prices. First, the recent increase in oil prices has been driven mainly by strong global demand, not supply disruptions, as had occurred in the past. With supply disruptions, the physical shortage of oil leads to an immediate disruption in overall economic activity, whereas a demand-driven price rise has a far less adverse effect on growth. Second, both inflation and inflationary expectations are lower worldwide than during the previous oil shocks. Third, the oil intensity of consumption and production, particularly in developed countries where services contribute almost 70 per cent of output, is significantly lower than in the 1980s, so that the economic impact of even a large increase in oil prices is lower now than then.

Rising oil prices have a negative impact on growth, inflation and trade balances

The impact of rising oil prices on economic growth, inflation and a country's trade balance is influenced not only by the extent of the rise and its persistence but also by the country's oil and energy dependence, measured by oil self-sufficiency, the energy intensity of GDP and the intensity of oil use in energy consumption. On all these counts, the Asian and Pacific region ranks as highly dependent on oil.

Table I.5 summarizes the short-run economic impact of a permanent increase of $10 per barrel in the price of oil in selected Asian economies: GDP growth would fall in all Asian economies. The Philippines, Singapore and Thailand would be the most severely affected, as they are large net oil importers and highly dependent on imported oil and energy. Inflation, measured by the consumer price index, would tend to increase in all cases, with India, Malaysia, the Philippines and Thailand experiencing the highest increases. The current account balance would worsen in all countries except Malaysia, where the oil self-sufficiency index is positive. Hong Kong, China; the Republic of Korea; and Taiwan Province of China would be the most severely affected, with current account balances declining by about 1 per cent of GDP.

Table I.5. Impact of a $10 increase in oil prices on selected Asian economies

(Percentage)

	GDP growth	*Inflation*	*Current account balance (percentage of GDP)*
China	−0.5	0.2	−0.6
Hong Kong, China	−0.3	0.0	−1.0
India	−0.5	1.1	−0.3
Indonesia	−0.5	0.6	0.0
Japan	−0.2	0.4	−0.4
Malaysia	−0.5	0.9	0.1
Philippines	−0.7	0.9	−0.1
Republic of Korea	−0.3	0.5	−1.0
Singapore	−0.8	0.8	−0.7
Taiwan Province of China	−0.1	0.3	−1.1
Thailand	−0.8	1.0	−0.6

Source: United Nations Economic and Social Commission for Asia and the Pacific calculations, based on the Oxford Economic Forecasting Model, released in September 2005, <www.oef.com>.

Several factors should mitigate the impact of a rise in oil prices in the region, however. First, widespread State intervention in petroleum product price-setting acts as a limit on the pass-through from higher oil prices to domestic inflation and output costs. Some degree of State intervention is practised in about half the countries in the region and prices are set administratively in Bangladesh, China, India, Indonesia, Malaysia and Viet Nam. Thailand had set prices previously but has ended subsidies on petroleum products. In per litre terms, the Government of India provides the highest subsidies. Such subsidies have added significantly to fiscal burdens. The fiscal burden in Indonesia was equivalent to 3 per cent of GDP in 2004 and to 4.4 per cent in 2005. Lower but significant fiscal costs prevail in India, Malaysia and Viet Nam. A second mitigating factor is the low level of inflationary expectations. With inflationary pressures contained, pressures for higher wages have not emerged, at least for the time being.

Given the demand-driven nature of the oil price increase and the prevailing supply constraints, prices are expected to remain high throughout 2006 and possibly beyond, which is referred to in some quarters as a "permanent oil shock". The impact would depend, however, on specific country circumstances, which are briefly discussed in the following paragraphs.

Policy actions are needed for net oil importers

Net oil-importing countries need to take steps to adjust to this reality. Having recognized that the continuation of oil subsidies may not be fiscally sustainable, many countries have scaled down subsidies since the second quarter of 2005. Inflationary pressure has been increasing as a result. Some degree of monetary policy tightening may be required to pre-empt higher inflation in the months ahead. The prevailing low-interest environment in the region should make it easier for policymakers to pursue tighter monetary policies for some time to come.

The streamlining of subsidies is clearly warranted, particularly when they do not reach the intended group: the poor. Governments could start by phasing out subsidies on fuel types that are not widely used by the poor. For example, diesel subsidies, though widespread, do not directly benefit the poor as do, for instance, subsidies on liquefied petroleum gas (LPG) or kerosene. A better approach would be to replace oil subsidies with direct income-targeting instruments for the poor, as the Indonesian authorities have done. In that country payments in cash are to be made to 15 million of the poorest families who are affected by rising kerosene prices.

Over and above the fiscal burden, subsidies create distortions in other areas. They increase fuel and energy inefficiency, reduce incentives to develop and diffuse cleaner technologies and encourage smuggling and other illegal activities.

The low-income, net oil importers of the Asian and Pacific region face significant external vulnerabilities as a result of rising oil prices. Since these countries have little access to financing to cushion a temporary balance of payments instability caused by an oil price shock, international financial institutions need to provide assistance to them, as was done in the 1970s through the International Monetary Fund "oil facility". However, to be useful to countries such as the least developed countries, such mechanisms have to be highly concessional.

Policy actions are necessary for net oil exporters

Net oil exporters in the region, for example Central Asian countries, also need to adjust to rising oil prices. The focus should be on how to manage oil windfalls efficiently without jeopardizing short-term macroeconomic stability, as there will be pressure on the real exchange rate to appreciate (the so-called Dutch disease). Even though such appreciation may be inevitable, the monetary authorities can use "sterilization operations" to reduce the impact. With regard to fiscal policy, the windfalls should be used to improve the country's overall fiscal position through refinancing previously issued high-interest debt or to reduce the absolute level of such debt. Alternatively, the windfalls could be invested in much needed infrastructure, human capital development and social safety nets.

Long-term policy actions are required

Both oil-importing and oil-exporting countries need to develop a longer-term policy response to reduce oil dependency, improve energy efficiency and promote energy conservation. As industry, road transport, construction, buildings and domestic appliances are major energy consumers, energy-efficiency policy initiatives need to be formulated to target these areas. Capacity-building in energy management, rationalization of energy pricing, greater public awareness of alternative energy options, regulations to ensure a minimum level of energy efficiency and fiscal incentives to reduce energy consumption have proven effective in various settings. Such initiatives need to be promoted more widely as a matter of priority in the region.

THE PROBLEM OF GLOBAL IMBALANCES

The United States current account deficit is increasing

The widening imbalances in the external accounts of major economies are emerging as a risk for the global economy, with potentially serious repercussions for Asian and Pacific economies. A precipitous unwinding of these imbalances could create large upheavals in international financial markets, causing exchange rate instability involving the dollar and several currencies in the region. Both consumers and investors could become more risk averse, with negative impacts on the global real economy. The United States current account deficit is the largest single contributor to the global imbalances. Since 2001, that country's fiscal situation has deteriorated sharply and household savings have virtually disappeared. The United States now has both current account and fiscal deficits, a repeat of what occurred in the 1980s, and correcting them will have a major impact on monetary policy and the future course of interest rates in the United States.

Contrasting with this development have been the widening current account surpluses of Japan, China, several other Asian countries and recently the oil-producing developing countries (figure I.1). Until the technology bubble ended in 2001, the United States deficit was financed largely by private capital inflows. Since then, as the fiscal deficit grew alongside the current account deficit, it has been increasingly financed by foreign Governments, especially some in Asia, that are now buying United States government securities. Such Governments seem content to continue buying dollar-denominated assets despite the capital losses incurred by the depreciating dollar; it has depreciated 12 per cent since 2002 in real effective terms and even more on a bilateral basis against a number of

Figure I.1. Current account balances for selected economies, 2004-2005[a]

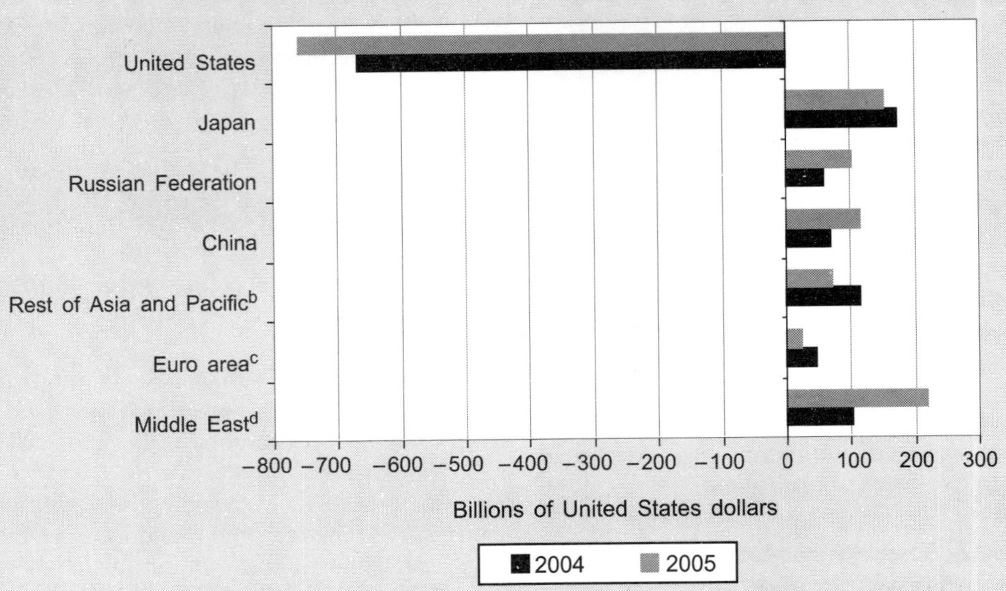

Source: International Monetary Fund, *World Economic Outlook, September 2005: Building Institutions* (Washington, D.C., IMF, 2005).

a Data for 2005 are IMF projections.

b Rest of Asia and Pacific comprises Bangladesh; Bhutan; Cambodia; Fiji; Hong Kong, China; India; Indonesia; Kiribati; Lao People's Democratic Republic; Malaysia; Maldives; Myanmar; Nepal; Pakistan; Papua New Guinea; Philippines; Republic of Korea; Singapore; Samoa; Solomon Islands; Sri Lanka; Taiwan Province of China; Thailand; Tonga; Vanuatu; and Viet Nam.

c Euro area comprises Austria, Belgium, Finland, France, Germany, Greece, Ireland, Italy, Luxembourg, Netherlands, Portugal and Spain.

d Middle East includes Bahrain, Egypt, Islamic Republic of Iran, Iraq, Jordan, Kuwait, Lebanon, Libyan Arab Jamahiriya, Oman, Qatar, Saudi Arabia, Syrian Arab Republic, United Arab Emirates and Yemen.

other currencies. This willingness may not continue indefinitely as investors are likely to demand progressively higher risk premiums to invest in dollar-denominated assets. The greatest risk in the imbalances lies in the possibility of market sentiment changing suddenly, with foreigners switching away from dollar-denominated assets within a short span of time. In an extreme case scenario, a global recession could follow as:

- A sharp depreciation of the dollar leads to a drastic reduction in the value of foreign exchange reserves in Asian countries that have accumulated substantial reserves in recent years. The dollar depreciation could also hurt the export competitiveness of Asian economies;
- High interest rates, in turn, lead to large capital losses on official dollar-denominated bond portfolios held by many Asian countries. High rates impose an additional debt service burden on Asian developing countries. Considerably higher interest rates would reduce the level of activity virtually across the board in the global economy.

There is considerable uncertainty about the federal funds rate

There is considerable uncertainty regarding the trajectory of United States interest rates over the next 18 to 24 months. Not only are the current account and fiscal deficits a concern, but inflation has reached 3.5 per cent, the highest level among developed countries, and it is expected to remain at this level for most of 2006. Thus, there is a strong possibility that nominal interest rates could rise substantially to fund the current account and fiscal deficits and to restrain price pressures. The United States Federal Reserve Board has increased its benchmark interest rate (the federal funds rate) in a series of steps from 1 per cent in mid-2003 to 4.50 per cent in January 2006 to bring borrowing costs into a range consistent with keeping the economy operating near its non-inflationary potential (see figure I.2).

In the light of the uncertainty, three simulations were conducted by the ESCAP secretariat to examine the impact of changes in the Federal Reserve's rate on Asian economies.[2] The first scenario assumes that the Federal Open Market Committee increases the federal funds rate by 25 basis points from the base case in the first quarter of 2006 and maintains that rate until 2007. The second scenario assumes a further increase in the third quarter of 2005 by 25 basis points so that the rate reaches 5 per cent in the third quarter. The third scenario assumes that the rate reaches 5.5 per cent at the end of 2006.

Such increases will affect Asian economies through two main channels: the exchange rate and the interest rate. An increase in the United States interest rate would tend to depreciate nominal and real exchange rates in Asian economies relative to the dollar, stimulating exports, particularly to the United States. However, a rise in the interest rate would simultaneously generate a negative income effect in the United States economy, cancelling out at least some of the increased export effect. An increase in the United States interest rate is also likely to trigger increases in interest rates in other countries, generating a negative income effect on overall demand. The net impact remains ambiguous, depending on the relative magnitudes of the positive impact from the exchange rate deprecia-

Figure I.2. Federal funds rate, 2004Q1-2007Q4

(Percentage)

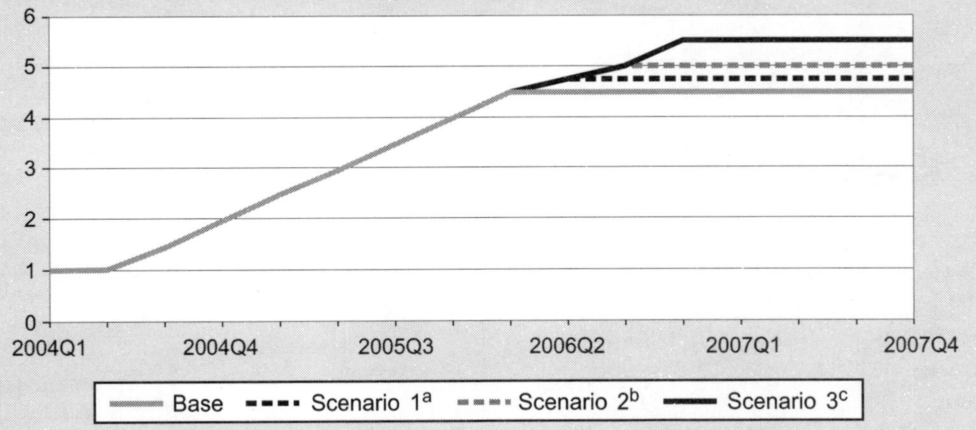

Source: Board of Governors of the Federal Reserve System, <www.federalreserve.gov>.

[a] Assumes that federal funds rate increases by 25 basis points in the first quarter of 2006 and maintains that rate until 2007.

[b] Assumes that the federal funds rate increases in the third quarter of 2005 by 25 basis points so that it reaches 5 per cent.

[c] Assumes that the federal funds rate increases to 5.5 per cent at the end of 2006.

[2] Based on the Oxford Economic Forecasting Model.

tion and the negative income effects from higher interest rates in the United States and in the Asian and Pacific economies (see table I.6).

The simulation exercise suggests that the negative impact from a slowdown and a higher interest rate in the United States exceeds the positive impact from the exchange rate channel. In all three scenarios, economic growth in the Asian economies would slow. GDP growth would slow most in scenario 3 and least in scenario 1. In the Asian economies GDP growth would decline by 0.04 percentage point in 2006 and by 0.30 percentage point in 2007 under scenario 1 and by 0.08 points in 2006 and by 0.84 points in 2007 under scenario 3. Developing economies would be the most seriously affected group in the Asian and Pacific region, especially China; Hong Kong, China; Singapore; and Thailand, the economies of which are the most closely linked with the United States.

The impact of a rise in the federal funds rate on inflation in the region would be minimal, however, because of two effects that would tend to dampen inflation on balance in most countries. Depreciation of the exchange rate in Asian economies would tend to increase inflation, with the increase varying depending on the degree of exchange rate pass-through into domestic prices. The decline in aggregate demand from an increase in interest rates and a slowdown in the United States economy would reduce inflationary pressure, with this effect more than offsetting the

Table I.6. Three simulated impacts of a rise in the federal funds rate on GDP growth

(Change relative to baseline scenario, percentage points)

	Scenario 1[a]		*Scenario 2*[b]		*Scenario 3*[c]	
	2006	*2007*	*2006*	*2007*	*2006*	*2007*
United States	−0.10	−0.40	−0.10	−0.70	−0.10	−1.10
Australia	0.00	−0.10	0.00	−0.10	0.00	−0.20
Japan	0.00	−0.20	0.00	−0.30	0.00	−0.50
North-East Asia						
China	−0.10	−0.70	−0.20	−1.20	−0.20	−1.90
Hong Kong, China	−0.10	−0.40	−0.10	−0.80	−0.20	−1.30
Republic of Korea	−0.10	−0.30	−0.10	−0.50	−0.20	−0.90
Taiwan Province of China	−0.10	−0.20	−0.10	−0.40	−0.10	−0.80
South-East Asia						
Indonesia	−0.20	−0.40	−0.20	−0.80	−0.30	−1.40
Malaysia	−0.10	−0.30	−0.10	−0.60	−0.10	−1.00
Philippines	−0.10	−0.40	−0.20	−0.70	−0.20	−1.20
Singapore	−0.20	−0.60	−0.20	−1.10	−0.30	−1.80
Thailand	−0.10	−0.51	−0.20	−0.90	−0.20	−1.50
South Asia						
India	−0.10	−0.20	−0.10	−0.40	−0.10	−0.60
Asian countries	**−0.04**	**−0.30**	**−0.06**	**−0.51**	**−0.08**	**−0.84**
Developing countries	**−0.11**	**−0.46**	**−0.15**	**−0.82**	**−0.18**	**−1.35**

Source: United Nations Economic and Social Commission for Asia and the Pacific calculations, based on the Oxford Economic Forecasting model.

[a] Assumes that federal funds rate increases by 25 basis points in the first quarter of 2006 and maintains that rate until 2007.

[b] Assumes that the federal funds rate increases in the third quarter of 2005 by 25 basis points so that it reaches 5 per cent.

[c] Assumes that the federal funds rate increases to 5.5 per cent at the end of 2006.

inflationary effect of the exchange rate depreciation. As a result, inflation in the region as a whole and in the developing countries would be reduced. All in all, the simulations suggest that an increase in the federal funds rate would have a negative growth effect on Asian economies, and on emerging Asian economies in particular, especially if the rate exceeds 4.75 per cent. The effect on inflation would be more limited.

Exchange rates become an issue

The large United States current account deficit has already set off a protectionist backlash in the United States against Asian countries, particularly China. This sentiment is partly reflected in the increasing number of anti-dumping actions against Asian countries, action in the United States Congress at the beginning of 2005 for a bill to impose trade restrictions on China in the absence of a revaluation of the yuan and political clamour for appreciation of other currencies in the region.

The widening global imbalances and their unsustainability thus do not bode well for the Asian and Pacific region, which is highly dependent on a favourable external environment for economic growth. ESCAP estimates show that a sharp and abrupt depreciation of the dollar could bring the United States current account deficit down to 3 per cent of GDP within a year, but at a significant cost to partner trading countries, particularly in Asia. On average, Asian currencies would experience an immediate real appreciation of about 33 per cent, with Singapore, the Philippines, Malaysia and Thailand experiencing the highest appreciation, in that order. This would be followed by current account balances across the region deteriorating by about 2.4 percentage points. The most seriously affected countries would be Malaysia, the Republic of Korea and Singapore. Finally, the unwinding of the global imbalances would lead to a substantial slowdown in economic activity, with Asia's GDP growth declining by about 2.6 percentage points. Singapore, the Republic of Korea, Indonesia and China would be the most seriously affected, in that order.

One way to address global imbalances is to focus on the current account balances themselves, ignoring their underlying causes, such as a deficiency or surplus of domestic savings. Since one country's deficit is another's surplus, one approach would be to cause the currencies to depreciate in deficit countries and to appreciate in surplus countries. Deficit countries would improve their export competitiveness and thus improve their current account balances. The opposite would be true for surplus countries.

This approach is unlikely to prove effective, however, for several reasons. First, the price elasticities of internationally traded goods tend to be limited in the short term, and consumer choice is not a matter of price alone. Hence, while the dollar has depreciated by 12 per cent in real effective terms since 2002, the current account deficit has continued to grow. Second, pressing for exchange rate adjustments in one country, such as China, or in one region, such as Asia, may not solve the problem either. For example, the United States–China bilateral deficit accounted for 26 per cent of the overall United States deficit in 2005. At this level, even a massive appreciation of the yuan may not make a meaningful dent in the United States current account deficit. Third, large exchange rate adjustments are likely to be excessively contractionary in their impact on output in the countries where the exchange rate appreciates.

Current account imbalances tend to reflect deeper structural problems. Unless these problems are addressed, a pure exchange rate adjustment is unlikely to provide a lasting solution.

Countries with excess savings over investment tend to run current account surpluses. The opposite is true for countries with low savings. Remedying the imbalances therefore requires higher investment in and by the surplus countries, and higher savings in deficit countries, particularly the United States.

Investment in Asia needs to be bolstered

Asian countries with current account surpluses need to bolster investment in their economies. In the aftermath of the 1997-1998 Asian financial crises, Asian countries have seen a build-up of excess savings over investment in the form of reserves. East Asia, in particular, has cut back on public sector investment. This partly reflects a deliberate effort to make economies less vulnerable to future financial crises by cutting back public sector expenditures (especially investment expenditure), maintaining high liquidity, running current account surpluses and accumulating foreign reserves. However, low public sector investment, especially in essential public goods, is likely to have negative consequences for competitiveness and long-term growth.

Asian countries have made tentative progress in promoting regional financial integration that could facilitate the profitable reduction of Asia's huge pool of savings. At the national level, countries are deepening their capital markets by issuing investment-grade securities and they are also strengthening corporate governance. As a result, domestic bond markets have grown rapidly, but cross-border activity in financial markets remains limited. At the regional level, the Asian Bond Market Initiative is a welcome development, but much remains to be done to deploy the region's pool of savings profitably within the region. There is great scope for investment in Asia, particularly given the enormous need for new investment in physical and social infrastructure.

If left to financial markets alone, an abrupt and large-scale unwinding of global current account imbalances could have widespread negative implications. A concerted global response is needed that is commensurate with the risk. Rather than trying to correct imbalances that may lead to sharp contractions in the global economy, a more effective solution would be a balanced, medium-term approach of exchange rate adjustments over time rather than suddenly. However, a lasting solution requires addressing structural imbalances in savings and investments across the world. It is also the case that the threat of a sudden unwinding of global imbalances can, perhaps, be overstated. Indeed, with United States interest rates going up, a sharp dollar depreciation in the short term is unlikely.

Table I.7. Change in real estate prices in selected Asian and Pacific economies from 2004 to 2005

(House price indices)

	Q3 2005 compared with Q3 2004	*Rate of inflation (percentage)*
Republic of Korea	20.0[a]	2.9
India	20.0[a]	4.5
Hong Kong, China	14.1	1.1
New Zealand	14.5	2.8
China	6.6	2.4
Singapore	3.3	0.5
Australia	1.0	2.4
Japan	−4.7	−0.1

Source: The Economist, various issues; *Seoul Times*, 18 October 2005.

[a] For major cities.

IS THERE A PROPERTY BUBBLE IN THE REGION?

There is no evidence of a bubble yet

The Asian and Pacific region has witnessed a sharp increase in property prices over the last few years, with this trend continuing in 2005 (see table I.7). In certain parts of the region, the increase has been extraordinary in real terms given the relatively low rates of inflation currently prevailing. The increase in real estate prices is virtually a worldwide phenomenon taking in much of the developed world, although there are important exceptions such as Germany and Japan. The following paragraphs examine whether there is a real estate bubble in the region and what policy implications the current situation might have.

The Organisation for Economic Co-operation and Development (OECD) defines an asset bubble in housing as occurring when the ratio of house prices to house rents exceeds a "fundamental ratio", with prices taking into consideration property taxes, tax relief and maintenance costs. Another definition of a bubble occurring is when average house prices are significantly higher than historical multiples of average annual earnings. While comparable data for a sufficient number of countries are not readily available in the Asian and Pacific region, a widening gap between the ratio of house prices and house rents has undoubtedly emerged in several countries in the region. Yet evidence of a property bubble in the region in the strict sense of the word has not been found except in particular locations. As table I.7 indicates, the real estate sector is not booming uniformly in the region.

The notion of a bubble also implies that sooner or later the bubble will burst and property prices will come crashing down. In the Republic of Korea, for instance, house prices slumped by 45 per cent in the immediate aftermath of the Asian financial crises. Similarly in Hong Kong, China, the average price of luxury homes tumbled 58 per cent in 1998 from their peak in mid-1997. However, there are no signs yet that property prices in the Asian and Pacific region are likely to fall dramatically in the near future.

Before a bubble forms, the real estate market usually displays evidence of buying and selling to take advantage of the capital gains available in the market rather than for owner occupation. In the United States, for instance, there are signs that home loans for the purchase of a second house for purposes other than owner occupation are playing a major role in the housing market and thus keeping prices higher than they would be otherwise.

In principle there is nothing wrong in borrowing to buy real estate for investment rather than for owner occupation. The action can be regarded as rational profit-seeking behaviour so long as borrowers are able to sell at a profit. The buying becomes speculative when people begin to borrow to buy, regardless of price or of their ability to service the debt, in the expectation of selling at an even higher price. Since prices cannot rise forever, some speculative buyers will inevitably take a loss. Losses on assets purchased with debt generate systemic risk that might affect the health of the financial system, and that is why real estate bubbles or potential bubbles have policy implications for Governments and central banks.

Reports from some parts of the region, especially Seoul and Hong Kong, China, suggest some speculative real estate buying activity. A further sign of speculation is a rise in the number of people buying property with a loan and selling it before their first mortgage payment becomes due. This phenomenon was common in many parts of East and South-East Asia before the 1997 financial crisis and has been reported to have resurfaced in places such as Hong Kong, China, and some cities of China. Such risky behaviour is giving rise to concerns about a potential real estate bubble in parts of the region.

A property bubble collapse could be devastating

The collapse of a property bubble is likely to prove even more devastating than a stock market crash, as many more people own houses than shares. The direct loss of asset value is compounded if property owners, propelled by a wealth effect, borrow for consumption against the inflated price of their property, as has happened in the United States over the past two to three years. If property prices crash, borrowers are left with huge personal debts that can lead to bankruptcy and misery for themselves and their families. There is another important social dimension to the problem. The construction sector is a major employment generator in both rich and poor countries. By one estimate, half of all private sector jobs created in the United States since 2001 have been in housing-related sectors. In developing countries, too, construction, with its many low-skill jobs, is a major employer, often acting as a "pull" for surplus labour in agriculture. A real estate collapse can therefore jeopardize the future of tens of thousands of workers living on the margins of the economy.

Is there a real estate bubble in the region? Not yet. First, house prices, though inflated in many countries of the region, are on the whole lower than they were in the mid-1990s. In Hong Kong, China, for instance, despite recent rises, prices for luxury homes in the second quarter of 2005 were still about 80 per cent of what they had been at their peak in 1997.[3]

Second, the funds that are fuelling the current property boom differ from those that fuelled the last one. In the 1990s, the property bubble in East Asia was built largely on money borrowed from abroad since global interest rates were lower than domestic rates. This, along with full current account convertibility, gave speculators access to a huge pool of overseas funds that were channelled into speculative deals in the property and stock markets. Currently, there is no significant interest rate differential across countries. Greater regulatory surveillance by central banks to ensure that foreign funds are not borrowed indiscriminately means that the bulk of

---

[3] *International Herald Tribune*, 22 April 2005.

funds going into the real estate sector are domestic in origin. Thus, the total sum of funds available for property investment is smaller than in the 1990s, so the boom is less extravagant this time.

Third, the chief cause of the current rise in property prices is low interest rates, which have caused home loan rates to fall to record lows in several countries. As interest rates move up, albeit gradually, this should dampen demand in the coming months. The remedy therefore suggests itself: property markets can be cooled down by the proper use of policy instruments, as has already begun in countries such as China, where real estate prices began to taper off in 2005 after four years of rapid increases, especially in Beijing, Hangzhou and Shanghai. Elsewhere, Australia is another location where the property boom appears to have come to an end.

Against this background, it would be safe to conclude that, while some Asian and Pacific property markets are certainly overheated, there is no property bubble of the magnitude seen in the past decade. However, what are the chances of a bubble building up in the near future? With property prices softening in developed countries, investors are likely to look for profitable avenues in the Asian and Pacific region. However, the two countries with scope for the highest returns suffer from either high risk (absence of a developed legal system, in China) or barriers to entry (individual foreign investors cannot buy property in India as yet). Regulators in many countries have also learned from the experience of the Asian financial crises of 1997-1998 and are more likely to intervene swiftly against speculative activity in real estate this time, as happened in China in 2005. There are therefore a number of constraints to any property bubble build-up in the Asian and Pacific region.

What measures could countries take to minimize the risk of a property bubble? One possible step is the imposition of a capital gains tax or a surcharge on the sale of property owned for less than a reasonable period (say, two years), a rise in margin requirements for home loans and a ban on the registration of property sales that occur before the first mortgage payment becomes due. There would also be some merit in building up awareness through the media to warn prospective buyers about the pitfalls of purchasing property in an overheated market. Governments could also enforce a practice that has been successfully used in financial markets: requiring real estate developers to list prominently in their prospectuses the potential risk factors.

THE CHALLENGE OF AVIAN INFLUENZA

Avian influenza is a viral infection primarily affecting birds but sometimes also mammals, such as pigs, tigers and humans. The current outbreak is caused by the H5N1 strain. The infection is spread by migratory birds and mechanical vectors, such as contaminated cages and clothing. Crowded poultry markets exacerbate the problem. International trade in live poultry could also spread the disease. The main mode of transmission to humans has been exposure to infected birds; almost all cases have been traced to this mode or the handling of infected carcasses.

Until recently, the current outbreak of avian influenza has affected mainly poultry in East and South-East Asia, although it has the potential to spread to humans under certain conditions. Between December 2003 and February 2006, there have been 161 human cases of avian influenza in the region with 86 deaths. No vaccine is yet available to protect humans from avian influenza. Anti-viral drugs (such as oseltamivir phosphate and zanamivir) have proved to be of some use for treating H5N1 infection.

The region has already suffered significant human and economic losses as a result of the outbreak. Losses in GDP resulting from the damaged poultry sector in Asia total roughly $10 billion. The impact has been hardest on small and medium-sized farmers, whose flocks are often not insured and who have no alternative sources of income. This is especially the case in poorer countries, where small backyard producers, usually individual rural households, supply the bulk of poultry output.

Consumer confidence in poultry has plummeted and poultry prices have dropped, adding to the financial burden on producers and affecting the poultry industry even in countries where poultry has not been infected. Approximately 140 million birds were destroyed as a result of the 2003 and 2004 avian influenza outbreaks in Asia. Trade in poultry at the domestic, regional and international levels has been adversely affected. Many countries ban imports of poultry meat from affected countries.

Estimates of human deaths from a possible global pandemic of the highly pathogenic avian influenza range from 5 million to 150 million people. As a conservative estimate, the global loss in GDP from a pandemic would amount to $200 billion in just one quarter and in a worst case scenario could plunge the global economy into recession. The costs of dealing with the wider spread of the disease have so far been limited, for example, about 0.1 per cent of GDP in Viet Nam but, should it emerge as a pandemic involving rapid human-to-human infection, it will inevitably cause massive disruption to everyday life through overloaded health-care systems, widespread quarantines and travel restrictions.

Tourism accounts for about a tenth of GDP in East and South-East Asia. A global pandemic that causes severe restrictions on people's movement and reduced consumer spending would result in a sizeable loss of global output and large increases in unemployment. Restrictions on the movement of people across regions could also adversely affect long-term economic growth through the destruction of human capital. The need for collective preparedness in the region is urgent, involving the stockpiling of medicines and vaccines (when they become available) and joint action on possible control measures such as travel restrictions to prevent the spread of the disease. From a cost-effectiveness standpoint, it is important to concentrate resources and action on controlling avian influenza at the source before it develops into a more rapidly spreading disease.

THE ISSUE OF INEQUALITY

High growth and increasing inequality are of growing concern

Of growing concern in the region is the number of countries experiencing increasing inequality in tandem with high growth. Inequality emerges in a number of guises. The most obvious is income inequality. Perfect equality is prcbably unattainable. However, inequality becomes a problem when differences in income across sections of society are deemed to be excessive, with the definition of "excessive" varying across countries and societies, or self-perpetuating. Also important are inequalities in the social sphere, for instance, unequal access to public services such as health and education, a problem compounded in many countries by gender, ethnic and cultural biases.

Income inequality is evident in many forms: the income gap between countries, between the poorest and richest citizens within a country, between rural and urban dwellers and between regions in a country. The Gini coefficient is one way of expressing this phenomenon, as is measuring the proportional income gap between social groups.

Within countries, there is ample evidence of high rates of growth being accompanied by growing inequality. This is an unfortunate departure from the region's reputation until the 1990s of having managed to retain a significant degree of equity along with the growth in incomes. Inequality manifests itself across a great diversity of circumstances. For example, inequality is increasing in the rapidly growing large economies of China and India, in the middle-income developing economies of the Republic of Korea and Thailand, in Viet Nam, the Lao People's Democratic Republic and Georgia, as well as in the Philippines, Nepal and Sri Lanka. In some countries, such as in China, India and Thailand, the income gap has a significant urban-rural bias and these income differences have increased over the 1990s.

Social inequalities, the most important being in access to health care and education, continue in many countries. Access depends on income, on rural or urban location and on gender. Although there have been some advances in extending primary education, the slow progress in reducing the gender divide in secondary education in South Asia remains a matter of great concern. At the current pace of progress, achieving the Millennium Development Goal of eliminating gender disparity in education by 2015 will prove a great challenge. Health inequalities are seen in the disproportionate numbers of poorer people who are affected by diseases and illnesses related to HIV infection and AIDS and smoking.

Least developed countries in the region display only a quarter of the average income of all Asian and Pacific countries, despite the impressive growth of the region as a whole. No least developed country in the region has yet graduated from that status. Extending the fruits of the region's development to the least developed countries is important for addressing the special needs of such countries, one of the targets of the eighth Millennium Development Goal.

Inequality has many facets

The problem of inequality has many facets. At the ethical level, it is an affront to social conscience if large numbers of people are excluded from the fruits of progress and development. Inequality also has serious negative functional attributes. Extensive research indicates that inequality is hampering progress towards achieving the Millennium Development Goal of eradicating extreme poverty and hunger. Countries can also gain through the effects of increased efficiency and productivity if inequality is less. For instance, health inequalities lead to lower worker productivity and higher national health care costs. Gender discrimination affects efficiency through the inability of girls to achieve their educational potential and to access adequate business-related facilities, such as credit. Gender and income inequalities have also played an important role in the spread of HIV/AIDS. Unequal access to sexual and reproductive health services, unequal rights in the home and community, and early marriage make women especially vulnerable to infection and less likely to receive adequate treatment. While the relationship between income inequality and HIV/AIDS is complex, the two are correlated in developing countries. At the social and political levels, there are clear links between income inequality and social unrest and violence.

Governments need to be aware that inequality may follow from particular growth-enhancing policies and other such measures. However, there are country examples of growth both with and without a negative effect on equality. Hence, growth and equality are not irreconcilable. The causes of the increase in inequality in some countries in the region include rapid population growth, trade and labour policies, the state of rural development and the lack of social protection mechanisms, in particular the inadequacy of public health and education services. FDI-led growth has widened the gap between skilled and unskilled labour in some countries, with the notable exception of FDI in the textile and apparel subsector. Rural areas have often lagged behind their urban counterparts in physical infrastructure and health and education opportunities and have received insufficient investment in agricultural research and extension services. The Asian financial crises of the 1990s had important longer-term negative consequences for equality in some of the countries affected. These include underemployment and higher school dropout rates at the primary and secondary levels.

More robust measures are needed

There can be little doubt that Governments need to adopt more robust measures to tackle inequality. Indeed, appropriate policy measures at both the country and regional levels could foster greater equality without sacrificing the benefits of growth. At the national level secondary schooling should be emphasized and should impart vocational skills that are relevant to the evolving globalized workplace. This would help to narrow gaps in knowledge and skills and reduce the income differences between skilled and less skilled workers. The rewards of secondary education are known to be large. It is particularly important to provide equal access to secondary schooling for girls. Adequate social safety nets are also necessary to provide coping mechanisms in the event of macroeconomic shocks. "Workfare" programmes, with sufficient credit and transfers, may be considered to enable the poor to return to employment.

While the paucity of public resources is a fundamental constraint for all developing countries, it is nonetheless important that the overall thrust of their fiscal policy should be to reduce inequality. On the expenditure side, fiscal policy needs to ensure that sufficient funds are available for poverty reduction in rural areas and for disadvantaged groups in times of growth. The health of the poor can benefit from the reduction or waiving of charges for health care and the provision of incentives to families for health check-ups for children. It is generally seen that the most effective way to ensure community health is by helping mothers and children directly. At the same time, tax systems should guard against excessive tax collection from the poor in the form of indirect taxes and high user charges for public services, in order to ensure that growth is maintained.

At the regional level, true tariff- and quota-free access for least developed countries to developed country markets will enable the poorest countries to share more equally in the benefits of globalization. While the Sixth WTO Ministerial Conference, held in Hong Kong, China in December 2005, offered least developed countries greater openness in terms of market access and the European Union already permits unrestricted access, some of the most important tariff lines remain excluded in some major developed countries. Greater support should be provided to international migrant workers in and from the region. Work by poor migrants and the remittances they send to their families can be an important tool to reduce income inequality in their home countries. Measures to facilitate such work include the provision of adequate social security by the labour-receiving countries and improvement in the mechanisms for transferring remittances. Asian and Pacific countries can gain from greater sharing of information on best practices among themselves, as they often have similar issues and concerns. One of many relevant areas is the regulation and delivery of inequality-reducing social programmes, for example, pro-poor public-private partnerships in the delivery of public services.

REMITTANCES: A RESOURCE FOR DEVELOPMENT

Remittances make a major contribution to development

Over the last two decades or more, remittances by migrants or temporary workers in foreign countries to their countries of origin have made a major socio-economic contribution in many countries. At the social level, remittances have added to family incomes and boosted consumption. At the national economic level, remittances have reduced, in some cases substantially, the current account deficit of many developing countries. Recent data indicate that remittances from high-income countries to developing countries reached more than $167 billion in 2005, an unprecedented sum, amounting to twice the level of official development assistance from all sources. Indeed, total remittances worldwide reached $232 billion in 2005, underlining their growing importance as a source of external finance. If remittances sent through informal channels are added, totals could be as much as 50 per cent higher. Of the top five remittance-receiving countries in the world in 2004, three were in the Asian and Pacific region: India ($21.7 billion), China ($21.3 billion) and the Philippines ($11.6 billion). The other major remittance-receiving countries in the region include Bangladesh, Pakistan and Sri Lanka. Countries such as Cambodia, the Lao People's Democratic Republic, Myanmar, Nepal, Thailand and Samoa also benefit from remittance flows. For many countries in the region, remittances now far exceed inflows of FDI and official development assistance (table I.8). In the Asian and Pacific region, flows between developing countries and flows from developed countries are important. Within the region, Australia; Hong Kong, China; Japan; New Zealand; the Republic of Korea; and Singapore are major sources of remittances for several developing countries. For the Lao People's Democratic Republic and Myanmar, Thailand is a major source of remittances, although the precise level is unknown. Outside the region, Canada, the United States, the United Kingdom, France, Saudi Arabia and the Gulf States remain the largest sources of remittances for the developing countries of the Asian and Pacific region. A growing number of remittance-senders are female workers.

Several factors have contributed to the recent surge in remittances. Liberalization of financial markets has made it easier to remit money from one country to another. A surge in the number of bank branches seeking remittance-related business in host countries and providing an increased range of financial services has also played an important role. Changes in the skill composition of workers going abroad has further contributed to the higher remittance flows of the last two to three years.

It needs to be emphasized, however, that remittances should not be seen as substitutes for development assistance. They do, nonethe-

Table I.8. Receipts of workers' remittances, foreign direct investment, official development assistance and merchandise exports for selected development countries of the Asian and Pacific region

(Millions of United States dollars)

	Remittances[a]		*Foreign direct investment[b]*		*Official development assistance and official aid*		*Merchandise exports*	
	Amount	*Percentage of GDP*	*Amount*	*Percentage of GDP*	*Amount*	*Percentage of GDP*	*Amount*	*Percentage of GDP*
Bangladesh	3 400	5.8	102	0.2	1 393	2.6	8 151	14.0
China	21 300	1.3	53 505	3.8	1 325	0.1	593 393	35.9
India	21 700	3.3	4 269	0.7	942	0.2	59 338	10.3
Lao People's Democratic Republic	1	0.0	19	0.9	299	14.2	311	17.7
Myanmar	78	0.9	134	1.6	126	1.5	2 927	42.5
Nepal	785	12.9	15	0.2	467	7.7	764	12.0
Pakistan	3 900	3.8	534	0.6	1 068	1.2	13 353	12.9
Philippines	11 600	13.7	319	0.4	737	0.9	38 728	45.7
Samoa	45	15.1	0	0.0	33	11.1	18	7.9
Sri Lanka	1 438	7.9	229	1.3	672	3.7	5 757	27.8
Thailand	1 601	1.1	1 949	1.4	−966	−0.7	94 979	58.1

Source: World Bank, *World Development Indicators* (CD-ROM) (Washington, D.C., 2005); and *Global Economic Prospects 2006* (Washington, D.C., 2006).

Notes: Data in the table refer to 2003. Data for merchandise exports refer to 2004, except for India (2003), the Lao People's Democratic Republic (2001) and Samoa (1999).

[a] Data are defined as workers' remittances and the employees' compensation. Data for Bangladesh, China, India, Pakistan and the Philippines are for 2004.

[b] Data refer to net inflows and are calculated based on the balance of payments.

less, play an important developmental role, particularly in helping countries to achieve some of the targets of the Millennium Development Goals. For instance, there is considerable evidence that remittances reduce household poverty through increased consumption and investment in housing, health and education. They also facilitate the formation of small businesses by other members of the household. The countries sending workers abroad benefit as migration eases unemployment pressure and results in a better allocation of labour at home.

It is not only the worker-exporting countries that benefit. The worker-receiving countries also benefit as the migrant workers enable them to meet their need for specific skills at lower cost and without long lead times. Several worker-receiving countries also use migrant workers to smooth out seasonal variability in the demand for labour, as in agriculture.

Remittances have an important macroeconomic impact

Remittances have important macroeconomic impacts too. They add to a country's foreign exchange earnings, enabling it to boost imports and spur growth. Indeed, as remittances are a non-debt-creating external resource, many developing countries find it more useful than other forms of external finance. Remittances increase a country's international creditworthiness and lead to lower borrowing costs. If financial institutions in the home countries can securitize remittance deposits, they can increase their access to and participation in international capital markets, thus enhancing the home countries' integration in such markets. Furthermore, remittances tend to be stable and may be countercyclical, thus smoothing out household consumption and investment patterns during episodes of unemployment and high inflation in the home countries.

Although remittances have grown rapidly, high transaction costs remain a disincentive to sending money home. Fees charged by remittance service providers are very high in comparison to the actual costs incurred in transferring the funds. For small transfers, fees can reach as high as 10 to 15 per cent of the money sent home. For poor migrant workers, who generally send small sums of money, this has encouraged the growth of informal channels for remittances. With declining transaction costs associated with more competition in the remittance market, a greater volume of funds could be remitted through formal channels. While measures must remain in place to eliminate the use of informal channels for criminal and terrorist activities, such measures should be implemented carefully so that the cost of transferring funds through formal means does not go up. One option is to increase the efficiency of the postal system. Identity cards for migrant workers have also proved useful.

There is no doubt that more can be done to increase the volume of home remittances and to enable recipients to use them more effectively. Additional measures should be taken to increase the access of poor migrant workers and their families to formal financial institutions. The establishment of more home-country bank branches in host countries and allowing microcredit institutions and credit unions to transfer funds to rural households could significantly increase the access of remittance senders and receivers to financial services.

Over the medium term, investments by sending countries in training to produce workers with higher skills could create a larger pool of workers who could respond to changing market conditions in the worker-receiving countries. Once workers can move beyond unskilled jobs and secure higher paying semi-skilled and skilled jobs, their earnings should rise, enabling them to send more money home. Making information available on job opportunities can improve the chances of migrants in securing stable, safe and remunerative employment abroad. Many poor families spend huge sums of money, sometimes their life savings, and incur large debts to send a family member abroad, only to find that the earnings are not sufficient to recover the costs incurred. Public policy can play a key role in providing timely and appropriate information so that potential migrants can avoid such financially devastating consequences.

Remittances are private flows of money

Policymakers need to recognize that remittances are private flows of money that need to be treated as such. Therefore, these flows should not be taxed, for at least two reasons. First, these flows have already been taxed in the originating countries. Second, taxes would only discourage the transfer of funds through formal channels. Measures to guide remittances to specific end-uses or sectors by creating matching-fund programmes should also be avoided, by and large, as they have proven to be ineffective.

Migrant worker-sending countries need to devote sufficient resources to monitoring the changing labour-demand patterns in receiving countries and to make this information widely available. Policymakers also need to tighten up regulatory and enforcement mechanisms to ensure that their citizens do not fall prey to unscrupulous agents. The level of remittances and the rate at which these flows increase over time are intimately connected with the safety and security of migrant populations. This is particularly pressing for countries that send large numbers of women workers abroad, as they remain highly vulnerable to misinformation, mistreatment, exploitation and physical violence.[4]

Finally, official data on remittances do not always capture the flows to the developing countries. Data on remittances are sometimes scattered across overlapping categories and institutions. In some instances, remittances to buy real estate or business assets are classified as FDI. Remittances in the form of imports of durable goods are also difficult to record. Financial institutions in some countries treat such flows in ways that make it difficult to classify and accurately estimate them. These problems indicate the need for better data management and improvements in the reporting systems of both the remittance-sending and remittance-receiving countries.

---

[4] Freer movements of natural persons, as envisaged under Mode 4 of the WTO General Agreement on Trade in Services negotiations could bring significant benefits to many developing countries of the region. A more formalized approach under WTO could foster long-term human resources development in developing countries and simultaneously ensure better working conditions for their citizens abroad.

THE OUTCOME OF THE SIXTH WTO MINISTERIAL CONFERENCE

The Sixth WTO Ministerial Conference, held in Hong Kong, China, adopted a 44-page Ministerial Declaration. Haunted by the Doha round's past failures (numerous missed deadlines and the collapse of the Fifth Ministerial Conference in Cancun, Mexico, in September 2003), the Declaration is the product of a fractious preparatory process, punctuated by a flurry of cross-continental mini-ministerial meetings seeking to bridge significant divergence among WTO members before the Ministerial Conference. In the lead up to the Conference, it became clear that positions were too wide apart and that its outcome would not re-establish the primacy of the multilateral trading system. Finally, pragmatism prevailed, all the members agreed to lower their expectations in favour of consensus rather than breakdown. The Conference thus delivered no surprises.

New elements in the Declaration include the following:

- An end to all agricultural export subsidies would take place by the end of 2013, with a progressive phase-out of subsidies so that a substantial part would be realized by the end of the first half of the implementation period, and an end to all export subsidies for cotton by developed countries in 2006.
- For non-agricultural market access, the Swiss formula for the reduction of tariffs was adopted. Under the formula, higher tariffs are reduced more steeply than lower tariffs, leading to a more harmonized (flatter) tariff structure across all WTO members. The details of the tariff-reduction formula (the starting point, the extent of reductions, the timeline and the flexibilities for developing countries) all remain unresolved. The differential values of the coefficient for developed and developing countries have yet to be determined.
- Duty- and quota-free access "on a lasting basis" was accepted by developed and developing countries declaring themselves in a position to do so, for at least 97 per cent of exports (as defined at the tariff line level) from the 32 least developed countries that are WTO members, by 2008 or no later than the start of the implementation period. The term "lasting basis" raises questions on the legally binding nature of such commitments and possible reversals of commitments. Furthermore, the products most likely to fall into the 3 per cent category, textiles and clothing products, are the very products in which least developed countries are the most competitive and would stand to gain the most from unfettered access to developed markets. Notwithstanding these concerns, this represents a step forward on an issue that has been on the agenda for more than a decade.
- Intensification of the request-offer negotiations in services, which remains the main method of negotiation, was accepted with a view to securing substantial commitments. A second round is to be conducted by 31 July 2006, while a draft schedule of commitments in services is scheduled for completion by 31 October 2006.

While the Declaration puts the Doha round back on track, an issue of fundamental importance is whether it holds the promise that the Doha round will correct the "development deficit" of the Uruguay round. In other words, is the development aspect of the Doha round back on track? Among ESCAP members and associate members, and other WTO members outside the region, there is not complete agreement on the extent to which the Doha round will deliver on development issues. While it is true that as long as the Doha round is in process, no answer is definitive; however, expectations have been lowered. A key challenge facing ESCAP members and associate members over the next year will be how to deal with raised development expectations. Trade-dependent nations of the region can ill afford to lose yet another opportunity for turning trade into a poverty-fighting mechanism. The larger traders among the developing countries of the region could turn this into an opportunity if they seize the moment to exert new leadership.

In the months ahead, developing countries in the Asian and Pacific region will consider making concessions with a commercial value that will ensure that developed countries find it attractive to remain committed to the process. Thus, the task facing trade-dependent countries of the region is how to harness the traditional reciprocity dynamics of WTO to move forward on their market-access expectations. At the same time, service industries in developed countries are seeking access to new markets. A jump-start from Asia and the Pacific is needed to open up the services sector, and efforts made in this regard by one or two increasingly dynamic service exporters are worthy of further support by other developing countries in the region. A novel display of developing countries leading and maintaining a negotiating coalition in this sector, even though specific national interests may differ, could inject dynamism and renewed confidence into the Doha negotiations. Careful preparation and coordination among ministries and a range of private sector interests are needed. Private sector interests involve not just import-competing firms but, more importantly, those with export interests and those that are large consumers of services. ESCAP members and associate members would need to embark on measures aimed at achieving the potential benefits to be realized from such coalitions.

II. MACROECONOMIC PERFORMANCE, ISSUES AND POLICIES

REGIONAL OVERVIEW

Rapid economic growth and macroeconomic stability are widely recognized as central objectives of development policy. All developing countries need rapid output growth to fulfil the rising aspirations of their citizens for a better standard of living. Poorer developing countries need more rapid growth to generate the resources needed to develop the social and physical infrastructure to make progress towards achieving the Millennium Development Goals. Macroeconomic stability is a prerequisite for rapid socio-economic growth since high inflation rates, high interest rates and fluctuating exchange rates can be devastating for both economic growth and sustained social progress, as shown by the economic and financial crises that have affected different parts of the world over the years. According to this measure, the developing economies of the Asian and Pacific region have been quite successful in achieving both social and economic objectives, enjoying average GDP growth of 6.6 per cent and an average inflation rate of just below 5 per cent between 2003 and 2005 (see table II.1).

Following a strong performance in 2004, the economic growth rate of developing countries in the Asian and Pacific region slowed moderately to 6.6 per cent in 2005, a deceleration of 0.8 percentage point. This was the result largely of high oil and commodity prices and a global slowdown in trade. From the perspective of countries in the region, much of 2004 and 2005 was characterized by a cyclical downturn in the world's information and communication technology industry in which many of the region's economies enjoys considerable competitive strength. The slowdown in 2005 was fairly uniform, with all subregions and country groups experiencing some loss of momentum in economic activity.

China, India and Pakistan saw high economic growth in 2005 despite high oil prices

However, a number of individual economies, principally the energy producers, registered higher economic growth in 2005 than in 2004. By far the most striking performers were China, India and Pakistan, countries that are net oil-importers, where growth accelerated in 2005. In those countries, growth is increasingly being driven by buoyant domestic investment and consumption and, significantly, neither the higher energy prices nor the global trade slowdown affected their dynamism. In China, however, exports remain a major component of growth. From a more global point of view, despite the modest slowdown, the Asian and Pacific region had the highest rate of economic growth of all regions of the world. For the third year in succession, no country in the region experienced a negative rate of economic growth.

Inflation remained low in 2005

The rise in oil and other commodity prices did, however, nudge inflation up in 2005 over that in 2004, although price increases throughout the region remained mild by historical standards at less than 5 per cent, the average level in recent years. North and Central Asia, despite being a net oil-exporting area, saw inflation rise to 12 per cent, fuelled mainly by high inflation in the Russian Federation. The North and Central Asian subregion continues to remain susceptible to price pressures, primarily because of chronic supply-demand mismatches and high rates of growth in money supply in the transition to a market-based system among countries of the former Union of Soviet Socialist Republics. Inflation declined in East and North-East Asia as food prices fell following good harvests in China and the price of manufactured goods in that subregion trended lower; in addition, there was subdued aggregate demand growth in the Republic of Korea. Similarly, average inflation was close to zero in the developed countries of the region because of continuing deflation in Japan. All other subregions experienced only a moderate increase in price pressures as economies adjusted well to the higher oil and commodity prices. Some countries attenuated the effects of

Table II.1. Rates of economic growth and inflation in selected Asian and Pacific economies, 2003-2006

(Percentage)

	Real GDP				*Inflation*[a]			
	2003	*2004*	*2005*[c]	*2006*[d]	*2003*	*2004*	*2005*[c]	*2006*[d]
Developing economies[b]	6.5	7.4	6.6	6.5	4.8	4.7	4.8	4.4
East and North-East Asia	6.5	7.7	6.9	6.5	1.4	3.2	2.2	2.2
China	10.0	10.1	9.6	8.4	1.2	3.9	1.9	2.0
Hong Kong, China	3.2	8.1	7.5	5.4	–2.5	–0.4	1.1	1.6
Mongolia	5.6	10.6	6.0	6.0	4.6	11.0	10.0	6.0
Republic of Korea	3.1	4.6	3.8	4.9	3.6	3.6	2.8	2.9
Taiwan Province of China	3.3	5.7	3.8	4.1	–0.3	1.6	2.3	1.6
North and Central Asia	7.5	7.4	6.9	6.1	12.9	10.2	12.0	9.9
Armenia	13.9	10.1	13.9	7.0	4.8	6.9	0.6	3.0
Azerbaijan	11.2	10.2	26.4	24.8	2.2	6.7	9.6	7.4
Georgia	11.1	6.2	7.7	9.0	4.8	5.7	8.2	3.0
Kazakhstan	9.3	9.6	9.2	8.6	6.4	6.9	7.6	6.7
Kyrgyzstan	6.7	7.1	–0.6	3.0	3.1	4.1	4.3	4.7
Russian Federation	7.3	7.2	6.4	5.7	13.7	10.9	12.7	10.3
Tajikistan	11.0	10.6	6.7	6.8	17.1	6.8	7.8	7.3
Turkmenistan	13.0	9.0	11.0	9.0	6.5	10.0	10.5	11.0
Uzbekistan	4.2	7.7	7.2	7.0	13.1	1.7	7.1	7.4
Pacific island economies	3.0	3.3	2.7	3.0	10.7	3.0	2.2	3.4
Cook Islands	3.1	3.4	3.2	3.0	2.0	0.9	2.9	2.0
Fiji	3.0	4.1	1.7	2.0	4.2	3.3	3.0	3.0
Papua New Guinea	2.9	2.9	3.0	3.5	14.7	2.1	1.0	3.4
Samoa	3.3	3.7	5.6	3.0	0.1	11.7	7.8	3.0
Solomon Islands	5.3	5.0	2.9	2.6	10.0	7.1	6.2	5.0
Tonga	3.1	1.6	2.8	2.8	11.6	11.0	9.6	9.0
Vanuatu	2.4	3.2	2.9	2.2	3.0	1.4	2.5	2.5
South and South-West Asia[e]	7.3	7.4	7.0	7.0	10.4	6.5	7.0	5.7
India	8.5	7.5	8.1	7.9	3.9	3.8	4.5	4.0
Iran (Islamic Republic of)	6.7	4.8	5.0	7.4	15.6	15.2	14.5	11.5
Pakistan	5.1	6.4	8.4	7.0	3.1	4.6	9.3	8.0
Sri Lanka	6.0	5.4	5.5	6.0	6.3	7.6	11.6	6.4
Turkey	5.8	8.9	5.0	5.0	25.3	8.6	7.7	5.8
South-East Asia	5.0	6.4	5.4	5.9	3.1	3.9	5.8	6.0
Indonesia	4.9	5.1	5.6	6.2	6.6	6.1	10.5	11.4
Malaysia	5.4	7.1	5.2	5.9	1.2	1.4	2.9	2.8
Philippines	4.5	6.0	4.8	5.2	3.5	6.0	7.6	7.0
Singapore	1.4	8.4	6.4	6.0	0.5	1.7	0.4	1.2
Thailand	6.9	6.1	4.5	5.7	1.8	2.8	4.5	4.0
Viet Nam	7.3	7.7	8.4	8.0	3.1	7.8	8.4	7.4
Least developed countries	5.6	6.1	5.2	5.8	4.7	5.8	6.3	6.6
Bangladesh	5.3	6.3	5.4	6.0	4.4	5.8	6.5	7.0
Bhutan	6.8	8.7	8.8	8.0	2.1	4.6	5.5	5.0
Cambodia	7.1	7.7	6.3	6.1	0.5	5.6	5.5	3.5
Lao People's Democratic Republic	5.8	6.5	7.2	7.5	15.5	10.5	8.0	7.0
Myanmar	13.8	5.0	4.5	3.5	8.0	..	..	..
Nepal	3.1	3.7	2.6	4.5	4.8	4.0	4.5	5.0

(Continued on next page)

Table II.1 *(continued)*

(Percentage)

	Real GDP				Inflation[a]			
	2003	2004	2005[c]	2006[d]	2003	2004	2005[c]	2006[d]
Developed economies	1.9	2.4	2.5	2.1	–0.1	0.2	0.0	0.5
Australia	3.3	3.3	2.5	3.2	2.8	2.3	2.8	2.9
Japan	1.8	2.3	2.5	2.0	–0.3	0.0	–0.3	0.3
New Zealand	3.8	4.4	2.2	2.0	1.8	2.3	2.8	3.0

Sources: United Nations Economic and Social Commission for Asia and the Pacific, based on national sources; International Monetary Fund, *International Financial Statistics* (CD-ROM) (Washington, D.C., IMF, 2005); Asian Development Bank, *Key Indicators of Developing Asian and Pacific Countries 2005* (Manila, ADB, 2005); Economist Intelligence Unit, *Country Reports* and *Country Forecasts* (London, EIU, 2005 and 2006), various issues; Commonwealth of Independent States Inter-State Statistical Committee, <www.cisstat.com>, accessed on 9 January 2006 and 10 February 2006.

[a] Changes in the consumer price index.

[b] Data are based on 38 developing economies representing more than 95 per cent of the population of the region (including the Central Asian countries); GDP figures at market prices (in United States dollars) in 2000 (at 1995 prices) have been used as weights to calculate the regional and subregional growth rates.

[c] Estimate.

[d] Forecast or target.

[e] The estimates and forecasts for countries relate to fiscal years defined as follows: fiscal year 2004/05 = 2004 for India, the Islamic Republic of Iran and Myanmar; and fiscal year 2003/04 = 2004 for Bangladesh, Nepal and Pakistan.

those higher prices by continuing to subsidize oil products and others by pre-emptively tightening monetary policy, thereby dampening inflationary expectations.

The strong growth momentum in 2005, despite the rising energy prices, suggests the rise in overall prices that has manifested itself in an outward shift in the aggregate demand curve owing to the huge growth in the demand for goods and services from the region's fast-growing economies, especially China. This change has been accompanied by an equally large outward shift in the aggregate supply curve. As a result, the higher demand has been satisfied with an equally robust supply response rather than being dissipated in the form of higher prices, as had happened in previous oil shocks when "stagflation" resulted. Success in keeping inflation in check was also helped by the relatively low inflation rate prevailing in past few years, the lower intensity of energy needed per unit of higher output, especially in economies with a large preponderance of services, and more effective monetary policies that have been built on the experience gained in previous episodes of oil price increases.

Growth should continue in 2006, but there are some challenges ahead

The region as a whole is expected to grow at about the same pace in 2006 as in 2005, absent any new adverse developments such as a further large increase in oil prices, an influenza pandemic or a major realignment of exchange rates. Even as the Chinese economy is predicted to slow somewhat, the slack is likely to be taken up by India and the South-East Asian economies, by strong domestic consumption growth in India and by a cyclical upturn in the information and communication technology industry in South-East Asian economies. The countries of South and South-West Asia, recently affected by two major natural disasters within a 10-month period, have been fortunate in that the disaster zones were not major contributors to national output, except where tourism is a major activity.

Optimism for 2006 also stems from the hope for a sustained economic recovery in Japan, while continuing high commodity prices should help the region's commodity producers. On the other hand, a sharper than expected slowdown in the United States economy would adversely affect export momentum from the region, even though intraregional trade has become a strong driver of growth over the last two to three years. The following paragraphs examine the principal near- and medium-term policy issues and challenges likely to confront the region in the coming months. Policy issues with a global dimension, such as oil prices, regional imbalances, threat of avian influenza, the post-Hong Kong, China, WTO agenda and others, were discussed in chapter I.

Near-term policy issues

Tighter fiscal and monetary policies could produce adverse impacts

An important issue for economies in the region in 2006 is the potentially adverse impact on growth of tighter fiscal and monetary policies. For several years, many countries have been following a policy of fiscal consolidation with a view to reducing the growing burden of public debt and providing more space for private investment. Inflationary pressures induced by higher oil prices have resulted in a tightening of monetary policy and rising interest rates across the region, though with some notable exceptions. Reinforcing the effects of long-term fiscal consolidation, especially in countries that are cutting government spending rather than improving tax revenues, higher interest rates are bound to have some negative effect on the pace of economic activity. A particular danger is where low interest rates have fuelled strong growth in debt-financed private consumption and also created asset bubbles. Higher interest rates should prove less deleterious for economic growth than cuts in government spending, especially in poorer developing countries where government development expenditure is often the key to the pace of development. However, in the richer developed countries, where real interest rates are already high, a further increase could trigger a hard landing of the economy through a sharp fall in asset prices.

China faces excess capacity

Several economies in the region have become closely tied to the Chinese economy through trade and investment links, as in much of the East and North-East Asian subregion. After years of furious growth, the Chinese economy is now faced with excess capacity in a number of sectors, such as steel, cement, consumer electronics and construction. Among the various adjustment measures that are being taken by the Chinese authorities to cool the economy, a reduction in imports related to these sectors is probable. That would adversely affect other economies, the exports of which have been driven by the strong pace of Chinese demand in the last two to three years. China is the largest destination for exports from the Republic of Korea and Taiwan Province of China; China ranks second to the United States among Japan's main export destinations. Commodity exporters such as Australia have also benefited hugely from Chinese demand. All the above-mentioned countries, including China's smaller neighbours, would have to make suitable adjustments in their external sectors, especially as slower growth in Chinese demand could weaken overall commodity prices in the region.

A potentially positive development in the Asian and Pacific region is the Japanese economy's recovery from a decade of stagnation. The prospects of more sustained growth in that country over the next few years have led to remarkable buoyancy in Japan's stock markets, isolated but significant increases in property prices and the likelihood that the country will overcome deflation in 2006. In addition, corporate investment activity has increased and unemployment has begun to decline. Together, these developments should strengthen consumer confidence and provide a more durable basis for sustained output growth over the medium term. As one of the main sources of foreign direct investment and an important destination of exports for many countries, the recovery of the world's second largest economy has great significance for the region as a whole. However, Japan's recovery is at a nascent stage, and its real impact on the region will depend on the revival of domestic consumption and on how it deals with its massive public debt.

Medium-term policy issues

Poverty reduction remains the most significant challenge for the region

Despite growing faster than most regions of the world for more than two decades, poverty reduction remains the most important challenge for the Asian and Pacific region. It is a chastening reality that the region contains two thirds of the world's poor, with 40 per cent of the extremely poor who earn less than $1 a day living in South Asia and in the least developed countries. Pockets of extreme poverty also exist in parts of South-East Asia and in some Pacific island States.

It should be emphasized that elimination of poverty has no general solution that would be applicable equally in all countries and at different levels of development. The handful of economies in the region, such as Hong Kong, China; the Republic of Korea; Singapore; and Taiwan Province of China, that have effectively overcome poverty during the past quarter century have done so by applying individual approaches and policies. The one common feature in their diverse experience is that a fast pace of economic growth is vitally important. Rapid growth not only provides ever-increasing opportunities for employment in both the formal and informal sectors but also generates resources for the public sector to use in addressing issues of non-income poverty, such as insufficient or poor quality public goods: education, health, transport and housing.

Rapid growth alone is not enough

However, rapid growth alone may not be enough. The impressive growth of China and, of late, India is widely believed to have pulled millions of people out of extreme poverty. These successes, welcome as they are, have nevertheless been skewed in their impact. For instance, in China growth has been most visible in the coastal areas, with income levels growing more slowly in the interior and in the western part of the country. In India, the information and communication technology boom has reduced the incidence of poverty in urban areas, but large parts of the rural economy have been left behind. It thus appears that in countries where poverty is widespread, jobs and income growth alone will not eliminate non-income poverty. Governments need to expand the provision of public goods and ensure better access for the poor. Without such intervention, even rapid economic growth will deliver inequitable outcomes and will be unsustainable over the long term.

While the private sector, including civil society, can provide critical support in widening access to public services, through public-private partnerships and other means, government intervention remains essential for scaling up individual successes and creating a favourable environment, through regulation, for promoting and sustaining universal access to public services. A good example is Viet Nam, where the Government has not only created a favourable business environment for domestic and foreign investors but also has extended the benefits of economic growth to the wider society by investing in education, medical facilities, roads, drinking water and electricity in rural areas. Governments would do well to re-examine dispassionately their successes and failures in tackling the challenge of poverty and address decisively the constraints that could prevent them from attaining the Millennium Development Goals.

Inequitable growth is an important issue

The problem of inequitable growth is not confined to specific geographic areas and it is not specific to certain levels of development (discussed at length in chapter I). Inequitable growth is an important issue in many of the smaller economies, including the least developed countries and the Pacific island States. In such countries, national efforts can be severely undermined by the paucity of financial and non-financial resources; these efforts are also made more difficult owing to the physical remoteness of the countries. Their prospects for sustained long-term growth and, hence, for reducing poverty are very limited without regional and indeed, international aid and support, such as the global compact envisioned as one of the Millennium Development Goals. In that context, the temporary movement of workers on contract employment abroad is an option with enormous potential for reducing poverty. This option is not capital-intensive and, with its relatively short lead time, it could deliver visible results quickly.

Remittances help to raise living standards

Remittances sent to their families by temporary migrants and workers on contracts abroad have helped enormously to raise the standard of living in some of the poorest sections of society in Bangladesh and Nepal in South Asia; Cambodia, the Lao People's Democratic Republic and Myanmar in South-East Asia; and Samoa and Tonga in the Pacific. Governments in these and other economies with high levels of underemployment and with limited opportunities in formal sector employment could follow the example set by the Philippines and systematically promote the temporary export of workers as part of a national development and poverty-reducing strategy. However, countries facing labour shortages or shortages of people with specific skills would also have to allow migrant workers to enter and work in their economies legally, without fear of harassment, and to treat them with dignity.

An issue with which many ESCAP developing countries will have to contend over the medium term is the emergence of China as a manufacturing powerhouse for the rest of the world. Several economies, mainly in East and South-East Asia, have prospered as relatively open economies, with international trade serving as the engine of growth. These economies, which have also benefited from the inflow of FDI and its various spillover effects, are listed in the two right-side quadrants of figure II.1. The figure depicts the relative openness of selected Asian

Figure II.1. Relative openness of selected Asian and Pacific economies

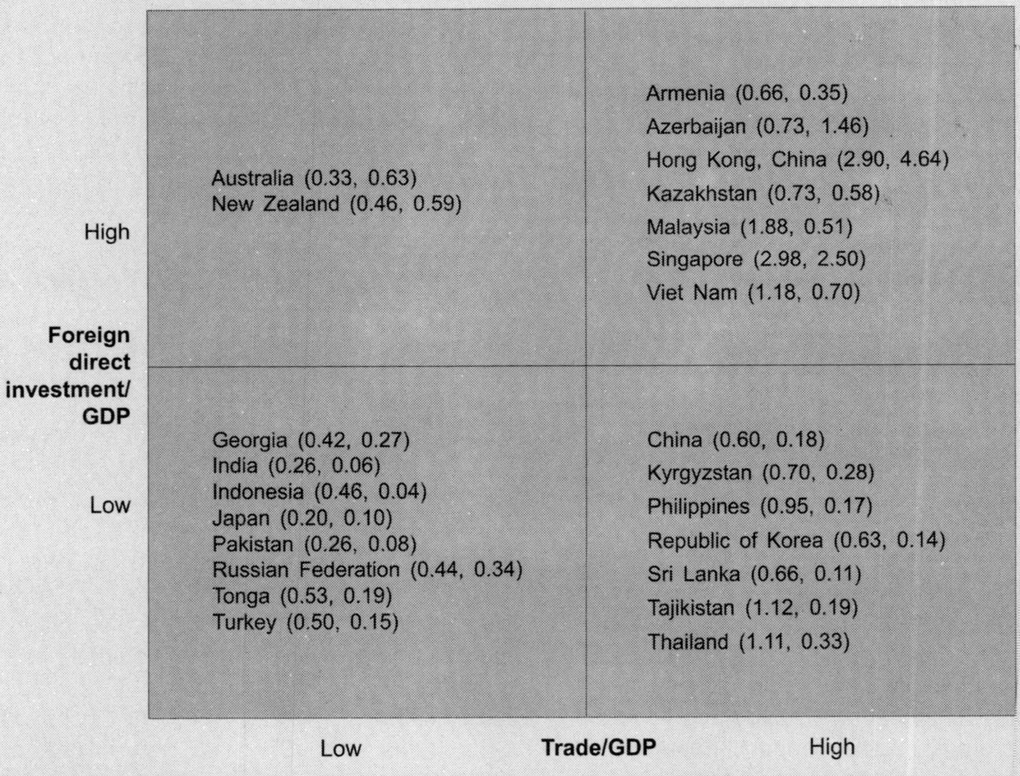

Sources: International Monetary Fund, *Direction of Trade Statistics* (CD-ROM) (Washington, D.C., IMF, December 2005) and *World Economic Outlook, September 2005*, (Washington, D.C., IMF, 2005); United Nations Conference on Trade and Development, Foreign Direct Investment online database <http://stats.unctad.org>, accessed on 16 December 2005; and national sources.

Notes: Trade data refer to annual average exports and imports of merchandise goods for the period 2002-2004. Foreign direct investment refers to the annual average stock of FDI for the same period. The cut-off point between "High" and "Low" has been defined as 60 per cent in the case of total trade/GDP and 35 per cent in the case of FDI/GDP. Individual country ratios for trade/GDP and FDI/GDP respectively have been shown in parenthesis.

and Pacific economies. The position of China as the most attractive FDI destination in the region is changing, yet the country has a vast reservoir of workers and huge internal market. Thus, these phenomena will pose new and challenging issues with which economies in the region will have to deal if the overall regional growth momentum is to be maintained.

Although the sum of FDI is not fixed, that is, more FDI for China does not necessarily mean less for others, China enjoys a huge competitive advantage over other producers and exporters of labour-intensive manufactured goods in the region. As described in the section on the East and North-East Asian subregion, China dominates the world in textile and clothing exports and it is developing prowess in the export of information and communication technology equipment. In the near future it might emerge as an important base for automobile exports. Several established producers of information and communication technology goods have already felt China's impact. Other industries are likely to be affected by China's growing competitiveness in industries that are not labour-intensive. These developments suggest that South-East Asia could experience sharply reduced inflows of FDI and of access to the technology and markets that FDI brings.

The restructuring experience of Singapore (see discussion in the section on the South-East Asian subregion) suggests some of the alternatives available to South-East Asian economies. These include a radical restructuring of the manufacturing sector in order to benefit from China's economic development by moving from labour-intensive to more technology- and capital-intensive production niches. Expanding the service sectors with information and communication technology is another option, but this would require major investment in human resources and cannot be done in just a few years. Moreover, investment in education is only one element in improving human resources. Better standards of governance in both the public and private sectors of the region's economies are also required in order to maximize total factor productivity. The way in which individual economies cope with the challenges posed by China will depend on a variety of considerations, involving a strong interaction between all stakeholders in pursuing a common vision and agenda for the future.

North and Central Asia should expedite economic reforms

Finally, greater economic diversification is needed in the economies in transition in North and Central Asia. The subregion is going through a sustained period of growth, with the energy sector, helped by high oil and gas prices, providing the main source of growth in many economies, especially Azerbaijan, Kazakhstan, the Russian Federation and Tajikistan. In Azerbaijan, where foreign capital inflows into the energy sector constitute an unusually high proportion of GDP, the need for broad-based growth is particularly strong in order to prevent the Dutch disease phenomenon in which the exchange rate appreciates and the economy loses competitiveness in the non-energy sectors. The Central Asian economies also need to expedite their economic reforms, particularly in the macroeconomic arena, that have been going on since 1992. Only two countries, Kazakhstan and the Russian Federation, have achieved market-economy status thus far.

DEVELOPING COUNTRIES

East and North-East Asia

Overview

Robust growth continues in the subregion

The economies of the East and North-East Asian subregion differ greatly in size and level of development. China accounts for two thirds of subregional GDP. In purchasing power parity terms, however, that country's GDP per capita of $4,500 is exceeded by a wide margin by that of Hong Kong, China, at $27,000, and the Republic of Korea, at $17,000. Those two economies also have a much higher ranking than China in the human development index of the United Nations Development Programme. Nonetheless, the economy of the subregion is hugely influenced by the increasing weight and power of China as a trading nation and its remarkable impact on the prices of manufactured goods, raw materials, exchange rates, financial flows, services and tourism.

Powered by the spectacular performance of the Chinese economy in 2005, the East and North-East Asian subregion forged ahead with strong growth in GDP and exports. Although the subregion's performance was a little less impressive in 2005 than in 2004, it continued on its robust growth path. Significantly, domestic demand appears to be replacing export demand as the primary source of growth, but Hong Kong, China, is likely to continue to depend mainly on trade, especially trade with China, including re-exports.

Several downside risks emerged during the year, as concerns heightened over rising global macroeconomic imbalances, steeply rising oil prices, the growing threat of an influenza pandemic and dollar interest rates trending upwards. The overall impact in 2005 was limited. Although dramatic change is not expected in 2006, investor sentiment may well be affected by the way in which the risks evolve and the measures that Governments of countries in the subregion take to deal with them.

Steep rises in oil and other commodity prices left an imprint on the economies of the East and North-East Asian subregion. China and the Republic of Korea performed better than others in coping with the upward pressure on prices, China doing so through a system of administrative controls on oil prices. In any event, price increases remained muted overall, although there was some modest upward pressure on prices in Taiwan Province of China.

On the positive side, global markets in information and communication technology began a cyclical recovery, affecting the Republic of Korea and Taiwan Province of China positively.

China became the largest destination for exports from the Republic of Korea and Taiwan Province of China in 2005, underpinning the growing interdependence in the subregion, but especially the crucial role that China plays in the region as a whole. The return to growth in Japan strengthened the subregion's prospects. In terms of global imbalances, in which the Chinese current account surplus features prominently, there was a 2.1 per cent appreciation in the trade-weighted exchange rate of the Chinese yuan in mid-2005. Indications of a further modest rise in the yuan's value in the coming months also emerged as the central bank of China executed its first ever swap transaction in the domestic foreign exchange market. Indeed, of the likely scenarios of how the global imbalances could unwind, one could include a significant appreciation of Asian currencies, including the Republic of Korea won.

GDP growth performance

China's economy maintains spectacular growth

The East and North-East Asian subregion may be the most dynamic in Asia and the Pacific. Its economies specialize in high-technology industries and are increasingly developing new technologies in the information and communication technology field, particularly in semiconductors and telecommunications.

The subregion has one of the world's most sophisticated financial centres in Hong Kong, China, providing world-class services in commerce, financial intermediation and capital markets.

China continued its spectacular growth of the last two decades; average GDP growth was 10 per cent per year in the period 1987-1996 and 8.4 per cent in the period 1997-2005, making China the world's greatest economic success story in recent history. New official figures released by the National Bureau of Statistics resulted in an upward revision by almost 17 per cent of the 2004 GDP of China (equivalent to $285 billion), with most of the increase in the service sector. This indicates that the economy of China is more diversified than previously thought. On the basis of the revised data the country's GDP is estimated to have grown by 9.6 per cent in 2005 (see figure II.2). On the social front, strong GDP growth was also manifested in a further reduction in income poverty in 2005 as growth in industrial production further reduced registered unemployment in urban areas.

Robust growth in China has been sustained by three broad factors: surging net exports, domestic investment, especially in infrastructure and, increasingly, domestic consumption. Strong export demand propelled much of the growth, particularly in the second half of 2005. Based on current data and trends, exports

Figure II.2. GDP and sectoral growth in selected East and North-East Asian economies, 2003-2005

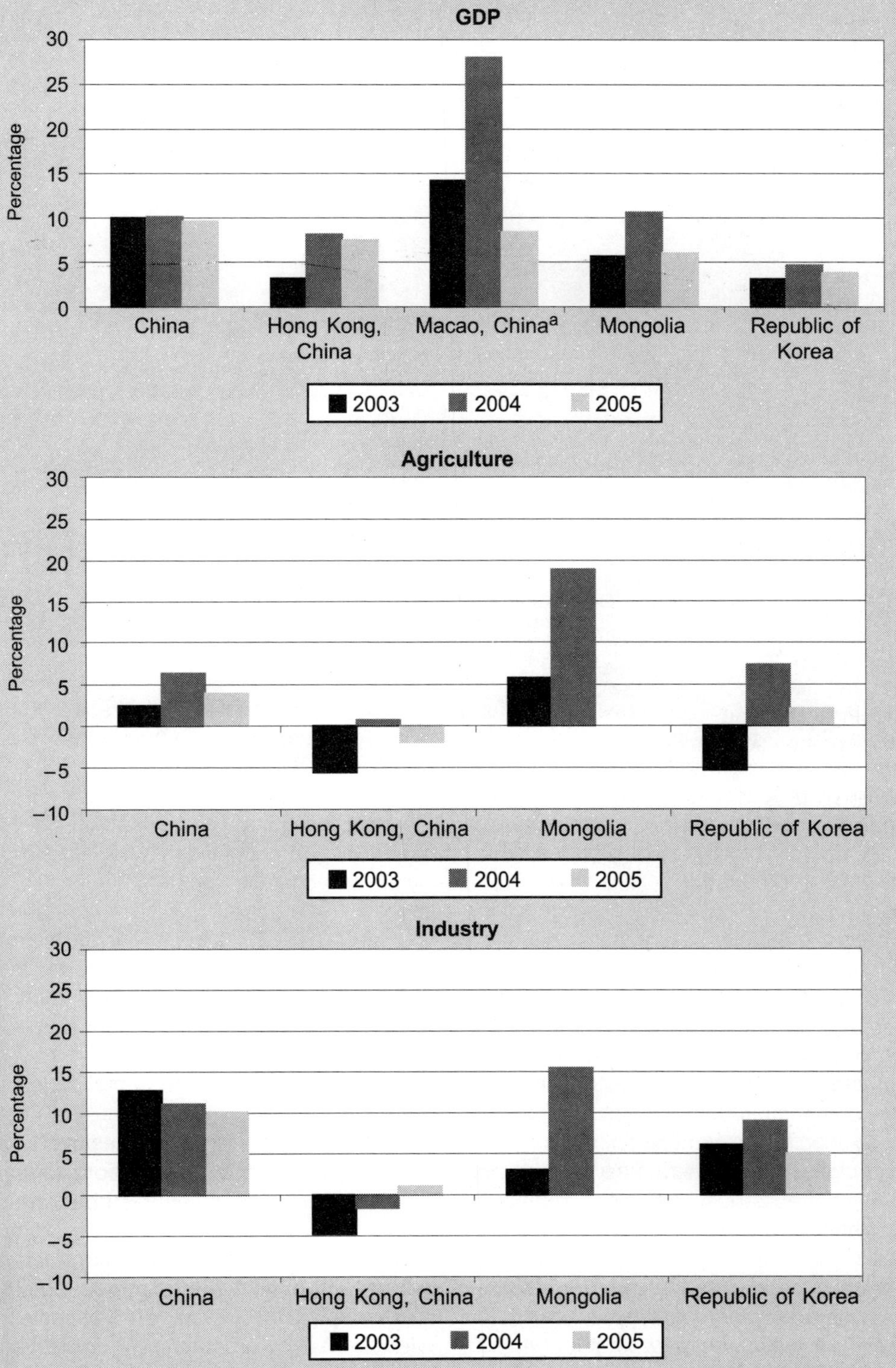

(Continued on next page)

Figure II.2 *(continued)*

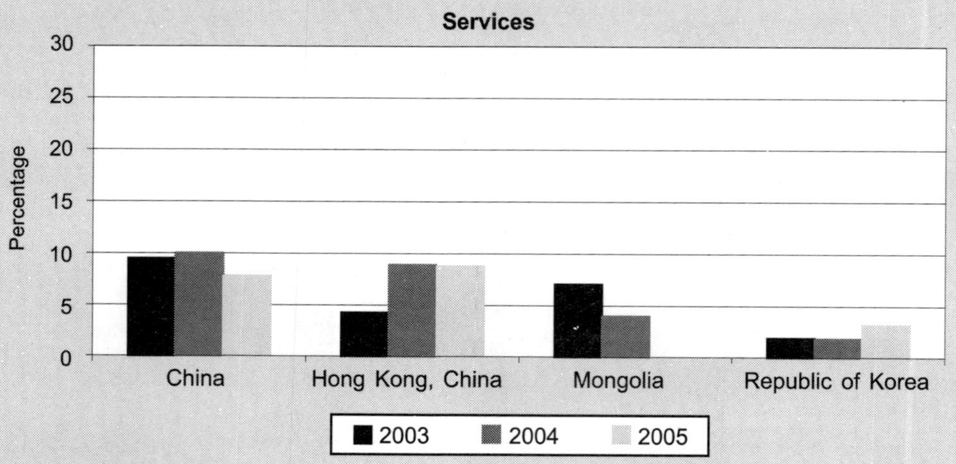

Sources: United Nations Economic and Social Commission for Asia and the Pacific, based on national sources; National Bureau of Statistics of China, *China Statistical Yearbook 2005* (Beijing, China Statistics Press, 2005); Asian Development Bank, *Key Indicators of Developing Asian and Pacific Countries 2005* (Manila, ADB, 2005); and Economist Intelligence Unit, *Country Forecasts* (London, EIU, 2005 and 2006), various issues.

Notes: Growth rates for 2005 are estimates. Industry comprises mining and quarrying; manufacturing; electricity-generation, gas and power; and construction.

[a] Data (provisional) for 2005 refer to the period January-June of that year.

from China are expected to have exceeded $760 billion in 2005, the third highest level in the world. In the last few years, the export of a wide spectrum of products has played the most important role in sustaining the recent growth momentum in China. Indeed, one of the striking features of 2004-2005 is that China has overtaken the United States in high-technology information and communication technology exports. In addition, the GDP growth rate held steady at nearly 10 per cent in 2005 because of continuing strong investment demand, aided by an increase in private consumption. Overall, the data suggest that China's economic growth could be shifting away from improvements in total factor productivity to capital accumulation, with large investments in physical infrastructure in the last few years, which traditionally have had relatively low financial rates of return.

There are indications to suggest that the economy of China will lose momentum marginally, with GDP projected to grow at the rate of about 8 per cent in 2006. Export growth is expected to taper off slightly, but overall domestic demand with regard to investment and consumption is expected to increase. Import growth, too, is expected to gather some momentum in 2006 over that in 2005.

Savings as a percentage of GDP continued to grow significantly, surpassing the high levels reached in the early years of the current decade (see figure II.3) and may soon exceed 50 per cent of GDP. Investment as a percentage of GDP, however, slowed to 42.3 per cent in 2005 from a high of 45.3 per cent in 2004. During the first eight months of 2005, investments in fixed assets increased by 27.4 per cent, down from 30.3 per cent during the same period in 2004.

The slowdown in investment growth was due largely to the introduction of administrative controls to curb investment growth in certain sectors, including the real estate sector that has seen explosive growth in demand virtually across all of China. The Government imposed a 5 per cent capital gains tax on the sale of houses owned for fewer than two years and raised mortgage rates and down payments. However, the ability to curb aggregate investment demand through administrative means has come under

Figure II.3. Savings and investment in selected East and North-East Asian economies, 2003-2005[a]

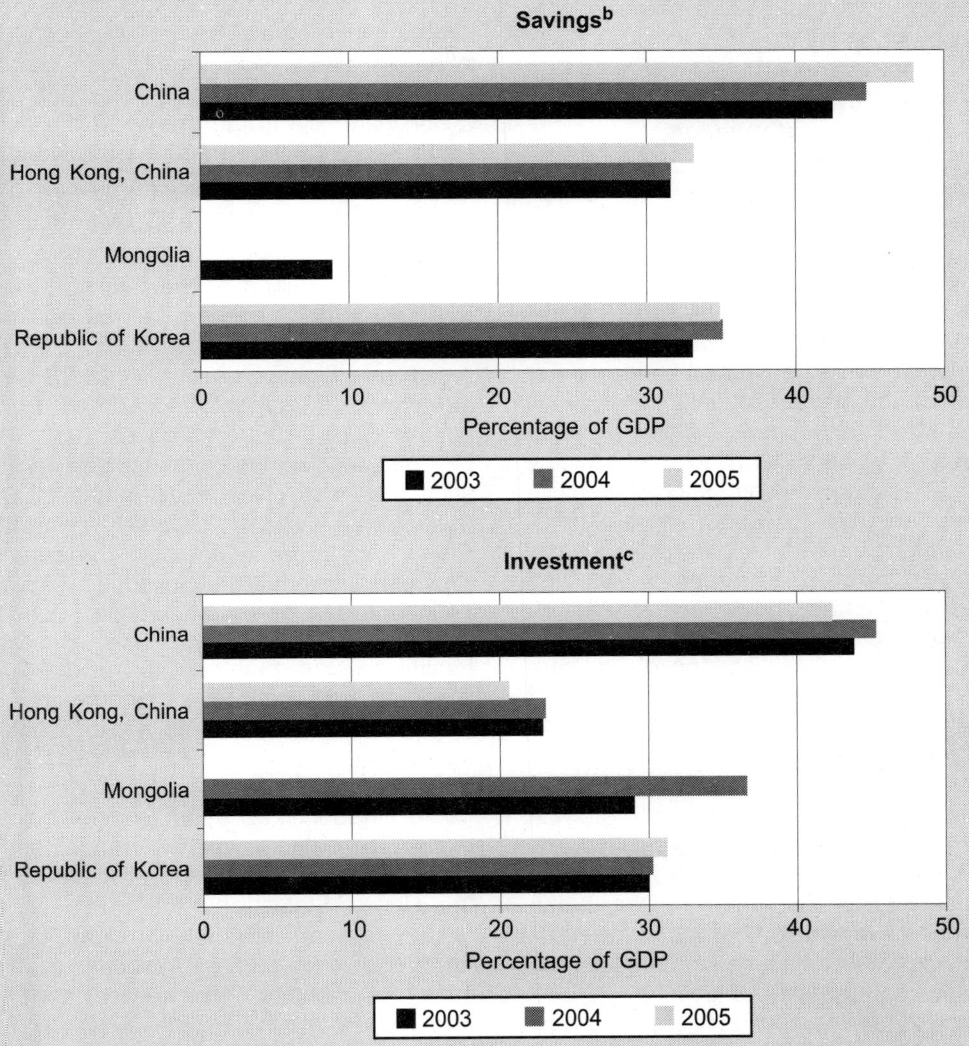

Sources: United Nations Economic and Social Commission for Asia and the Pacific, based on national sources; Asian Development Bank, *Key Indicators of Developing Asian and Pacific Countries 2005* (Manila, ADB, 2005); Economist Intelligence Unit, *Country Forecasts* (London, 2005), various issues.

[a] Data for 2005 are estimates.
[b] Gross domestic savings.
[c] Gross domestic investment.

pressure as China has moved progressively towards a market-based financial system. The increased autonomy enjoyed by enterprises and local authorities is another factor that hampers efforts to curb demand, as these entities tend to be guided more by local considerations than by national policies. Against this background, the considerable liquidity in the banking system indicates that investment demand, whether for real estate or manufacturing, could continue to increase the risk of overheating the economy.

In agriculture, production slowed to 4 per cent in 2005 from 6.3 per cent in 2004. Industrial growth, also slowed down to 10.1 per cent from 12.7 per cent in 2003 and 11.1 per cent in 2004. Industrial growth was supported by a growth rate of 7.8 per cent in the service sector in 2005, slightly down from an average of just over 8 per cent since 2000.

China's industrial scene undergoes massive transformation

The industrial sector in China has undergone a massive transformation in the recent past. By some estimates, the number of manufacturing enterprises exceeded 250,000 by mid-2005, while the number of State-owned enterprises declined to about 29,000 as a significant number of units were privatized, merged or closed. Most of the privatized units were small and medium-sized enterprises. China is also expected over the near term to move away from traditional resource-based, energy-intensive manufacturing activities towards more knowledge-based industries with a greater emphasis on employment creation in urban areas and increasing space for the private sector. Improving the efficiency of capital is also high on the agenda, with more equitable sharing of the benefits of growth between the dynamic coastal belt and the interior and between the urban and rural areas generally.

One area in manufacturing, the growing importance of which became apparent towards the close of 2005, was the export of parts and components to Boeing and Airbus for the manufacture of civilian airliners. China has signaled its determination to develop its own technological base and industrial capacity in both the aircraft and aerospace industries, until now a preserve of developed countries. Apart from its well-publicized success in sending persons into space, China is rapidly developing its capacity in the area of launch technology for commercial satellites.

Hong Kong, China, grows robustly

The economy of Hong Kong, China, grew by 7.5 per cent in 2005 following its strong recovery in 2004 when it grew by 8.1 per cent. This slowdown was led by a moderate decline in consumer spending as interest rates rose, though this was offset somewhat by sustained growth in investments in machinery and equipment and a surge in exports propelled by import demand from China.

Savings as a percentage of GDP picked up, reaching 33.1 per cent in 2005. However, investment as a percentage of GDP slowed to 20.6 per cent from 23.0 per cent in 2004. Most of the growth in GDP came from the service sector, which grew by 8.8 per cent in 2005. Although growth was slightly less than in 2004, it was clear that services would continue to play a dominant role in the growth of the economy in Hong Kong, China, in 2006 and beyond.

Sharp decline in Mongolia

After growing at the rate of 10.6 per cent in 2004, the economy of Mongolia slowed sharply to 6 per cent in 2005, primarily as a result of higher energy prices. Before the slowdown, investment had surged to 36.6 per cent of GDP in 2004 from less than 30 per cent in 2003 as demand for metals and minerals stimulated new investments in the mining industry. Strong external demand, principally from China, had given a boost to the mining sector. Agricultural production picked up significantly in 2004 and this had a favourable impact on poverty reduction. Industry, after growing at a healthy rate of 15.4 per cent in 2004, a significant increase over the performance in 2003, slowed in 2005 in response to higher energy prices and other factors. The textile and garments industry suffered a heavy blow as Mongolia lost ground to other competitors with the expiration of the Multifibre Arrangement in January 2005. This led the Government to approach the United States and the European Union to secure bilateral treatment in order to safeguard its textile and garment exports to these two important markets. The service sector showed only modest growth in both 2004 and 2005 after having performed well in 2003.

Domestic demand slows in the Republic of Korea

GDP in the Republic of Korea grew by an estimated 3.8 per cent in 2005, down nearly 1 percentage point over that of 2004. The growth momentum was affected in recent years by the relatively slow growth in domestic demand, as credit card debt mounted rapidly and had to be curbed, although the slowdown was offset by buoyant exports. The country's economy is again becoming more reliant on external demand, primarily from China, which has emerged as the country's largest export market.

Overall, GDP is projected to grow at the rate of 4.9 per cent in 2006, as private consumption regains strength. Private consumption began to strengthen after the last quarter of 2004 and by August 2005 the real consumption sales index had grown by 6.0 per cent on a year-on-year basis, its healthiest growth rate since 2002. Consumption demand for semi-durable goods and services picked up further after the second quarter of 2005, a trend that was likely to be maintained as household debt burdens eased and an appreciating won meant lower prices for imported goods. Overall, the savings rate remained at around 35 per cent of GDP in 2005. Investment held steady at 31.2 per cent of GDP in 2005.

During the year, high oil prices blunted business confidence and may have been instrumental in the deferment of new investment in manufacturing. Moreover, the cyclical downswing in 2003-2004 in the global high-technology industry also adversely affected economic growth in the Republic of Korea, although the effect was short-lived as the economies of both Japan and the United States grew fairly strongly in 2005. A new and dynamic source of demand for the Korean economy in 2005 was import demand from China.

Agricultural growth declined by more than 5 percentage points in 2005 following declines of negative growth of more than 5.3 per cent and 3.5 per cent respectively in the two previous years. Industrial growth also fell to 5 per cent following a growth rate of 9 per cent in 2004. Textile exports declined as low-cost producers made inroads with the phasing out of the previously mentioned Multifibre Arrangement on 1 January 2005.

Despite the overall recovery of the economy, investment spending remained hesitant as small and medium-sized enterprises rebuilt their balance sheets. Corporate profits suffered as oil prices soared and the exchange rate appreciated in 2005. Although the leading indicators for equipment investment showed moderate improvement, monthly indicators failed to exhibit signs of a lasting recovery. Investment growth in construction turned positive in the second quarter of 2005, after recording negative growth rates in the preceding three quarters.

Growth in the service sector improved, growing at the rate of 3.2 per cent in 2005 compared with only 1.8 per cent in 2004. Financial sector performance improved considerably. The ratio of non-performing bank loans fell across the board. The major credit card service providers increased their profitability as the average delinquency ratio continued to decline. The stock market displayed remarkable strength in 2005 with the Korean Composite Stock Price Index rising nearly 50 per cent, the best performance by a stock market in the region.

Key macroeconomic policy developments

Price pressures moderate

Inflation remains benign in the subregion despite higher oil prices. Headline inflation in China fell to around 2.0 per cent in 2005, a significant reduction from the level of 2004, largely as a result of falling food prices (see figure II.4). Food prices are expected to remain low following a series of good harvests, improving yields, and the Government's efforts to reduce the tax burden on the farming community. Prices of raw materials, fuel and power rose more slowly than in the previous year as lower investment demand relieved pressure on their supply.

On the fiscal side, the budget deficits in all economies of the subregion except Hong Kong, China, widened in 2005 after having contracted in 2004 (see figure II.5). Higher fiscal deficits were occasioned primarily by increased government spending rather than lower tax revenues. Although the fiscal situation deteriorated in 2005, this is not a cause for concern as the deficits remained below 3 per cent of GDP in all the economies except Mongolia.

The Chinese central bank has undertaken several measures to tighten monetary conditions and to slow growth in lending. The more rapid pace of reserve accumulation in late 2004 and the first half of 2005 led to a substantial spike in the money supply and ample liquidity remained in the banking system. However, inflationary pressure remained moderate as global commodity prices fell and grain production rose. Increasing competition among manufacturers kept prices low on a wide range of goods, such as consumer durables.

Figure II.4. Inflation and growth of money supply in selected East and North-East Asian economies, 2003-2005[a]

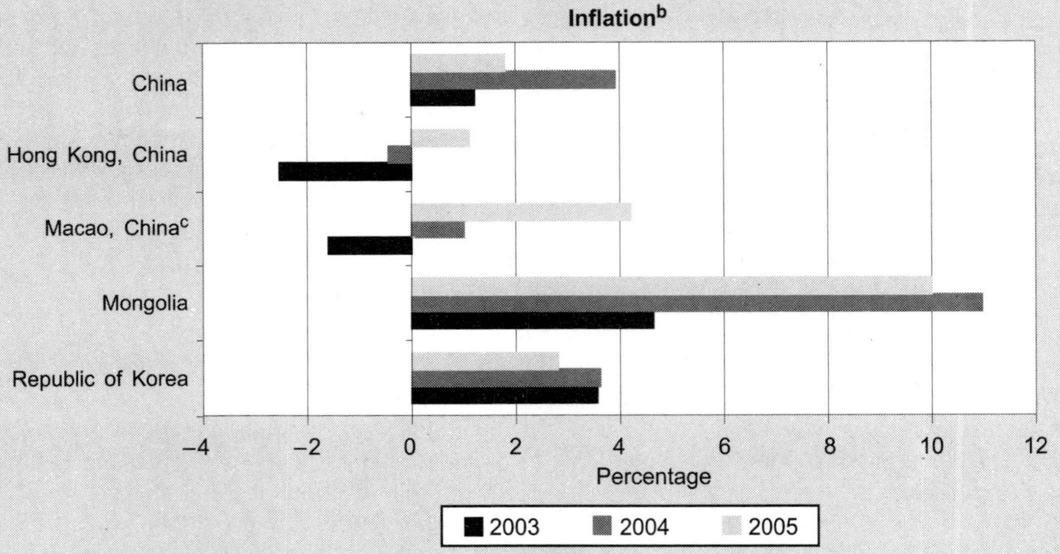

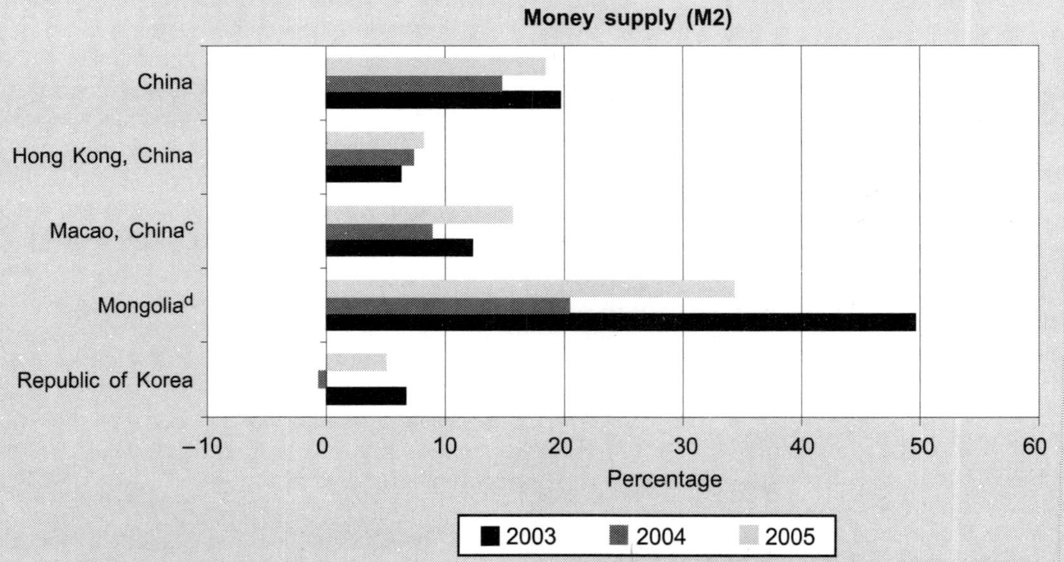

Sources: United Nations Economic and Social Commission for Asia and the Pacific, based on national sources; Asian Development Bank, *Key Indicators of Developing Asian and Pacific Countries 2005* (Manila, ADB, 2005); Internation Monetary Fund, *International Financial Statistics* (CD-ROM) (Washington, D.C., IMF, September 2005), and *Mongolia: Selected Issues and Statistical Appendix,* IMF Country Report No. 05/400, November 2005; and Economist Intelligence Unit, *Country Forecasts* (London, 2005), various issues.

[a] Data for 2005 are estimates.
[b] Inflation refers to changes in the consumer price index.
[c] Inflation for 2005 refer to January-October in that year; money supply for 2005 refers to January-August in that year.
[d] Data for 2005 refer to January-September.

Figure II.5. Budget balance in selected East and North-East Asian economies, 2003-2005[a]

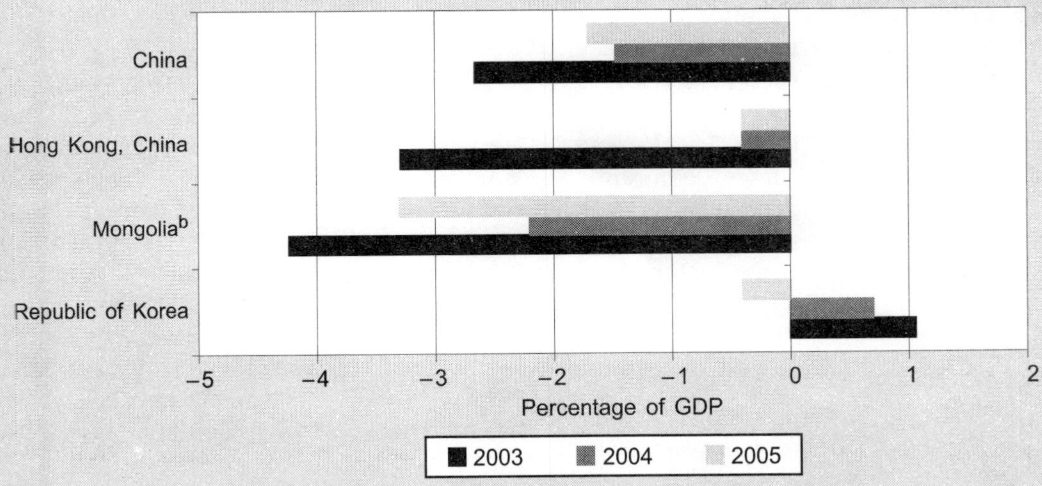

Sources: United Nations Economic and Social Commission for Asia and the Pacific, based on national sources; Asian Development Bank, *Key Indicators of Developing Asian and Pacific Countries 2005* (Manila, ADB, 2005); International Monetary Fund, *Mongolia: Selected Issues and Statistical Appendix,* IMF Country Report No. 05/400 (2005); and Economist Intelligence Unit, *Country Forecasts* (London, EIU, 2006), various issues.

[a] Data for 2005 are estimates.
[b] Budget balance including grants.

Hong Kong, China, emerges from deflation

In Hong Kong, China, inflation edged up to the rate of 1.1 per cent in 2005 after several years of deflation. A buoyant economic upturn, progressive feed-through from the earlier rental rebound and the modest impact of higher fuel costs added to upward pressure on headline inflation in the economy. The persistent downward pressure on prices over the past several years was halted by the third quarter of 2005. However, the inflationary environment was expected to remain benign as productivity and productive capacity increased. Growth in the money supply was held at 8.2 per cent in 2005, an increase from that of the previous year. Overall, inflation was expected to remain at under 2.0 per cent in 2006.

In Mongolia, inflation more than doubled to 11.0 per cent per year in 2004 from 4.6 per cent in 2003. This was despite a sharp contraction in the growth of money supply from 49.6 per cent in 2003 to 20.4 per cent in 2004. Steep increases in oil prices and adjustment of domestic heating and electricity prices contributed to the inflationary pressure. Some easing of the monetary policy also contributed to the price rise. The latest data for 2005 suggest that price pressures have eased somewhat but remain close to 10 per cent. More stable energy prices should remove some of the pressure on prices in the remainder of 2005.

Appreciation of the won moderates price pressures in the Republic of Korea

Headline inflation fell to 2.4 per cent in the Republic of Korea in November 2005 on a year-on-year basis, although the money supply grew by 5.0 per cent from negative growth of 0.6 per cent in 2004. This was despite the steep increase in oil prices. The appreciation of the won in early 2005 also helped to keep inflation low. House prices came under significant pressure in the first half of 2005, reflecting a prolonged shortage of housing and speculative transactions fueled by the low interest rates that had prevailed in the country in the recent past. A variety of tax measures were introduced to contain the upward pressure on housing prices. The overnight call rate went up to 3.5 per cent in October, the first rise in more than three years, and interest rates were increased again in December 2005 to 3.75 per cent in order to pre-empt a more generalized rise in the price level.

Developments in the external sector

Foreign trade and other external transactions

China's foreign trade maintains robust growth

The subregion accounts for more than 60 per cent of the region's foreign trade with the rest of the world and more than two thirds of the trade within the region. China is a major trading power of global importance in a wide range of both low- and high-technology goods, the Republic of Korea and Taiwan Province of China are at the forefront of high-technology production and export, while Hong Kong, China, apart from its role as an entrepôt for China, is a substantial exporter of goods and services in its own right. As such, the subregion exercises a large and growing influence in both trade and output in the development of technology in the region as a whole.

Exports from China declined to 31 per cent in 2005 after an increasing trend since 2002 (figure II.6). This slight easing in the export growth rate was caused by slower growth in electronic exports to the United States and the European Union in the earlier part of 2005. The export of textiles and clothing took up some of the slack, showing a strong increase subsequent to the ending of the Multifibre Arrangement through the WTO Agreement on Textiles and Clothing in January 2005; however, this provoked protectionist measures by both the United States and the European Union. China's large and modern textile and garment industry expanded rapidly as its exports to the European Union increased by 40 per cent in value during the first six months of 2005.

Export growth has been more durable than in other countries owing to China's diversified manufacturing base. The economy continues to expand capacity in a wide range of areas, such as steel, cement and automobiles. Remarkably, exports of automobiles exceeded imports for the first time in 2005. Automobile production reached record levels as new plants opened. Steel production, already exceeding 330 million tons, was 27 per cent higher in the first nine months of 2005 than in the previous year, with exports reaching 21.7 million tons.

Going forward, electronics exports are likely to maintain their recovery, which began late in 2005. However, textile and clothing exports will be constrained by limits agreed with both the United States and the European Union.

Import growth also slowed in 2005 from its very high pace during the previous three years. This was the result of slightly lower investment growth in the economy as well as new factories becoming operational, which allowed for greater substitution of imports. Weaker investment led to slower growth in imports of intermediate goods, which have been important in the past, such as chemicals, raw materials, equipment components and plastics.

The investment slowdown can also be seen in lower foreign investment in 2005 and reflects the Government's moves to cool the economy. Policies to temper growth have been in place since mid-2004, through monetary, fiscal and administrative measures in the steel, cement, aluminium, automobile and real estate subsectors. Once China implements all its current expansion plans in the steel industry, its imports are likely to decline drastically. This could have major repercussions for the global steel industry, which could be faced with large overcapacity and persistent weaker prices in the future.

Figure II.6. Growth rates in merchandise export earnings and import spending in selected East and North-East Asian economies, 2003-2005

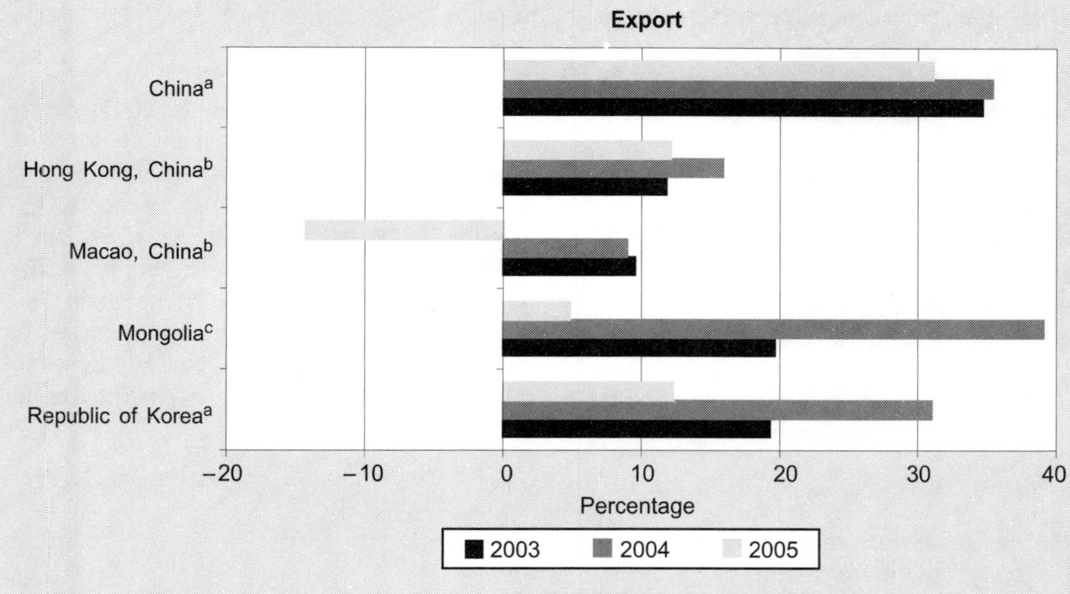

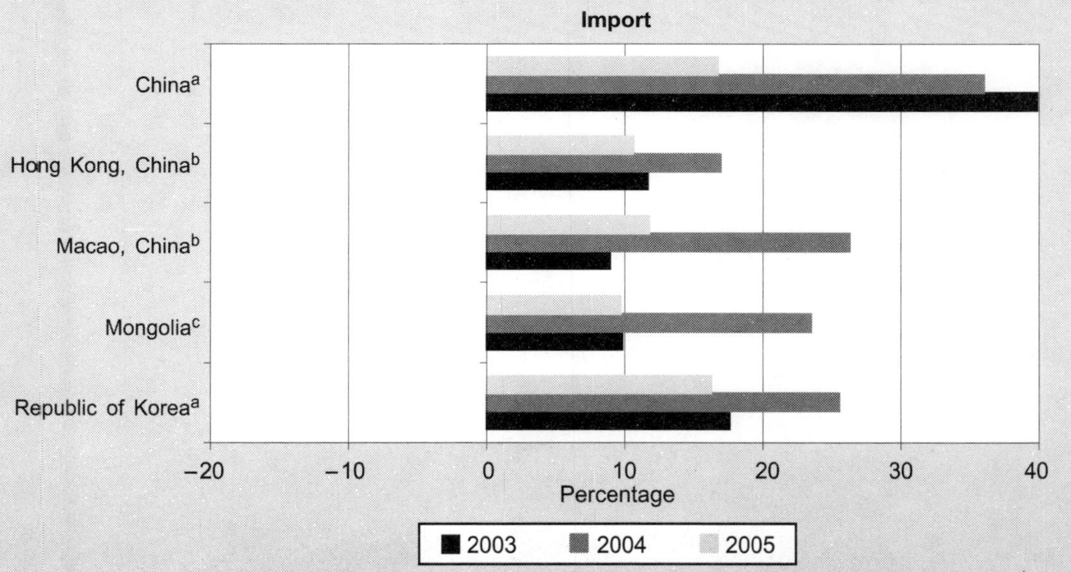

Sources: National Bureau of Statistics of China website <www.stats.gov.cn>, accessed on 21 October 2005; Ministry of Commerce of the People's Republic of China website <http://english.mofcom.gov.cn>, accessed on 12 January 2006; Hong Kong Census and Statistics Department website <www.info.gov.hk>, accessed on 7 September 2005; Macao Special Administrative Region Government website <www.gov.mo>, accessed on 13 January 2006; Monetary Authority of Macao website <www.amcm.gov.mo>, accessed on 13 January 2006; Macao Special Administrative Region Economic Services website <www.economia.gov.mo>, accessed on 13 January 2006; Korea Development Institute website <www.kdi.re.kr>, accessed on 28 December 2005; and International Monetary Fund, *IMF Executive Board Concludes 2005 Article IV Consultation with Mongolia,* Public Information Notice (PIN) No. 05/140 (6 October 2005).

[a] Growth rates for 2005 refer to January-October of that year.
[b] Growth rates for 2005 refer to January-November of that year.
[c] Growth rate for 2004 is an estimate and for 2005 is a projection.

The merchandise exports of Hong Kong, China, suffered a downturn in the first few months of 2005, with slower growth in the United States and in neighbouring Asian countries, though the pace subsequently improved. This led to an overall reduction in export growth for the year, from 15.9 to 12.1 per cent of 2005. Slower expected export growth for China in 2006 could have parallel effects on Hong Kong, China, which handles the bulk of China's re-exports. Textile and clothing exports, which declined with the expiration of the Multifibre Arrangement quotas in January 2005 (see box II.1), have now expanded owing to the re-export of finished Chinese goods to overcome the limits imposed on mainland companies by the European Union and the United States. A boost to export services came from implementation of the Individual Visitor Scheme and the opening of Disneyland in September 2005, helping to attract record numbers of visitors from the mainland. The number of tourists from China to Hong Kong, China, has tripled over the past five years.

Import growth slowed in 2005, from 16.9 to 10.6 per cent. The merchandise trade deficit shrank in 2005 as export growth outstripped import growth. The deficit is expected to increase if exports improve less in the year ahead. Imports should remain strong because of robust consumption and investment in the economy. The current account surplus increased as the merchandise trade deficit was offset by the large and growing services surplus (figure II.7).

Figure II.7. Current account balance in selected East and North-East Asian economies, 2003-2005[a]

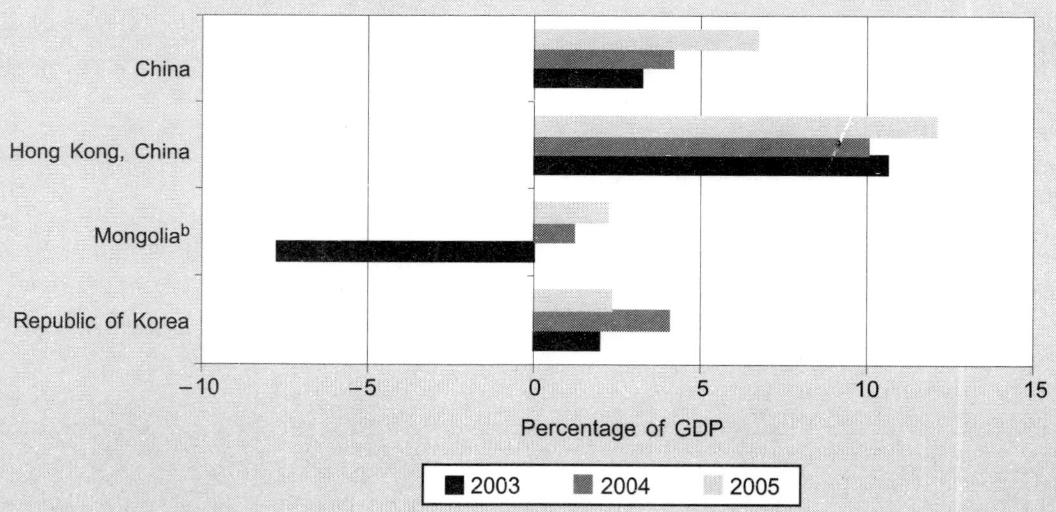

Sources: United Nations Economic and Social Commission for Asia and the Pacific, based on national sources; Asian Development Bank, *Key Indicators of Developing Asian and Pacific Countries 2005* (Manila, ADB, 2005); International Monetary Fund, *Mongolia: Selected Issues and Statistical Appendix,* IMF Country Report No. 05/400 (2005); and Economist Intelligence Unit, *Country Forecasts* (London, EIU, 2005), various issues.

[a] Data for 2005 are estimates.

[b] Current account balance includes official transfers.

Box II.1. The new scenario for textile and clothing exports from China

The end of the Multifibre Arrangement in January 2005 had a dramatic impact on Chinese exports to developed countries. The United States saw a 60 per cent increase in Chinese textile and clothing exports and a 180 per cent increase in the newly liberalized categories, in the first three months of 2005 alone.[a] The European Union witnessed a 40 per cent increase in the value of Chinese textile and clothing exports in the first six months of 2005, with a 95 per cent increase in the liberalized categories.[b]

The size and rapidity of these changes provoked protectionist reactions in these markets. The European Union in June 2005 and the United States in November 2005 set limits with China on annual textile export growth in a number of categories. The agreement with the European Union covers "mass market" items likely to cause major disruption to European producers: pullovers, men's trousers, blouses, T-shirts, dresses, brassieres, flax yarn, cotton fabrics, bedlinen and table and kitchen linen. Growth in exports in these areas was limited to 8-12.5 per cent a year in 2005, 2006 and 2007. The limits affect a large portion of textile exports to both the United States and the European Union.

The agreement with the United States, following tougher unilateral limits in mid-year, will limit the export growth of most Chinese textile and clothing goods to 8-10 per cent in 2006, 12.5 per cent in 2007 and 15-16 per cent in 2008. The agreement also restricts growth in Chinese exports of 14 "core" apparel products by more than any quotas that could have been imposed under WTO safeguards. The limits are 5.5 per cent in 2006, 7.8 per cent in 2007 and 10.3 per cent in 2008, compared with 7.5 per cent annually under the safeguard mechanism. Products classified as core apparel include cotton knit shirts, synthetic fibre knit shirts, woven shirts, cotton trousers, brassieres and underwear.

The effects of these restrictions on the composition and direction of Chinese exports will depend on how Chinese textile producers react. They could divert production into the non-limited categories or move production bases to countries in the region in order to avoid quotas. Other textile-exporting countries in Asia have had to react to the new scenario without quotas. Some are trying to upgrade to higher value-added products. Others have asked for special consideration from the United States and the European Union. The United States has reduced tariffs by granting normal trade relations status to the Lao People's Democratic Republic and Viet Nam. The European Union has removed tariffs and duties on nearly all exports from the least developed countries.

Sources: European Commission, "EU-China textile agreement 10 June 2005", press release dated 12 June 2005; and Office of the United States Trade Representative, "Benefits from establishing quotas on certain Chinese apparel exports to the United States", *Policy Brief,* November 2005.

[a] International Monetary Fund, *IMF Survey*, 23 May 2005, vol. 34, No. 9.

[b] European Commission, "Evolution of EU textile imports from China 2004-2005", 28 November 2005.

The export growth rate of Mongolia dropped from 39.1 per cent in 2004 to 4.8 per cent in 2005. The main negative impact was due to lower textile and clothing sales following the end of quotas under the Multifibre Arrangement. This problem is likely to persist, although there should be some improvement in exports owing to the mid-2005 Generalized System of Preferences Plus scheme with the European Union, which allowed approximately 7,200 goods to be exported to the European Union at a preferential rate. High copper and gold prices, strong tourism flows and private transfers also had a positive effect on exports. Copper exports should continue to benefit from strong demand in China, the country's main export market. However, there may be a sharp downturn in export growth going forward if the copper price falls significantly from its record levels during the year.

The value of imports increased by 9.7 per cent, mainly as a result of higher oil prices. Oil products account for about a quarter of imports. The current account may worsen in 2006 if the copper price falls or demand from China slackens, but there could also be a positive effect if oil prices stabilize or fall.

Export growth slows in the Republic of Korea but exports of information and communication technology pick up

The export growth rate sharply declined in the Republic of Korea, from 31.0 per cent in 2004 to 12.3 per cent in 2005. Export growth in the third quarter of 2005 marked the first upturn in five quarters. The earlier poor performance was caused primarily by low international demand for information and communication technology–related products. Those products, including semiconductors, electronic components and telecommunications equipment, account for 40 per cent of merchandise exports. Textile and clothing exports have also declined sharply following the end of the international quota system. A positive factor has been the continuing rapid increase in exports to China. The recovery in Japan could further aid exports in the future.

Despite the rise in oil prices the country saw a large drop in the import growth rate from 25.5 to 16.2 per cent. The current account balance has a surplus of about $17 billion, but it is showing a tendency to decline. In 2006 high oil prices should continue to erode the current account balance, in view of the country's nearly total dependence on imported oil. Domestic demand, which has begun to recover, could also lead to higher imports.

Capital flows and external debt

China is becoming a source of foreign direct investment

Although China remains one of the largest destinations in the world for inflows of foreign direct investment, FDI growth into China was close to zero in 2005. This was essentially a reaction to the large quantities of investment that entered the country following the accession of China to the World Trade Organization in 2001. The Government is also attempting to cool investment in several overheated sectors, which is making foreign investors more circumspect. FDI is likely to grow moderately in coming years. The pace could even slower further as profit opportunities diminish somewhat with greater competition and increasing labour costs. On the other hand, China is emerging as a significant outward investor, with Chinese FDI stock abroad standing at $39 billion in 2004. The Government has provided encouragement by relaxing sector controls, streamlining procedures and easing foreign exchange restrictions.

An important investment objective for China has been to secure long-term access to foreign energy and mining assets to satisfy the country's growing demand for natural resources. Since India shares the same need, there has been cooperation in several cases between State-owned companies from the two countries in natural resource investments abroad. China is also displaying greater interest in developed country corporate acquisitions to secure new markets and acquire technologies and skills. A notable example was the takeover of the personal computer business of IBM by Lenovo. Portfolio inflows also increased during 2005 on speculation of a revaluation of the yuan. A 2.1 per cent revaluation of the currency in July was not large enough to substantially affect the real economy, although inflows of speculative funds appear to have eased as is evident in the slower growth in reserves in the second half of 2005. The country's external debt continues to be relatively small, mainly long term and easily covered by its reserves.

Hong Kong, China, in addition to its large current account surplus, experienced a strong inflow of FDI during the year. The expansion of the Closer Economic Partnership Arrangement with the mainland in January 2005, which provides tariff-free access and preferential treatment for service providers, helped to attract FDI. There has been increasing entry of mainland investors into the Special Administrative Region with many establishing regional or global headquarters. There were both large gross outflows and inflows of portfolio investment in keeping with Hong Kong, China's role as a financial centre. The exchange rate maintained its dollar peg after the yuan's revaluation, the only remaining currency in the region to do so after Malaysia adopted a managed float in July 2005.

The balance of payments of Mongolia saw strong remittances from overseas workers, FDI in mining and continued aid flows. Studies have upgraded mineral prospects, and large mining multinationals are displaying investment interest in mineral development. Privatization of a number of companies will also help to attract FDI. External debt remains high, at around 90 per cent of GDP, but it is manageable, with most of it being concessional public sector borrowing. A prudent monetary policy is helping to maintain a stable exchange rate and prevent debt-servicing from becoming a concern.

Portfolio inflows taper off; outward foreign direct investment from the Republic of Korea increases

Inward direct foreign investment in the Republic of Korea was down from the previous year's unusually high level. Outward direct investment increased substantially. Inward flows were affected by energy prices, global overcapacity, and Chinese competition in key sectors such as steel, automobiles and shipbuilding. Outward investment has been stimulated by the increasingly globalized enterprises in the Republic of Korea and has been directed primarily towards the United States and China. Portfolio investment recorded a net deficit by mid-2005, compared with a surplus in 2004, with such investment abroad increasing steadily because of low interest rates at home. There was increased borrowing from abroad as foreigners were prepared to increase their exposure to Korean debt. Continued surpluses on the current and capital accounts led to a sharp increase in reserves to $210 billion in December 2005, more than three times the short-term debt. In response, the Government set up an investment company in July 2005 to place some of the reserves in overseas stocks and bonds. The exchange rate strengthened against the dollar during 2005, leading to pressure on profit margins for exporters (see figure II. 8).

Medium-term prospects and key policy issues

Growth in China will moderate

There is little doubt that the pace of economic growth and development in China will be the preponderant factor regarding medium-term prospects for the subregion as a whole. On that basis, there is a consensus that the economy of China will grow somewhat slower than it did over the last 8-10 years. Along with a slower pace of growth in investment and a shift towards services, some moderation in the growth of the country's international trade is also likely, with the growth rate of exports and imports slowing to about 15-16 per cent a year, down from average growth rates of close to 30 per cent in the last five years. These changes will have a direct impact not just on the East and North-East Asian subregion but on the entire Asian and Pacific region and on the global economy. Reacting and adjusting to what happens in China thus poses the main challenge for the other economies in the subregion in terms of trade and investment flows and financial market developments and the domestic policy issues that arise as a result.

Achieving greater flexibility in exchange rates emerged as a key policy issue in 2005. The yuan was revalued against the United States dollar by 2.1 per cent in July. This meant that the yuan would no longer be pegged to the dollar but would move in keeping with market demand and supply with reference to a basket of foreign currencies, and be allowed to fluctuate within a band of plus or minus 0.3 per cent around a predetermined exchange rate target. In the short run, the revaluation could theoretically hurt exports, employment and GDP growth but any negative impact is likely to be negligible in view of the strong competitive advantage China enjoys. Most analysts agree that in the long run an exchange rate more in line with market conditions could benefit the Chinese economy by producing a positive impact on China's terms of trade, export pattern and allocation of resources. In addition, it would provide the authorities with another instrument for policy transmission.

Figure II.8. Index of exchange rates against the United States dollar in selected East and North-East Asian economies, 1996-2005[a]

(1996Q4=100)

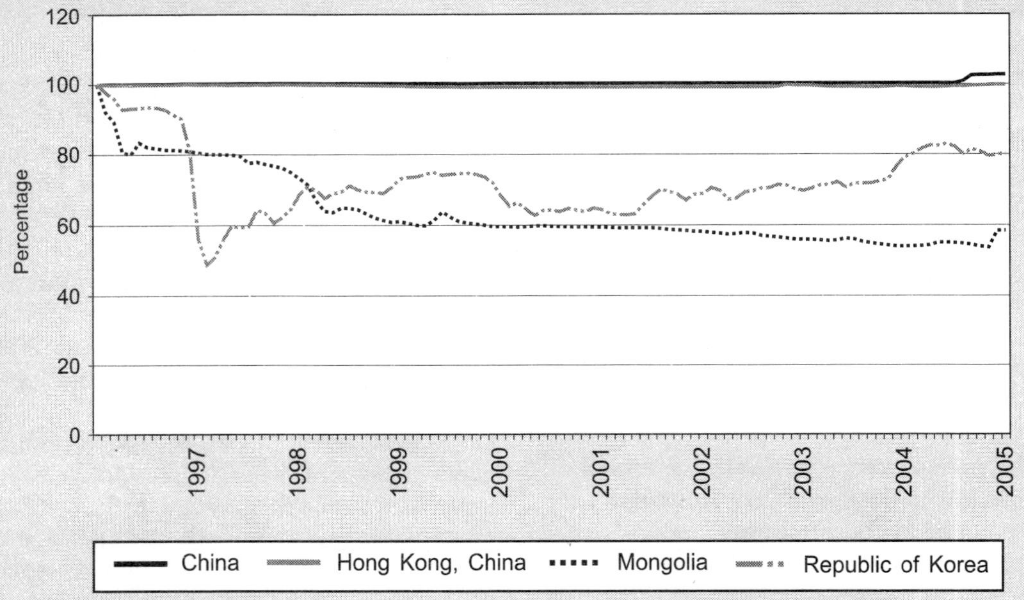

Sources: International Monetary Fund, *International Financial Statistics* (CD-ROM) (Washington, D.C., IMF, 2005); and *The Economist*, various issues.

[a] Data for 2005 are estimates.

Combined with its spectacular economic growth, China has managed to drastically reduce the incidence of income poverty from 33 per cent in 1990 to 17 per cent in 2001. More than 160 million people have been taken out of poverty. Thus, China has continued to make steady progress in reducing poverty, indicating that it is well on its way to achieving this important Millennium Development Goal. In recent years, however, concerns about growing income inequality and regional disparities have mounted as the country's economy has became technologically more sophisticated and earnings in manufacturing have risen rapidly, especially for those possessing useful skills. As a result, the bottom 25 per cent of the population accounted for only 4.7 per cent of total consumption in 2001.

China plans to create a more harmonious society

Policy attention has accordingly shifted towards a more balanced model of economic growth so that groups and regions left behind by the rapid growth of the Chinese economy would enjoy more benefits from the country's progress in coming years. The draft eleventh five-year plan for economic development, approved by the National People's Congress in October 2005, set the stage for the most important national economic and social development blueprint for the next five years (2006-2010). The plan focuses on improving the quality of growth to create a more harmonious society. Three broad areas are identified for policy attention: improving efficiency, raising technological standards and narrowing the income gap between the rich and the poor and between cities and the countryside.[1] Public spending on social protection and rural

[1] International Monetary Fund, *People's Republic of China: 2005 Article IV Consultation – Staff Report; Staff Supplement; and Public Information Notice on the Executive Board Discussion*, IMF Country Report No. 05/411 (Washington, D.C., IMF, 2005).

areas has begun to rise, but major initiatives are needed in the short term.

For Hong Kong, China, several policy issues seem to be gaining importance. Maintaining investor confidence is the key as the economy is the premier financial centre in the region and its prosperity is strongly linked to how investors and users of its services perceive policy changes and the functioning of the Government, particularly moves towards greater democratization and popular participation in decision-making. The fiscal deficit and the accumulation of public debt need attention as they conflict with the low tax regime that Hong Kong, China, has traditionally enjoyed. The Hong Kong, China, government expects to restore fiscal balance in 2008-2009.

Another issue concerns administrative changes and policy continuity. Under the "Strong governance for the people" policy, the Chief Executive announced several administrative changes on 12 October 2005, including the reorganization of the Chief Executive's Office to increase its effectiveness. The size of the civil service would continue to be reduced in order to maintain a small government. Plans have been announced to recruit more talented professionals from the mainland and abroad. Professionals would be allowed to stay in Hong Kong, China, without having to have a prior job offer. The Hong Kong, China authorities expect to sustain the pre-eminent position of the economy as a regional financial and commercial centre through these means.

Significant challenges faced by Mongolia are to increase the value added in its mining sector and to diversify into new export areas. Greater value added domestically in mining would provide increased employment opportunities. Moving up the value chain from raw material exports, such as through the establishment of smelters and refineries, would require investment in capital and technology. This may be achieved by greater foreign investment in the sector. The country relies on a narrow range of export products, with minerals, cashmere and textiles accounting for more than 80 per cent of exports. Further development of tourism services could diversify foreign earnings. There has been growth in the sector over the past few years, although visitor numbers are still low. The country possesses attractive adventure and cultural opportunities. To fully benefit from these advantages, the general tourism infrastructure needs improvement.

Oil prices and appreciation of the won are the main policy issues

After successfully negotiating post-Asian financial crisis-related challenges and regaining strong growth momentum in the last two to three years, the economy of the Republic of Korea is expected to face two broad policy issues as it enters 2006. First, as an energy importer, high and volatile global oil prices pose considerable risks for the economy. High oil prices could cause aggregate demand in the economy to contract, with possibly severe implications for GDP growth. High oil prices could also affect global demand for exports from the country, adversely affecting its growth prospects. Second, dollar interest rates are on the rise; this could put upward pressure on Korean interest rates, putting downward pressure on housing prices. Higher interest rates could lead to a sharp contraction in new construction activity, with significant downstream effects. The large current account imbalances in the global economy suggest that significant exchange realignments should take place over the medium term. The won already appreciated by nearly 5 per cent against the dollar in 2005. Any further appreciation could undermine export competitiveness, particularly in the information and communication technology industry.

North and Central Asia

Overview

The subregion enjoyed the seventh successive year of GDP growth

The countries of North and Central Asia experienced the seventh successive year of GDP growth in 2005, the longest sustained expansion since the beginning of their transition to a market-based system in 1992. Positive GDP growth was recorded virtually across the subregion in 2005. The growth performance of the countries, with the exception of Kyrgyzstan, remained strong as a result of high export commodity prices. Domestic demand also played an important role, with retail turnover growing at double digit rates in most of the economies. However, increases in the prices of fuel and food products, and higher domestic utility tariffs, pushed up consumer price inflation in virtually all the countries of North and Central Asia.

The strong economic expansion over much of the subregion in 2005 was underpinned by the continuing growth in external trade and foreign investment. Owing to favourable international conditions for the principal exports of Kazakhstan and the Russian Federation and increased global oil and gas prices, those countries increased their trade surpluses in the first 11 months of 2005. However, the other economies were expected to experience wider trade deficits owing to the strong growth in imports, primarily of intermediate and capital goods, food and raw material.

GDP growth performance

High international prices of natural resources provided robust growth in 2005

Robust growth in the subregion in 2005 was driven largely by the high international prices of oil, gas and other natural resources. Proportionately, the energy sector and net exports contributed more to economic growth in most of the countries of the subregion than in previous years. On the demand side, private consumption remained the main source of economic growth, and growth of domestic demand was driven by rising household incomes and large inflows of foreign remittances.

In individual economies, Azerbaijan registered a remarkable 26.4 per cent growth in GDP in 2005, a result of high capital investment in oil and gas and strong overall industrial performance (see figure II.9). The industrial sector benefited from the construction of the Baku-Tbilisi-Ceyhan oil pipeline completed in May 2005 and from new investment in the South Caucasus gas pipeline project. Industrial output grew by 33.5 per cent in 2005. The mining sector accounted for more than 50 per cent of total industrial production and was one of the main drivers of economic growth. The agricultural sector grew by 7.5 per cent in 2005 and remained the largest employer in the country.

Armenia continued its high rate of GDP growth and maintained progress in macroeconomic reform in 2005. GDP growth averaged

Figure II.9. GDP and sectoral growth in North and Central Asian economies, 2003-2005

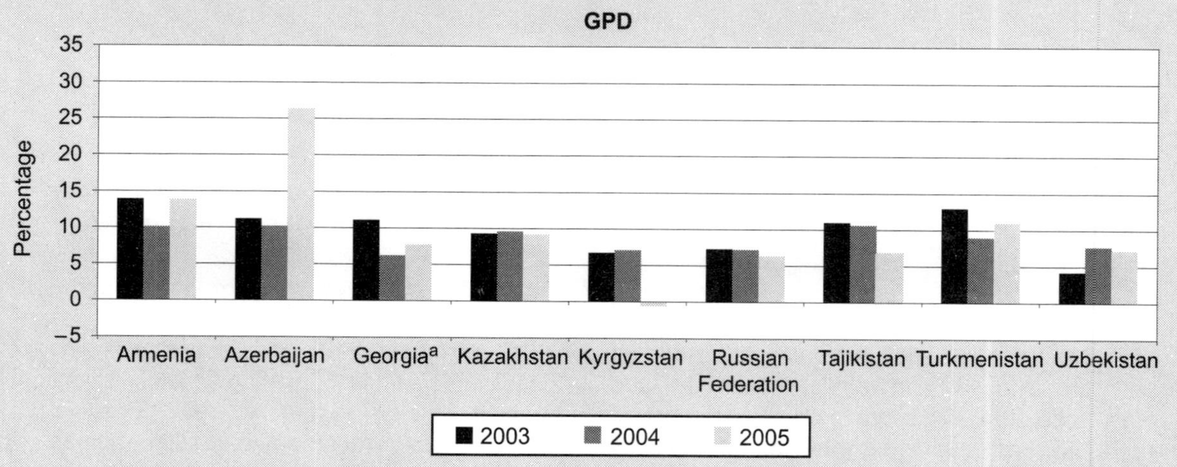

(Continued on next page)

Figure II.9 *(continued)*

Agriculture

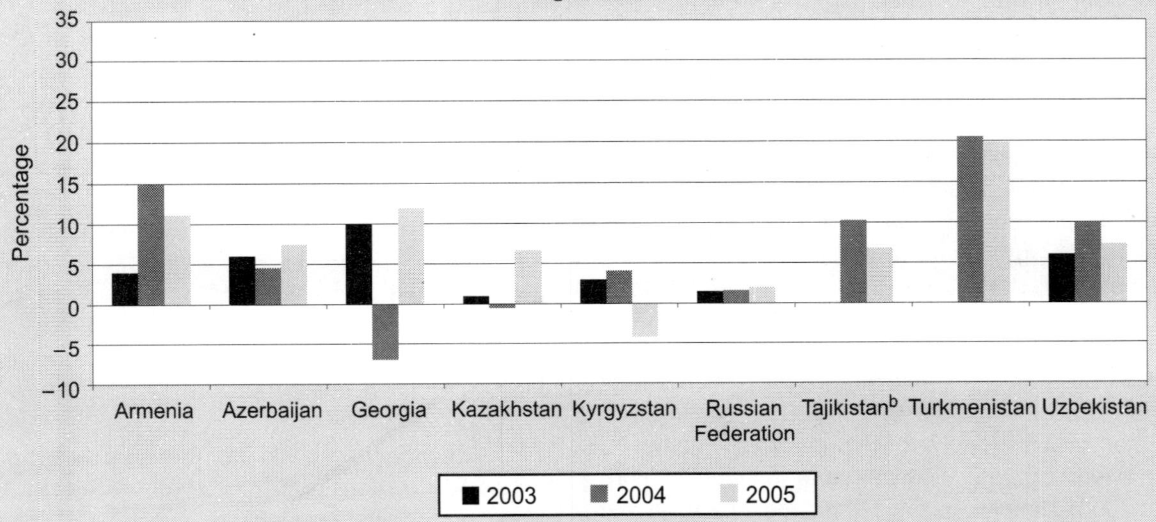

Industry

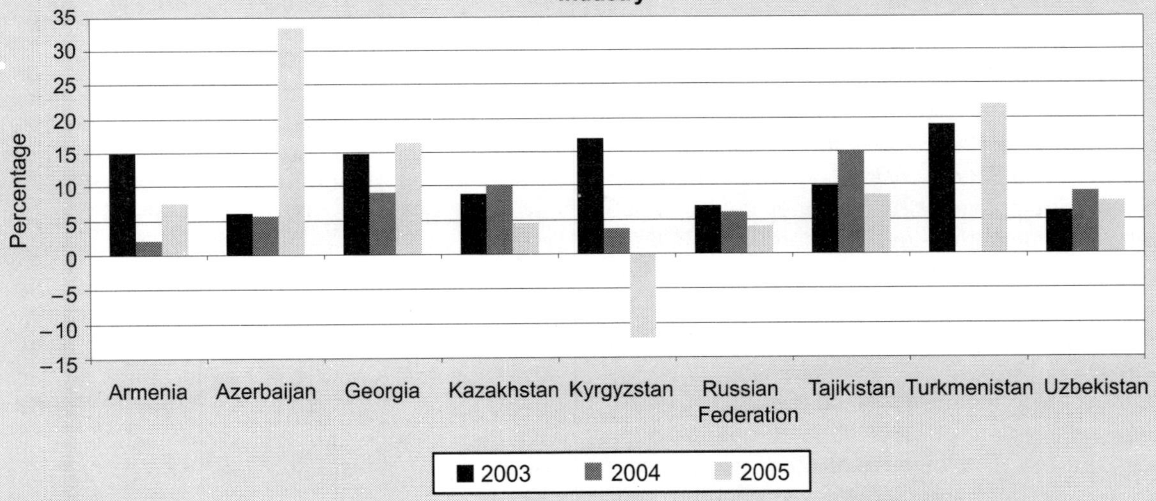

Sources: United Nations Economic and Social Commission for Asia and the Pacific, based on United Nations Economic Commission for Europe, *Economic Survey of Europe 2005,* No. 1 (United Nations publication, Sales No. E.05.II.E.7); website of the Commonwealth of Independent States Inter-state Statistical Committee, <www.cisstat.com>, accessed on 6 January 2006 and 10 February 2006; and Economist Intelligence Unit, *Country Reports* (London, EIU, 2006), various issues; and national sources.

[a] Growth rate for 2005 refers to January-September.

[b] Growth rate for 2005 refers to January-August.

more than 11 per cent annually in the period 2000-2004 and was 13.9 per cent in 2005. Construction and agriculture were the fastest growing sectors. Owing to a good fruit harvest, agricultural output grew by 11.2 per cent in 2005. A growth rate of 7.5 per cent in industry in the same year was boosted by FDI and inflows of remittances. These capital flows were used to renovate public infrastructure and build new productive capacity in the trade and service sectors. These sectors also supported growth in domestic demand, reflected in the 9.3 per cent growth in retail turnover in 2005. Remittances helped to increase personal incomes, which rose almost 9 per cent in the first five months of 2005.

Kazakhstan, a principal energy producer in the subregion, achieved rapid growth of more than 9 per cent annually in the period 2002-2004. GDP grew by 9.2 per cent in 2005 owing to new investment, particularly FDI, and expansion in domestic demand. Broad-based growth was recorded in all sectors: industrial production grew by 4.6 per cent and agricultural output grew by 6.7 per cent in 2005. The construction sector grew strongly, owing to rapidly rising investment in new pipelines and residential construction. Despite bad weather, the grain harvest amounted to 13.8 million tons for 2005, an increase of 11.4 per cent.

The rapid GDP growth that Georgia achieved in the period 2002-2004 continued in 2005, with a 7.7 per cent increase in the first nine months of 2005. The fastest growing sectors were industry, construction and agriculture. Industrial output grew by 16.4 per cent in 2005, owing to hydrocarbon development in the Caucasus area. The completion of the oil pipeline from Azerbaijan to Turkey through Georgia and the beginning of a new gas pipeline in the South Caucasus became an increasingly important source of economic growth in Georgia. In addition, construction of new oil and gas pipelines promoted the development of other sectors such as telecommunications, hotels and catering. Agricultural production increased by about 12 per cent in 2005, accounting for one fifth of GDP in the same year. Additional land reforms, including privatization, were planned for 2005-2006 to improve agricultural production.

Economic growth in the Russian Federation, the largest economy in the subregion, was expected to slow to 6.4 per cent in 2005 compared with 7.2 per cent in 2004 and 7.3 per cent in 2003. The growth rates of industrial output were also below the rates recorded in 2004. The slowdown was essentially the result of the slow pace of industrial restructuring. The main sources of growth in industry are manufacturing, mining and extraction, led by oil and gas. Oil and gas were particularly buoyant in 2005. Agriculture continued to be a weak performer in the economy, growing by 2.0 per cent in 2005 due to problems in the livestock sector. The grain harvest, at 78-79 million tons, was expected to be the same as in 2004. The main drivers of economic growth in the Russian Federation in 2005 were domestic demand, net exports and investment. Domestic demand was met mainly by domestic output and its growth was reflected in strong retail sales, which rose by 12.0 per cent in 2005. Net exports and investment were stimulated by the strong performance of the energy sector.

Economic growth in Tajikistan was also expected to decelerate in 2005 owing to the slow progress achieved in agricultural reform and industrial restructuring. GDP rose by 6.7 per cent in 2005 compared with more than the 10 per cent growth recorded annually in the period 2002-2004. Industry continued to be the fastest growing sector, increasing by 8.5 per cent in 2005. There was also a considerable increase in the production of consumer goods, which resulted in a growth rate of 9.6 per cent in retail trade turnover in 2005. Rising wages in Tajikistan and continued inflows of worker remittances boosted domestic demand and private consumption. The service sector became an increasingly important source of growth in the country. Growth in agricultural production decelerated from 10.3 per cent in 2004 to 6.8 per cent in the first eight months of 2005 owing to unfavourable weather conditions and floods.

With high capital investment in the gas and oil sectors and strong industrial performance, overall economic growth of 11 per cent was expected in Turkmenistan in 2005. Hydrocarbons remain the main contributor to the growth of industrial output, which rose by 22.0 per cent in 2005. Cotton and wheat also played a significant role in boosting economic growth. However, the cotton harvest was expected to be below the 2005 target, which could have negative implications for the textile sector and the trade balance.

Hydrocarbons and agriculture remained the leading sectors for economic growth in Uzbekistan in 2005. New investment from the Russian Federation and China in oil and gas production and recovery in the manufacturing sector contributed to the 7.7 per cent growth rate in industrial production in 2005. Agricultural production increased by 7.3 per cent in the same year owing to an improved harvest of the main export earner and the largest source of employment in the country, the cotton sector. Also contributing to strong expansion of both industry and agriculture was the introduction of convertibility to the som currency, which boosted exports and improved the competitiveness of local manufacturing of consumer goods. GDP growth in Uzbekistan was expected to be 7.2 per cent in 2005.

Total output, after rising by 7.1 per cent in 2004, decelerated to 0.6 per cent in 2005 in Kyrgyzstan. A marked slowdown in the production of gold, which accounts for more than 40 per cent of the country's industrial production, resulted in a 12.1 per cent decline in industrial output in 2005. The agricultural sector also posted a 4.2 per cent drop in the same year. However, private consumption was strong owing to rising wages and large inflows of remittances from abroad.

Key macroeconomic policy developments

Fiscal policy developments

The reform process continues but the pace slackens

In 2005, much of the subregion continued to make progress in strengthening revenue collection and fiscal consolidation and improving public expenditure policy, although in comparison with previous years the pace appears to have slackened somewhat (see figure II.10).

Figure II.10. Budget balance in North and Central Asian economies, 2003-2005[a]

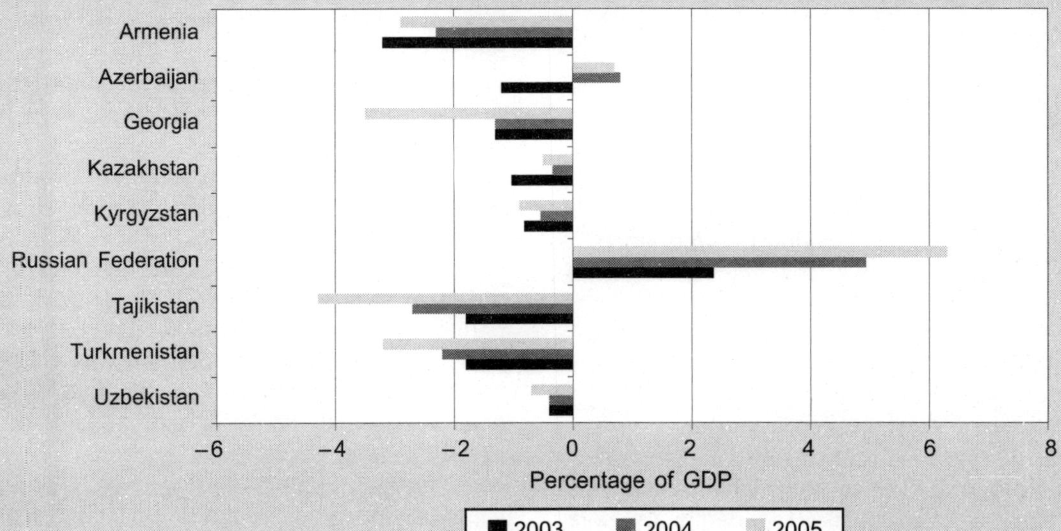

Sources: United Nations Economic and Social Commission for Asia and the Pacific, based on International Monetary Fund, *International Financial Statistics* (CD-ROM) (Washington, D.C., IMF, 2005), and *World Economic Outlook databases* (Washington, D.C., IMF, 2005); and Economist Intelligence Unit, *Country Reports* (London, EIU, 2005 and 2006), various issues.

[a] Data for 2005 are estimates.

During 2005 the Government of the Russian Federation revised the federal budget to reflect the improved revenue position as a result of higher than expected oil and natural gas prices and better tax collection. Taxes on fossil fuel extraction, on profits and on value added made up the bulk of tax collections. In addition, tax collection improved as a result of greater efficiency by the tax authorities, reflected especially in the payment of substantial tax arrears by some large oil companies. Federal budget revenues exceeded the Government target for 2005 and should provide a budget surplus of 6.3 per cent of GDP by the end of the year. On the spending side, three fourths of the excess revenue was earmarked for social welfare, including increasing the salaries of public sector workers and for investment promotion. To further improve tax collection, the Government planned to implement an amnesty on the repatriation of capital flight allowing individuals to transfer money from foreign to domestic banks with a proposed payment of 13 per cent or even 7 per cent income tax on the amount being transferred. It was expected that this amnesty would have a positive effect on business confidence.

High oil and gas prices also supported budget revenues in Azerbaijan in 2005. Higher than expected revenue should provide the State budget with a surplus of 0.7 per cent of GDP in 2005. The main sources of revenue were the taxes on value added, corporate profits and income, while major budget outlays were for education, social security and infrastructure development.

Owing to high commodity prices, especially for oil and gas, budget performance in Kazakhstan was strong in the first half of 2005, with a surplus of 3.1 per cent of GDP. However, the budget was expected to have reverted to a small deficit of 0.5 per cent of GDP by the end of 2005.

In 2005, Armenia increased its tax collection owing to improved tax and customs administration and a crackdown on endemic tax evasion. Overall, tax collection increased by nearly 25 per cent in the first five months of 2005, which enabled the Government to meet increased expenditure targets. Excise and value added taxes accounted for almost 60 per cent of total tax revenues and they remained the principal source of budget revenues. However, underreporting of corporate taxes was a serious problem, at about 17 per cent of tax proceeds. A 1 per cent minimum turnover tax was introduced in 2004 to increase corporate taxes, thus ensuring greater compliance with tax laws by the country's largest taxpayers. Social spending increased significantly in 2005 owing to increases in public sector wages, pensions and poverty-related benefits. The Government budget deficit target for 2005 was 2.9 per cent of GDP.

In Georgia, the likely budget deficit of 3.5 per cent of GDP in 2005 was expected to be covered mainly by inflows from foreign multilateral organizations. Some additional revenue was also expected from the privatization of State property. Among the main budget priorities in 2005 were paying off pension arrears and reducing poverty. The budget provided for raising the minimum monthly wage of State sector employees to $65 and the minimum monthly pension to $15 in 2005. The Government also introduced a financial amnesty on undeclared assets and a new tax code to strengthen revenue performance in 2005. The tax code reduced the number of taxes from 21 to 7 and the rates of the social, income and value-added taxes.

In 2005, Tajikistan introduced a new tax code that established a two-tier income tax system, a minimum tax on corporate turnover and removed several exemptions. The new code was expected to improve compliance in the payment of taxes and bring in more revenues from the country's shadow economy. However, the budget deficit target for 2005 was revised upwards from 0.5 to 4.3 per cent of GDP.

Uzbekistan was expected to have a lower deficit of 0.7 per cent of GDP in 2005. Budget performance was solid in the first half of 2005, with a surplus of 1.2 per cent of GDP and budget revenues boosted by the effects of high gold prices and delays in expenditure. In October 2005, the Government increased by 20 per cent minimum State sector wages, pensions, stipends and other social benefit payments. The expanded State spending put the budget back into deficit by the end of the year.

Monetary policy developments

The subregion had two key policy targets in monetary policy in 2005: preventing excessive real exchange rate appreciation, the so-called Dutch disease (the tendency of the exchange rates to appreciate in price-inelastic natural resource-producing economies) and curbing inflation. The loosening of monetary policy in the subregional economies was attributed to the clearance of wage and pension arrears and growth in net foreign assets. A further indication of the gradual loosening of monetary policy was the periodic cuts in benchmark interest rates, the refinancing rates of the central banks. This policy approach created a dilemma for the authorities, as it tended to undermine the fight against inflation (see figure II.11).

In the Russian Federation the monetary policy in 2005 was aimed at reducing inflation to a target of 11 per cent and preventing excessive real appreciation of the ruble, which would reduce competitiveness. However, high oil prices led to an increase in the money supply and in inflation. High inflation of 12.7 per cent in 2005 was driven primarily by increases in the costs of food products, housing and communal services. This level of inflation is regarded as being very high for country attempting to attain sustained economic growth. Therefore, one of the key goals of the Russian Federation in 2006 was expected to be a gradual decrease in inflation to 7-8.5 per cent and management of money supply growth consistent with the inflation target; money supply growth is a problem created by an enormous trade surplus of close to $143 billion in 2005. Monetary policy was expected also to be consistent with efforts to prevent real appreciation of the ruble. In 2005, the central bank succeeded in preventing the ruble from strengthening. The inflation target was also met, but only just, and reserves rose to $165 billion by November 2005.

Robust economic expansion and surging hard currency inflows in Azerbaijan resulted in strong growth in the money supply, which accelerated consumer price inflation. Consumer price inflation stood at 9.6 per cent in 2005. The high level of inflation forced the National Bank of Azerbaijan to tighten monetary policy. The bank

Figure II.11. Inflation[a] in North and Central Asian economies, 2003-2005[b]

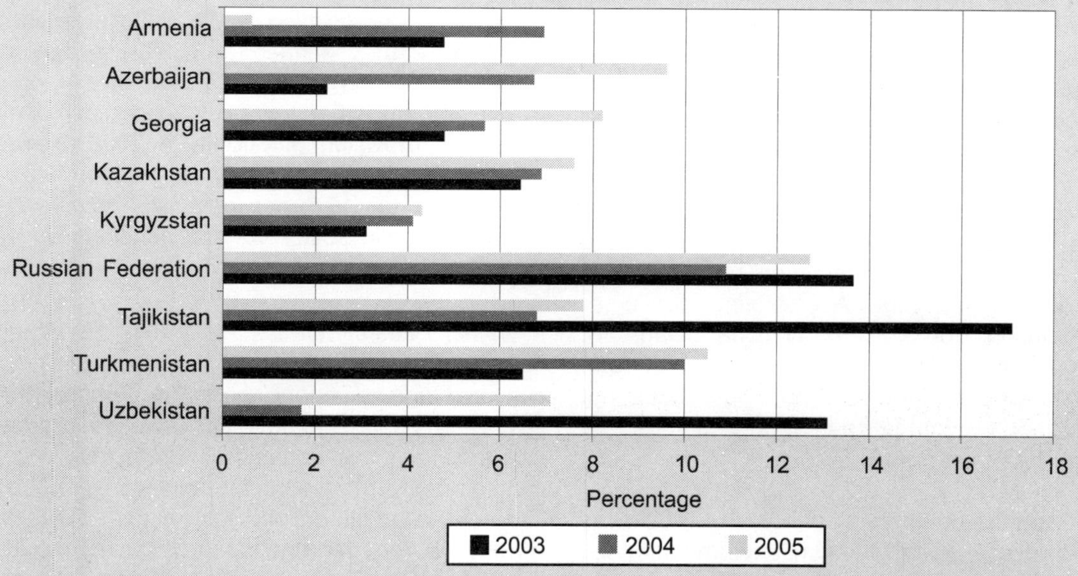

Sources: United Nations Economic and Social Commission for Asia and the Pacific, based on the website of the Commonwealth of Independent States Inter-state Statistical Committee, <www.cisstat.com>, accessed on 6 January 2006 and 10 February 2006; and Economist Intelligence Unit, *Country Reports* (London, EIU, 2006), various issues.

[a] Inflation rates refer to percentage changes in the consumer price index.
[b] Data for 2005 are estimates.

raised its benchmark interest rate, the refinancing rate, from 7 to 8 per cent in 2005, making the refinancing rate positive in real terms. The higher interest rates and appreciation of the exchange rate were expected to rein in inflation in 2005 and 2006, causing the average annual consumer price index to fall substantially in 2006.

Tajikistan, too, maintained a relatively tight monetary policy in 2005 to curb inflation and ensure currency stability. However, a sudden jump in gas and oil prices led to a 10 per cent increase in the price of basic food products in the country in September 2005. In 2005, consumer price inflation was 7.8 per cent compared with 6.8 per cent in 2004. Other factors contributing to the increase in the overall price level were rises in domestic utility tariffs, public sector salaries, pensions and the minimum wage. In addition, robust inflows of workers' remittances contributed to growth in domestic demand, pushing up prices. Average annual inflation in 2005 was higher than the central bank's 7 per cent target. In response, the national currency, the Tajikistan somoni was expected to depreciate by 5 per cent in 2005.

Massive foreign exchange inflows caused rapid growth in all monetary aggregates in Kazakhstan, and this had an inflationary effect. Large hard currency inflows resulting from the oil boom caused consumer price inflation to accelerate from 6.9 per cent in 2004 to 7.6 per cent in 2005. Additional inflationary pressure came from wage growth and producer prices, which rose at double-digit rates. The inflation rate exceeded the annual consumer price inflation target of 5.7 per cent. Accelerating consumer price inflation forced the National Bank of Kazakhstan to raise its benchmark interest rate, the refinancing rate, from 7 to 8 per cent, but that did not prevent a real appreciation of the tenge in 2005.

Georgia's monetary policy in 2005 was also aimed at curbing inflation and ensuring the stability of the national currency. However, consumer price inflation was 8.2 per cent in 2005. High oil prices, rising food prices, increasing household energy consumption and a rise in excise taxes on some leading commodities exerted greater upward price pressure than expected. Strong capital inflows and increased budget and export earnings strengthened the lari against the dollar in 2005 and thus mitigated the upward pressure to some extent.

Price stability also continued as the focus of monetary policy in Armenia in 2005. Following inflation of 6.9 per cent in 2004, which reflected robust expansion in the demand for money, inflation decelerated sharply to 0.6 per cent in 2005. To reduce inflationary pressure, the central bank refrained from intervening in the currency markets and broadened its policy tools to keep the national currency stable. However, in the first half of 2005, the Armenian dram appreciated by almost 20 per cent against the United States dollar.

In Uzbekistan, inflation was expected to accelerate from 1.7 per cent in 2004 to 7.1 per cent in 2005 because of money supply growth, increases in utility tariffs and payment of wage and pension arrears. The introduction of currency convertibility in 2003 and the removal of restrictions on the purchase of hard currency allowed the Uzbekistan som to depreciate against the United States dollar by about 1 per cent per month during 2005.

To lessen the impact of the Turkmenistan manat's depreciation, the Government of Turkmenistan continued to pursue a tight monetary policy and maintained extensive price controls and subsidies on basic goods, as well as the free provision of utilities in 2005. Nevertheless, annual consumer price inflation was expected to be 10.5 per cent in 2005, owing to rises in public sector wages, pensions and various household benefits.

Financial sector policies

Ongoing financial sector reforms in the Russian Federation in 2005 included conversion of in-kind social benefits to cash payments and an amnesty for the repatriation of the outfow of money in capital flight that occurred in recent years. Anyone repatriating such capital would pay a flat 13 per cent or even 7 per cent of the amount concerned. The funds would be deposited in a bank in the country and invested in the national economy. The amnesty could be offered for a six-month period in 2006. Proposals for simplifying legalization of undeclared domestic income were also under preparation.

Tajikistan continued banking sector reforms aimed at increasing competition, improving access to credit and promoting microcredit and small enterprises. All limits on foreign bank activities in the country were abolished and banking laws were amended, as needed. The reforms enabled Tajikistan to improve operational efficiency and increase public confidence in the sector. However, further efforts are needed to improve financial discipline in large industrial enterprises and to streamline business regulations in order to encourage private sector development.

Despite improvements in banking sector supervision in Kyrgyzstan in recent years, greater consolidation and a higher level of financial intermediation are still needed. Industrial enterprises, for example, still have limited access to commercial bank financing, and only a small percentage of bank credit is provided on a long-term basis.

In contrast, growing confidence in the banking system of Armenia contributed to a higher demand for money and greater financial intermediation. A strengthened banking system improved the business environment in 2005, and there was a 30 per cent increase in domestic credit from commercial banks to companies. Financial intermediation by the banking sector was also increasing more generally in the economy, with the introduction of new services and savings media.

Developments in the external sector

Current account, exports and imports

External balance improves but not in all economies

The Russian Federation, Kazakhstan and Uzbekistan recorded substantial current account surpluses in 2005 (see figure II.12) owing to growing trade surpluses (see figure II.13). In the process these economies built up their international reserves and repaid a part of their foreign debt. Other subregional economies continued to have current account deficits that deteriorated slightly.

Figure II.12. Current account balance in North and Central Asian economies, 2003-2005[a]

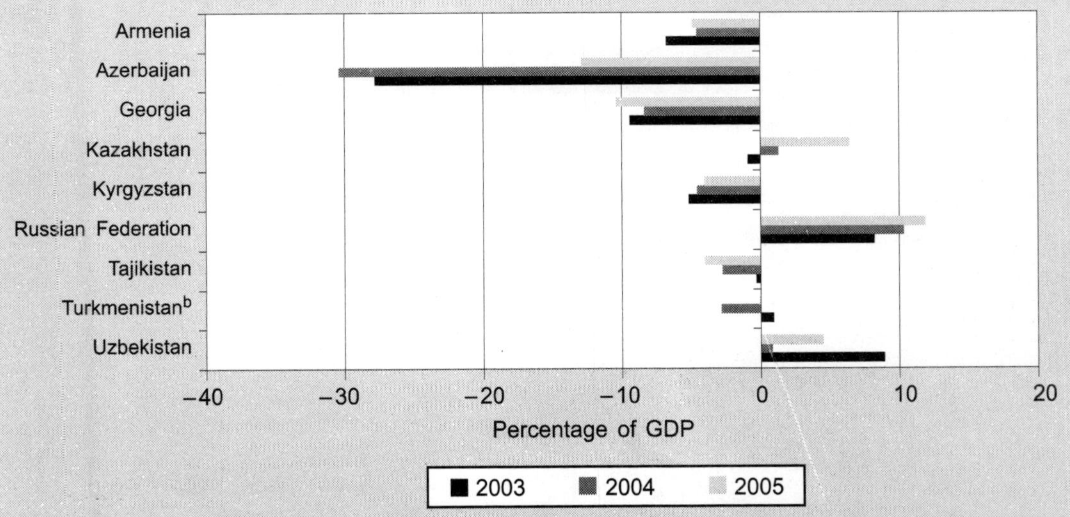

Sources: United Nations Economic and Social Commission for Asia and the Pacific, based on International Monetary Fund, *International Financial Statistics* (CD-ROM) (Washington, D.C., 2005), and *World Economic Outlook databases* (Washington, D.C., IMF, 2005); and Economist Intelligence Unit, *Country Reports* (London, EIU, 2005), various issues.

[a] Data for 2005 are estimates.
[b] Current account balance is calculated using official exchange rates.

Figure II.13. Growth rates in merchandise export earnings and import spending in North and Central Asian economies, 2003-2005

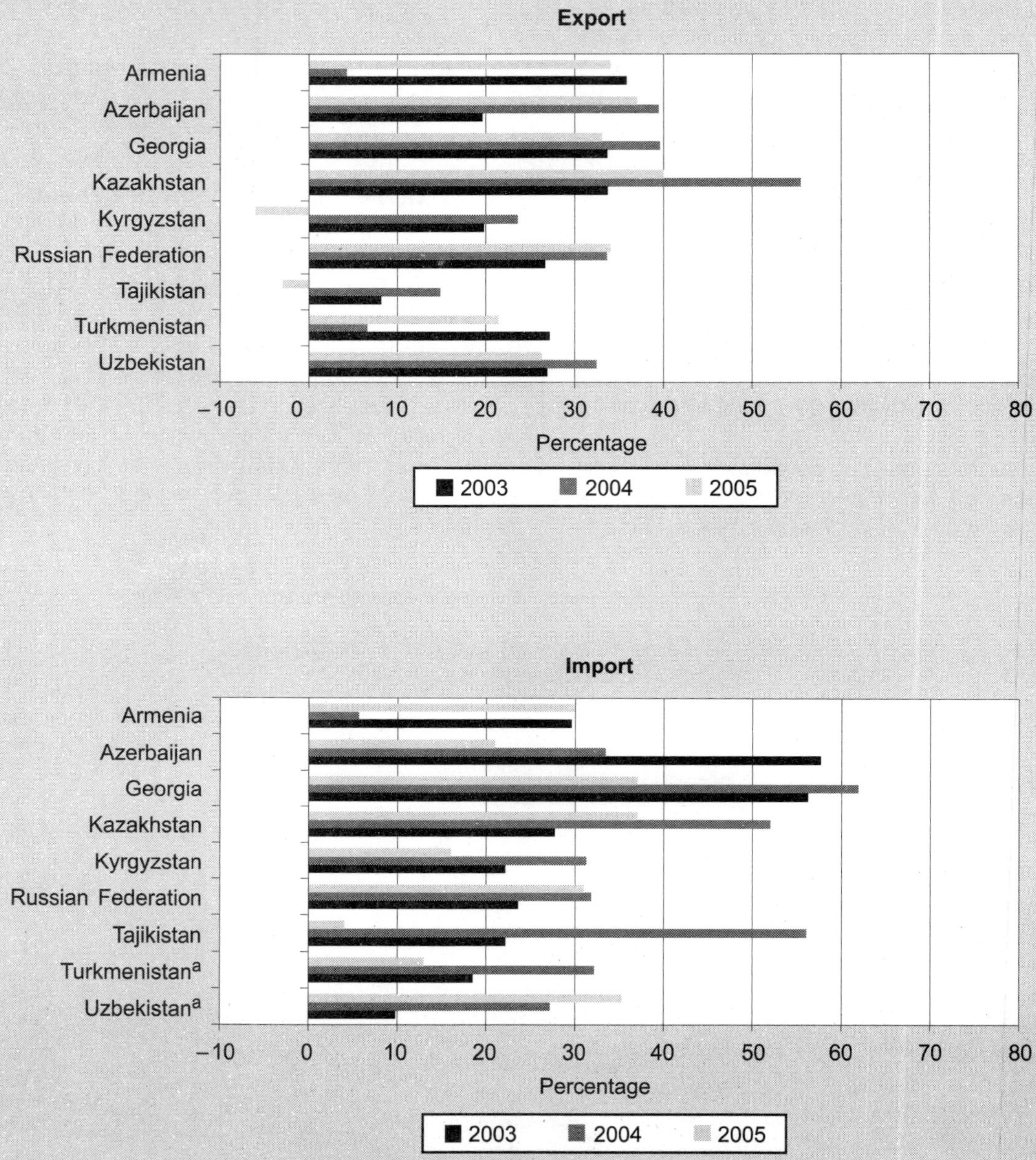

Sources: Website of Commonwealth of Independent States Inter-State Statistical Committee, <www.cisstat.com>, accessed on 22 February 2006 and Economist Intelligence Unit, *Country Reports* (London, EIU, 2005), various issues.

Note: Growth rates for 2005 are estimates for Turkmenistan and Uzbekistan.

[a] Valued free on board (f.o.b.).

The Russian Federation enjoyed higher current account and trade surpluses in 2005. Its trade surplus increased from $106 billion in 2004 to more than $140 billion in 2005, while the current account surplus topped $100 billion in the same year. This outcome was the result almost entirely of the high prices and general buoyancy of energy exports. The Russian Federation became a major supplier of energy to the major energy consumers in the region, including China, India, Japan and the Republic of Korea in 2005. The volume of exports rose by 37.2 per cent in 2005 to countries outside the Commonwealth of Independent States (CIS) compared with 10.6 per cent to CIS countries. Imports from non-CIS countries rose by 37.5 per cent and from CIS countries by 6.8 per cent in 2005.

Rising world oil prices increased the merchandise trade surplus of Kazakhstan from $7.3 billion in 2004 to $9.4 billion in the first 11 months of 2005. As a result, the current account was expected to record a surplus of 6.4 per cent of GDP in 2005 following strong growth in oil and gas exports. In the first 11 months of 2005, oil and gas contributed more than three fifths of merchandise export earnings, which grew by 40.0 per cent and reached $25 billion. Merchandise imports grew by 37.0 per cent to $15.8 billion in the same period. The growth in import spending remained high owing to larger imports of capital goods, machinery and equipment needed to implement the Government's import-substitution policy.

Owing to high prices of the main export commodities, cotton and gold, Uzbekistan was expected to record a trade surplus of $1.2 billion and a surplus of 4.5 per cent of GDP in its current account in 2005. Export earnings were estimated to have grown by 26.3 per cent for a total of $5.4 billion, while merchandise imports were expected to grow by 35.3 per cent, to $4.1 billion in 2005. The Government of Uzbekistan continued to exercise control over the import of consumer goods in order to protect domestic industries and to keep trade and current account balances in surplus.

FDI inflows into hydrocarbon projects were expected to reduce the current account deficit of Azerbaijan from 30.4 per cent of GDP in 2004 to 12.9 per cent in 2005. The economy ran a trade surplus of $338 million in the first 11 months of 2005, compared with $110 million in 2004. Imports rose by 21.0 per cent to $3.8 billion in the first 11 months of 2005. Among the largest imports were energy, capital goods (primarily machinery and equipment) and foodstuffs. Oil and refined petroleum products accounted for the largest share of export earnings, which increased by 37.0 per cent in the first 11 months of 2005.

The growing trade imbalance of Tajikistan widened its current account deficit from 2.7 per cent of GDP in 2004 to 4.0 per cent in 2005. The trade deficit exceeded $330 million in the first 11 months of 2005 compared with $460 million in 2004, a result of unfavourable trends in global commodity prices. Export revenue fell 3.0 per cent to $823 million in the first 11 months of 2005 as a result of a decline in the price of cotton. Cotton remained the country's second largest export commodity, while aluminium provided the bulk of total earnings. Import expenditures rose 4.0 per cent to $1.2 billion in the same period owing largely to higher fuel prices. Imports of consumer goods continued to increase, in line with rising foreign remittances and higher wages, which boosted the purchasing power of domestic households.

The current account of Kyrgyzstan was expected to remain in deficit at 4.0 per cent of GDP in 2005 owing to rapidly rising imports and falling exports. Imports grew by 16.0 per cent to $979 million and exports fell by 6.0 per cent to $618 million in the first 11 months of 2005. The trade deficit increased from $222 million in 2004 to more than $360 million in the first 11 months of 2005. The growing trade imbalance was the result of the country's narrow export base, strong domestic demand and considerable energy requirements.

The current account deficit of Georgia deteriorated in 2005 as a result of a worsening of the trade balance. The trade deficit rose from $1.2 billion in 2004 to more than $1.4 billion in the first 11 months of 2005. Merchandise imports grew by 37.0 per cent and reached $2.2 billion in the first 11 months of 2005 as a result of a rise in capital imports related to pipeline construction and increased spending on consumer goods. Export revenue grew strongly by 33.0 per cent in the first 11 months of 2005 to $785 million owing to buoyant global prices for the main export item, metals, and to an increase in the trade in wine and mineral water. However, the country remained vulnerable to changes in the external economic environment because of its narrow export base.

Despite a substantial increase in the merchandise exports of Armenia, its trade deficit widened from $628 million in 2004 to $715 million in the first 11 months of 2005. Export earnings rose more than 30 per cent to $867 million in the first 11 months of 2005, owing to favourable prices for base metals and investment-related growth in the main export-producing sectors of the country. However, high global prices for the main import commodities raised import costs by 30.0 per cent to $1.6 billion in the first 11 months of 2005. The growing trade deficit was expected to widen the current account deficit from 4.5 per cent of GDP in 2004 to 4.9 per cent in 2005.

Capital inflows

Armenia was expected to approve a new law by the end of 2005 to promote greater foreign investment by easing restrictions on access to the country's market. FDI in Armenia increased from $121 million in 2003 to $218 million in 2004 and by more than 11 per cent to almost $140 million in the first six months of 2005. The bulk of the foreign investment from more than 30 countries was concentrated in metallurgy, food services, telecommunications and energy. Among the main foreign investors were Argentina, France, Germany, Greece, the Russian Federation and the United States.

The Russian Federation and the United States were also among the largest investors in Georgia in 2005. Inflows of FDI declined slightly, however, from $172 million in 2003 to $169 million in 2004. The service sector was the main recipient of FDI. In addition to FDI, Georgia was expected to receive a new $300 million aid package from the United States Millennium Challenge Account over the next five years. The aid package is aimed at developing and modernizing the infrastructure of the poorest and remotest regions of the country.

Foreign investment in the Russian Federation reached $11.6 billion in 2004, up from $8 billion in 2003 thanks to an improved investment climate and the removal of cumbersome restrictions on capital repatriation. FDI was expected to increase by a further 60 per cent in 2005, driven by high energy prices and the country's huge untapped potential in this area. In 2005, interest in the Russian Federation in new investment in the energy field was extended to Asian countries such as China, India, Japan and the Republic of Korea to construct and modernize the country's energy infrastructure. China, for example, was evaluating an investment in a new strategic oil pipeline from the far eastern area of the Russian Federation to the Chinese border, with a total throughput of 30 million tons of oil annually. The Russian Federation was also expected to participate in a new consortium of companies from China, Malaysia, the Republic of Korea and Uzbekistan to develop gas fields in the Aral Sea area.

FDI inflows in Kazakhstan reached $4.3 billion in 2004, double the $2.1 billion received in 2003. More than 40 per cent of FDI inflows went into the oil and gas sector.

FDI inflows in Azerbaijan, another oil-producing country, exceeded $3 billion in both 2003 and 2004. However, the level of FDI was low compared with that to other hydrocarbon-producing countries in the subregion. One third of FDI was allocated to the transport and communication sector, about 20 per cent to light industry and 13 per cent to the oil and energy sector.

Foreign debt

High oil and gas prices enabled the energy-producing countries of the subregion to accelerate repayment of external debt and to replenish and enlarge their foreign exchange reserves. In 2005, the hard currency reserves in the Russian Federation exceeded total foreign debt, enabling the country to pursue an active policy of debt reduction, repaying about one third of outstanding debt to the Paris Club of leading creditor countries on an accelerated schedule. The repayment was expected to save about $6 billion in interest annually. This repayment is considered to be the largest early repayment in the Paris Club's history. Even after this repayment, the country's foreign debt still amounted to about $80 billion at the end of the year. The stabilization fund of the Russian Federation was expected to reach $30 billion in 2005, while foreign exchange reserves were nearly $165 billion in November 2005.

The gross foreign debt of Kazakhstan rose from $22.8 billion in 2004 to about $35 billion in the first half of 2005. Sovereign foreign debt accounted for 10 per cent of the total and private sector debt for 90 per cent. The foreign debt was the equivalent of 78.6 per cent of the country's GDP in 2005.

Tajikistan's foreign debt was expected to be reduced from 70 per cent of GDP in 2000 to 40 per cent in 2005, owing to the conclusion of several debt-rescheduling and write-off agreements. The country, for example, concluded a debt-for-equity swap with the Russian Federation in October 2004. The direct government debt accounted for almost 80 per cent of the total of $905 million debt in 2005. Among the main creditors were the World Bank, the Asian Development Bank, the Islamic Development Bank, the European Commission and the OPEC Fund for International Development.

Kyrgyzstan reduced its external debt from more than $2 billion in 2004 to $1.93 billion in the first three months of 2005 through a restructuring deal reached with the Paris Club.

Armenia also improved its prospects for external debt sustainability through a debt-for-equity swap agreement concluded with the Russian Federation, which reduced its bilateral debt by about $100 million. Debt rescheduling agreements were also concluded with the country's other main creditors. Since the bulk of the external debt that Armenia owed to multilateral creditors was provided on concessional terms, the debt service burden has not been onerous. Total external debt amounted to $1.18 billion, or 33 per cent of GDP in 2004 compared with 39 per cent of GDP in 2003.

Medium-term prospects and key policy issues

Integration into the global and regional economies is an important challenge for the subregion

At the macro level the subregion has to address five basic sets of policy issues. First, integration of the countries into the global economy will provide new opportunities to maintain growth momentum. Accession to WTO is one of the main medium-term goals to that end. Armenia, Georgia and Kyrgyzstan are full members of WTO. The other economies, except Turkmenistan, have observer status at WTO and are at different stages in accession negotiations. In 2005, Kazakhstan and the Russian Federation made encouraging progress in negotiations and were expected to become WTO members in the near future. WTO membership could help the countries in North and Central Asia to establish legal frameworks and market-based institutions supportive of international trade and widen access to markets and investment inflows through the provision of unconditional most-favoured-nation status. However, since most of the subregional economies are still in transition to a market-oriented system it is important for them to assess the costs and benefits of WTO membership before making commitments that may not be in their best interests.

Second, participation of the countries of North and Central Asia in regional economic cooperation in Asia could facilitate their integration into the global economy. Currently, these countries participate mainly in two regional trading arrangements: Commonwealth of Independent States and the Economic Cooperation Organization. Little progress has been made in reintegrating the economies of the former Union of Soviet Socialist Republics, despite the numerous agreements adopted and the institutions created under CIS auspices. The achievements of the Economic Cooperation Organization have also been limited by the failure of members to comply with commitments and regulations.

The Eurasian Economic Community (EurAsEC), created by Belarus, Kazakhstan, Kyrgyzstan, the Russian Federation and Tajikistan in 2000 as a customs union, has had a more constructive role in promoting regional economic cooperation. In 2005, Uzbekistan joined EurAsEC after the Organization of Central Asian Cooperation merged with EurAsEC. The North and Central Asian countries are expected to promote their economic integration into a single, free-trade, economic zone within EurAsEC. The economic dynamism of Asia, particularly China, could provide significant new economic opportunities for the economies of North and Central Asia, enhancing trade and financial links with the rest of Asia. New growth hubs centring on East, South and South-East Asia are emerging in the broader Asian and Pacific region where growth has outpaced that of the rest of the world over the past decade; these trends are likely to continue at least over the medium term.

Third, sustaining a high rate of growth in the countries of North and Central Asia requires diversification of production and exports and of export markets. Many economies in the subregion continue to have a high degree of concentration in domestic production and external trade. This concentration makes them more vulnerable to external shocks, as was demonstrated in the Russian Federation in 1998. Promoting diversification requires sustained, high-quality investment in both hard and soft public goods, well-maintained physical infrastructure and reliable public services, including legal and regulatory systems, and the development of new technologies and products, since most private sector enterprises still lack the resources to conduct such activities. Above all, diversification requires realistic exchange rates that do not undermine international competitiveness (see figure II.14). Virtually all countries in the subregion produce primarily natural resources, the demand for which is relatively price inelastic. In such economies, an overvalued exchange rate could gravely undermine diversification.

Fourth, economic diversification and cooperation of the North and Central Asian countries require an unwavering commitment to reform and to building on the gains already achieved. The essential components of reform are a commitment to macroeconomic stability and prudence, keeping inflation low and maintaining exchange rate stability. Higher energy and commodity prices might not be a blessing in disguise, however, because in the current phase they appear to dilute the reform effort. They could also be masking still unaddressed structural weaknesses

Figure II.14. Index of exchange rates against the United States dollar in selected North and Central Asian economies, 1996-2005[a]

(1996Q4=100)

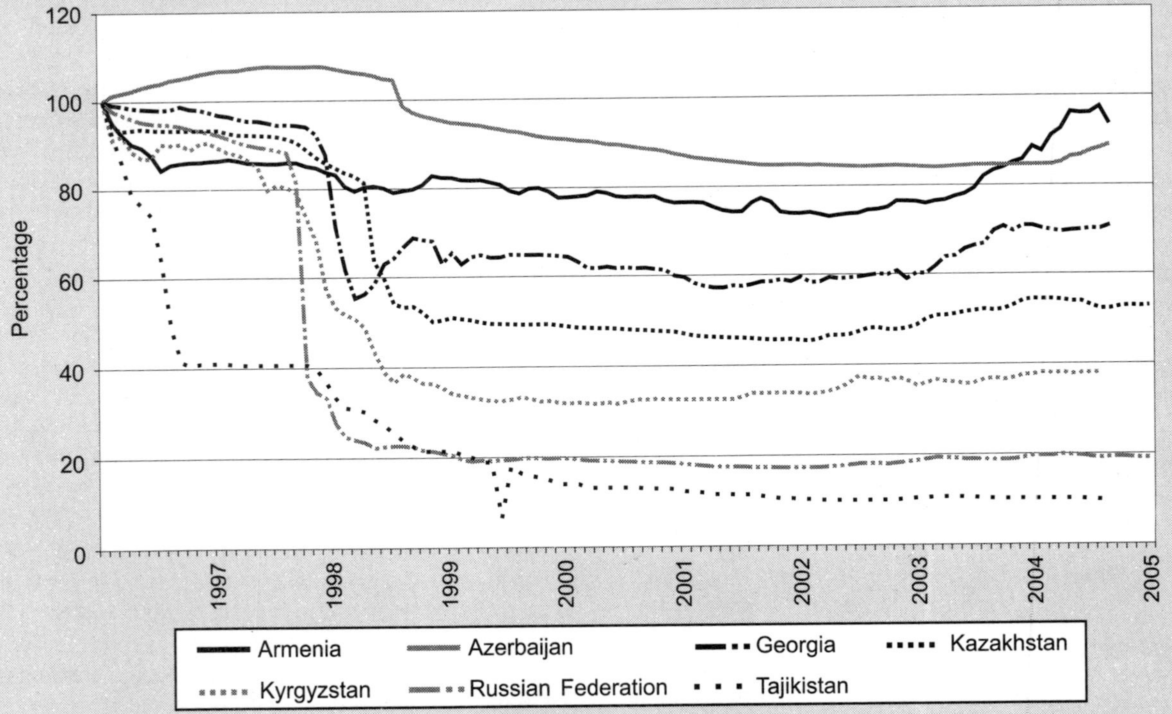

Sources: International Monetary Fund, *International Financial Statistics* (CD-ROM) (Washington, D.C., IMF, 2005); and *The Economist*, various issues.

[a] Data for 2005 are estimates.

in the economies of the subregion. The current phase should therefore be a spur to further reform. Further financial sector reforms are needed for the development of a forward-looking, more harmonized subregional tax policy framework and an integrated economic space for cross-border trade and investment. In this area the subregion could follow the example of the various areas of cooperation agreed by the Association of Southeast Asian Nations (ASEAN) and the ASEAN Free Trade Area.

Fifth, while regional and bilateral trade preference schemes can play a useful role in promoting subregional trade in North and Central Asia, closer economic cooperation in the future needs to extend beyond trade. The construction of regional infrastructure is necessary for meaningful economic cooperation, expansion of exports and greater inflows of FDI. Improvement in transport could enable people and goods to move more easily and rapidly among countries, reduce the cost of trade and enhance the value of business. The subregion's transportation infrastructure is adequate for supporting the needs of the economies and for facilitating their trade and development interests in the former Union of Soviet Socialist Republics. However, that aspect of the infrastructure should be reoriented and improved to meet the goals of expanded trade and closer economic cooperation among countries in the subregion and with other countries. The most important problem facing the transportation sector in North and Central Asia is the rapid deterioration of physical infrastructure as a result of inadequate investment in maintenance, repair and rehabilitation.

Growth will continue in the subregion in 2006 and unemployment will decline

GDP growth in the Russian Federation is forecast to be 5.6-5.8 per cent in 2006; it will be driven by buoyant private consumption and strong investment spending. The budget plan of the country for 2006-2008 reflects significant spending in order to double public sector wages by 2008 and to improve transport infrastructure. The plan also calls for the creation of a 700 billion ruble ($25 billion) investment fund to finance large-scale infrastructure projects. The fund was to be financed with surplus budget revenues stemming from high oil prices and from cost savings arising from early repayment of a portion of the external debt of the country. Based on current trends, the budget surplus should continue for the next three years.

The economy of Kazakhstan is expected to expand by more than 9 per cent annually for the next five years, transforming it into a dynamic developing country with a high standard of living. During this period, GDP per capita could reach $8,000-$9,000 a year, bringing the average monthly salary to 70,000 Kazakhstan tenges (about $500). By 2012, oil production and industrial production are expected to double. Through the higher household incomes that growth will bring in its wake, small and medium-sized businesses should form the basis of the economy, generating up to 40 per cent of GDP. Among other mid-term goals of the economy are ensuring greater cooperation and dialogue between State and private sector businesses, promoting and protecting private property, orienting the economy towards exports and improving the business climate.

Economic growth in Armenia in 2006 is expected to subside from the double digit growth of the period 2002-2005 to 7.5 per cent in 2006.

Azerbaijan is likely to continue investing in the energy sector and raising energy production. GDP growth is forecast to reach an extraordinary 25 per cent in 2006 owing mainly to a substantial increase in oil and gas output. Maintaining macroeconomic stability during a period of rapid economic growth has increasingly appeared as a key policy issue. Over-reliance on hydrocarbons could have an adverse affect on the economic structure and on the development of the oil and non-oil sectors alike in the long term.

Tajikistan's new country assistance strategy for the period 2006-2009 envisages strengthening the financial sector to improve the business environment, targeting more financial resources at the health and education sectors and increasing the efficiency of the domestic energy sector through greater exploitation of the country's hydropower potential.

Georgia is expected to attain 9 per cent GDP growth in 2006 owing to a rapid rise in investment linked to the construction of pipelines. Inflation could be reduced from 8.2 per cent in 2005 to 3 per cent GDP in 2006 and remain within the Government's target rate of 3 per cent of GDP. The Government is expected to implement further reforms of the tax and customs administration in order to mobilize greater tax revenues, enhance fiscal transparency and strengthen the financial sector.

The GDP of Turkmenistan is expected to grow by 8-9 per cent in 2006-2007, assuming that the high international prices of hydrocarbons persist. The hydrocarbon sector and construction should be the main contributors to economic growth. Strong export revenue from the sale of gas would keep the current account in surplus in 2006.

The growing investment of China and the Russian Federation in the oil and gas sector of Uzbekistan could provide a major impetus to economic growth in that country, which could average 5.6 per cent annually in 2006-2007. High gold prices would enable the economy to maintain surpluses in its trade and current accounts and allow greater freedom in domestic policies. The textile sector's contribution to economic expansion should increase with a more competitive exchange rate for the national currency.

High GDP growth will expand employment opportunities in most of the subregion

Owing to high rates of growth, employment opportunities are expected to expand in most of the economies of North and Central Asia in 2006. The Russian Federation, for example, improved its labour-market conditions considerably in 2004-2005. Employment rose 2 per cent in 2004, owing to restructuring of industry and expansion of the service sector. In the first nine months of 2005, 2.4 million jobs were created and the unemployment rate fell by 1.7 per cent.

The unemployment rate in Kazakhstan declined steadily as a result of continuing economic growth and stood at an average of 7.8 per cent of the economically active population of just over 8 million in the first eight months of 2005. At this level, however, the country had the highest reported unemployment rate in the subregion, but other countries in the subregion report only registered unemployment, which is not comparable and may not measure unemployment accurately. The high rate also indicates that there was a greater measure of structural reform in Kazakhstan than elsewhere in the subregion.

The labour market of Armenia developed favourably in 2004, and wages and incomes rose. However, progress in job creation slowed in 2005. The unemployment rate hardly changed, falling from 9.0 per cent in 2004 to 8.9 per cent in the second quarter of 2005 despite a high rate of emigration.

Output growth in Georgia in recent years has resulted in slow job creation, and the overall labour-market situation remains unfavourable. The unemployment rate rose from 10.7 per cent in 2003 to 12.5 per cent in 2004 due to large-scale cuts in public sector employment. The unemployment rate was much lower in rural areas than in urban areas owing to family, largely subsistence, farming although there was some seasonal work for the rural population.

The rate of labour migration from Tajikistan to neighbouring countries declined from more than 420,000 people in the first quarter of 2004 to 320,000 in the first quarter of 2005. Although the Russian Federation continued as the destination for roughly 90 per cent of this labour outflow from Tajikistan, the decline was due to greater job opportunities in Tajikistan, including new jobs related to the construction of hydroelectric power plants.

The slow pace of structural reform continues to dampen job creation in Kyrgyzstan. As a result, unemployment was higher than 4 per cent in the first four months of 2005. It is worth mentioning, however, that the actual number of people unemployed was much higher, possibly by one third more than the officially reported unemployment numbers.

Pacific island economies

Overview

Modest growth continues

Pacific island countries face many daunting problems in their quest for economic growth and sustainable development. These include the physical disadvantages of remoteness, smallness and dispersion, significantly raising transport and other development costs and limiting opportunities for realizing economies of scale. In many cases, rapid population growth exerts pressure on scarce resources and frustrates efforts to raise living standards. The severe shortages of professional and technical skills, paucity of domestic savings and vulnerability to external shocks pose further constraints.

Most Pacific island economies registered modest real GDP growth in 2005 (figure II.15). However, at growth rates of less than 3 per cent for most countries, there was little change from the figures in 2004, and for Fiji and Solomon Islands the GDP growth rates were almost halved. Economic conditions in Pacific island countries in 2005 were relatively favourable, with good growth in tourist numbers, favourable movements in primary commodity prices other than petroleum and a strong performance from remittances. Moreover, there was no significant economic damage from natural disasters during the year.

Most Pacific island countries continue to experience declining living standards as popula-

Figure II.15. GDP and sectoral growth in selected Pacific island economies, 2003-2005[a]

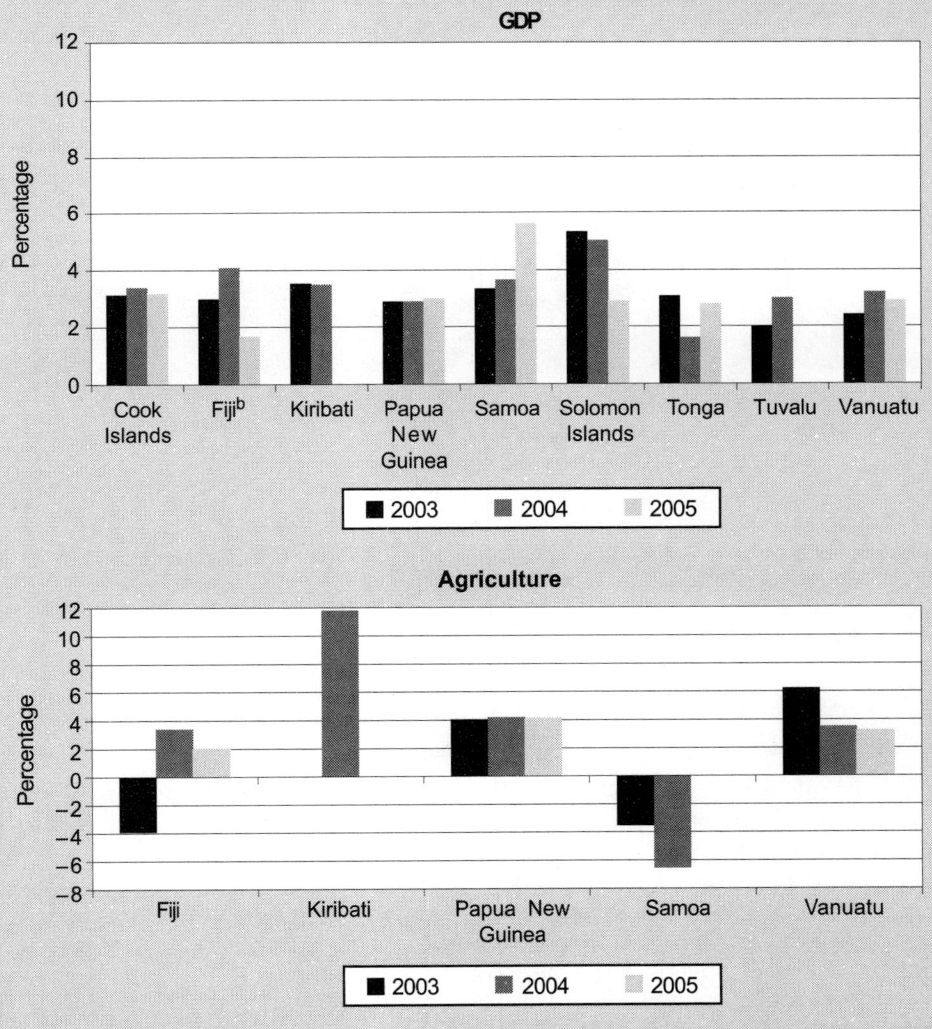

(Continued on next page)

Figure II.15 *(continued)*

Industry[c]

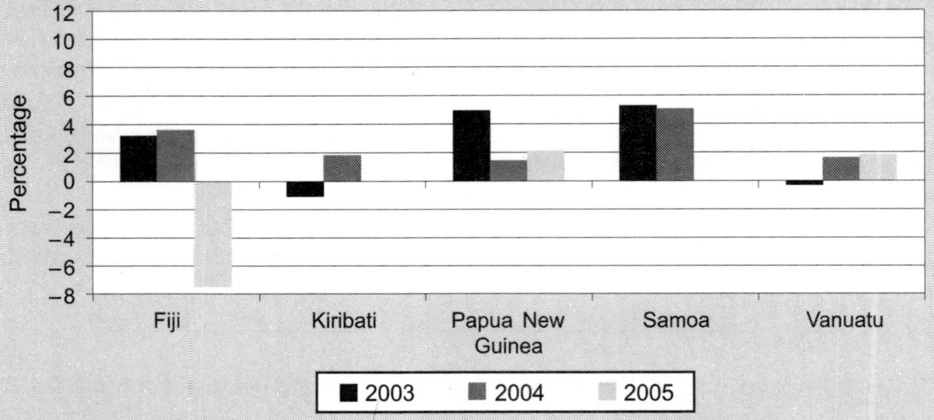

Services

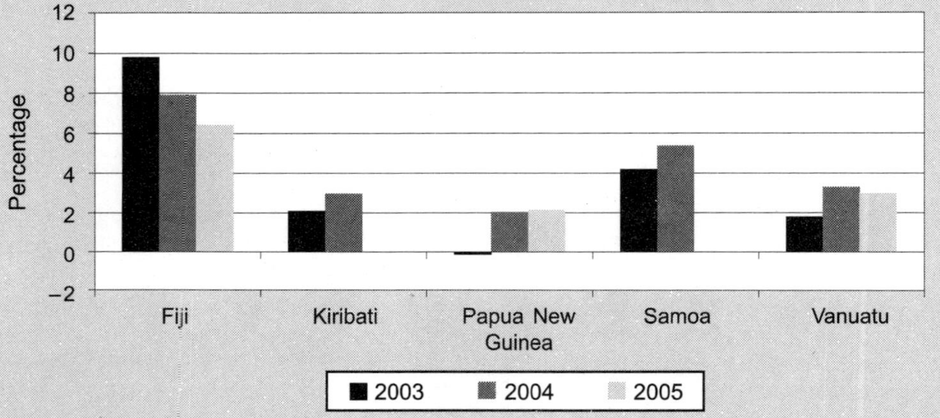

Sources: United Nations Economic and Social Commission for Asia and the Pacific, based on national sources; Department of Treasury and Planning, Papua New Guinea, *2006 National Budget* (Port Moresby, 2005); Asian Development Bank, *Key Indicators of Developing Asian and Pacific Countries 2005* (Manila, ADB, 2005) and *Asian Development Outlook 2005 Update* (Manila, ADB, 2005).

[a] Growth rates for 2005 are estimates.

[b] Real GDP at factor cost.

[c] Industry comprises mining and quarrying; manufacturing; electricity-generation, gas and power; and construction.

tion growth rates outpace modest GDP growth rates. Also, average economic performance in these economies hides the fact that a small proportion of the people earn high incomes, while the bulk of the population is doing poorly and a larger proportion is slipping into poverty. The three major causes of poverty are a lack of employment and economic opportunities, lack of access to basic services (education and health) and lack of response by government institutions to the people's needs.

The small proportion of people who are doing well in Pacific island countries are mainly those benefiting from privileged monopoly positions, which were created largely by Governments. Conditions for the development of an open-market, competitive private sector are generally highly unfavourable. This is manifested in the frustration expressed by the private sector with the difficulties faced in trying to establish businesses in these countries.

Agriculture is an important source of income and employment in the majority of Pacific island countries, so investment in this sector is important. For land-rich countries such as Fiji, Papua New Guinea, Solomon Islands and Vanuatu, their development strategy has to focus on the rural sector. Investment must be aimed at improving agricultural productivity to increase rural people's incomes and savings so that they can be invested in activities servicing the rural sector. Increased research in new and improved varieties of crops and farming systems is also needed.

Infrastructure, human resources and the investment climate need strengthening

Costly and unreliable utilities and poor transport infrastructure are widespread problems in Pacific island countries. Most Pacific island countries have been unwilling to introduce a level of competition into utility industries, and where they have made markets more contestable, they have been slow to adopt effective regulatory arrangements. They have adopted monopoly positions, often public-private joint venture monopolies, that have led to internationally uncompetitive telecommunications costs.

Primary and secondary education is of relatively poor quality throughout most Pacific island countries. It is stronger in countries that have easy emigration access to metropolitan countries, for example, in Samoa and Tonga, where the prospect of higher-paying jobs overseas provides an incentive for investment in education. In countries such as Papua New Guinea, Solomon Islands and Vanuatu, the weak prospects of formal sector employment discourage investment in education. A better educated labour force is a prerequisite for increased investment and economic growth, but unless other constraints to investment are reduced, training will be insufficient or the trained labour force will leave the home country for overseas work.

The tourism industry makes an important contribution to many Pacific island economies. The recent increase in tourism numbers in some countries reflects a combination of factors, including the growing demand for safe destinations, increased marketing and increased air capacity and the entry of low-cost carriers. The South Pacific Tourism Organisation estimates that tourism is worth more than $1.5 billion to the Pacific subregion. The challenge is to ensure political stability, to encourage private investment in infrastructure such as hotels and roads and to step up marketing efforts in new tourist-originating markets, such as China.

Remittances, mainly from long-term emigrants, have also given strong support to Pacific island economies. However, the nature of remittances has been changing, with short-term offshore employment opportunities becoming more widely available and with countries such as Fiji taking advantage of these opportunities. In addition, the rapid population ageing of high-income countries is providing job opportunities for Pacific island countries, which have large proportions of people in the under-25 age groups.

To accelerate GDP growth, increase employment opportunities (see box II.2) and reduce poverty Pacific island countries must improve their investment climate. Governments will have to develop secure rights to land; remove restrictions against the free movement of goods and services, investment, labour and technology; provide reliable transport infrastructure; reduce the costs of utilities; improve the regulation of natural monopolies; reduce red tape and bureaucratic control over the establishment of businesses and improve people's access to education and health.

GDP growth performance

GDP growth declines in Fiji

The real GDP growth of 2005 is estimated at 1.7 per cent, much lower than the 4.1 per cent achieved in 2004. GDP growth is projected to be 2.0 per cent for 2006 and 2.4 per cent for 2007, well below the nearly 4 per cent average for the period 2002-2004. The poor prospects for the sugar and the garment industries that led to a pessimistic outlook in the 2005 budget have not improved. The tourism industry is performing well, with resort hotels fully booked for the current tourist season; construction is under way on four resorts, and other resorts are planned. Remittances from overseas employment in nursing and teaching and from army and security personnel are continuing to grow: from F$50 million in 2000 to F$300 million in 2004 and F$500 million expected in 2005. The Reserve Bank of Fiji estimates that an additional F$150 million could be remitted in unrecorded transfers in 2005.

This boom in remittances is helping to sustain the economy in the face of the sharp decline in garment exports and the long-term decline in sugar production and exports. The expiration of the WTO Agreement on Textiles and Clothing on 1 January 2005 has led to the loss of 5,000 to 8,000 jobs in Fiji. The closure of one garment plant that was dependent on the United States market meant the loss of 3,000 jobs. The Government of Australia has extended the South Pacific Regional Trade and Economic Co-operation Agreement (SPARTECA) by seven years, giving some breathing space to the Fiji garment industry. However, the value of this access will decline as Australia lowers its tariffs in line with the global WTO agreement. The Government of Fiji is requesting the Government of Australia to lower local content requirements under the SPARTECA rules of origin from 50 per cent to 25-30 per cent. This would provide Fijian garment firms and employees some relief, but it would advantage mainly other countries exporting materials for the garment industry to Fiji. Fiji cannot hope to compete with major producers in standard products because of its high trade costs, small scale, remoteness and high wages relative to other garment-manufacturing countries. The only hope for the garment industry in Fiji is to find and exploit niche markets. The country's ability to move in this direction will depend on many factors, most importantly on product design and marketing.

The tourism sector in Fiji is continuing to grow strongly. Visitors increased by an estimated 7.7 per cent in the first six months of 2005, following an 18 per cent increase in 2004, when tourist numbers topped 500,000 for the first time. The Fiji Visitors Bureau forecast that visitor arrivals would reach a new record of 532,000 in 2005. Most tourists are from Australia and New Zealand, followed by European countries and the United States. With the terrorist bombings that occurred in some other tourist destinations and the avian influenza scare, tourism numbers in the Pacific subregion should grow robustly. Because China is expected to be a new growth market, Fiji and other Pacific island countries have been negotiating easier visa entry for tourists from China.

Growth in the country's tourism sector could be held back by the shortage of suitable accommodations, although resort developments under construction and in the planning stage will add over the next two years 2,000 first-class rooms to those currently available. The Government has initiated a public-private partnership policy to encourage private sector participation. Construction of resort hotels is being facilitated by agreements between landowner groups and hotel owners for 99-year leases on land held under customary ownership. There are problems in the construction industry, however, with the continuing loss of skilled tradesmen in the wake of the 2000 coup. In the 2006 budget, the Government introduced a 5 per cent "bed" tax for resort owners, responding to claims that only 40 per cent of the tourist dollar remains in the country.

The sugar industry, with annual foreign exchange earnings of about F$200 million, well below remittances and tourism, now accounts for only 6 per cent of GDP and 8 per cent of foreign exchange earnings. The Fijian sugar industry is in deep trouble with the upcoming loss of preferential prices for exports to the European Union and the United States. The Fiji Sugar Corporation, owner of the country's four sugar mills, has been losing money consistently in recent years, even though it sells two thirds of its sugar at two to three times the price on the global market. Farm yields are only half those of major producers, such as Australia and Brazil. In an attempt to stave off the necessary adjustment to the liberalization of the global sugar market under WTO, Fiji and various African, Caribbean and Pacific countries are petitioning the European Union to slow the pace of reduction in the preferential sugar price and to provide adjustment assistance. A subsidized loan of F$86 million from the Government of India is being used to upgrade machinery in the four mills to improve efficiency. Sugar output has fallen from a peak of 517,000 tons in 1994 to an estimated 320,000 tons in 2005.

For the sugar industry to become viable, farm yields would have to improve substantially, the cost of transporting sugar cane to the mills would have to drop substantially and milling efficiency would have to rise. To achieve higher yields farmers will need more secure access to land, farms will need to be consolidated so that machine-harvesting can be used and the area of marginal land will have to be reduced substantially. The Asian Development Bank has provided a loan and technical assistance to help farmers displaced from their leaseholds land and farmers wishing to move out of farming sugar cane, so that they can develop new livelihoods.

Private investment in Fiji is well below the level needed to generate economic growth in the 5 per cent plus range and provide jobs for the 15,000 or more young people entering the labour force each year. Although increasing in recent years, total investment is still only about 17 per cent of GDP, and only about a quarter of this amount is private investment. Investment in public enterprises is earning poor returns, as most State-owned enterprises are losing money or earning close to zero returns on their investments. If growth is to move beyond the 2-3 per cent range, the challenge for the Government will be to create an environment in which private investment could increase rapidly and raise total investment to about 25 per cent of GDP. Increasing private investment will depend on a significant reduction in political instability and law and order problems. The Government should focus on actions, such as providing better transport infrastructure, ending the monopoly status of the telecommunications industries to reduce costs, resolving the impasse over land leases and reducing the red tape facing potential investors.

Stable growth continues in Papua New Guinea

The improvement in economic activity in Papua New Guinea that began in 2003 continued with a modest real GDP growth rate of 3 per cent expected for 2005. This three-year period of modest growth followed a three-year period of decline in real GDP, which eroded average per capita incomes. The construction sector is expected to drive growth in 2005, with several new projects under construction. The combination of low interest rates and strong domestic demand has translated into several new residential and commercial building projects. GDP in the agricultural, forestry and fishing sectors is expected to grow by 4.1 per cent in 2005, while the non-mining sector will grow by 3.2 per cent. The sector's strong performance reflects new fisheries licenses and increased production of cash crops as the maintenance and rehabilitation of feeder roads increase producers' access to markets. The petroleum sector is expected to grow by 11 per cent during the year, while the mining and quarrying sector is expected to decline by 4.5 per cent in 2005 reflecting a 6 per cent decline in gold production.

GDP growth for Papua New Guinea is projected at 3.5 per cent for 2006, underpinned by a 5 per cent increase in construction activity resulting from the initiation of work on the Ramu Nickel Project. Initial construction work on the Papua New Guinea-Australia gas pipeline will also contribute to growth. The mining sector is projected to grow by 5.8 per cent in 2006, with better productivity expected from all mines except the Porgera Gold Mine. It is hoped that the expected boom in government revenues from the gas project and related activities will be handled better than during the mining boom in the early 1990s.

Solomon Islands recorded GDP growth of 5 per cent in 2004. Growth for 2005 is estimated at 2.9 per cent, because of reduced earnings from tuna fishing and copra production. Receipts from fishing over the first nine months of 2005 declined by 49 per cent owing to seasonal conditions and the poor performance of the country's ageing fishing fleet. The fishing company in Solomon Islands, now under government control, is not performing as well as it was when it was privately owned, in part because of the loss of Japanese expertise and the links to the marketing network of Japan. The poor performance in the fishing and copra industries has meant greater dependence on logging for export and foreign exchange earnings. Log exports remained fairly stable during the years of internal conflict because logging is confined to the Western Province, a region of the country that has experienced relatively little fighting.

The rehabilitation of palm oil plantations on Guadalcanal Island has proceeded well, and production and export were expected to resume at the end of 2005. Gold production from the Gold Ridge Mine, closed during the period of civil unrest and considerably damaged, is expected in late 2006. This will be important for the economy as the mine was contributing about 30 per cent of GDP before the conflict.

Real GDP growth for Samoa in 2005 is estimated at 5.6 per cent compared with 3.7 per cent in 2004. Credit for the improved performance is due to the upswing in the construction sector in preparation for the 2007 South Pacific Games and a turnaround in agriculture and fishing. The construction industry grew by 29 per cent in nominal terms as of the end of June 2005, and a further increase in real GDP of 3 per cent is expected for 2006, with the construction for the Games completed and the further improvements made in the agricultural and fishing sectors. Because of the much-improved performance of the Samoan economy over the past decade, per capita GDP has increased from about WS$1,000 in 1995 to about $2,000 in 2005.

The agricultural sector in Samoa has been performing poorly since damage was caused by Cyclone Heta in January 2004 and subsequently by drought. The fishing industry recovered somewhat in 2005 following the poor tuna catches since mid-2002. The recent difficult conditions have led to a rationalization of the fishing fleet, with marginal operators dropping out. This should result in a more resilient industry, better able to weather the inevitable fluctuations in catch and in global prices.

The economy of Samoa was supported strongly again in 2005 by remittances and tourism, the two largest contributors to national income and the balance of payments. Remittances account for up to 20 per cent of GDP, while tourism receipts account for about 15 per cent. Efforts are being made to increase tourism earnings, particularly through resort hotel construction. The recent joint venture between Polynesian Airlines and Virgin Blue should reduce the high costs of travel to Samoa.

Real GDP growth in Tonga recovered to an estimated 2.8 per cent in 2005 from 1.6 per cent in 2004 on better performance in agriculture and tourism and ongoing construction projects. Similar performance is expected in 2006 but will depend primarily on continuing growth in remittances, on an improved tuna catch, on the performance of the squash industry and on the Government's management of the fiscal problems resulting from large pay increases for public servants following a nationwide public strike in 2005.

Because of the high rate of emigration, Tonga's population growth rate is well below 1 per cent per year so, even with modest GDP growth rates, average income levels continue to rise. Private remittances average from T$80 million to T$90 million and can be expected to continue if economic growth in Australia and New Zealand continues at its recent pace. Official estimates of remittances are likely to be low because of the large amount of cash that enters the country unofficially.

Apart from remittances, agriculture, fishing and tourism are the mainstays of the Tongan economy. The contributions of the squash and vanilla industries depend heavily on prices, which tend to be highly volatile. The fishing industry has also been in difficulty, with lower catches and lower prices, but better performance is expected. Tonga's tourism industry has been performing well, with increasing tourist arrivals and expenditures. The declining level of the pa'anga against the Australian and New Zealand currencies and the safe environment offered by Pacific island countries appear to have encouraged visitors. However, the number of visitors to Tonga fell over the first six months of 2005.

A modest expansion of economic activity was expected in Vanuatu for 2005, underpinned in part by rising output in the forestry and beef industries and a pickup in tourism following the start-up of low-cost flights from Australia by the "no frills" Pacific Blue Airlines. The economy has grown while inflation remained low. Vanuatu also maintains low interest rates and a reasonable level of international reserves, despite the political instability of the past few years and the disappointment over the absence of the growth dividend expected from the partially implemented Comprehensive Reform Programme. However, with the population growing faster than the economy, the long-term lack of improvement in average incomes persists. GDP per capita in real terms is reported to have fallen below the level of 20 years ago. The obstacles to achieving a much higher growth path appear to be the continuing political instability, the difficulties in mobilizing land for investment and the monopolies in key areas, particularly essential services.

The one bright spot has been the growth in tourist numbers over the past two years. In 2004, visitors to Vanuatu increased by 20.3 per cent and in the first six months of 2005, numbers increased by a further 11 per cent. The increases are attributed to the entry of low-cost carriers into the market and to better marketing. The safety of the Pacific subregion from terrorism and disease may be another reason, as is the continued good economic performance of Australia and New Zealand. Important for income generation and distribution is the extent to which tourist expenditures flow through to local labour and producers of goods and services used in tourist resorts. Growing confidence in Vanuatu's tourism industry is reflected in plans for new hotels and extensions to existing properties that will significantly increase capacity. The industry's growth prospects could, however, be frustrated by financial troubles and political interference in the management of the national airline, Air Vanuatu.

In the longer term, Vanuatu's GDP growth is forecast to remain in the 2-3 per cent range. In its Article IV consultations on exchange arrangements, IMF has argued that Vanuatu has the potential for much improved economic performance, particularly in agriculture and tourism. Achieving this would require a reorientation of fiscal spending towards social and infrastructural needs, further financial sector reform and creation of a more investor-friendly environment. Areas for increased spending on the infrastructure include roads, electricity, water and transportation.

Key macroeconomic policy developments

Fiji enjoys greater macroeconomic stability

The budget deficit of Fiji for 2005 is expected to be 4.3 per cent of GDP, up from 3.2 per cent in 2004 (see figure II.16). The Government has announced an expansionary fiscal policy for 2006, with an expected deficit of 4 per cent of GDP in 2006, which appears quite optimistic. With the next general election to be held in 2006, this is widely seen as a pre-election budget. It includes several concessions to the poorer sections of the population, including a zero value added tax rate on several basic food items and tax concessions on fuel-related items. However, the concessions will reduce revenue collection. The Government has also granted substantial income tax exemptions for new investment activities in several areas, thus forgoing additional revenue collections. The public debt is projected to increase substantially over the period 2006 to 2008 in order to fund the

Figure II.16. Budget balance[a] in selected Pacific island economies, 2003-2005[b]

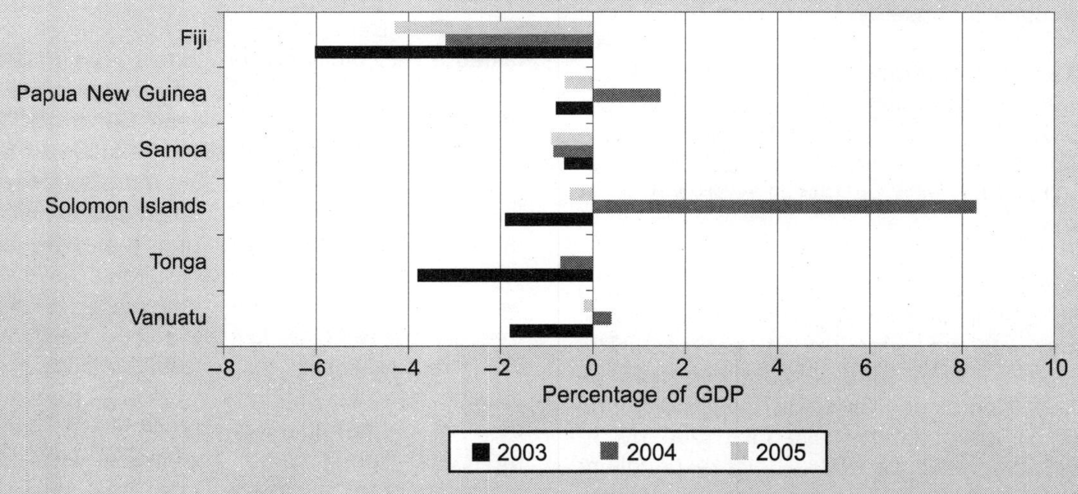

Sources: United Nations Economic and Social Commission for Asia and the Pacific, based on national sources; International Monetary Fund, *Samoa: Selected Issues and Statistical Appendix,* IMF Country Report No. 05/221 (2005) and *Solomon Islands: Selected Issues and Statistical Appendix,* IMF Country Report No. 05/364 (2005); and Asian Development Bank, *Key Indicators of Developing Asian and Pacific Countries 2005* (Manila, ADB, 2005).

[a] Budget balance includes grants.
[b] Data for 2005 are estimates.

deficit, so debt-servicing costs will continue to rise. The public arbitrator has granted a cost-of-living adjustment to public service salaries that is not funded in the budget, and no initiatives were announced for reducing the number of civil service staff, which is believed to be quite high.

The Reserve Bank of Fiji raised the official interest rate from 1.75 to 2.25 per cent in October 2005, the first increase since May 2004. It justified the increase on the grounds that consumer credit growth remained strong and that robust domestic demand growth was resulting in rapidly increasing imports and rapid growth in mortgage lending, which if left unchecked, risked straining households' capacity to service rising debt. Total domestic credit rose by a further 22.6 per cent over the year as of September 2005, fuelled primarily by private sector credit, which grew by 23.4 per cent.

The Fiji dollar appreciated by 1.87 per cent against the Japanese yen, by 0.08 per cent against the New Zealand dollar and by 0.33 per cent against the United States dollar, and depreciated by 1.25 per cent against the Australian dollar in September 2005. After rising for much of the year, the effective exchange rate index of the Fiji dollar fell by 0.1 per cent in September 2005, pointing to an improvement in the country's international competitiveness, thanks mainly to lower domestic inflation (see figure II.17).

The inflation rate for 2004 was 3.3 per cent, and it was expected to be close to 3 per cent for 2005. In 2006, high global oil prices are expected to have a greater impact on other prices. The 2006 inflation rate is projected to be 3.0 per cent.

The budget deficit of Papua New Guinea for 2005 is projected to be 0.6 per cent of GDP, compared with the target of 1.0 per cent. The turnaround is due mainly to improved revenue performance and good fiscal discipline. Revenue for 2005 is estimated to have increased by 16 per cent over that of 2004. Total expenditure and net lending in 2005 is projected to increase by 24 per cent, reflecting mainly the Government's intention to use 400 million kina to assist in funding its equity interest in the Papua New Guinea-Australia gas project. Interest rates on government securities have fallen steadily with tight government expenditure controls and the related drop in inflation.

The Government is targeting a budget deficit of 0.6 per cent of GDP for 2006. A risk built into the 2006 budget may well be the expected prices for gold and oil for the next three years. The budget assumes that these prices will decline from current high levels, but only gradually; however, primary commodity price declines from peaks are characteristically quite rapid.

Good public expenditure control, together with the increased revenues from high prices for gold and petroleum, has provided scope for the Government to substantially reduce its public debt. When the current Government took office in 2002 the public debt to GDP ratio was about 80 per cent. This figure was expected to be 49.8 per cent of GDP at the end of 2005, reflecting prudent fiscal management and exchange rate appreciation. The improvement in budget performance, low interest rates, low inflation and the high level of foreign exchange reserves reflect improved macroeconomic management, which should provide an encouraging environment for investment. However, the country's coalition Governments have remained unable to implement the necessary changes in microeconomic policies, to lower the high cost and improve the reliability of the infrastructure and to tackle the significant law and order problems needed to improve the investment climate.

The Bank of Papua New Guinea maintained an accommodative monetary policy stance in 2005. The Kina Facility Rate remained unchanged at 7 per cent between December 2004 and August 2005 before being reduced to 6 per cent in September 2005. This measure reflected the good progress made in reducing inflation over the past few years and the absence of price pressures. Market interest rates have fallen well below the indicator rate, with short-term treasury bill rates as low as 3-4 per cent during the year, reflecting the excess liquidity in the market. The accommodative policy stance has been made possible by prudent fiscal management and strong global conditions, which have supported the exchange rate and moderated prices. Monetary policy is likely to remain accommodative in 2006 as long as inflation pressures remain subdued. The year-on-year average inflation rate for the quarter ending in June 2005 was 1.2 per cent and the rate is expected to rise to 3.4 per cent in 2006, largely because of higher global oil prices and the flow-through

Figure II.17. Inflation and money supply growth in selected Pacific island economies, 2003-2005[a]

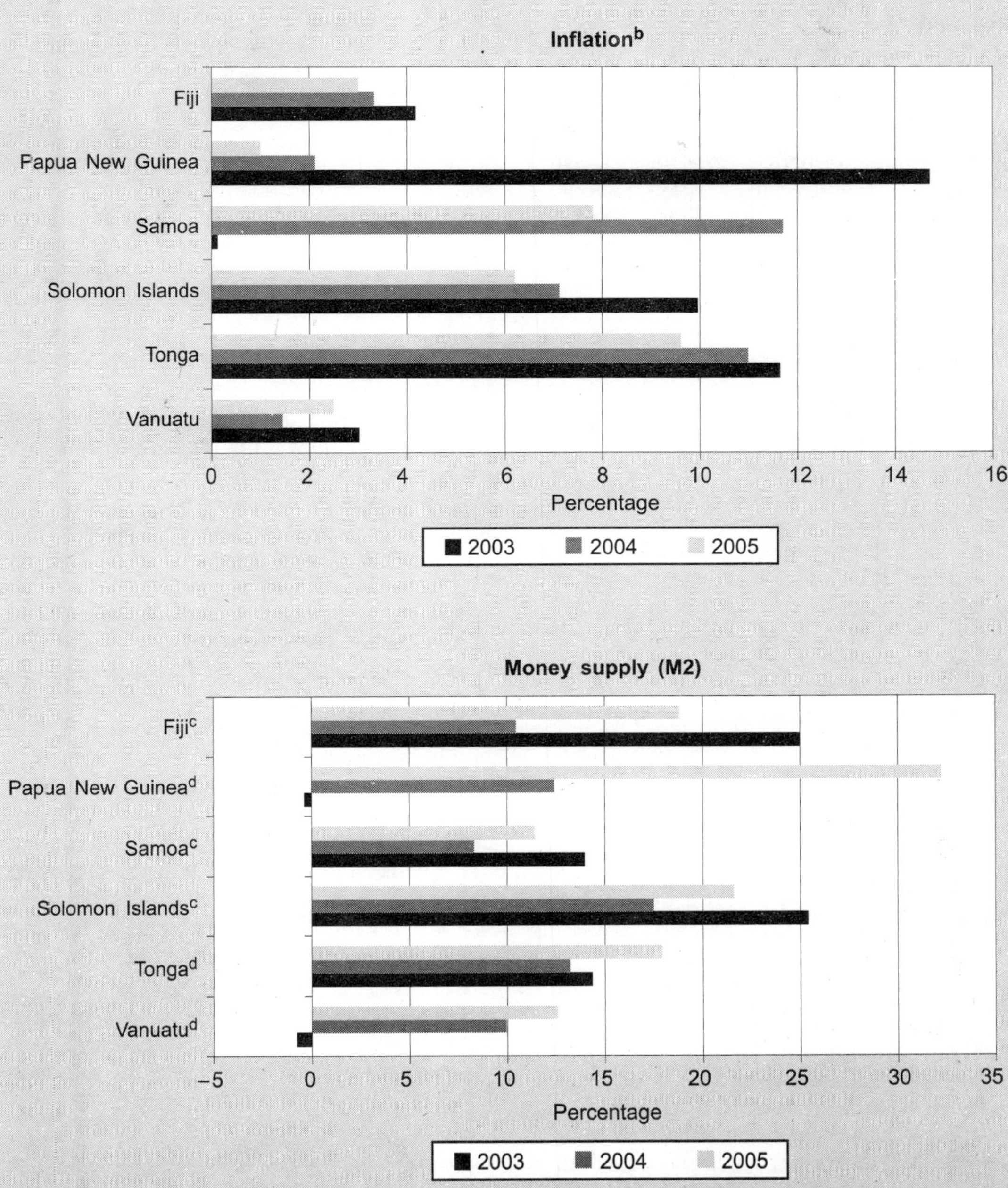

Sources: United Nations Economic and Social Commission for Asia and the Pacific, based on national sources; Asian Development Bank, *Key Indicators of Developing Asian and Pacific Countries 2005* (Manila, ADB, 2005); and International Monetary Fund, *International Financial Statistics* (CD-ROM) (Washington, D.C, IMF, 2005).

[a] Data for 2005 are estimates.
[b] Inflation rates refer to changes in the consumer price index.
[c] Money supply for 2005 refers to January-September.
[d] Money supply for 2005 refers to January-October.
[e] Money supply for 2005 refers to January-August.

to most transport and production activities. However, with the expected construction boom the challenge to monetary policy will be increased.

The kina exchange rate was generally stable in 2004 and steadily appreciated through 2005, appreciating by 2 per cent against the United States dollar and 3.8 per cent against the Australian dollar in the first nine months. The stability of the currency reflects both an increase in the terms of trade from higher international prices of the country's key commodity exports and lower inflation reflecting the Government's sound economic management.

Average per capita income in Solomon Islands has been recovering slowly since the arrival of the Regional Assistance Mission to Solomon Islands in July 2003; it is now back to about 80 per cent of its level before the civil unrest during the period 1999-2003. The achievements since the arrival of the Mission have been significant. Law and order was quickly restored. Fiscal prudence has been developing and the public debt has been reined in; foreign exchange restrictions have been relaxed and foreign reserves have been increased to about eight months of import cover. Public services are also slowly recovering. These achievements have been realized because of considerable donor support. For example, donors funded about 55 per cent of the recurrent budget and almost the entire development budget for 2005. Since this level of donor support cannot be expected to continue indefinitely, the country will have to create an environment in which domestic savings and investment can play the major part in development.

Some relief on the fiscal front was provided when international creditors agreed to grant Solomon Islands a two-year moratorium on its debt repayments. The Honiara Club of creditors agreed on a framework for consultations on reducing the country's debt, provided Solomon Islands maintains its planned programme of fiscal discipline and economic reform. The 2005 budget had allowed for the use of up to 20 per cent of revenues for debt-servicing.

Investors in palm oil production and in the restoration of the Gold Ridge Mine have been given substantial tax concessions for a considerable period, a matter of concern because of the loss of potential government revenue. If over-logging of the country's forests leads to a sharp decline in log exports and log export revenue within five years or so, this will create a large gap in government revenue. A major question is how this gap will be filled.

The 85 per cent of the population living outside the urban areas of Solomon Islands form the backbone of the economy, and enhancing their capacity to increase their livelihood is the most important factor in achieving significantly improved living standards. Most communities in rural areas were able to function during the previously mentioned unrest, which prevented what could have been much more widespread hardship. However, the productivity of rural activities is very low. Improving rural productivity will require government investment in physical and social infrastructure such as transport, safe water, power and health and education services. Research into new and improved plant species is also needed as are improved farming systems to lift productivity, improvements in the provision of market information and the means to raise and maintain quality standards and trade facilitation. The loss of resource rents from exploitation of forests and from mining gold and cultivating oil palm will make it very difficult for the Government to fulfil its functions.

The inflation rate in Solomon Islands in the three months to the end of October 2005 was 10 per cent, a considerable increase over that of the same period in 2004. The higher inflation has been due in part to the increase in fuel prices; inflation has flowed into transport and utility costs. In addition, the Mission exercise is being reflected in a surge in the housing rental component of the consumer price index.

A major concern for economic prospects in Samoa is the pre-election 2006 budget. Public sector salaries and wages are to be increased by up to 50 per cent over the next three years, an increase equivalent to 4 per cent of GDP. The rise in public service salaries and the expenditure commitments for the South Pacific Games are projected to sharply increase the budget deficit to 4.5 per cent of GDP, from its average range of 1-2 per cent over the past decade. The Government proposes to issue government bonds worth $26.5 million to fund the 2006 deficit, in contrast to previous years when the much smaller budget deficits were funded from government savings held in the banking system.

Inflation in Samoa was expected to be about 7.8 per cent in 2005. This rate is lower than the rate in 2004 when Cyclone Heta damaged crops, which led to higher prices for local produce and import costs rose because of increased fuel costs. The continuing high fuel costs, the public service salary and wage increases and construction expenditures for the South Pacific Games present a severe challenge to the central bank in managing inflation and protecting foreign exchange reserves. Some budget relief may be provided by the Polynesian Airlines-Virgin Blue joint venture, which means that the Government will no longer have to cover airline losses. The central bank has announced that it will be tightening monetary policy to protect foreign exchange reserves. As a result, interest rates will rise, credit will be restricted and demand will be compressed.

The Government of Tonga has taken measures to improve revenue collection. Technical assistance is being provided with donor support to improve customs duty collections; current inefficiency in duty collection accounts for the loss of an estimated $20 million in revenue annually. A new 15 per cent consumption tax has replaced the 20 per cent ports services tax levied on all imports as well as the 5 per cent sales tax and fuel tax. The consumption tax does not discriminate between imports and domestically produced goods and services and therefore does not distort resource allocation. Compliance costs are being kept low by requiring only businesses with an annual turnover of $50,000 or more to register for the tax.

In Tonga, the monetary expansion from support provided to loss-making public enterprises that have been unable to meet their debt commitments appears to underlie the continuing high level of inflation and depreciation of the pa'anga. The inflation rate was expected to remain high in 2005 and 2006 because of high international oil prices and the increases in public service salaries agreed at the time of a sector-wide strike. Wage increases as high as 80 per cent are well in excess of the increases planned in the budget. The increases have no basis in labour productivity gains and therefore the real value of the nominal increases will be quickly lost to inflation through depreciation of the exchange rate unless the Government somehow reduces expenditures in other areas; however, this is highly unlikely. The expected revenue increase from the value added tax will not be enough to shore up government finances.

The high inflation in Tonga will continue to place downward pressure on the exchange rate and the country's international competitiveness. The loss of international competitiveness may already be reflected in the downturn in tourist numbers in the first six months of 2005. Concerns over the sustainability of foreign exchange reserves and high inflation will likely see the Reserve Bank of Tonga attempt to maintain a tight monetary policy in order to dampen domestic demand and investment. However, past performance casts doubt on whether the Bank will be able to maintain this discipline.

Prudent fiscal and monetary management in Vanuatu has ensured continuing good performance on the inflation front. The inflation rate has been held to 2-3 per cent in recent years. High petroleum prices, reinforced by the rising United States dollar, present considerable challenges for restraining inflation and maintaining foreign reserves. Moreover, because of the low growth and lack of benefits arising from the Comprehensive Economic Reform programme, there could be strong public pressure for fiscal stimulus to promote economic growth, resulting in increased budget deficits in coming years.

Developments in the external sector

Higher commodity prices will aid growth but higher oil prices remain a problem

Higher world prices for primary commodities over the past three years have been a mixed blessing for Pacific island countries, except for Papua New Guinea. The sharp rise in the prices of oil, gold, copper and agricultural commodities enabled the Government of Papua New Guinea to reduce substantially the public debt and take the pressure off interest rates.

Increases in the prices for cocoa, copra and coconut oil have also benefited Solomon Islands and Vanuatu. However, palm oil prices declined between 2004 and 2005, and cocoa and copra prices fell in the third quarter of 2005, which may herald a period of lower prices for these commodities.

Pacific island countries other than Papua New Guinea rely heavily on petroleum imports for energy production and transport, and the sustained high prices for petroleum products have increased the costs of production and made it more difficult for the Goverments to control inflation and the balance of payments.

Exports from Fiji have been declining because of the decline in sugar production and exports, the loss of kava markets due to the bans (since lifted) on the product in Europe and the United States and stagnant fish exports (see figure II.18). Total merchandise exports (in local currency terms) fell 11 per cent in the 12

Figure II.18. Growth rates in merchandise export earnings and import spending in selected Pacific island economies, 2003-2005

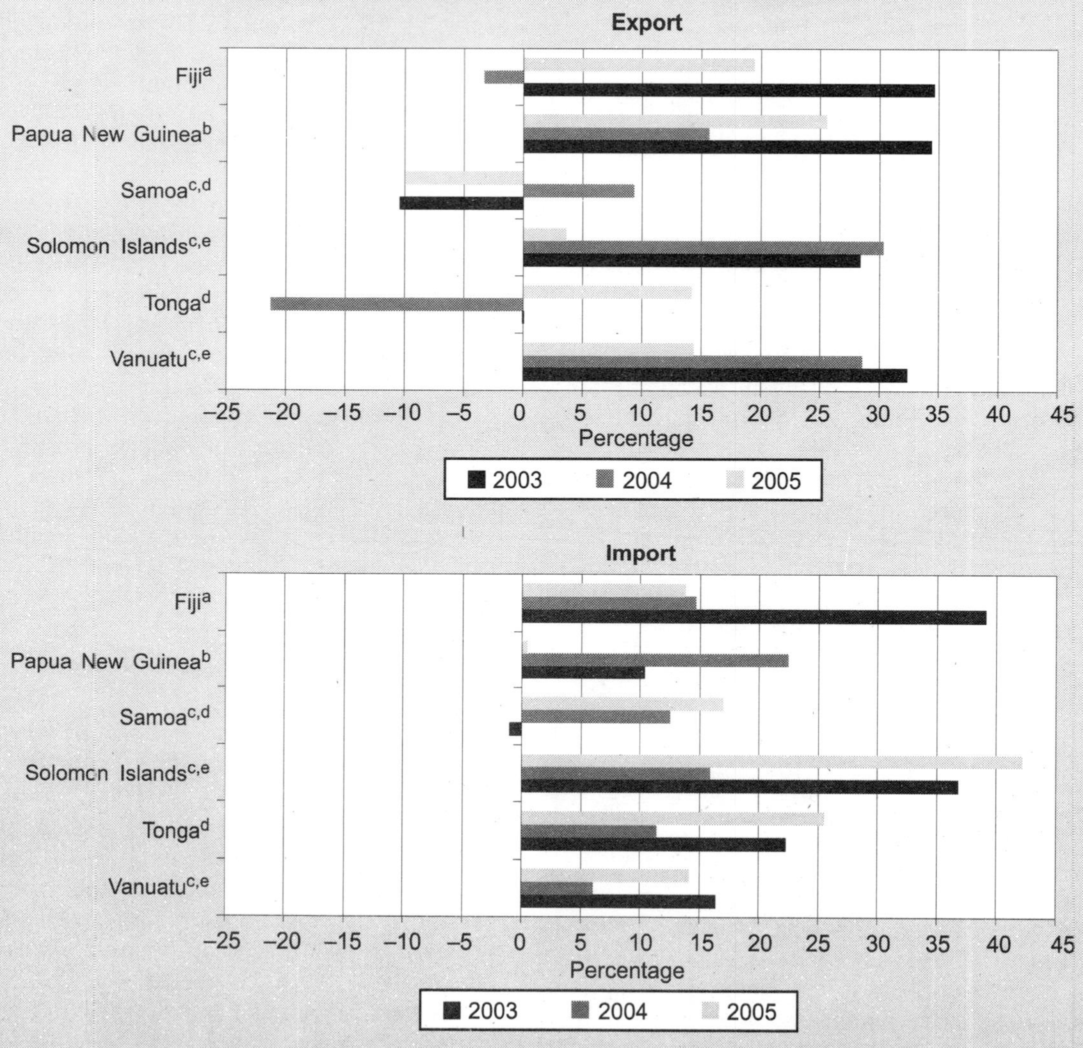

Sources: International Monetary Fund, Country Report No. 05/221 (2005), and *Public Information Notice*, various issues; Reserve Bank of Fiji website <www.reservebank.gov.fj>, accessed on 16 January 2006; Bank of Papua New Guinea website <www.bankpng.gov.pg>, accessed on 9 January 2006; and National Reserve Bank of Tonga website <www.reservebank.to>, accessed on 17 January 2006.

[a] Growth rate for 2005 refers to January-June of that year.
[b] Growth rate for 2005 refers to January-September.
[c] Growth rate for 2005 is a projection.
[d] Fiscal year data.
[e] Data for 2004 are estimates.

months to September 2005, largely attributable to negative contributions from textiles, clothing and footwear and from fish that more than offset the positive contributions from sugar, re-exports of mineral fuel, ginger and mineral water. During the same period, merchandise imports rose about 20 per cent, with delivery of greater quantities of goods for consumption, investment and intermediate use. Imports grew by 13.7 per cent in the first six months of 2005. Garment exports to the United States declined in 2005, and market opportunities there and in the rest of the world are expected to worsen considerably as Fiji and other countries face the full force of East Asian exporters. A bright spot for the balance of payments has been the sharp increase in remittances from teachers, nurses and army and security personnel employed overseas (see figure II.19). Remittances were expected to rise from more than F$300 million in 2004 to reach almost F$500 million in 2005. The country's official foreign exchange reserves fell from F$992 million at the end of June (equivalent to 5.6 months of import cover) to F$940 million at the end of September 2005 (5.3 months of import cover), reflecting sluggish export receipts and rising import costs. Exports were affected by the modest appreciation of the Fijian dollar in 2004. However, the exchange rate stabilized in 2005 (see figure II.20).

Papua New Guinea recorded a current account surplus of K 273 million in the first half of 2005 compared with a surplus of K 2 million in the first half of 2004, mainly because of a larger surplus in the balance of trade in goods and services (K 897 million in the first half of 2005 compared with K 461 million in the first half of 2004), which more than offset a larger deficit in the balance of income and transfers. This was mainly due to a higher merchandise trade account, which recorded a surplus of K 4,624 million in the first half of 2005, reflecting the higher export values of major commodities driven higher as a result of the increase in international prices. The value of Papua New Guinea's merchandise imports increased by 0.4 per cent in the first nine months of 2005 compared with the same period in 2004. The rise reflects increased business investments and an

Figure II.19. Current account balance in selected Pacific island economies, 2003-2005[a]

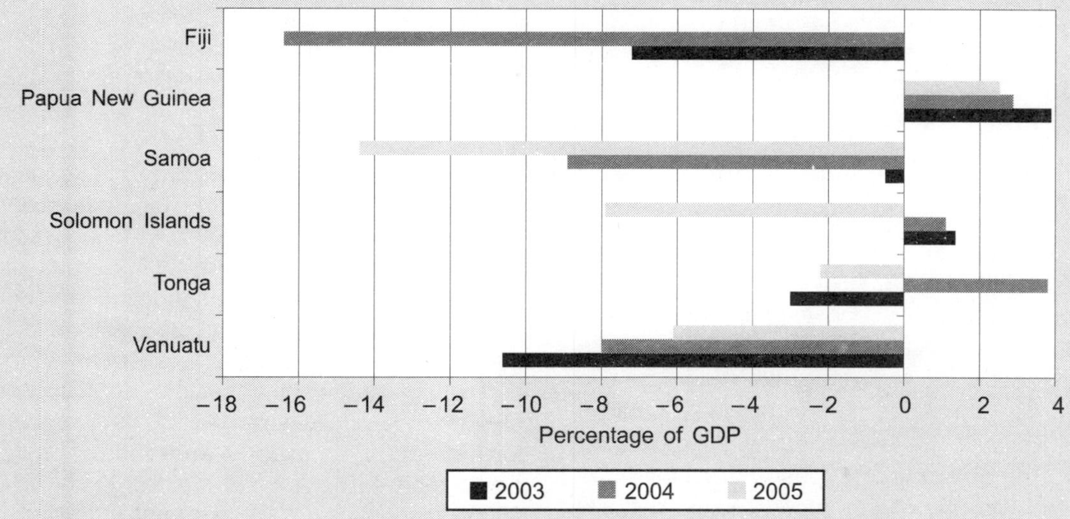

Sources: United Nations Economic and Social Commission for Asia and the Pacific, based on national sources; International Monetary Fund, *Solomon Islands: Selected Issues and Statistical Appendix,* IMF Country Report No. 05/364 (2005); and Asian Development Bank, *Key Indicators of Developing Asian and Pacific Countries 2005* (Manila, ADB, 2005).

[a] Data for 2005 are estimates.

Figure II.20. Index of exchange rates against the United States dollar in selected Pacific island economies, 1996-2005[a]

(1996Q4=100)

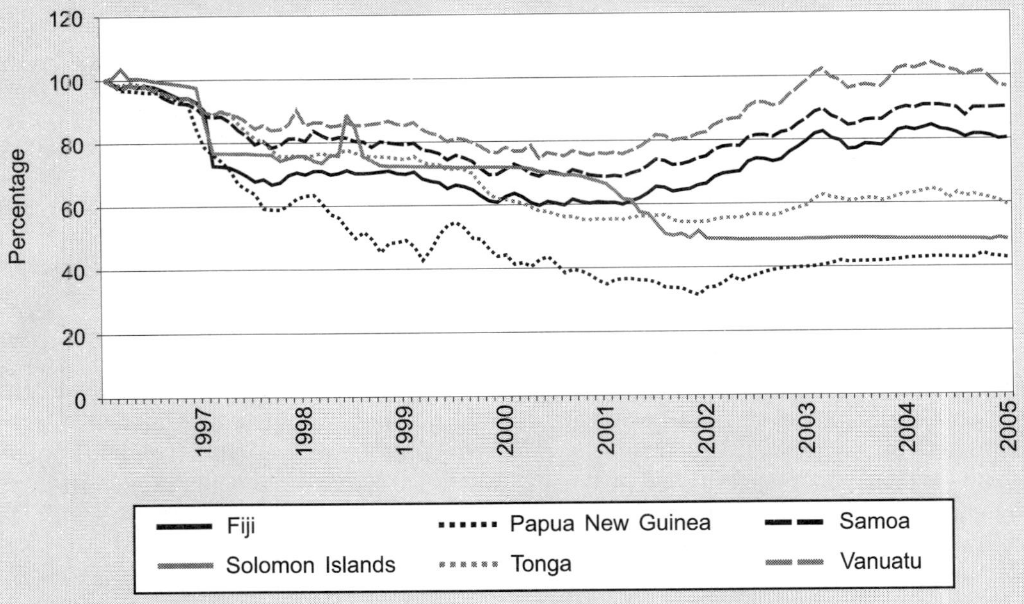

Sources: International Monetary Fund, *International Financial Statistics* (CD-ROM) (Washington, D.C., IMF, 2005); and *The Economist,* various issues.

[a] Data for 2005 are estimates.

increase in domestic demand. Holdings of gold and foreign exchange reserves totaled K 2,135 million as of August 2005, sufficient for 5.2 months of import cover.

The underlying balance of payments position of Papua New Guinea is expected to be healthy in 2006, with solid global growth and high commodity prices boosting export receipts, and steady domestic demand and moderate price increases for imports curbing increases in the volume of imports. However, the country's external account could be heavily affected over time by the goods and services and capital flows associated with the Papua New Guinea-Australia gas project and the Ramu Nickel project. If the projects proceed as expected, this will result in a substantial rise in imports and a turnaround in the current account from a surplus in 2005 to a large deficit in 2006 in the range of 4-5 per cent of GDP.

The external trade deficit of Samoa widened to 45.7 per cent of GDP in 2004 as a result of sluggish export growth and higher import growth owing to rapid growth in the construction sector, which is largely externally financed, and higher prices for imported fuel. Slow export growth in 2004 was the result of weak performance in the agricultural and fishing sectors. The current account deficit was almost eight times larger than that of 2004, at 8.9 per cent of GDP. With better performance in the agricultural and fishing sectors in 2005, export performance is likely to record an improvement for the year. Fish exports were the top merchandise export earner for the quarter ending in June 2005, accounting for 39 per cent of exports. For that quarter, total exports increased 18.3 per cent over the same period in 2004. However, with imports increasing even faster, the trade deficit increased to 65 per cent of GDP in that quarter, and the current account deficit reached 14.4 per cent of GDP. Foreign exchange reserves as of June 2005 were equivalent to 5.9 months of import cover. The central bank expects that pressures on reserves, particularly from rising fuel costs, will cause import cover to fall to about 4.8 months in 2006.

Samoa and New Zealand recently reached an agreement that should enhance the access of Samoa to New Zealand markets. Niche markets in products such as taro, woven mats and tapa cloth are developing for countries such as Samoa and Tonga that have large overseas populations in New Zealand, Australia and the United States. Organically grown foods with eco-labelling certification could also provide export growth in products that fetch premium prices. Such export diversification will also enable the economy to better withstand external shocks. Development of niche markets that can command a premium price is also the only way to overcome the high costs of international trade that these small, isolated economies face.

Foreign exchange reserves of Solomon Islands at the end of October 2005 were at record levels owing to inflows of donor aid, improved export receipts and some investment inflows, mainly linked to the rehabilitation of the gold mine and oil palm plantation damaged during the civil unrest. Foreign reserves of SI$705 million were equivalent to six months of import cover. With the fishing sector decline in diversification of exports is urgently needed to reduce the dependence on the forestry sector, which is said to be logging at three to four times the sustainable rate. Progress in getting the palm oil plantation back into operation has been rapid, and production was expected to begin at the end of 2005, which will contribute to export diversification. Imports are expected to increase, in view of the high import content of the investment rehabilitation projects under way and the high international fuel prices.

International prices for cocoa and copra, the main agricultural exports of Vanuatu, continued to be favourable in the first half of 2005. However, prices declined in the third quarter quite sharply for copra. Although bans on kava exports to Europe and the United States have been lifted, until the results of ongoing tests of the effects of kava on human health are known, it is unlikely that exports will be resumed. The kava industry in the Pacific is optimistic about the test results and expects that exports will be resumed as early as 2006. There are prospects for new markets for kava in Asia, particularly in China, for pharmaceutical uses, but these markets also are not likely to open up until the scientific tests are concluded.

A trade dispute between Fiji and Vanuatu led to a six-month ban on kava exports from Vanuatu to Fiji, which had recently developed as an important market for Vanuatu. While the two countries are members of the Melanesian Spearhead Group, the lack of an effective mechanism for resolving disputes appears to present an important obstacle.

The foreign exchange reserves of Vanuatu rose further in the second quarter of 2005, owing mainly to an increase in donor funds and stronger foreign earnings from tourism. According to the Reserve Bank of Vanuatu, official foreign reserves rose from 6.8 billion vatu ($63 million) at the end of March 2005 to 7.1 billion vatu at the end of June 2005, equivalent to 5.8 months of import cover.

Medium-term prospects and key policy issues

Growth is expected to accelerate slightly in 2006 but longer-term challenges remain

Despite high oil prices, current indications are that most Pacific island economies will continue to grow in 2006-2007 largely because of the expansion of the tourism sector, diversification in the agriculture sector, and remittances. However, GDP growth rates are expected to be modest as countries in the subregion continue to experience high population growth rates; thus, living standards are likely to decline in the medium term. Most Pacific island countries also expect low inflation rates in 2006, although this situation could change if major natural disasters were to strike.

There are uncomfortable levels of poverty in most Pacific island countries. The three major causes of poverty are lack of employment and economic opportunities, lack of access to basic services (education and health) and lack of response by the Government to people's needs, all traceable to unsatisfactory economic performance. However, more people live under conditions of hardship rather than absolute poverty.

The level of poverty in Samoa and Tonga is not much lower than in the Federated States of Micronesia and the Republic of Marshall Islands, although it is well below the estimates of poverty in Papua New Guinea, Solomon Islands and Vanuatu.

The poverty situation has likely deteriorated considerably in Solomon Islands because of the disastrous impact of the civil unrest on economic activities, which reduced average per capita incomes by about 25 per cent.

Many reasons can be advanced for the low per capita GDP growth rates and the poor investment and employment performance of Pacific island countries. Overall, the poor investment environment is the most obvious proximate cause.

While data on investment, particularly private investment, is almost non-existent for Pacific island countries, comparative data are available on the difficulties faced by those attempting to establish businesses. The Doing Business study of the World Bank ranks countries in terms of the difficulties in starting a business, registering property, getting credit, protecting investors, trading across borders, enforcing contracts and similar activities. Samoa, which has done the most among Pacific island countries to create a favourable environment for domestic and foreign investment, performs most poorly in terms of the bureaucratic steps involved in starting a business.

Insecurity of access to land is a problem common to most Pacific island countries, although to varying degrees. Most land is held under some form of customary tenure, rather than individual tenure rights that can provide reliable collateral for commercial borrowing. For example, Fiji has developed its sugar industry on the basis of long-term individual leasehold of land owned under "customary" communal tenure by land-owning groups; however, the conditions on the transfer of such leases erode the land's value as collateral.

At the other extreme is Papua New Guinea, where even the little land that is held under freehold title is sometimes under threat because of claims over it by former landowners. Also, the widespread nature of claims for increased compensation from landowners when projects on leased land are seen to do well has created a climate of pervasive uncertainty.

Restrictive policies against trade in goods and services are another reflection of the antipathy towards open markets in Pacific island countries. Because of remoteness from major markets and the small size of domestic markets, Pacific island countries face very high costs in participating in international trade, except in mining projects where production costs may be internationally competitive. If these countries are to improve their economic performance, they have to take advantage of the economies of scale in trading with the rest of the world. Moreover, to compensate for the high costs of trade, they have to export products and services the prices for which would more than compensate for their high costs. This means they have to develop differentiated products in niche markets. They cannot depend on the export of basic primary commodities, for which they are at a cost disadvantage in relation to other producing countries. By placing barriers against the import of goods and services and capital, they increase the costs of producing for export markets by raising the costs of inputs. They should have completely open markets for trade, investment, labour and technology in order to maximize the opportunities for developing the differentiated products they need to export.

Pacific island countries need better infrastructure

Unreliable and high-cost utilities and poor transport infrastructure are other widespread problems in Pacific island countries. The rapid decline in the cost of telecommunications globally has accelerated the international fragmentation of firms, benefiting developing countries by offering new investment opportunities and jobs. The Pacific island countries have, for the most part, shut themselves off from this global phenomenon by adopting monopoly positions, often public-private joint venture monopolies, that result in internationally uncompetitive telecommunications costs. Pacific island countries have generally been unwilling to introduce competition into their utility industries, and where they have made markets more contestable, the countries concerned have been slow to adopt effective regulatory arrangements.

Law and order problems are confined mainly to Fiji, Papua New Guinea, Solomon Islands and Vanuatu. Political instability is also a problem in a few of these countries. At the extreme, those countries have experienced coups, as in Fiji and Solomon Islands. More common across the Pacific are weak coalition Governments that make economic reform, particularly microeconomic reform, especially difficult. Contributing to the law and order problems in these countries is the large number of unemployed and underemployed youth who threaten person and property.

Education at the primary and secondary levels is poor throughout most Pacific island countries. Commentators lament the dearth of vocational training and the concentration on university training for the elite. Certainly, a better-educated labour force is a prerequisite for a country wishing to attract increased investment and to stimulate economic growth. However, unless other constraints to investment are reduced, the trained labour force in these countries will leave for overseas work and investment in education will not be made in the first place.

Remittances play a major role in development

Remittances have long been playing a major role in Pacific island economies such as Kiribati, Samoa and Tonga, but their importance and volume have risen dramatically in recent years. Where emigration has been possible, remittances have grown substantially; in Samoa and Tonga, remittances account for up to half of gross national income.

Pacific island countries consider emigration and the possibility of overseas employment for their youth as a safety valve in an environment of continued high fertility rates and stagnant domestic employment opportunities (see box II.2). Many of these countries are exerting pressure on their developed Pacific neighbours, Australia and New Zealand, to increase the intake of migrants from Pacific island countries. However, overseas employment and remittances should not be a reason for Pacific island countries to relax efforts to improve domestic investment environments.

Box II.2. Lack of economic growth and employment opportunities in Pacific island countries

Unemployment data are unlikely to give a true picture of the extent of unemployment in Pacific island countries. There is little in the way of public unemployment insurance or unemployment benefits. If people become unemployed, their families usually have to support them until they find a job. Thus, there is little incentive for people to notify the authorities that they are unemployed. The high unemployment rates shown for economies such as Cook Islands, the Federated States of Micronesia and Marshall Islands reflect to some extent the desire for employment in the formal sector, while the low unemployment rates for Samoa and Tonga could reflect the lack of interest in finding local jobs because of the high levels of emigration. In contrast, however, because of the large share of the population living in rural areas, it is unlikely that the low unemployment rates for Kiribati and even for Vanuatu truly reflect the numbers searching jobs in the formal sector.

Formal sector jobs account for only a very small share of the total labour force in some Pacific island countries and a much larger proportion in others. In countries where the bulk of the labour force is engaged in semi-subsistence activity, a combination of subsistence activity and cash-earning activity, the labour force may be seen as a pool of potential workers for formal sector employment. In countries where formal sector workers form a large part of the total labour force, this has occurred largely because of the migration of workers in search of employment overseas .

In most Pacific island countries large numbers of people have moved from rural areas to urban centres, partly in search of formal employment.[a] They are also looking for better educational opportunities for their children, improved access to health care and perhaps the attractions of urban life. Because of high

[a] Urban centre populations in most of the Pacific island countries are growing at rapid rates, up to 5-6 per cent a year, as a result of rural-urban migration.

(Continued overleaf)

(Continued from preceding page)

fertility and high population growth rates, per capita agricultural production in Pacific island countries appears to be declining and it is probably becoming harder to maintain livelihoods in rural areas.[b] Because of the poor opportunities for formal employment, many rural migrants have not found jobs in the formal sector and therefore have to sustain themselves and their families with informal sector activity. Underemployment is a much more relevant issue for the Pacific island countries than unemployment.

Economies such as Cook Islands, the Federated States of Micronesia, Marshall Islands, Samoa and Tonga have relatively easy access to emigration, which reduces the working-age population and therefore increases formal sector employment as a percentage of the working-age population.

In the Pacific island countries that do not have such easy access to emigration, such as Papua New Guinea, Solomon Islands and Vanuatu, the bulk of the population (75 per cent or more) live in rural areas and earn their livelihood from mixed subsistence cash-crop activity. Most of those in rural areas are unskilled and would have little chance of migrating even if easier access to metropolitan countries were provided.

The Governments of Pacific island countries must improve the investment climate if they are to see increases in formal sector employment and reductions in unemployment and underemployment. Otherwise, workers will continue to leave for overseas employment or remain underemployed in the rural sector; another alternative is that they will continue to migrate to urban centres, where they will have to support themselves through legal or illegal informal activity.

---

[b] Mahendra, Reddy and Ron C. Duncan, "Causes of decline in Pacific island agriculture", (mimeo) (Suva, University of South Pacific, 2005); Marin Yari and Ron C. Duncan, "Food security: development issue for Pacific island countries", *Bulletin on Asia-Pacific Perspectives 2004/05* (United Nations publication Sales No. E.04.II.F.47), pp. 97-116.

Moreover, in the larger countries such as Papua New Guinea, Solomon Islands and Vanuatu, emigration and remittances cannot be expected to become as important as they are in the smaller and atoll economies.

For land-rich countries such as Fiji, Papua New Guinea, Solomon Islands and Vanuatu, where most of the populations continue to live and work in the rural sector, the development strategy should focus on the rural sector. Agricultural productivity has to increase so that rural incomes and welfare improve, helping to spur growth in rural services. Growth in the urban manufacturing and services sectors will create employment for labour that will be able to move out of the rural sector as its productivity improves. Increased research is needed to provide improved and new varieties of crops and improved farming systems. Improved access to markets for rural produce will demand improved infrastructure and better market information.

South and South-West Asia

Overview

Despite high oil prices, the momentum of growth was maintained ...

Despite high oil prices, the South and South-West Asian subregion maintained its growth momentum in 2005. The continuing reforms and structural changes of the last few years are bearing fruit. The subregion's increasing integration into an expanding global economy, rising consumer spending and generally accommodative policies are also helping to foster economic growth. Both India and Pakistan have achieved impressive growth rates in recent years. On the basis of sustained high economic growth, India is increasingly becoming a leading contributor to global growth. A strong earthquake in October 2005 resulted in massive loss of human life and damage to property and infrastructure in Pakistan, but the impact on GDP growth is expected to be minimal as the areas affected are mountainous and their contribution to GDP is small. Sri Lanka maintained its growth momentum despite the tsunami disaster in late 2004. After the immediate relief work in 2004 and 2005, the country is now engaged in reconstruction and rehabilitation in the affected area. Higher growth is projected for 2006, driven by improved performance in various sectors of the economy and the continuing reconstruction work. High oil prices are helping the Islamic Republic of Iran to maintain its growth momentum, while in Turkey growth has slowed to a more sustainable level in 2005.

... but inflationary pressures are emerging

Partly because of higher oil prices, inflationary pressures are emerging. In India, inflation increased by 0.7 percentage point in 2005 over that in 2004, while in Pakistan and Sri Lanka the increase has been much sharper, at more than 4 percentage points. In some countries food price increases outpaced overall consumer prices, becoming an extra burden for the poor, the bulk of whose income is spent on food items. The increase in the prices of domestic petroleum products in some countries was lower than the upsurge in international oil prices, because a part of the increase was absorbed by the Governments to contain inflation. In the Islamic Republic of Iran, inflation declined only marginally in 2005, while Turkey, which began a major stabilization programme in 2001, experienced lower inflation in 2005 despite the higher oil prices. In the subregion as a whole, inflationary pressures are expected to subside somewhat in 2006 as the impact of higher oil prices is absorbed and most countries pursue tighter monetary policies.

Higher oil prices are hurting current account balances

Currently high oil prices are hurting countries by threatening more sustained inflationary pressure and by eroding the current account of the balance of payments. While export growth remains strong in most countries, imports are growing faster, widening the gap between exports and imports. As a result, the current account surplus turned into deficit in fiscal year 2005 in Pakistan and the deficit widened in India, Sri Lanka and Turkey. If oil prices rise further, the balance of payments situation could deteriorate further in most countries in the subregion in 2006. The Islamic Republic of Iran, however, being a major exporter of oil, would have a much larger surplus on its current account.

Main challenge is to maintain growth with macroeconomic stability

The main challenges facing the subregion include sustaining the higher growth momentum while maintaining macroeconomic stability. Containing inflationary pressures while oil prices are rising has to be the main priority. Judicious use of fiscal and monetary policies can help to limit the increase in consumer prices. Several countries in the subregion are growing rapidly, in part fuelled by higher consumer spending financed by credit. There is a need to remain vigilant, especially where rapid economic growth is accompanied by a wider current account deficit and higher inflation. Containing credit booms usually requires strengthened surveillance of the banking system and close scrutiny of corporate borrowing during periods of rapid economic growth to prevent the impairment of asset quality in the financial system.

Fiscal consolidation should be high on the agenda in all countries

The Governments of virtually all countries in the subregion are trying to bring budget deficits down to more sustainable levels. In India, under the Fiscal Responsibility and Budget Management Act, 2003, the Government has formulated a medium-term strategy for putting the fiscal balance on a sustainable basis. Pakistan also passed similar legislation, the Fiscal Responsibility and Debt Limitation Act, 2005, to limit the fiscal deficit and public debt. The Government of Sri Lanka has reiterated its commitment to a phased reduction of the budget deficit over the medium term to ensure an orderly correction of the structural weaknesses in the fiscal system. Continuing budget deficits have led to high public debt in most countries of the subregion, although the public debt as a ratio of GDP is falling in some countries, including India and Pakistan. A large part of the public debt is domestically held, so when huge public financial resources are needed for debt servicing, Governments are forced to limit their expenditures on priority areas such as poverty reduction and social development. Containing public debt by limiting the budget deficit should therefore remain a major priority of all countries in the subregion.

GDP growth performance

India maintains high growth

India has achieved high GDP growth in recent years. Growth of 8.5 per cent in 2003 slowed to 7.5 per cent in 2004, as agricultural growth slowed (see figure II.21). GDP growth accelerated to 8.1 per cent in 2005, aided by growth in all the main sectors. In addition to the return to a near-normal harvest, the strong response of the private sector to emerging opportunities sustained robust growth in industry and services. Capital goods and consumer goods performed well, indicating an acceleration in both consumer and investment demand. The economy also benefited from substantial inflows of foreign investment and the Government's efforts to contain the fiscal deficit despite

Figure II.21. GDP and sectoral growth in selected South and South-West Asian economies, 2003-2005[a]

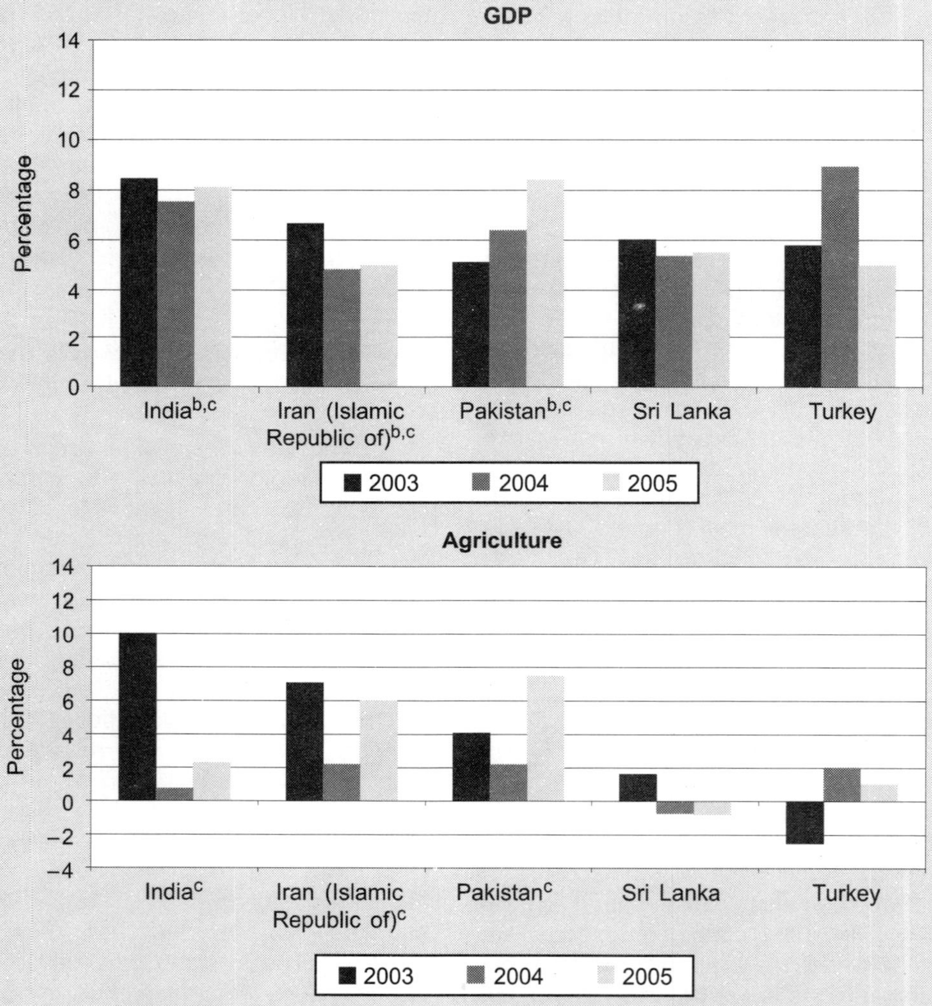

(Continued on next page)

Figure II.21 *(continued)*

Industry[d]

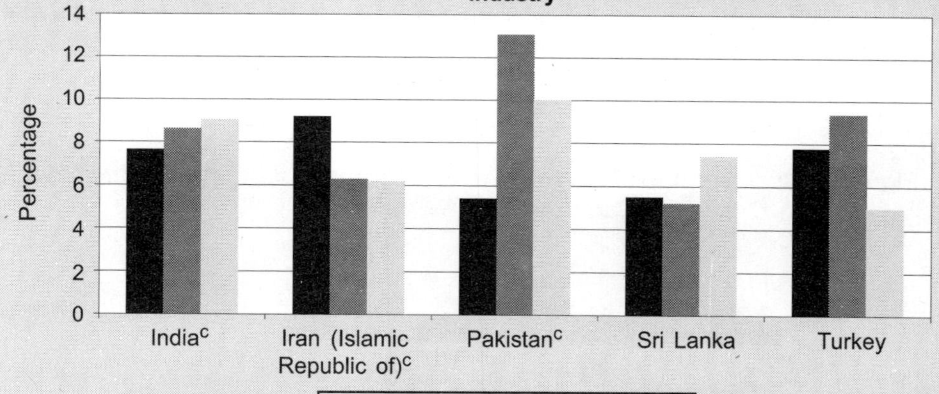

Services

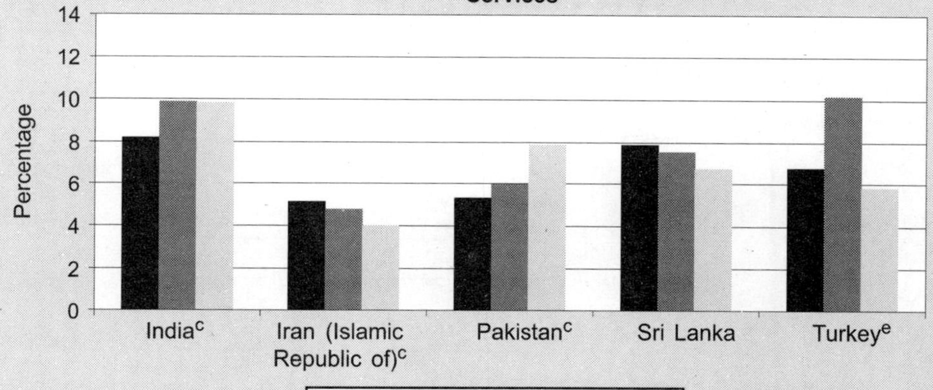

Sources: United Nations Economic and Social Commission for Asia and the Pacific, based on national sources; India, Ministry of Finance, *Economic Survey of India 2004-2005* (New Delhi, 2005); Central Bank of Iran, *Economic Trends* (Tehran, 2005); Pakistan, *Economic Survey of Pakistan 2004-05* (Islamabad, 2005); Central Bank of Sri Lanka, *Annual Report 2004* (Colombo, 2005); and Central Bank of the Republic of Turkey, *Annual Report 2004* (Ankara, 2005).

[a] Growth rates for 2005 are estimates.
[b] GDP growth rate refers to real GDP at factor cost.
[c] Fiscal year data.
[d] Industry comprises mining and quarrying; manufacturing; electricity-generation, gas and power; and construction.
[e] Construction is included under services.

higher public expenditure for employment generation programmes. The good performance of agriculture and industry in recent years has generated a strong demand for transport and communications, trade-related activities and financial services. Rapid increases in expenditure on public administration, social services and rural extension services have also had a favourable impact on growth in the service sector, which accounted for more than 50 per cent of GDP in 2005.

Growth accelerated in Pakistan in 2005

Pakistan appears to be in the midst of a strong economic upturn, recording its third straight year of impressive economic growth in

2005. GDP growth of 8.4 per cent in 2005 was the highest in the last two decades. Contributing to the acceleration were strong domestic demand, better weather conditions for agriculture, continuity of economic policies and a robust financial sector. There was a sharp increase in nominal investment supported by strong macroeconomic fundamentals, increased availability of credit and a significant rise in foreign direct investment. However, the investment to GDP ratio has remained at about 17 per cent in the last four years (see figure II.22). On the supply side, agriculture

Figure II.22. Savings and investment in selected South and South-West Asian economies, 2003-2005[a]

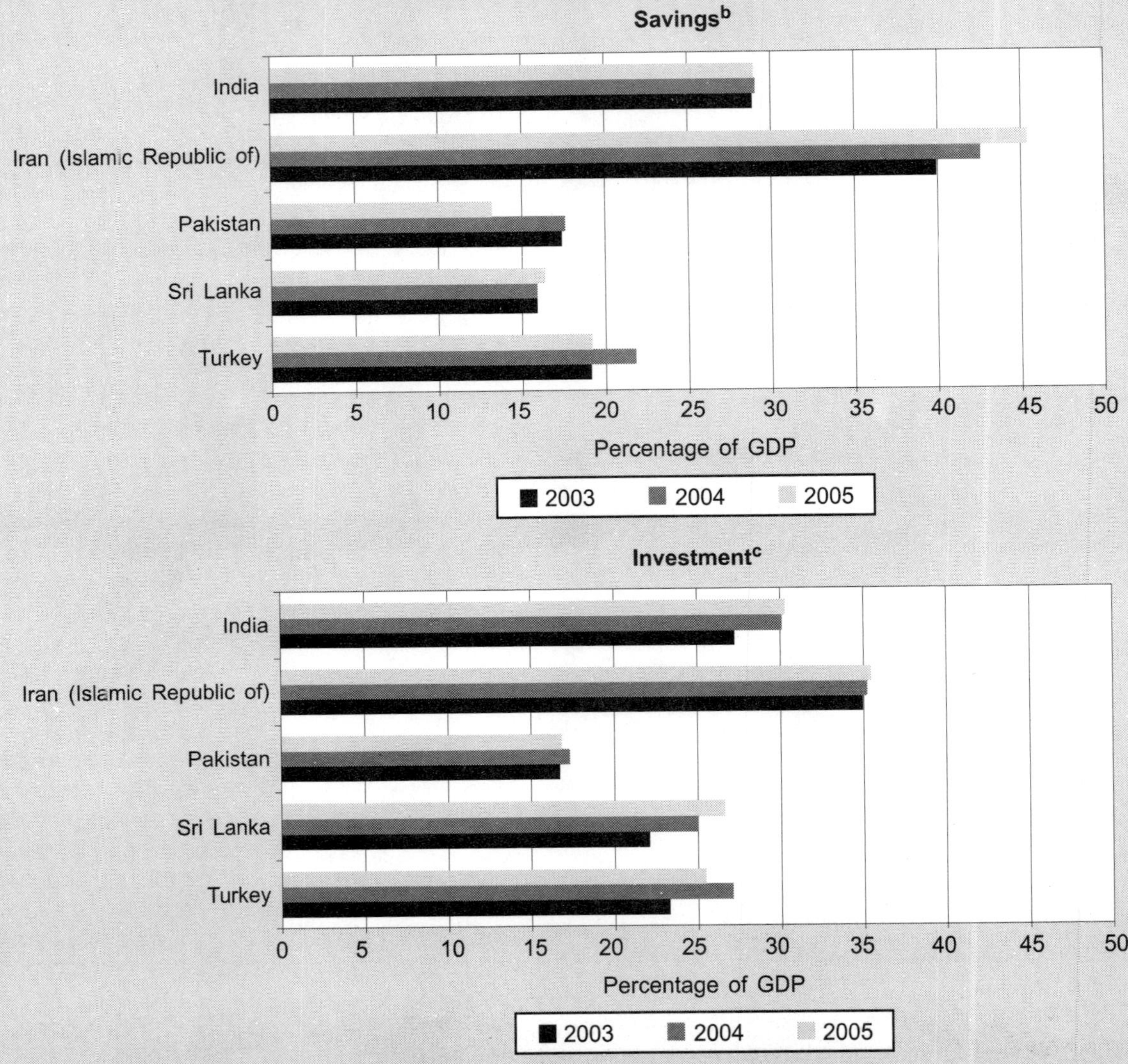

Sources: United Nations Economic and Social Commission for Asia and the Pacific, based on national sources; India, Ministry of Finance, *Economic Survey of India 2004-2005* (New Delhi, 2005); Central Bank of Iran, *Economic Trends* (Tehran, 2005); Pakistan, *Economic Survey of Pakistan 2004-05* (Islamabad, 2005); Central Bank of Sri Lanka, *Annual Report 2004* (Colombo, 2005); and Central Bank of the Republic of Turkey, *Annual Report 2004* (Ankara, 2005).

[a] Data for 2005 are estimates.
[b] Gross domestic savings.
[c] Gross domestic investment.

performed exceptionally well in 2005, with good weather and supportive government policies contributing a growth rate of 7.5 per cent, an increase over the 2.2 per cent rate in 2004. Large-scale manufacturing recorded an impressive and broad-based growth rate of 15.4 per cent in 2005. The service sector grew by 7.9 per cent in 2005, in line with the higher growth in the commodity-producing sectors.

Despite the tsunami disaster, Sri Lanka maintained growth momentum

The economy of Sri Lanka expanded by 5.4 per cent in 2004. Towards the end of the year the tsunami struck, leading to enormous human and material losses. Economic growth slowed to 4.4 per cent in the first quarter of 2005, reflecting negative impacts on the tourism and fisheries sectors. As these sectors recovered, GDP growth improved to 5.5 per cent for the year as a whole.[2] The service sector grew by 6.7 per cent and industry grew by 7.4 per cent. Agriculture, however, contracted by 0.8 per cent in 2005 on top of a 0.7 per cent contraction in 2004. Unfavourable weather conditions for certain crops and the adverse impact of the tsunami on the fisheries sector contributed primarily to negative growth in the agricultural sector. Investment, particularly from the public sector, was channelled towards rehabilitation and reconstruction activities to normalize life in the tsunami-affected areas. As a result, investment rose from 25 per cent of GDP in 2004 to 26.6 per cent in 2005, while savings rose from 15.9 per cent of GDP to 16.4 per cent over the same period.

Higher oil prices helped the Islamic Republic of Iran to sustain growth

In the Islamic Republic of Iran, GDP grew by 4.8 per cent in 2004 compared with 6.7 per cent in 2003. Oil sector growth was limited to 2.6 per cent because of lower production. Agricultural growth also slowed. However, the industrial sector registered somewhat higher growth on better performance of large-scale manufacturing. There was a slight deceleration in the services sector. GDP was expected to grow by 5 per cent in 2005, slightly faster than in the previous year, partly as a result of the increase in oil prices. Agriculture also staged a major recovery in 2005, and there was some expansion in the industrial sector. However, service sector growth slowed further. On the demand side, the ratio of savings to GDP rose faster than the ratio of investment to GDP, reflecting the growing current account surplus.

Growth in Turkey slowed to a more sustainable level

In Turkey, GDP grew by an impressive 8.9 per cent in 2004, driven mainly by private domestic demand, with almost equal contributions from consumption and investment expenditure. Growth is estimated to have slowed to 5.0 per cent in 2005, with both production and consumption adversely affected by higher energy prices. In 2004, lower interest rates and a credit boom fuelled spending on durable goods and machinery and equipment, while a tight fiscal policy reduced public consumption and investment spending. Domestic demand began to slow in the second half of 2004, bringing production to a more sustainable level and reducing the demand for imports.

Reducing unemployment and poverty requires maintaining high growth rates

In the subregion, high growth rates need to be maintained to tackle poverty, a key challenge in most countries, as the South Asian Association for Regional Cooperation also recognized at its thirteenth Summit in Dhaka in November 2005 (see box II.3). Unemployment and underemployment are among the major reasons for the high incidence of poverty in South Asia. Official figures place open unemployment in the subregion at about 8 per cent, although the rate varies across countries. There is a lack of data on underemployment, but it is likely to be high. More than half the labour force is employed in the informal sector, where people tend to be underemployed and their income levels are low.

Urbanization is progressing in the subregion, but the largest share of people still live in rural areas and most are dependent on agriculture. Rural industrialization, based on the processing of agricultural products, is thus the key to generating additional employment in rural areas. Although fertility rates are declining in all countries in South Asia, population pressure con-

2 Estimates based on data for the first three quarters of 2005.

Box II.3. Thirteenth Summit of the South Asian Association for Regional Cooperation: high priority for fighting poverty, managing natural disasters and combating terrorism

The South Asian Association for Regional Cooperation (SAARC), an intergovernmental organization that comprises Bangladesh, Bhutan, India, Maldives, Nepal, Pakistan and Sri Lanka, held its thirteenth Summit in Dhaka, Bangladesh, in November 2005.[a] The Dhaka Declaration, issued by the Summit, called for stronger efforts for alleviating poverty, managing natural disasters and combating terrorism.

Recognizing poverty as the greatest challenge in the region, the Summit declared the decade of 2006-2015 the SAARC Decade of Poverty Alleviation, calling on Governments to infuse poverty-reduction efforts at the national and the regional levels with a renewed sense of commitment and urgency. It called for the establishment of a "SAARC poverty alleviation fund" and for enhanced economic cooperation, the main emphasis of which would be securing a wider economic space to realize fully the economic potential of South Asia so that all can share in its benefits and opportunities. Efforts would be made to create dynamic complementarities in the development of human resources and the capacity of member States to address common challenges. For this, regional cooperation would be accelerated through all available means, including the exchange of information on best practices. Member States were encouraged to undertake projects, under SAARC auspices, in the economic and social sectors, including human resource development and poverty alleviation. Financial or technical assistance from international financial institutions, the United Nations or any non-member State can be sought for undertaking these projects.

The Dhaka Declaration also stressed the need for meeting the 1 January 2006 deadline for implementation of the South Asian Free Trade Area Agreement. The Declaration also reiterated the need for closer regional cooperation in information and communication technologies and for stronger transportation and communication links for accelerated and balanced economic growth.

In recent years, South Asia has suffered extensive loss of life and colossal damage to property as a result of natural disasters such as the 2004 tsunami and 2005 earthquake. Member States agreed to establish a permanent regional response mechanism for disaster preparedness, emergency relief and rehabilitation. National authorities would coordinate their activities in early warning, information exchange, training, sharing of best practices in emergency relief efforts and other disaster-management activities.

Terrorism was also identified as a critical threat to economic stability and social development. Member States expressed a determination to join together to combat terrorism in the region.

---

[a] Afghanistan has been admitted to SAARC as a full member subject to the completion of various formalities. A decision in principle has been taken to allow China and Japan to become observers.

tinues to be a serious problem. It is clear therefore that a comprehensive package of population policies and programmes is needed to tackle the problem of unemployment and poverty.

Key macroeconomic policy developments

Inflation

Inflation in India remains low despite some acceleration

In India, average inflation based on the consumer price index rose from 3.8 per cent in 2004 to 4.5 per cent in 2005 (see figure II.23). Higher oil prices exerted considerable upward pressure, but the less than full price adjustment in the domestic market cushioned the impact of those prices. Other anti-inflationary policies in recent years include strict monetary and fiscal discipline and an effective management of supply and demand for essential consumer goods and raw materials through liberal imports. These policies have been aided by a strengthening of the public distribution system for food grains, sugar and kerosene. Successive budgets have provided various fiscal concessions and extended the value added tax to ensure that indirect taxes do not create cascading effects and unduly add to the prices of essential items.

Figure II.23. Inflation and money supply growth in selected South and South-West Asian economies, 2003-2005[a]

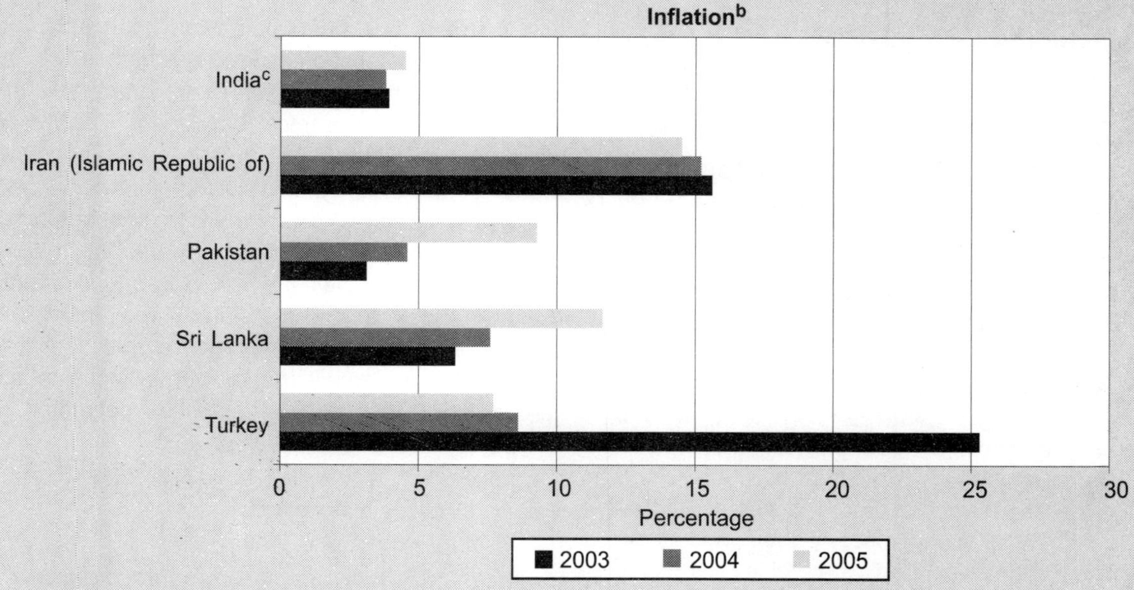

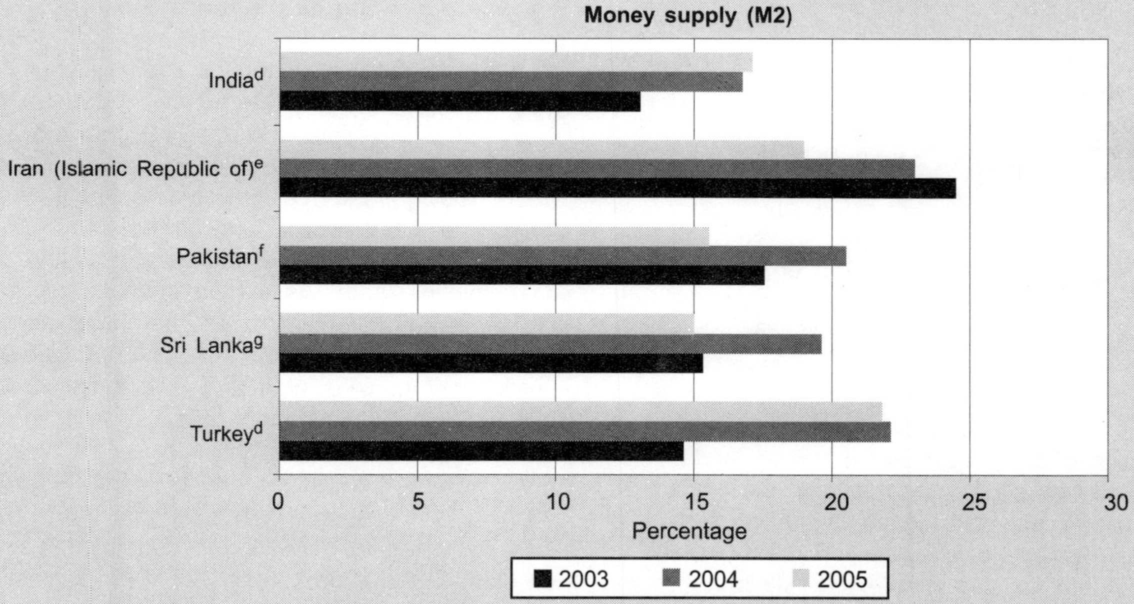

Sources: United Nations Economic and Social Commission for Asia and the Pacific, based on national sources; India, Ministry of Finance, *Economic Survey of India 2004-2005* (New Delhi, 2005); Central Bank of Iran, *Economic Trends* (Tehran, 2005); Pakistan, *Economic Survey of Pakistan 2004-05* (Islamabad, 2005); Central Bank of Sri Lanka, *Annual Report 2004* (Colombo, 2005); Central Bank of the Republic of Turkey, *Annual Report 2004* (Ankara, 2005); and International Monetary Fund, *International Financial Statistics* (CD-ROM) (Washington, D.C., IMF, January 2006).

[a] Data for 2005 are estimates.
[b] Inflation refers to changes in the consumer price index.
[c] Consumer price index for industrial workers.
[d] Data for 2005 are for January-September.
[e] Data for 2005 are for January-June.
[f] Data for 2005 are for January-October.
[g] Data for 2005 are for January-May.

Buoyant industrial growth improved the supply of manufactured items, while continuing government procurement built up stocks of food grains.

Inflation picked up in Pakistan and Sri Lanka

In Pakistan, inflationary pressure strengthened considerably in 2005, as inflation rose from 4.6 per cent in 2004 to 9.3 per cent. It is not uncommon to see price pressures build when economic activity accelerates because of various distribution bottlenecks in the country. Three years of strong economic growth, complemented by record low interest rates and the ongoing structural shift of many households towards higher consumption, have injected new life into domestic spending. This spending, coupled with rising oil and other commodity prices, contributed to a sharp increase in inflation in 2005. Food inflation reached double digits, a heavy burden on the poor who spend most of their income on food. The Government took several measures to ease inflationary pressures. It did not pass on to consumers, the entire increase in the international price of oil, and it began to tighten monetary policy to ease demand pressures. To improve the supply of food items, it allowed imports of food items from neighbouring countries.

Inflation also increased in Sri Lanka in 2005, rising from 7.6 per cent in 2004 to 11.6 per cent. Prices rose for both domestically produced and imported goods. Higher oil prices exerted substantial indirect pressure on consumer prices, although the full increase in oil prices was not passed on to consumers. The removal of the value added tax on certain imported products also dampened the impact of the rising cost of imported goods on consumer prices. Nonetheless, higher monetary expansion contributed to demand-driven inflationary pressures.

Inflation was on the decline in the Islamic Republic of Iran and Turkey

In contrast to the South Asian economies, the gradual downward trend in inflation in the Islamic Republic of Iran continued, falling from 15.6 per cent in 2003 to 15.2 per cent in 2004 and to 14.5 per cent in 2005. In general, prices rose faster for services than for goods. Also, price increases were greater than average for housing, fuel and electricity and fresh fruits and vegetables because of supply constraints.

Turkey has been particularly successful in bringing down inflation from very high levels to low levels in recent years as part of the stabilization programme begun in 2001. A stronger lira, tight fiscal policy, major improvements in productivity and falling inflationary expectations have all contributed to this outcome. In 2004, continued slack in the labour market and rising productivity prevented strong domestic demand from being translated into increased price pressures. The average annual inflation rate, as measured by the consumer price index, was 8.6 per cent in 2004 and was estimated at 7.7 per cent for 2005 as a whole.[3]

Fiscal policy developments

The public debt of India remains high, but is falling as a ratio to GDP

In India, the budget for 2005 was aimed at reducing marginally the central Government fiscal deficit to 4.3 per cent of GDP from 4.5 per cent in 2004 (see figure II.24). Under the Fiscal Responsibility and Budget Management Act, 2003, the Government has formulated a medium-term strategy to put the fiscal situation on a sustainable path. As a step in that direction, the Government implemented the value added tax at the state level on 1 April 2005. India's public debt remains high and is a major policy issue. Central Government debt as a ratio to GDP has decreased slightly in recent years, from 69.4 per cent at the end of March 2003 to 68.4 per cent at the end of March 2005 and was estimated to be 67.2 per cent by the end of March 2006. Most public debt is domestic. Nevertheless, a high overhang of domestic debt poses significant challenges, putting pressure on interest rates, crowding out private investment and creating problems for future debt servicing.

---

[3] Point-to-point inflation, which compares price levels at the beginning and end of year, was also less than 8 per cent in 2005, in line with the target of 8 per cent set by the Government.

Figure II.24. Budget balance and current account balance in selected South and South-West Asian economies, 2003-2005[a]

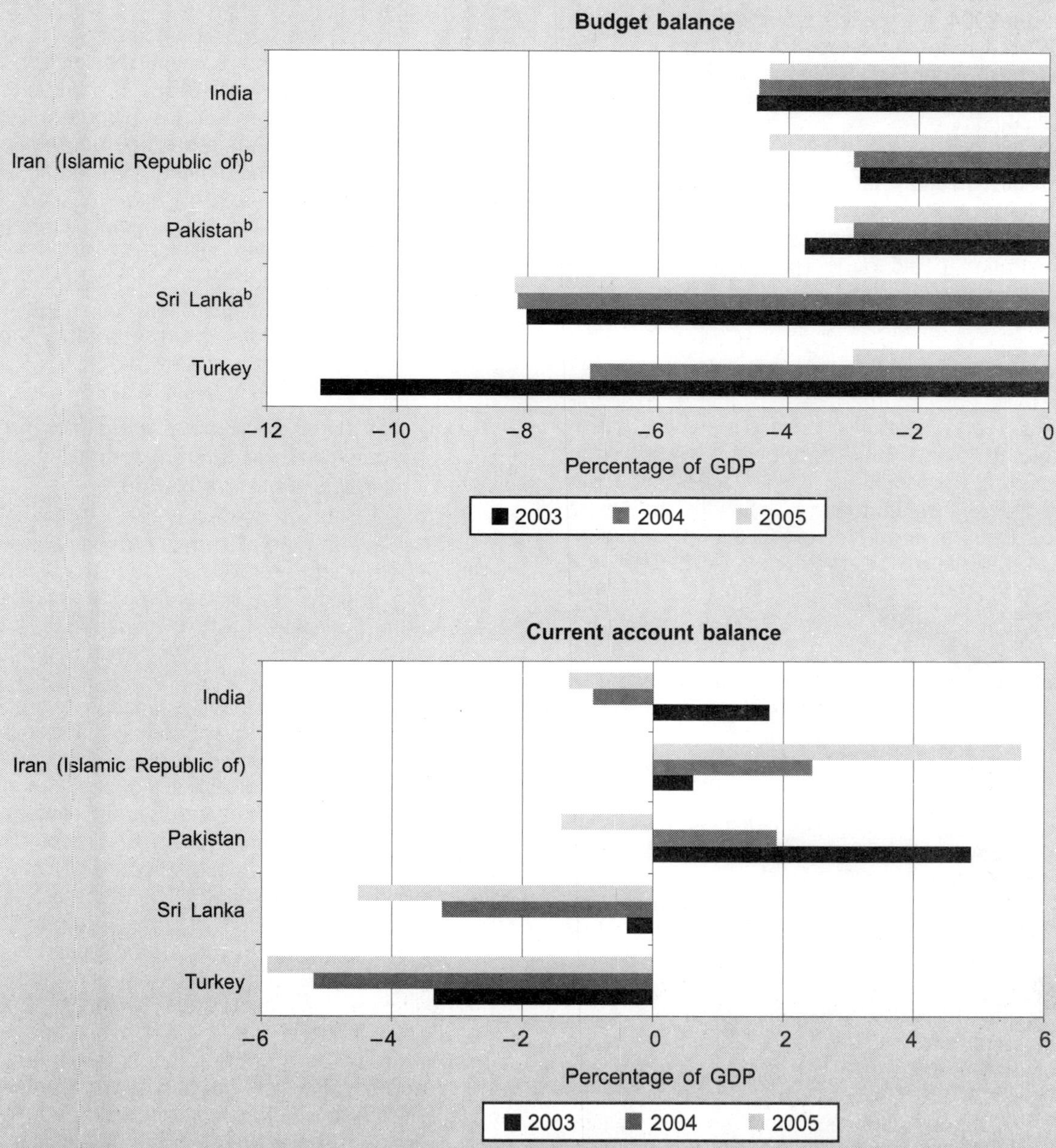

Sources: United Nations Economic and Social Commission for Asia and the Pacific, based on national sources; India, Ministry of Finance, *Economic Survey of India 2004-2005* (New Delhi, 2005); Central Bank of Iran, *Economic Trends* (Tehran, 2005); Pakistan, *Economic Survey of Pakistan 2004-05* (Islamabad, 2005); Central Bank of Sri Lanka, *Annual Report 2004* (Colombo, 2005); and Central Bank of the Republic of Turkey, *Annual Report 2004* (Ankara, 2005).

[a] Data for 2005 are estimates.

[b] Excludes grants.

Budget deficits were brought down in Pakistan but may rise again

The budget deficit in Pakistan has been brought down to a relatively low level in recent years. In 2004 the deficit stood at 3.0 per cent of GDP but rose slightly to 3.3 per cent in 2005. The Central Board of Revenue of Pakistan has been achieving its tax revenue targets in recent years. However, tax revenue buoyancy remains weak, as reflected in the continuing fall in the tax to GDP ratio that limits the Government's ability to provide adequate funds for infrastructure and social programmes. Strengthening tax administration could generate additional tax revenue by improving compliance. In Pakistan non-tax revenues have been making a significant contribution to the revenues of the federal Government. However, part of the increase has come form non-recurring items. On the expenditure side, rehabilitation and reconstruction activities related to the 2005 earthquake will increase government expenditure. This raises concern about the overall budgetary deficit in the years ahead. On the positive side, the public debt (explicit liabilities) has decreased to 64 per cent of GDP in 2005 from 71 per cent in 2004 and 93 per cent in 2001.

The budget deficit in Sri Lanka needs to be contained

The overall budget deficit of Sri Lanka for 2005 is estimated at 8.2 per cent of GDP, the same as in 2004. The high deficit in 2005 was due partly to tsunami-related relief, rehabilitation and reconstruction expenditure. The target for 2006 is to bring the deficit to below 8 per cent of GDP, and the Government of Sri Lanka has reiterated its commitment to a phased reduction of the budget deficit to ensure an orderly correction of the structural weaknesses in the fiscal system over the medium term. The reduction in outstanding public debt stock from 105.5 per cent of GDP in 2004 to an estimated 98 per cent in 2005 was due mainly to the appreciation of the rupee against major currencies and higher nominal GDP growth, which exceeded the rate of increase in the government debt stock.

The budget deficit of the Islamic Republic of Iran expanded despite a rise in oil revenue

In the Islamic Republic of Iran, the fiscal year 2005 budget continued the expansionary policy of recent years. Most of the surplus oil revenues resulting from higher oil prices went into the budget instead of the Oil Stabilization Fund, as had been expected. However, non-oil revenue and privatization receipts were overestimated, resulting in a revenue shortfall. Furthermore, capital outlays were budgeted to rise significantly. Efforts were made accordingly to improve tax collection and contain the growth of current spending. The fiscal policy objectives set forth in the Fourth Five-year Development Plan (2005-2009) are aimed at reducing the dependence on oil revenue and limiting growth in current expenditure. The reform agenda also includes a gradual phasing out of implicit energy subsidies (10 per cent of GDP in 2004). There is, nonetheless, a need for more sustained efforts to strengthen administration, eliminate tax exemptions and complete the preparatory work for introduction of a value added tax.

Turkey has taken innovative measures for achieving fiscal stability under fiscal decentralization

The Government of Turkey remains committed to implementing greater fiscal decentralization in order to improve basic services at the local level. Aware that this initiative could lead local governments to spend more than their revenues, thus raising the overall fiscal deficit, the central Government plans to submit legislation to parliament to ensure that the new spending mandates of local administrations are adequately matched by local tax instruments and revenue capabilities and supported by a stable and transparent system of revenue-sharing. Strict borrowing and debt limits for special provincial administrations and municipalities will be put in place. The debt stock of municipalities and special provincial administrations will be limited to no more than their annual revenue, while the debt stock of metropolitan municipalities will be limited to 1.5 times annual revenue. New borrowing by local administrations in excess of 10 per cent of their annual revenues will require authorization of the central Government. These limits will be closely monitored and tightened if needed to contain the budget deficit.

Monetary policy and financial sector developments

Monetary policy is tightened in India, Pakistan and Sri Lanka

The Reserve Bank of India is following a policy of gradual monetary tightening aimed at controlling inflation in response to a sharp pickup in private sector credit demand. It started publishing quarterly policy assessments in July 2005, paving the way for more frequent policy adjustments. In Pakistan, monetary policy witnessed a significant change during fiscal year 2005. After several years of accommodative monetary policy, the central bank switched to aggressive tightening in the second half of fiscal year 2005 in order to contain inflation. Sri Lanka also tightened its monetary policy during 2005 in order to reduce inflationary pressures and expectations. As a result, the interest rate structure moved upward during the year.

Turkey followed a formal inflation-targeting policy from early 2006

The central bank of Turkey has followed a strategy of implicit inflation-targeting in the past few years. The move to formal inflation-targeting from early 2006 should help in the fight against inflation. The central bank will be using short-term interest rates as its main policy instrument against inflation. Monetary policy transparency and predictability, critical elements of inflation-targeting, have been further enhanced by fixing the time of Monetary Policy Committee meetings and interest rate decisions in advance. After each meeting of the Committee, the central bank explains its decision and publishes as a report summarizing the inflation outlook and the deliberations of the Committee. The Committee was to assume full responsibility for setting interest rates in early 2006.

Developments in the external sector

Foreign trade

High growth of exports outpaced by even higher growth of imports and current account turned into deficit in India ...

In India the current account, after remaining in surplus for 2001-2003 with the pickup in economic activity, turned in a deficit of $6.4 billion (to 0.9 per cent of GDP) in 2004. While exports rose 24.9 per cent in 2004, imports rose even faster at 48.4 per cent, resulting in a widening of the trade deficit (see figure II.25). Although net invisibles, at $31.7 billion in 2004, increased by more than $5 billion over the previous year, the increase was too small to compensate for the substantial increase in the trade deficit. For 2005, exports were estimated to grow by 26 per cent on buoyant world demand and improvements in world commodity prices. Also contributing were export facilitating measures and good performance in key manufacturing sectors such as engineering goods, chemicals, automobiles and basic metals. Imports were expected to rise 28 per cent in 2005, due mainly to higher imports of crude oil and export-related products. As a result, the trade deficit as a percentage of GDP was estimated to increase from 5.5 per cent in 2004 to 6.3 per cent in 2005. The overall current account balance was again expected to be in deficit, at 1.3 per cent of GDP in 2005, higher than the deficit of 0.9 per cent of GDP in 2004.

... and in Pakistan also

In Pakistan, a $1.8 billion surplus in the current account in 2004 became a $1.5 billion deficit in 2005, as a result of a high trade deficit of $4.5 billion in 2005. While exports grew by the healthy rate of 16.9 per cent, imports grew almost twice as fast, by 32.3 per cent. Higher oil prices led to a substantial increase in import payments for oil and to higher shipment charges and so to higher prices for other imports as well. While growing domestic demand increased the demand for imports, machinery and raw material imports also increased substantially. These imports should improve the productive capacity of the economy and increase manufacturing activities and exports. Remittances from Pakistanis abroad have been about $4 billion in recent years and have been an important element in the balance of payments. Coupled with these large remittances, gains from the lower interest payments on the external debt and liabilities of Pakistan partially offset the impact of the large trade gap. As a result, the current account deficit was contained in 2005.

The current account deficit widened in Sri Lanka

In Sri Lanka, the trade deficit widened in 2005 as imports grew faster than exports. A significant increase in oil prices caused a strain on the balance of payments. Despite the foreign assistance for tsunami victims and a sharp increase in workers' remittances, the current ac-

Figure II.25. Growth rates in merchandise export earnings and import spending in selected South and South-West Asian economies, 2003-2005

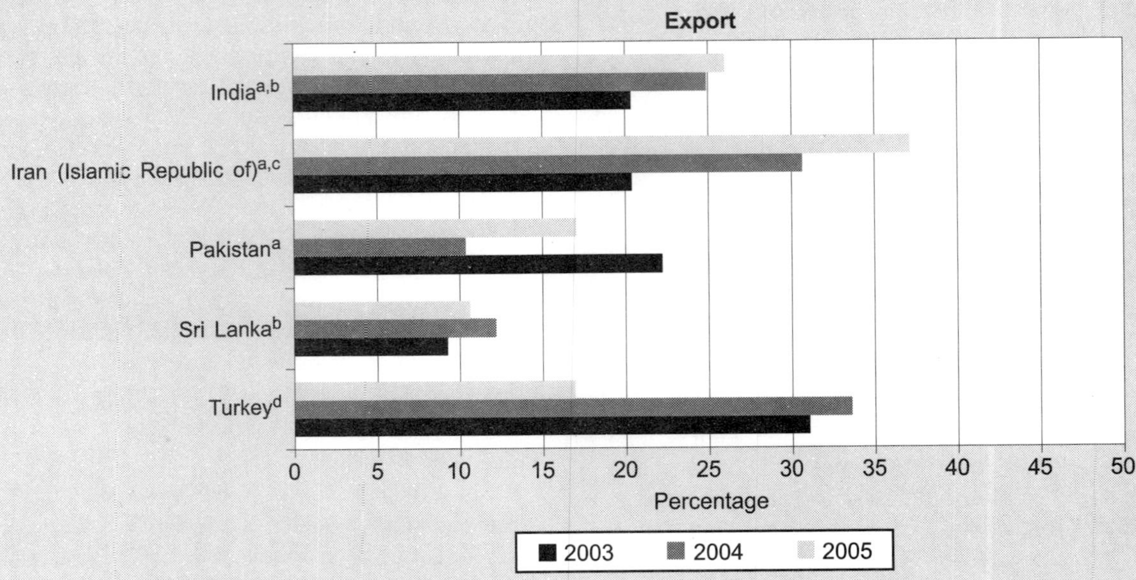

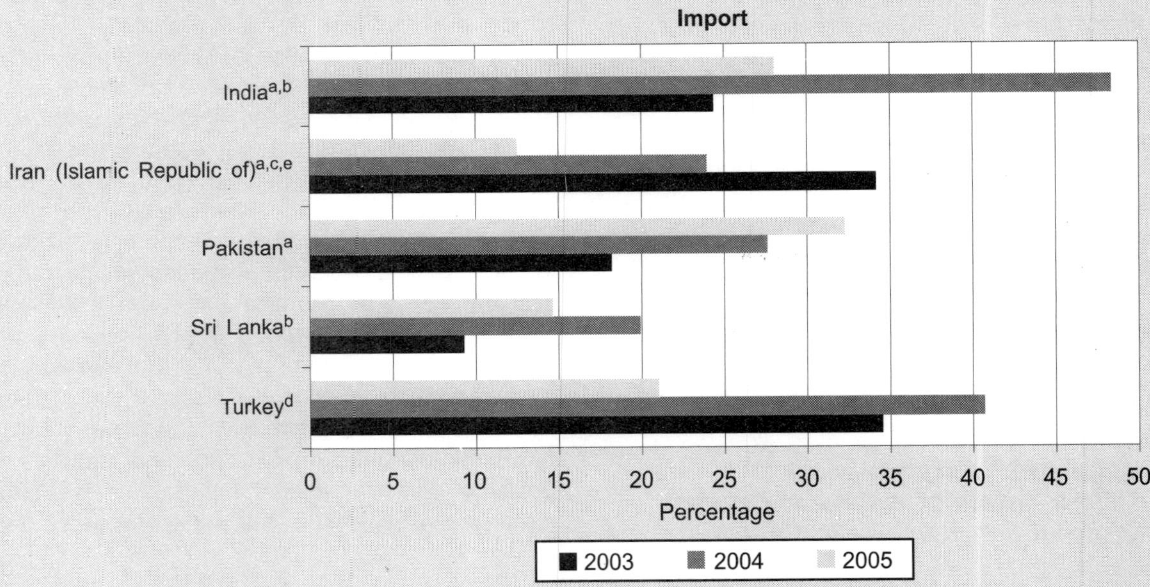

Sources: State Bank of Pakistan website <www.sbp.org.pk>, accessed on 5 September 2005; Central Bank of the Islamic Republic of Iran website <www.cbi.ir/publications/default.asp>, accessed on 28 December 2005; Central Bank of Sri Lanka website <www.lanka.net>, accessed on 28 December 2005; Republic of Turkey State Institute of Statistics website <www.die.gov.tr>, accessed on 28 December 2005; and national sources.

[a] Fiscal year.
[b] Growth rates for 2005 are projections
[c] Data for 2005 refer to 6 months.
[d] Data for 2005 refer to 10 months.
[e] Valued free on board (f.o.b.).

count deficit increased significantly in 2005. Exports increased by 11 per cent in 2005 compared with 12.2 per cent in 2004. Export growth resulted from modest price gains and substantial improvements in trade volume. Exports of textiles and clothing continued to grow despite the phase-out of the WTO Agreement on Textiles and Clothing in January 2005 and accounted for more than 46 per cent of exports in the first eight months of 2005. Imports grew by 15 per cent in 2005, the faster rate being partly due to the tsunami-related reconstruction work. The major contributors to overall import growth were petroleum and petroleum products, textile industry inputs, building materials, fertilizer and chemicals.

As a net exporter of oil the Islamic Republic of Iran recorded a higher current account surplus

Exports of the Islamic Republic of Iran increased by 30.6 per cent in 2004 compared with 2003. Most of the increase came from higher prices for oil and gas exports, amounting to $36.8 billion in 2004, an increase of 24.6 per cent over the comparable figure of the previous year. Non-oil exports increased by 14.9 per cent, due largely to the increased export of industrial goods. Imports rose by 23.9 per cent in 2004. Machinery and machine tools enjoyed the largest share of total goods imported in 2004, accounting for 29.6 per cent of the total value of imported goods. Both exports and imports increased with foreign trade liberalization and deregulation; these measures included the elimination of collateral and surrender requirements, greater freedom to use foreign exchange proceeds, gradual elimination of non-tariff barriers, exemption of exports from taxes and levies and stabilization of the foreign exchange market. As a result of the sharp increase in the export of oil and gas, the trade balance recorded a large surplus of $6.7 billion in 2004. Despite a $4.8 billion deficit in the services account, the current account recorded a surplus of about $4 billion, much higher than the $816 million surplus in 2003. High oil prices were expected to lead to a large current surplus in 2005 as well.

Turkey incurs large current account deficit

In Turkey, exports increased sharply by 33.6 per cent in 2004. Larger gains in productivity than in real wages helped firms to maintain their competitiveness in foreign markets and paved the way for handsome increase in exports. However, growth in imports outpaced the growth in exports. Imports grew by 40.7 per cent and this was partly the result of a rise in the import of intermediate goods to meet the demand for increased domestic production and exports. Strong domestic demand contributed to higher imports of durables and investment goods, while higher oil prices made the situation worse. The overvalued lira also contributed to the increase in imports. With imports growing faster than exports, the current account deficit widened to 5.2 per cent of GDP, even though growing revenues from tourism led to a substantial increase in services income. To contain the rapid growth in imports, the Government stopped the State banks' aggressive expansion of consumer credit, reduced generous tax credits for buying new cars and raised the intermediation tax on consumer credit. Such measures, in combination with a moderation of pent-up demand for consumer durables, caused import growth to slow somewhat in 2005, but it still outpaced export growth. The current account deficit was estimated at 5.9 per cent of GDP. The real effective exchange rate has appreciated significantly over the past few years. This, along with strong domestic demand, contributed to the large current account deficit.

Capital flows, foreign exchange reserves and exchange rates

Build up of foreign exchange reserves continues in India

In India, there has been a major shift in favour of long-term and non-debt-creating financial flows such as FDI and portfolio investment attracted by the sound macroeconomic environment, the stability of the exchange rate, further liberalization of foreign investment policies and relatively high returns on investment compared with that of other countries. There have been increases in both FDI and portfolio investment. Foreign investment inflows increased threefold, from $4.6 billion in 2002 to $14.8 billion in 2003, dropping to $12 billion in 2004. They were expected to exceed $12 billion in 2005, attracted by bullish stock markets, moderate inflation, sustained high economic growth and the strong rupee.

After a substantial build-up of foreign exchange reserves by $31 billion in 2003 owing to private transfers, receipts on travel and tourism on the current account and sustained foreign investment inflows on the capital account, there was a further build-up of $26 billion in 2004. Foreign exchange reserves stood at $144 billion at the end of December 2005 and were estimated to be $152 billion at the end of March 2006. The exchange rate of the rupee against major currencies exhibited some volatility during 2005, although on average it appreciated slightly against the dollar in 2005 as compared with 2004 (see figure II.26).

Foreign direct investment increased substantially in Pakistan

In Pakistan, too, there has been a significant increase in net inflows of capital. Capital inflows included mainly one-off inflows (such as $354 million through privatization and $600 million through sovereign debt issued internationally) and an increase in concessional long-term loans from the World Bank and the Asian Development Bank. FDI reached $1.5 billion in 2005, 61 per cent higher than in 2004. New FDI so far is concentrated in a few sectors such as telecommunications, finance and insurance and oil and gas exploration.

Foreign exchange reserves stood at $12.6 billion at the end of fiscal year 2005, $289 million higher than a year ago, and their pace of accretion appears to have slackened because of the deterioration in the external account. This also put pressure on the exchange rate of the rupee in the initial months of fiscal year 2005. The central bank intervened discreetly, injecting foreign exchange into the system; it made a

Figure II.26. Index of exchange rates against the United States dollar in selected South and South-West Asian economies, 1996-2005[a]

(1996Q4=100)

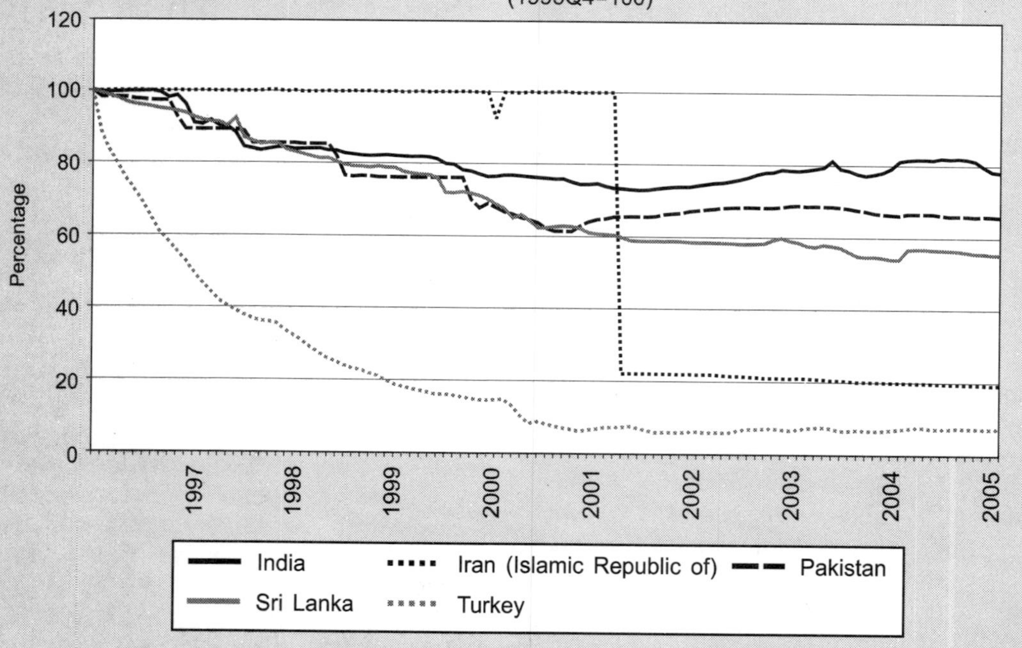

Sources: International Monetary Fund, *International Financial Statistics* (CD-ROM) (Washington, D.C., IMF, 2005); and *The Economist*, various issues.

[a] Data for 2005 are estimates.

public commitment to smooth the payments for oil imports. This had a positive impact on the value of the rupee, wiping out much of its losses during the initial months of fiscal year 2005. On average, the value of the rupee against the dollar depreciated by 3 per cent in fiscal year 2005.

Foreign funds flowed into Sri Lanka for the victims of the 2004 tsunami

In Sri Lanka, flows of FDI, portfolio investment and loan capital to the private sector showed marked improvements. Grants in aid for the victims of the tsunami and reconstruction of infrastructure enhanced the inflow of foreign funds to the Government. Net capital inflows were more than sufficient to finance the current account deficit, resulting in a surplus in the overall balance of payments.

Gross official reserves increased from \$2.2 billion at the end of December 2004 to \$2.4 billion at the end of August 2005. The value of the rupee began to appreciate against major currencies in the wake of the tsunami because of expected inflows of financial assistance. The rupee appreciated by 3.3 per cent against the dollar during the first nine months of 2005, as compared with a 6.7 per cent depreciation during the same period in the previous year.

Capital inflows increased in the Islamic Republic of Iran

In the Islamic Republic of Iran, the capital account of the balance of payments continued its upward trend. While net long-term inflows declined from \$2.1 billion in 2003 to \$1.2 billion in 2004, the surplus in short-term inflows rose from \$2.4 billion to \$4.4 billion. With surpluses in both the current account and capital account, the balance of payments registered a surplus of \$8.3 billion in 2004. This amount was added to the foreign exchange reserves of the country.

FDI and portfolio equity increased from \$1.7 billion in 2003 to \$2.7 billion in 2004. With a large market, the country offers many investment opportunities to foreign investors. However, few foreign firms outside the energy sector have established significant interests in the country. To build the confidence of foreign investors, the Government has taken several measures including membership in the Multilateral Investment Guarantee Agency. The foreign exchange market has operated smoothly in the recent past, and the exchange rate is not considered to be misaligned.

Short-term capital dominated capital inflows in Turkey

In Turkey, despite the large current account deficit in 2004, gross official reserves increased as a result of strong capital inflows, a major share of which, however, remained short-term debt and debt-creating inflows. The inflows consisted mainly of foreign borrowing (trade-related credits, interbank and corporate borrowing) as FDI remained low and portfolio investments going into government bonds were larger than going into equities. Gross official reserves, at \$37.6 billion in 2004, were estimated to have risen to \$44.8 billion in October 2005. The exchange rate of the lira appreciated slightly during 2005 against the dollar and the euro.

External debt

India and Pakistan made significant progress in reducing external debt as a ratio to GDP

In India, trends in various debt indicators such as the ratio of external debt to GDP indicate a marked improvement in the country's external indebtedness. The total external debt of India, that is; short- and long-term liabilities on both government and non-government accounts, increased from \$111.7 billion at the end of March 2004 to \$123.3 billion at the end of March 2005 and was expected to reach \$129 billion at the end of March 2006. Multilateral and bilateral debt constitutes 42 per cent of total debt stock and the share of concessionary debt was 34 per cent of total debt in 2005. The share of short-term debt has declined steadily in recent years and stood at 6.3 per cent of total external debt in 2005. The external debt to GDP ratio has also declined steadily from a high of 38 per cent in 1991 to 18 per cent in 2003 and 16 per cent in 2005.

Following the adoption of a robust strategy of debt reduction, Pakistan's external debt declined from $37.9 billion at the end of June 2000 to $36.6 billion at the end of March 2005. Contributing to this positive outcome have been the surplus in the current account, prepayment of expensive debt and debt write-offs. As a percentage of GDP, external debt has fallen from 51.7 per cent at the end of June 2000 to 33.1 per cent at the end of March 2005. There was a small increase of $576 million in external debt in 2005, owing mainly to fresh inflows from multilateral creditors and the issuance of a sovereign bond.

In Sri Lanka, the external debt has been increasing in recent years, reaching 65 per cent of GDP in 2004. This ratio was estimated to have declined slightly in 2005, due partly to appreciation of the domestic currency.

High share of short-term external debt is a source of concern in Turkey

In Turkey, dollar-denominated external debt increased from $145.5 billion in 2003 to $161.7 billion in 2004 and was estimated to have climbed to $168.7 billion in 2005. However, external debt as a ratio to GNP has been falling and stood at 48.3 per cent in 2005 compared with 53.6 per cent in 2004. More than 40 per cent of the external debt is owed by the private sector, 43 per cent of it short term. A high share of short-term debt is a concern as it implies strong roll-over pressures and high exposure to sudden changes in the exchange rate, interest rates and market sentiment.

Medium-term prospects and key policy issues

India to maintain high growth and low inflation

Assuming no major internal or external shocks, which could destabilize the economy, India should be able to sustain a real GDP growth rate of about 8 per cent over the period 2006-2008, supported by a growth rate of 2.5-3 per cent in agricultural value added, 8.5 per cent in industry and 9.0 per cent in services. The industrial and service sectors are expected to sustain their growth momentum driven largely by cyclical factors and induced by a rise in rural income and increased public spending on physical and social infrastructure. Higher growth over the medium term would be feasible with sustained fiscal reforms by both central and state Governments. Thus, increased public and private sector savings should boost the country's investment rate and provide resources for upgrading critical areas of infrastructure. While some increased use of foreign capital, particularly of FDI and portfolio investment, is consistent with external sector viability, the bulk of the savings would need to be generated domestically.

Both the wholesale and consumer price indices are likely to remain at about 4 per cent in the period 2006-2008, given the Government's commitment to reform, including strict fiscal prudence, monetary discipline, orderly movement of the rupee exchange rate, continued reduction of import duties and other indirect taxes and the removal of all quantitative restrictions on imports of consumer goods. It is important to lock in recent gains on the inflation front to protect the interests of the vulnerable and weaker sections of society.

Some slowdown in growth and inflation may be expected in Pakistan in 2006

The Government of Pakistan set a growth target of 7 per cent of GDP for 2006, less than the rapid 8.4 per cent achieved in 2005 but higher than the long-term growth trajectory of 6 per cent. A number of factors may interfere, however. Agriculture, prone to weather-related fluctuations, may perform below expectations. On the other hand, large-scale manufacturing could well exceed the target of 13 per cent, and growth in services is expected to remain strong. Sustaining a higher growth rate is thus possible.

A strong earthquake in October 2005 resulted in massive loss of human life and damage to property (including houses, schools, hospitals and other buildings) and infrastructure. More than 73,000 people died and even more were injured. More than 3 million people became homeless. Damage to assets was estimated at $5.2 billion or higher. The international community has responded generously, pledging more than $6 billion in soft loans and grants at a donor conference in November 2005 in Islamabad. The policy challenge is to convert these pledges into contributions and to create the machinery to effectively carry out the rehabilitation and reconstruction on a timely basis. For now, it is expected that the earthquake will have a minimal impact on economic growth. Although such natural disasters damage and destroy assets, the repair and rebuilding of these assets generates economic activity that can help to stimulate economic growth. Keeping all these factors in view, GDP should grow by 6.5 per cent in 2006.

Inflation is expected to drop to about 8 per cent in 2006, from 9.3 per cent in 2005, owing to the decline in aggregate demand implicit in the lower growth estimate, a high base effect for 2006 prices and an anticipated improvement in food supplies. However, prices of construction materials are expected to increase at a faster pace because of supply bottlenecks associated with the reconstruction work associated with the earthquake. Government expenditure related to the earthquake is likely to put pressure on the budgetary balance. However, with the continuing fiscal discipline, prudent monetary policy and focused attention on improving infrastructure and social sector indicators, the economy should maintain its medium-term growth trajectory. There is, nonetheless, a need to enhance the buoyancy of tax revenues to improve the tax to GDP ratio. In addition, growth in current expenditure needs to be curtailed and imbalances in the external sectors need to be addressed to ensure that the economy does not deviate from the growth path achieved in the past few years.

Sri Lanka to experience higher growth and lower inflation

In Sri Lanka, assuming that the current ceasefire agreement and improved political stability continue to hold and weather conditions remain favourable, GDP is projected to grow by 6 per cent in 2006. However, if the ceasefire agreement breaks down and internal conflict begins again, the growth rate could be lower. In any case, tsunami-related reconstruction work could further boost aggregate demand and output. The acceleration in economic growth is projected to be broad based. The agricultural sector is expected to benefit from better weather conditions and recovery in the fisheries sector. Four main categories of the industrial sector will make major contributions to higher growth of the sector: textiles, wearing apparel and leather products; food, beverages and tobacco; chemicals, petroleum, rubber and plastic products; and non-metallic mineral products. The service sector is also expected to grow more rapidly, due partly to reconstruction activities and new investments in the leisure industry and tourism-promotion activities. The government target is to boost both domestic and foreign investment levels to accelerate economic growth towards 8 per cent over the medium term. Inflation is expected to moderate to 9 per cent in 2006, with expected recovery of the agricultural sector and a drop in international oil prices.

There is a need for continuing fiscal consolidation by maintaining healthy growth in government revenue and rationalizing recurrent expenditures, strengthening debt management and restructuring public enterprises, while ensuring that public investment that supports pro-poor growth is not neglected. Moreover, domestic borrowing by the Government will be reduced to release resources for private sector activities, especially in small and medium-size enterprises.

The Islamic Republic of Iran plans for high growth

In the Islamic Republic of Iran, the Fourth Five-year Development Plan (2005-2009) targets an average annual real GDP growth rate of 8 per cent compared with 5.4 per cent during the previous plan period. This is expected to be achieved through higher private sector investment and improved efficiency resulting from accelerated implementation of structural reforms. GDP growth is forecast to rise to 7.4 per cent in 2006. Rapid expansion in oil and services are expected to accelerate GDP growth. With a growing population, the non-oil economy needs to develop much more rapidly to provide much-needed employment opportunities in the country.

In Turkey, growth to moderate and inflation to fall further

The Turkish lira is expected to depreciate against the dollar and euro in 2006. This should lead to a moderate rise in interest rates, which could dampen domestic demand. However, GDP growth is projected to be about 5 per cent in

2006 and over the next few years, supported by both the increases in the factors of production and productivity. For Turkey, the long-awaited European Union accession negotiations began in October 2005. Negotiations are likely to be long and difficult, lasting perhaps 10 years. If the negotiations proceed well and the economy of Turkey converges towards the economies of the European Union, the growing confidence of investors should attract increasing flows of foreign investment. The Government recently negotiated a new stand-by arrangement with the International Monetary Fund to support a three-year economic programme aimed at sustaining growth to raise living standards and reduce unemployment, delivering price stability and moving towards convergence with the economies of the European Union. Success in the programme would greatly aid the negotiating process.

South-East Asia

Overview

Growth eases in the subregion

Economic growth in the South-East Asian subregion eased in 2005 after an unusually good performance in 2004 when strong global demand for manufactures, especially electronics and information and communication technology products, drove the GDP growth rate up to 6.4 per cent. With the global electronics cycle subsequently experiencing a downturn, economic growth fell to about 5.4 per cent in 2005. The sharpest decline was in the trade-dependent economy of Singapore, which grew by 6.4 per cent after achieving an unusually high growth rate of 8.4 per cent in 2004. Against the general trend of the subregion, Indonesia and Viet Nam grew faster in 2005 than in 2004 (see figure II.27).

Fiscal and monetary policies in the subregion were tight during 2005, responding to the build-up of inflationary pressures caused by high oil prices. While oil prices doubled between 2002 and 2004, inflationary pressures did not emerge until the second quarter of 2005, because huge oil subsidies insulated final goods and services from the effects of the oil price increases. However, the high fiscal burden made the continuation of subsidies unsustainable from the middle of 2005. Many countries began phasing out oil subsidies, and inflation inched up to 5.8 per cent in 2005. In general, individual country policy responses to oil subsidies influenced the magnitude of their fiscal deficit. Thailand's elimination of oil subsidies in July 2005 increased the budget surplus, making it easier for the Government to finance the large infrastruc-

Figure II.27. GDP and sectoral growth in selected South-East Asian economies, 2003-2005[a]

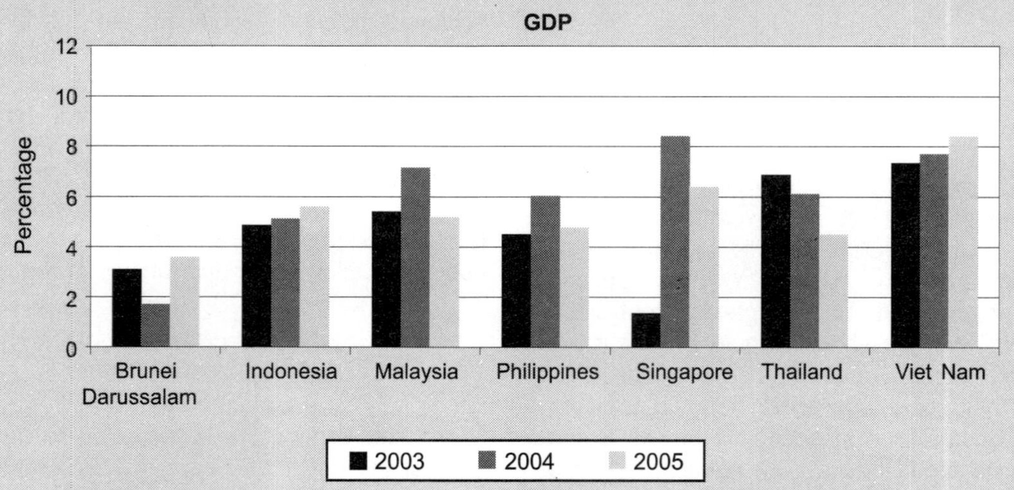

(Continued on next page)

Figure II.27 *(continued)*

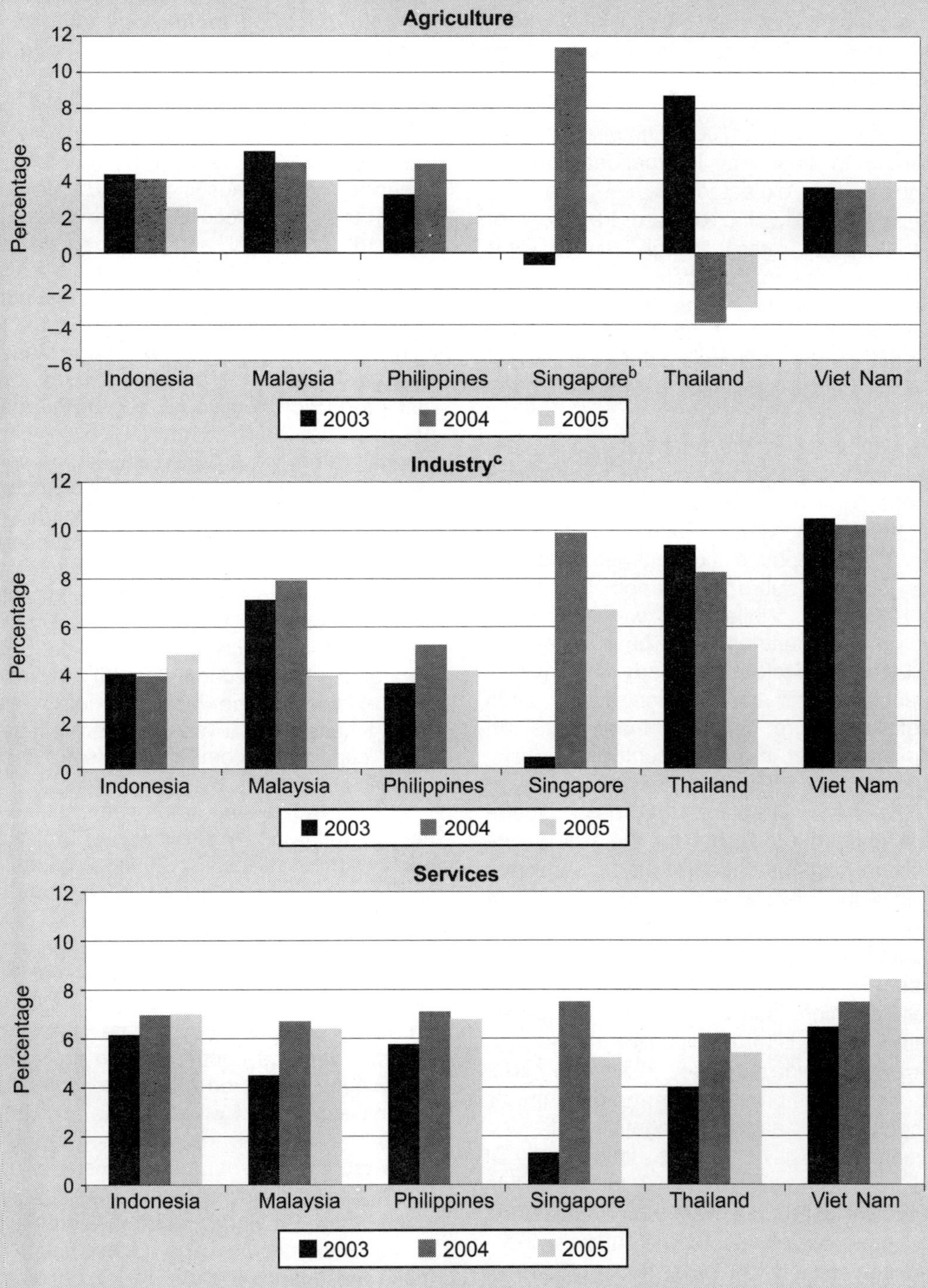

Sources: United Nations Economic and Social Commission for Asia and the Pacific, based on national sources; Asian Development Bank, *Key Indicators of Developing Asian and Pacific Countries 2005* (Manila, ADB, 2005), and Economist Intelligence Unit, *Country Forecasts* and *Country Reports* (London, EIU, 2005 and 2006), various issues.

[a] Growth rates for 2005 are estimates.
[b] Includes quarrying.
[c] Industry comprises mining and quarrying; manufacturing; electricity-generation, gas and power; and construction.

ture projects planned for 2006. A drastic cut in oil subsidies in Indonesia reduced the fiscal deficit. Malaysia, the Philippines and Viet Nam, however, retained substantial oil subsidies, managing the adverse fiscal effects through lower public expenditure.

Monetary policy in 2005 tightened across the subregion in line with international trends. Tight policies are expected to continue into 2006, keeping in view the upward trajectory of oil prices. Interest rates, though rising, were generally low except in the Philippines and particularly in Indonesia, where they rose to double-digit levels as the central bank attempted to neutralize the threat of spiraling inflation following a sharp cut in oil subsidies in October 2005.

Developments in the financial sector continue to be influenced largely by the assessment and lessons drawn from the Asian financial crises of 1997-1998, which placed much of the blame on the fast-paced financial liberalization undertaken in the subregion during the boom years of 1985-1996. While there were no major reform reversals, countries have been extremely reluctant to add to reforms already undertaken. Major financial sector liberalization during 2005 was therefore meagre, although there were important developments in some countries.

In the external sector, the major South-East Asian economies except for the Philippines and Viet Nam had merchandise trade surpluses in 2004. In 2005, the rate of growth of exports slowed in response to slower global demand. Only Indonesia registered a sharp rise, driven by an increase in non-oil and gas exports. In a largely oil-importing subregion high oil prices meant rising import bills, resulting in the narrowing of current account surpluses in several countries. In Thailand, pressure from oil imports turned the current account negative following several years of positive balance. Inflows of FDI increased from $17 billion in 2003 to $25 billion in 2004 for the subregion, with Singapore alone receiving nearly two thirds of the inflows. Indonesia, the only country to have had outflows of FDI in 2003, witnessed inflows of $1 billion in 2004 due to an upswing in mergers and acquisitions. International portfolio capital flows to the subregion were subdued, with investors preferring emerging markets in East and South Asia where potential returns were higher.

GDP growth performance

Higher oil prices and lower information and communication technology exports led to slower GDP growth in several economies

With a growth rate of 8.4 per cent, Viet Nam was the fastest growing economy in South-East Asia in 2005. Growth in Viet Nam remained dependent on domestic demand rather than exports; this was reflected in increasing import demand for capital and intermediate goods for the public sector. Private domestic consumption remained strong, with retail sales including sales from rapidly increasing consumer durable outlets rising nearly 20 per cent in 2005. Manufacturing was the main driver of the economy, and industrial production registered a growth rate of 10.7 per cent in 2005. Sectors showing impressive growth rates were fertilizers, automobiles, machine tools and coal. The service sector, including retail, financial and telecommunication services and the rapidly expanding tourism industry, also contributed significantly. A slight slowdown in economic growth is expected in 2006 owing to the effects of the avian influenza outbreak and the competition from China in textiles and garments, the second largest export of Viet Nam. However, the high rate of investment is likely to ensure that growth is sustained at about 8 per cent in the coming year (see figure II.28).

In Indonesia, improved business confidence, following the ending of political uncertainty with the October 2004 elections, appears to have contributed to the 5.6 per cent economic growth rate achieved in 2005. The service sector, led by the continuing expansion of telecommunications, drove economic growth during the year. Economic growth in Indonesia was also broad based, with both private consumption and external demand contributing to that growth. The inflationary impact on private consumption following the slashing of oil subsidies in October 2005 came too late in the year to seriously affect 2005 growth. The tsunami disaster of December 2004 also did not seriously affect GDP growth since Aceh Province contributes just 2 per cent of national income. The Government hopes to make the economy grow by 6.2 per cent in 2006 by increasing its spending. However, the actual growth rate may fall short of this target as high oil prices are likely to weaken private consumption. The Bali bomb blast of September 2005 may also dampen investor (in particular Australian) sentiment and reduce tourist arrivals.

Figure II.28. Savings and investment in selected South-East Asian economies, 2003-2005[a]

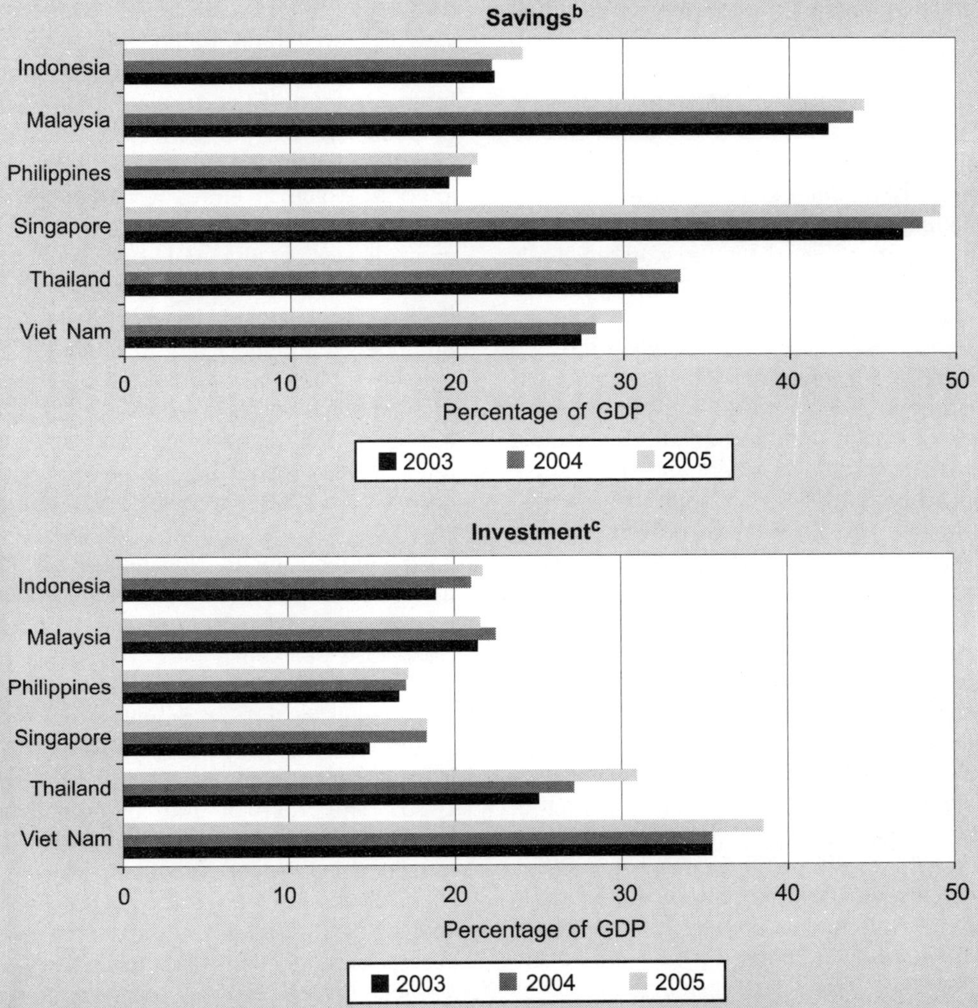

Sources: United Nations Economic and Social Commission for Asia and the Pacific, based on national sources; and Asian Development Bank, *Key Indicators of Developing Asian and Pacific Countries 2005* (Manila, ADB, 2005).

[a] Data for 2005 are estimates.
[b] Gross domestic savings.
[c] Gross domestic investment.

A downswing in global demand for electronic products caused GDP growth in Malaysia to decline from 7.1 per cent in 2004 to 5.2 per cent in 2005. The momentum for growth during the year was provided by the service sector, which grew faster than manufacturing, spurred by strong consumer spending and low interest rates, growth in financial and telecommunications services and a rise in tourism. Within manufacturing, commodity-based products such as rubber goods, petroleum products, paper and palm oil expanded faster during 2005 than electronic goods. GDP in Malaysia is expected to grow at a faster rate of 5.9 per cent in 2006, aided by the bottoming out of the global electronics cycle. Higher oil prices are also likely to provide short-term benefits to Malaysia, a net oil exporter. Economic growth in the coming year could be even higher except that rising global interest rates are likely to reduce overall demand for the country's exports.

After an outstanding performance in 2004, when the Philippine economy grew by 6 per cent, the growth rate declined to 4.8 per cent in 2005 as negative factors operated in different sectors of the economy. In the service sector, which makes the largest contribution to GDP, oil price-induced inflation and higher interest rates dampened private consumption and its contribution to GDP growth. The export of manufactures was adversely affected by lower global demand for electronic products, the country's main export, and stagnant growth in ready-made garments following the end of the Multifibre Arrangement. Positive contributions to economic growth came from the transportation, communication and storage service sectors and overseas workers' remittances, which rose considerably during 2005, boosting private domestic consumption. In 2006, the growth rate is projected to reach 5.2 per cent based on rising workers' remittances, which are increasing because of sustained demand for Filipino workers in high-income countries, improved tax revenues following successful implementation of the value added tax and renewed global demand for electronic products.

In Thailand, at least three factors contributed to the economic slowdown from a 6.1 per cent growth rate in 2004 to 4.5 per cent in 2005. The tsunami disaster that struck coastal areas in the Andaman Sea in December 2004 severely reduced the number of tourist arrivals during the first half of the year. The elimination of oil subsidies in July 2005 resulted in a sharp rise in inflation, from 2.8 per cent in 2004 to more than 4 per cent in 2005, slowing growth in private consumption. Lower global demand for electronics products, the country's leading export, also had an adverse impact on the country's economy. Manufacturing, the mainstay of the economy, grew 5.2 per cent. The electronics goods sector did particularly well, with hard-disk drive production being the top performer. The performance of the ready-made garments and vehicle manufacturing sectors was satisfactory, while textiles and the food and beverages sectors grew slowly during the year. In 2006, Government expenditure on large infrastructure projects, the normalization of tourist traffic and an upswing in the global electronics cycle are expected to contribute to a higher growth rate of 5.7 per cent.

Growth in Singapore, the fastest growing economy in South-East Asia in 2004, fell from 8.4 per cent to 6.4 per cent in 2005. The sharp decline in the rate of growth was the result of weaker global trade, particularly in information and communication technology products, the country's largest export. Export revenues, which had increased by 16.2 per cent in 2004, grew by only 4.4 per cent in 2005, and the rate of growth of imports, which in entrepôt Singapore are closely linked to exports, also declined from 19 to 5.5 per cent. However, the 6.4 per cent growth rate achieved in 2005 was impressive by the standards of the Organisation for Economic Co-operation and Development. Both the manufacturing and service sectors contributed led by a sharp revival in biomedical output, good performance by the transport and engineering industry and buoyant retail sales (especially of cars) and financial services. In 2006, improved global demand for the country's exports and an increase in capital inflows, particularly in real estate as the Government relaxes rules restricting foreign ownership of property, are likely to keep the GDP growth rate close to 6 per cent.

High oil prices meant a rise in the GDP growth rate for oil-exporting Brunei Darussalam from 1.7 per cent in 2004 to 3.6 per cent in 2005. The rest of the manufacturing sector, based largely on textile and garment production, remained depressed, however, following the abolition of quotas under the WTO Agreement on Textiles and Clothing. Agriculture, fisheries and livestock production also fell during 2005. The service sector, led by cars and retail sales, remained fairly buoyant, however. The rate of economic growth in 2006 will depend on international oil prices since the economy of Brunei Darussalam continues to be largely dependent on oil and gas exports, which contribute more than one third of GDP.

Key macroeconomic policy developments

Fiscal policy developments

After providing a fiscal stimulus to the economy for several years, the Malaysian Government has been following a policy of consolidating the fiscal deficit. In 2005 the deficit was 4.0 per cent of GDP (see figure II.29), well

Figure II.29. Budget balance in selected South-East Asian economies, 2003-2005[a]

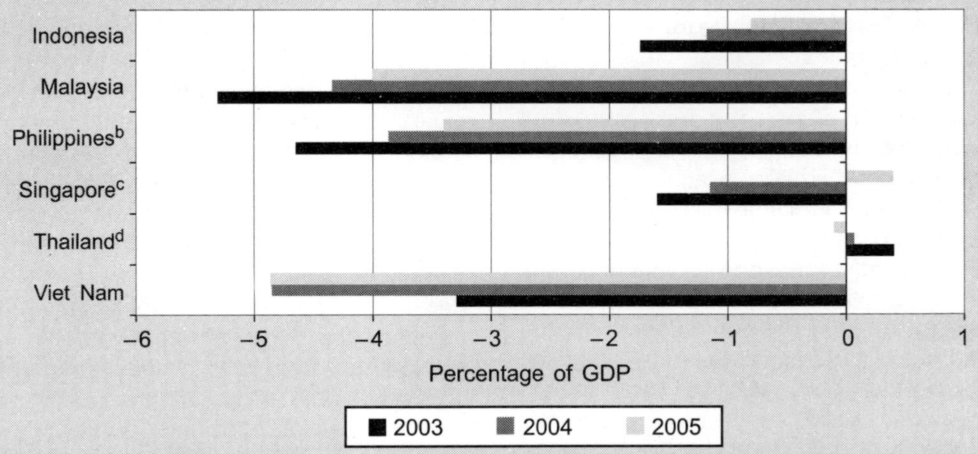

Sources: United Nations Economic and Social Commission for Asia and the Pacific, based on national sources; Asian Development Bank, *Key Indicators of Developing Asian and Pacific Countries 2005* (Manila, ADB, 2005); Economist Intelligence Unit, *Country Forecasts* (London, EIU, 2005 and 2006), various issues; and website of the Ministry of Finance of Singapore, <www.mof.gov.sg/budget_2005/budget_speech/downloads/>, accessed on 20 November 2005.

[a] Data for 2005 are estimates.
[b] Includes grants.
[c] Computed from government operating revenue minus government operating expenditure minus government development expenditure.
[d] Government cash balance comprising the budgetary balance and non-budgetary balance.

below the Government's target of 3.8 per cent. This was achieved in part by a reduction in government expenditure on development and construction projects. On the revenue side, there was strong growth in direct tax revenues, especially from the higher petroleum income tax and an increase in road toll charges. Indirect revenues also increased, owing mainly to higher duties on cigarettes and liquor. Non-tax revenues were also buoyant, including income from the government-linked oil giant Petronas. Despite cuts in oil subsidies, fuel prices in Malaysia are among the lowest in the subregion. A substantial subsidy remains, and a sales tax exemption on diesel and petrol costs the Government an additional 8 billion ringgit per year. With oil prices expected to remain high, the opportunity costs of the subsidy and concessions in terms of the developmental expenditure forgone appear to be considerable, particularly in view of the 7.7 per cent annual growth rate estimated to be required to achieve the country's Vision 2020 goal of becoming a fully developed country.

In the Philippines, the fiscal consolidation that began in 2003 continued, and the budget deficit shrank from 3.9 per cent of GDP in 2004 to 3.4 per cent in 2005. Lower government spending was assisted by an unexpected saving in interest payments as rates remained lower than projected. Not much headway was achieved in tackling the country's long-standing shortfalls in the collection of personal income tax and customs duties, which remained below annual targets. Extra revenue did begin to flow towards the end of the year after imposition of a wider value added tax in November that ended exemptions on power, fuel for air transport, medical and legal services and several other items. The Government has used administrative measures such as staggering working hours to curb fuel consumption instead of eliminating or reducing oil subsidies. Some pressure on the fiscal deficit can therefore be expected in 2006.

Indonesia has taken a conservative fiscal policy stance in the past few years in line with its structural adjustment package. The budget deficit in 2005 was 0.8 per cent of GDP, down from 1.2 per cent in 2004. The most important fiscal development in 2005 was the drastic cut in oil subsidies in October, which raised fuel prices 126 per cent. While this reduced the oil subsidy bill by 25 trillion rupiyah per year, the Government sought to ease the contractionary effect on consumption spending by providing cash grants of 100,000 rupiyah to each of the 16.5 million poorest households in the country. Notwithstanding the likely positive fiscal impact of this measure, questions remain about the efficacy of the policy package for the economy of Indonesia. How will the local government machinery ensure that the cash compensation reaches eligible households without leakage? Since the cash compensation payout is targeted only at low-income households, which are not major contributors to aggregate demand, can the payout prevent national consumption levels from falling and adversely affecting GDP growth? In view of these questions, it seems that additional steps may be required to boost demand since the economy is already facing both rising interest rates and a depreciating currency.

In July 2005, Thailand became the first South-East Asian economy to eliminate subsidies on petroleum products; the bold approach helped to increase the budget surplus slightly in 2005. Specifically, diesel subsidies that had cost the Government 92 billion baht in the year and a half prior to July 2005 were abolished. In order to compensate for the higher fuel costs, the Government introduced an economic stimulus package, including a higher minimum wage, a 5 per cent salary hike for civil servants, higher pensions and an additional outlay of 20 billion baht for a village fund. The overall budget impact for the year was neutral. With GDP projected to grow faster in 2006, by 5.7 per cent, tax revenues are also likely to rise. However, other policies are likely to cause a small budget deficit in 2006, including debt relief, investment in infrastructure and a delay in the privatization of State-owned enterprises such as the Electricity Generating Authority of Thailand.

In contrast to the fiscal consolidation occurring in most of South-East Asia, Viet Nam has maintained a relatively expansionary fiscal policy over the years. The budget deficit in 2005 was 4.9 per cent of GDP, the same as in 2004 and the largest in the subregion. A significant portion of the national budget was financed through oil revenues, which, owing to high oil prices, contributed 21 per cent of total receipts during the year. Other government revenues were also on the upswing because of higher corporate tax collections in an expanding economy. On the expenditure side, an important portion of outflows went to clear the wage burden of workers in an economy that is still dominated by the public sector. Even with fuel prices revised upwards three times during 2005, there is considerable scope for fiscal policy reform in Viet Nam as oil subsidies, particularly on diesel and kerosene, remain large.

After three years of deficits, Singapore delivered a budget surplus of 0.4 per cent of GDP during fiscal year 2005 owing mainly to higher tax revenues and the continuing good performance by State-owned enterprises, which are run on commercial lines. A budget surplus is in keeping with stated government policy that is aimed at sustaining surpluses over the medium term, possibly with the objective of containing inflationary pressures under the prevailing oil price conditions. Budget surpluses also provide the necessary flexibility for social security and pension schemes in a society with adverse demographics.

With oil revenues constituting the bulk of government income, the budget of Brunei Darussalam remained in surplus in 2005, aided by high global oil prices. However, the Government's plans to increase expenditures on several new initiatives, including the Pulau Muara Besar port project which is largely financed by the Government, and the improvement of the country's information and communication technology infrastructure, may cause the budget surplus to narrow in the coming year.

Monetary policy developments

In Indonesia, investor frustration over legislative delays in improving the investment climate triggered capital outflows in mid-2005, causing the rupiyah to slide in international currency markets. Bank Indonesia raised interest rates six times during the year, increasing the benchmark one-month rate from 8.5 per cent in July 2005 to 12.75 per cent in December. Inflation had spiraled from 6.1 to 10.5 per cent when fuel prices increased rapidly following the drastic cut in oil subsidies in October 2005 (see figure II.30). The aggressive use of interest rates by

Figure II.30. Inflation and money supply growth in selected South-East Asian economies, 2003-2005[a]

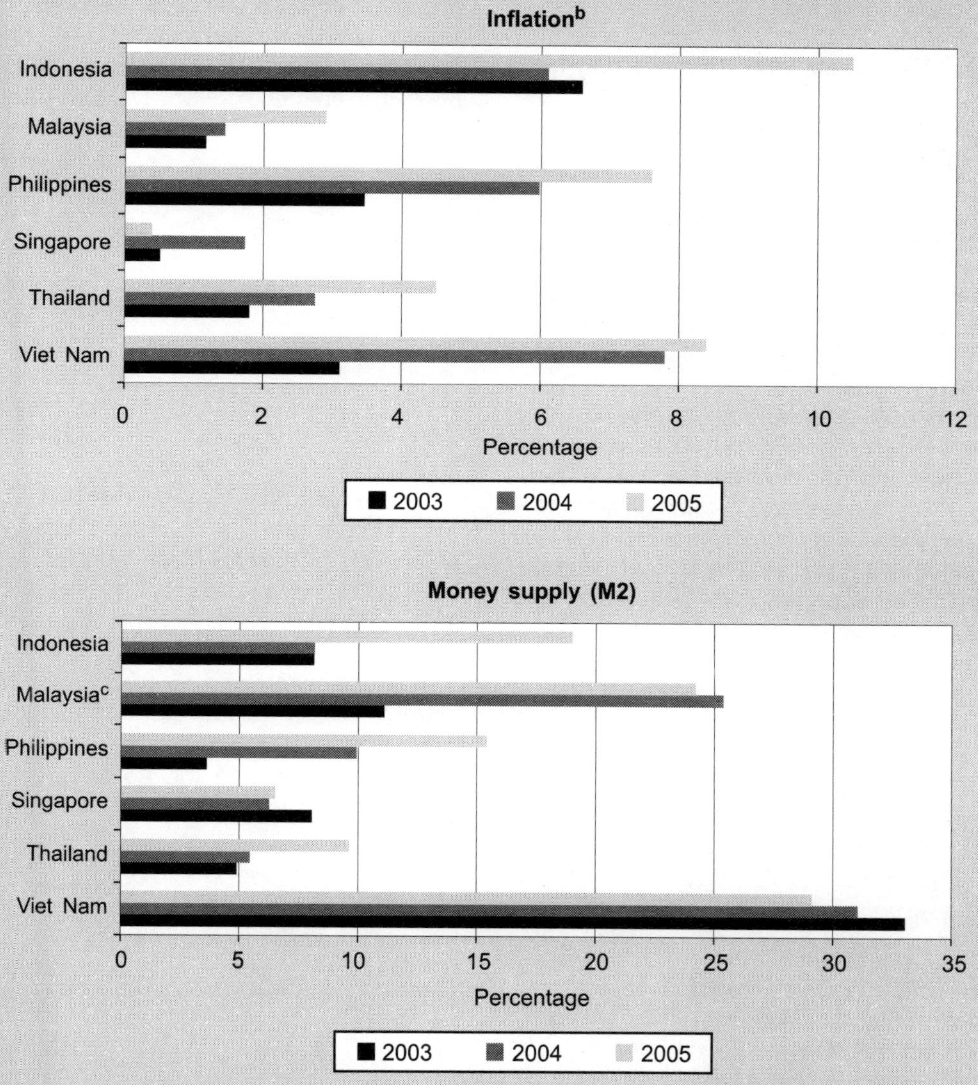

Sources: United Nations Economic and Social Commission for Asia and the Pacific, based on national sources; Asian Development Bank, *Key Indicators of Developing Asian and Pacific Countries 2005* (Manila, ADB, 2005); International Monetary Fund, *International Financial Statistics* (CD-ROM) (Washington, D.C., IMF, January 2006); Economist Intelligence Unit (EIU), *Country Forecasts* (London, EIU, 2005 and 2006), various issues.

[a] Data for 2005 are estimates.

[b] Inflation refers to changes in the consumer price index.

[c] Data for 2005 refer to January-September.

the Bank differs from the prevailing practice among most central banks, which favour incremental changes in monetary policy. While the rate of inflation might slow, the net impact of the policy on consumer spending and GDP growth is likely to be adverse. High interest rates will also increase the burden of servicing domestic debt and add to the fiscal costs of servicing foreign debt, which is due to commence in 2006 when the moratorium granted to Indonesia by the Paris Club of creditors expires.

In the Philippines, with inflation rising from 6 per cent in 2004 to 7.6 per cent in 2005, the central bank tightened monetary policy by raising the overnight borrowing rate to 7.25 per cent and lending rate to 9.25 per cent and raising the reserve requirement by 1 percentage point. This squeezed domestic credit significantly compared with the situation in 2004. On the positive side, commercial banks began responding to incentives offered by the Government to eliminate bad debts, and the percentage of non-performing loans declined to single digit levels. On the whole, monetary policy was driven more by the need to check inflation than to promote growth, which is not inappropriate in an environment where inflationary pressures induced by oil prices were coupled with a 19 per cent increase in the price of utilities (fuel, light and water) and an increase in the money supply faster than the 13 per cent target during the first three quarters, owing to a rise in net portfolio inflows and a surge in workers' remittances.

In Thailand, the non-performing loans of commercial banks declined to 10.5 per cent of total outstanding loans by August 2005 from 11.6 per cent in July 2004. With inflation climbing from 2.8 per cent in 2004 to 4.5 per cent in 2005, the central bank continued tightening monetary policy by raising overnight borrowing rates to 3.75 per cent in two phases, in September and in October 2005. In November 2005, the central bank announced its intention to keep interest rates above international levels in order to attract foreign capital. This is likely to have had important signaling effects. In anticipation of the rise in interest rates domestic investment is likely to have risen in the last quarter of 2005. Foreign capital inflows may have been postponed, however, as foreign investors waited for rates to go up, taking the announcements as credible.

Inflation peaked earlier in 2004 in Viet Nam, at 7.8 per cent, than in most other South-East Asian countries, which felt the impact of oil prices only in 2005. Tight monetary policy accordingly came into play as early as July 2004, when the State Bank of Viet Nam increased the reserve requirements of commercial banks. With inflation running at 8.4 per cent in 2005 due to commodity production shortfalls caused by drought and the avian influenza outbreak and the continuing high prices of imports, including petroleum products, steel ingots and chemical fertilizers, the authorities took further steps, including raising interest rates in September 2005. Deposit rates went up by between 0.24 and 0.6 percentage point (to between 7.56 and 8.4 per cent) while lending rates rose by 1.2 to 3.4 percentage points (to between 9.6 and 12.39 per cent), indicating greater concern over lending, especially the rapidly expanding credit lines to State-owned enterprises. A lending ceiling of 40 per cent of short-term funds available with credit institutions was imposed. Despite these steps, growth in Viet Nam is likely to continue unabated, riding on the momentum of broad-ranging structural reforms.

In Malaysia, despite the build-up of inflationary pressure, the overnight policy rate held steady at 2.7 per cent for most of 2005 except for 90.25 point increase in November 2005, enhancing the credibility of the central bank, which had announced in 2004 that, in order to sustain economic growth, interest rates were unlikely to be raised. In July 2005 the fixed exchange rate policy, under which the ringgit had been pegged to the dollar, was abandoned in favour of a managed float against a basket of currencies. The fixed exchange rate had outlived its utility. The Malaysian economy had fully recovered from the effects of the 1997 financial crisis, with a strong build-up of foreign exchange reserves from $44.9 billion in early 2004 to $75.7 billion by mid-November 2005 and regional initiatives under way to prevent currency volatility. The switch to a managed float restores to the central bank a critical policy tool for handling external shocks in a relatively open economy such as that of Malaysia.

There was little change in the exchange-rate-based monetary policy of Singapore. Despite the stance of the Monetary Authority of Singapore to allow a gradual appreciation of the Singapore dollar to prevent imported inflation, the unexpected strength of the United States dollar in the international currency markets in the second half of the year meant that the currency depreciated nominally by 1.18 per cent during 2005. Inflation, which declined to just 0.3 per cent, was contained by slower growth in the demand for imports as well as weakening domestic demand. The end result was a small real depreciation consistent with the parallel policy objective of sustaining export growth. Interest rates in Singapore have been following the movement of interest rates in the United States, with the three-month domestic interbank rate falling to 2 per cent at the end of July and rising to 2.38 per cent by the end of September. There was no dramatic change in foreign exchange reserves, which rose from $112 billion at the end of 2004 to $115.6 billion by November 2005, the highest reserves in the subregion.

The monetary policy of Brunei Darussalam remained unchanged during 2005, with the reserve requirement for banks and finance companies maintained at 6 per cent of liabilities. The country does not have a central bank but the Brunei Currency and Monetary Board. Its monetary policy is focused on managing the exchange rate which is pegged to the Singapore dollar on a 1:1 basis. This has provided the economy with an effective instrument for price stability. Inflation remained modest at 1 per cent during the year. Broad money increased significantly during the year as a result of higher oil income. However, because the Government expected the price rise to be temporary, most of the extra revenue was saved, so there was no effect on inflation. Domestic interest rates have remained low in contrast to international trends, but credit growth has been moderate, except for consumer lending. One weak link in the monetary system is non-performing loans, which remain high compared with neighbouring countries. Official foreign exchange reserves rose from $534 million at the end of 2004 to $590 million at the end of 2005, supported by the higher oil revenues.

Financial sector developments

Symbolic of the steady transition to a market-based economy in viet Nam, a second stock exchange was inaugurated in Hanoi in March 2005, five years after the first one opened in Ho Chi Minh City. In September 2005 the Government agreed to partially privatize the Bank for Foreign Trade of Vietnam (Vietcombank), one of the country's four large State-owned commercial banks. This was an important policy breakthrough in a country where the pace of public sector reforms has otherwise been slow.

The Indonesian economy witnessed both positive and negative developments in the financial sector. On the positive side was the replacement of the blanket sovereign guarantee on bank liabilities with a new deposit insurance scheme. That scheme provides for a gradual decrease in coverage so that by March 2007 a maximum of 100 million rupiyah ($10,000) per depositor will be covered by a guarantee. The blanket guarantee had been introduced in 1998 during the Asian financial crisis to prevent a run on the banking system. The limited guarantee substantially reduces the moral hazard risk in commercial bank lending in Indonesia. On the negative side was the crisis in the country's mutual fund business, one of the fastest growing in Asia. Panic withdrawals took place when fixed-income instruments started falling in value in March 2005, with investors claiming that risks were not adequately explained by the fund managers. As a result, the net asset value of mutual funds fell 60 per cent on average by September 2005, temporarily disabling mutual funds as instruments for converting household savings into investment capital for the Indonesian economy.

The first Philippine Fixed-income Exchange became operational in March 2005. While only government bonds were initially listed on the exchange, the long-term benefits to the economy of an alternative system of credit allocation are likely to be substantial, given that net domestic credit distributed by commercial banks has been sluggish, rising by only 2.8 per cent in July on a year-on-year basis, down from 9.4 per cent per year in 2004. The Philippine economy also witnessed a sharp rise in net portfolio inflows, resulting in a surge in domestic liquidity. The stock market index was by nearly 13 per cent higher by November 2005 over the level at the end of 2004, although this hides the fact that portfolio investments were volatile during the year, with outflows rising sharply in response to such domestic shocks as the political crisis surrounding the country's president in June and the Supreme Court's decision to postpone implementation of the value added tax in July.

By contrast, the efforts of Thailand to increase the role of the stock market in the economy have met with only partial success.

Stock market activity was fairly subdued during 2005, with the stock index declining marginally by 0.4 per cent in dollar terms by November compared with the end of 2004. Tax incentives granted to new firms listing on the Stock Exchange of Thailand, in place for four years, expired in September 2005, having had very little impact in encouraging new listing during 2005. The Ministry of Finance is drawing up plans to further develop the country's capital markets, including introduction of a market for futures and derivatives in 2006. There were also concerns in the country's financial sector about the fall-out from the Government's plans to grant debt relief (50 per cent debt write-off of principal and a 100 per cent write-off of interest) to about 100,000 debtors whose loans had turned bad during the financial crisis of 1997. Apart from conflicting with the central bank's efforts to reduce domestic credit at a time when inflationary pressures abound, the plan could be creating a moral hazard even before implementation in 2006 as customers of commercial banks and non-banking financial institutions could put off repayments in anticipation of similar concessions.

In Malaysia, a number of new initiatives were taken with regard to Islamic banks, which neither charge nor pay interest but share the profits on their investments with depositors. For the first time foreign ownership of up to 49 per cent was permitted for these banks. Two bond indices, called the Dow Jones – RHB Islamic Index and the Citigroup Malaysian Government Bond Index, were launched by the country's central bank, Bank Negara Malaysia. Islamic bonds contributed significantly to the Malaysian bond market in 2005, growing by 50 per cent during the year.

In Singapore, earnings from the foreign operations of several banks and financial institutions were on the rise and contributed increasingly to the acceleration in the growth of the country's financial services sector, which grew 6.8 per cent in the second quarter of 2005 on a year-on-year basis. An important cross-border bank purchase was also carried out by the Government's investment firm Temasek Holdings, which purchased $1 billion in shares of China Construction Bank (3 per cent of the total equity), one of the four biggest State-owned banks in China. This marks the first entry of a Singapore company into the banking sector of China and comes at an opportune moment when State-owned banks in China have begun to improve their portfolios by shedding bad debts.

A series of financial sector reforms were also announced in Brunei Darussalam, including the merger of two local banks, the Islamic Development Bank of Brunei and the Islamic Bank of Brunei. Greater financial strength of the merged institution would probably enhance the role of Islamic banking in the economy. Amendments to the Banking Act, Financial Companies Act, Insurance Act and the Pawn Broking Act have also been announced with the objective of raising the country's regulatory standards to international levels. The amendments come into effect in 2006.

Developments in the external sector

Current account positions deteriorate

Merchandise exports from Viet Nam rose by an estimated 20 per cent during 2005 to $31.8 billion, helped by higher international prices of crude oil, the principal export commodity, and the export of rice, wood, coal and electronics products (see figure II.31). Garment exports benefited from the imposition of non-tariff barriers against China. Merchandise imports rose by 22.5 per cent during 2005, to $37.3 billion, as robust construction activity led to a rise in imports of steel and escalating demand for car and motorcycle components and chemicals. Counterbalancing flows took place in the services account, where earnings from a rise in tourist traffic were offset by larger imports in other service sectors. Remittances from overseas Vietnamese continued to be strong, and the current account deficit narrowed from 2 per cent of GDP in 2004 to 0.9 per cent in 2005 (see figure II.32). Exchange rates remained stable against the dollar and against other South-East Asian currencies (see figure II.33).

With regard to the capital account, the efforts of the Government of Viet Nam to facilitate FDI continued to be rewarded, with realized and committed FDI totalling $3 billion, a rise of 14.5

Figure II.31. Growth rates in merchandise export earnings and import spending in selected South-East Asian economies, 2003-2005

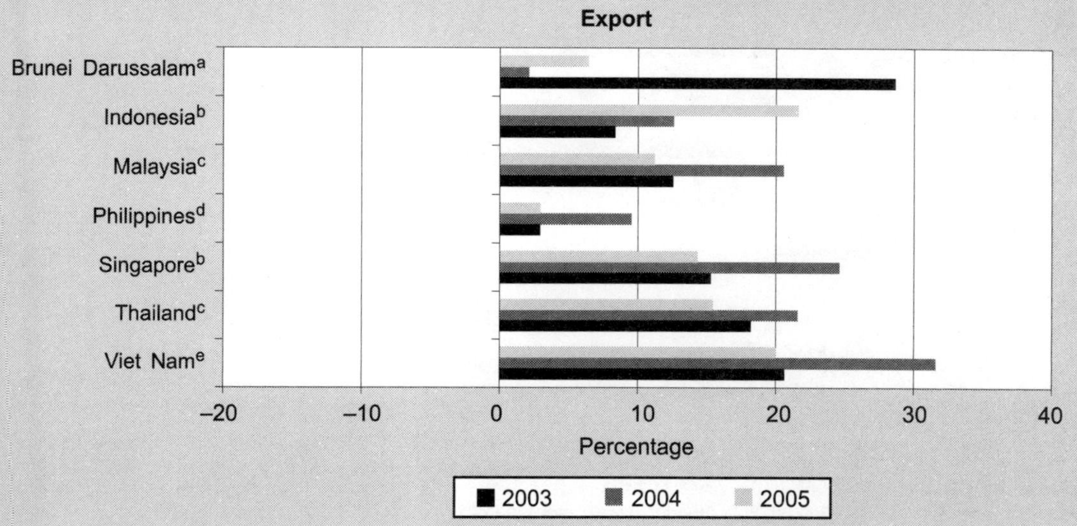

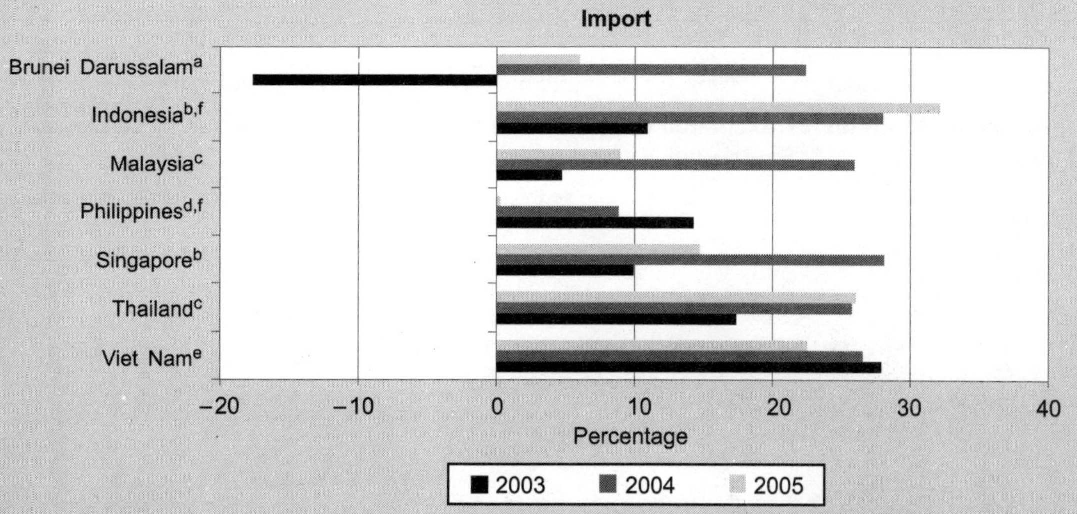

Sources: International Monetary Fund, *Direction of Trade Statistics* (CD-ROM) (Washington, D.C., IMF, 2005); Bank Indonesia website <www.bi.go.id>, accessed on 20 January 2006; Malaysia Economic Planning Unit website <www.epu.jpm.my>, accessed on 6 September 2005; Department of Statistics Malaysia website <www.statistics.gov.my>, accessed on 23 January 2006; Philippines National Statistics Office website <www.census.gov.ph>, accessed on 24 January 2006; Singapore Department of Statistics website <www.singstat.gov.sg>, accessed on 8 December 2005; Bank of Thailand website <www.bot.or.th>, accessed on 24 January 2006; and World Bank, *East Asia Update*, <http://siteresources.worldbank.org/INTEAPHALFYEARLYUPDATE/Resources/EAP-Brief-final.pdf>, accessed on 8 November 2005.

[a] Growth rate for 2005 refers to January-August.
[b] Growth rate for 2005 refers to January-September.
[c] Growth rate for 2005 refers to January-November.
[d] Growth rate for 2005 refers to January-October.
[e] Data for 2004 are estimates and data for 2005 are projections.
[f] Valued free on board (f.o.b.).

Figure II.32. Current account balance in selected South-East Asian economies, 2003-2005[a]

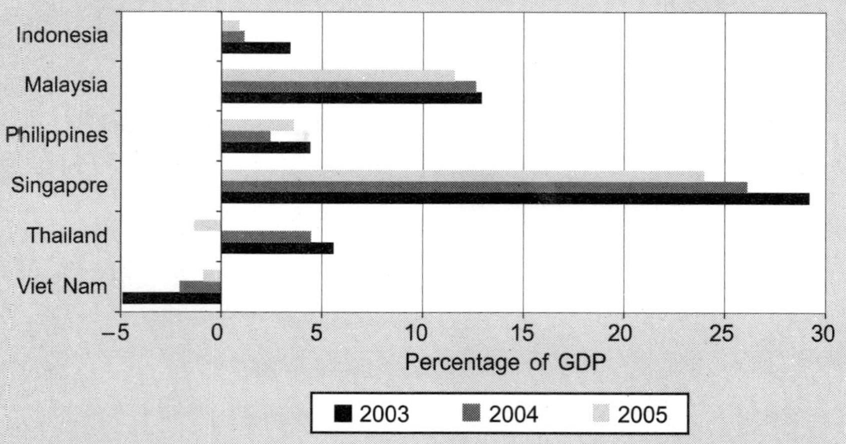

Sources: United Nations Economic and Social Commission for Asia and the Pacific, based on national sources; Asian Development Bank, *Key Indicators of Developing Asian and Pacific Countries 2005* (Manila, ADB, 2005); Economist Intelligence Unit, *Country Forecasts* (London, EIU, 2005 and 2006), various issues; and website of the Ministry of Finance of Singapore, <www.mof.gov.sg/budget_2005/budget_speech/downloads/>, accessed on 20 November 2005.

[a] Data for 2005 are estimates.

Figure II.33. Index of exchange rates against the United States dollar in selected South-East Asian economies, 1996-2005[a]

(1996Q4=100)

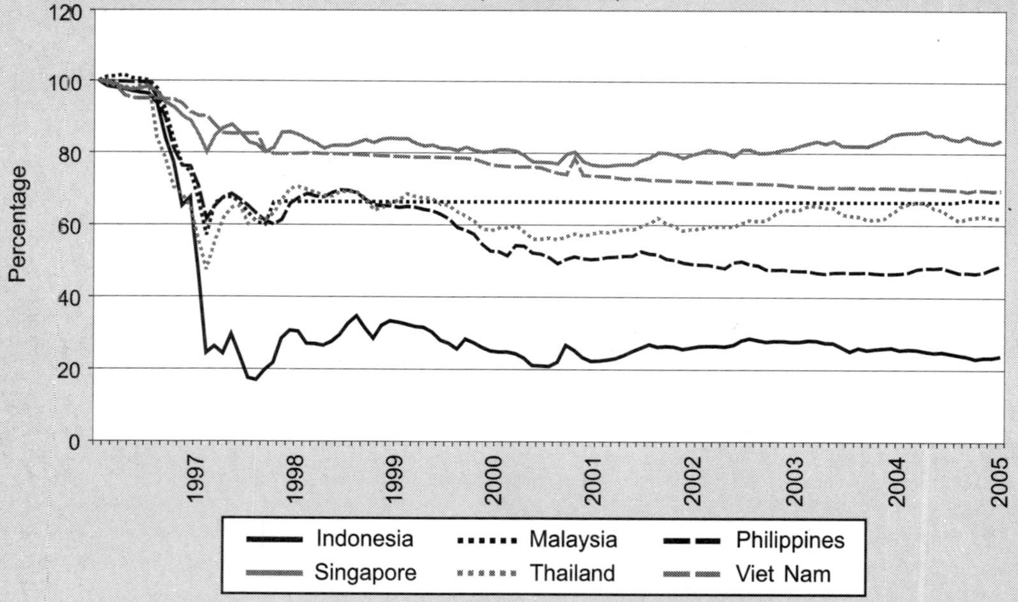

Sources: International Monetary Fund, *International Financial Statistics* (CD-ROM) (Washington, D.C., IMF, 2005); and *The Economist,* various issues

[a] Data for 2005 are estimates.

per cent. Telephone equipment and motorcycle components were some of the favoured sectors. The attractiveness of Viet Nam as an investment destination was also confirmed by the successful sale of government bonds worth $750 million in the international market in October 2005. The country remained an important destination for overseas development assistance, which reached $1.72 billion in 2005, up from $1.65 billion in 2004. On the whole, the current account deficit was more than compensated for by net inflows into the capital account, resulting in a balance of payments surplus of $1.9 billion in 2005.

In Thailand, weak global demand for electronics products and supply-side bottlenecks in agriculture caused merchandise exports to grow by 15.5 per cent in 2005, down from a growth rate of 21.6 per cent in 2004. A significant rise in the oil import bill and strong demand for imports of intermediate products and raw materials caused merchandise imports to grow by 26 per cent, slightly higher than the 25.7 per cent in 2004. In absolute terms, the merchandise trade balance registered a surplus, but there was a big rise in the deficit in the services trade account as tourism revenue fell following the December 2004 tsunami. As a result of these trends, the country's current account showed a deficit of 1.4 per cent of GDP for the first time since the 1997 financial crisis.

The capital account was supported by an increase in FDI and portfolio inflows and a rise in net transfers. The surplus in the capital account more than offset the deficit in the current account, resulting in a small but reduced balance of payments surplus during 2005. As a result, the reserves of Thailand exceeded $50 billion in December 2005 compared with $48.6 billion at the end of 2004. A free trade agreement signed with Australia in 2005, following similar agreements signed with China in 2003 and with India in 2004 and others before that, makes Thailand a leader in bilateral free trade agreements in South-East Asia.

The current account surplus in Indonesia fell from 1.1 per cent of GDP to 0.9 per cent in 2005 owing to higher import bill for petroleum products despite a strong export performance led by high global demand for natural resources such as coal and to textile and garment exports, helped by European Union and United States restrictions on such exports from China. Merchandise exports rose by 21.6 per cent to an estimated $84.4 billion, while merchandise imports grew at a faster rate, 32.1 per cent, to reach an estimated $62.9 billion during 2005. The main drivers for import growth were oil and petroleum products and gas, which rose as a consequence of high global prices and strong investment demand for capital and intermediate goods. The services account and net income from abroad remained negative during the year.

On the capital account, FDI outflows that had been persistent in Indonesia ever since its financial crisis in 1998 reversed for the first time in 2004 when net inflows totalled $1.02 billion. FDI flows into the Asian and Pacific region are mostly market-seeking, and a large potential market such as Indonesia is difficult to ignore for long. Sales of State-owned enterprises and foreign acquisitions of private firms, as for example in the banking sector, were mainly responsible for the reversal of this trend. In the first quarter of 2005, international transfers in the form of tsunami aid also boosted the capital account. However, by the second quarter FDI inflows were offset by portfolio outflows, and the overall balance of payments deteriorated as the oil import bill rose. The balance of payments position is unlikely to improve in 2006 as external debt servicing is scheduled to rise considerably.

In Malaysia, merchandise exports grew by 11.2 per cent in 2005, down sharply from the 20.5 per cent growth rate in 2004, an unusually good year for electronics goods, the country's "cash cow". Exports were sustained by strong growth in terms of value for crude oil and gas exports and rubber products and palm oil. Malaysian merchandise imports, which are closely linked to exports, also grew slowly by 8.9 per cent compared with 25.9 per cent in 2004. The trade surplus along with strong earnings from Malaysian investments overseas resulted in a large current account surplus of 12 per cent of GDP in 2005. With regard to the capital account, FDI inflows in 2004 amounted to $4.6 billion, a return to the levels seen before the crises in 1997 and 1998. These declined slightly during 2005; however, the decline was more than compensated by a surge in portfolio inflows, which kept the capital account in surplus during 2005.

Knowledgeable observers believe that the Malaysian economy is experiencing a period of excessive savings, with foreign exchange reserves more than doubling from $34 billion in 2002 to $70 billion by December 2005. Savings, at 44.5 per cent of GDP, are more than twice as large as investment. Given that the financial crisis in Malaysia began in 1997 with a run on the ringgit, government policy appears to be guided by a need to maintain a substantial cushion against currency volatility. If so, the policy is unlikely to change soon as another important protection against currency speculation, the dollar peg, has only recently been dismantled.

Philippine merchandise export growth slowed considerably from 9.5 per cent in 2004 to 2.9 per cent in 2005. Aside from weak demand in developed countries, electronic exports were also adversely affected by the transfer of a major electronic firm's processing and assembly plant to China. Although exports of textiles and garments were stagnant, automobile part exports performed better, helped by a policy decision to position the country as an automobile parts-manufacturing hub. Service receipts led by tourism increased substantially, growing by 10.9 per cent during the first half of 2005 thus far outpacing the 1.6 per cent growth rate achieved during the same period in 2004. Merchandise imports declined faster, registering growth of just 0.3 per cent compared with a 8.8 per cent growth rate in 2004. While the fuel import bill rose considerably, the increase was more than compensated by substantial declines in the import of telecommunications equipment and office machinery. On the whole, as imports were about 15 per cent higher than exports, there was a trade deficit of $5.8 billion in 2005. However, with a surge in workers' remittances of $4.8 billion in the first half of 2005, a 21.5 per cent year-on-year increase, the Philippine current account is estimated to have had a surplus amounting to 3.6 per cent of GDP in 2005, higher than the 2.4 per cent surplus in 2004.

Capital inflows to the Philippines have been languishing at below 25 per cent of their levels prior to the 1997 crisis for the past several years. FDI inflows in 2004 totalled $469 million, far below the high of $2.3 billion in 1998. During the first half of 2005, FDI rose to $450 million compared with $273 million over the same period in 2004, most of it going to manufacturing, real estate and the financial sector. There was a substantial turnaround in net portfolio inflows, as $2.1 billion entered the country in the first six months of 2005, compared with a net outflow of $114 million in the first six months of 2004. The improvement can be traced to the successful bond and note issuance by the Government and an improved investor outlook after the Government's success in controlling the fiscal deficit. However, the country's external debt stock stood at 56 per cent of GDP, higher than the World Bank's "safe" limit of 50 per cent.

With trade at three times GDP, the external sector plays a dominating role in the economy of Singapore. The growth rate of merchandise exports slowed to 14.3 per cent in 2005 after a high of 24.6 per cent in 2004 as global demand slowed for information and communication technology products, the country's main export. Exports of integrated circuits, computer peripherals and pharmaceuticals declined sharply. The growth momentum in exports was maintained, however, by petrochemicals, civil engineering equipment and electrical machinery. The imports of Singapore as an entrepôt are closely linked to its exports, and along with the decline in export growth, the rate of growth of merchandise imports also fell to 14.7 per cent in 2005 from 28.1 per cent in 2004. The service sector registered a small surplus led by exports of financial services that more than compensated the deficit in tourism and transport services. On the whole, the current account surplus remained high at 24.0 per cent of GDP.

Net FDI inflows to Singapore rose to $5.39 billion in 2004, and the positive trend continued in 2005 with the major recipients being finance, information and communication technology, biomedicine and food processing. However, there was a small deficit in the capital account as a result of the outflow of venture capital to overseas destinations, especially Hong Kong, China, and also by the reversal of foreign portfolio investments to more attractive destinations in emerging markets elsewhere. Other developments in 2005 were a bilateral free trade agreement with the Republic of Korea and the Closer Economic Cooperation Agreement with India, which included substantial tariff concessions on the country's imports from Singapore.

The main exports of Brunei Darussalam, oil and gas, account for 90 per cent of its export revenue. The rise in international prices for these products more than compensated the sharp decline in exports of textiles and garments following the abolition of quotas under the WTO Agreement on Textiles and Clothing, causing the overall rate of growth of merchandise exports to rise by 6.4 per cent in 2005 from 2.1 per cent in 2004. The country's main merchandise imports are machinery, manufactured goods and food products, and these grew more slowly in 2005 at 6 per cent than in 2004, at 22.4 per cent. One reason for the slower import growth could be the food product prices driven higher by rising oil prices. The merchandise trade surplus was supported by income from the country's substantial overseas investments, leading to a large current account surplus in 2005. In that year, Brunei Darussalam also acceded to the Trans-Pacific Strategic Closer Economic Partnership, granting considerable tariff concessions to New Zealand under the terms of the agreement.

FDI flows to Brunei Darussalam fell sharply to just $103 million in 2004, the lowest level in a decade after reaching a record high of $2 billion in 2003. Oil companies from the Netherlands and the United Kingdom account for the bulk of FDI in Brunei Darussalam. However, the Government is concerned that the country's oil reserves may run out within 12 years or so at current rates of production. The strong policy statement of the Government on the need to diversify away from the oil and gas sector may have been responsible for the decline in FDI.

Medium-term prospects and key policy issues

Prospects are encouraging, but the subregion faces important policy issues concerning competitiveness

With the revival in the global demand for electronics products and the improved performance of the economies of Japan and the United States, the economic growth rate in South-East Asia is expected to rise from 5.4 per cent in 2005 to 5.9 per cent in 2006. Oil prices are expected to remain above historic averages in both 2006 and 2007, benefiting oil exporters such as Brunei Darussalam, Malaysia and Viet Nam. Stronger export performance, larger remittances and higher income from overseas investments are likely to result in current account surpluses for most countries within the subregion. Monetary policy has been tightened in response to inflationary pressures since the second quarter of 2005, and this stance is expected to continue in 2006 with interest rates staying slightly ahead of international rates in order to attract foreign capital. Assuming that oil prices do remain higher than their 2005 levels, the overall inflation rate should rise modestly from 5.8 per cent in 2005 to 6 per cent in 2006 as subregional currencies are also expected to appreciate somewhat against the dollar, partially offsetting the higher prices of dollar-denominated oil imports. In addition, most countries in the subregion have been following a policy of fiscal consolidation, and this is expected to continue into 2006, with the exception of Thailand and Viet Nam, which are expected to use a moderate amount of fiscal stimulus to promote growth.

While the broad outlook for South-East Asia is promising, a number of risks and uncertainties remain because of recent regional and global developments. The phasing out of textiles and garments quotas under the WTO Agreement on Textiles and Clothing is likely to worsen the export performance of the subregion with countries such as Brunei Darussalam, the Philippines and Viet Nam losing out to China and the South Asian countries that have a comparative advantage in this sector. Economic restructuring aside, two medium-term policy options would seem to be available to South-East Asian countries for the textile and garment export problem: a move up the value chain (for example, manufacturers in Thailand developing the capacity for producing superfine luxury blends or those in Sri Lanka producing women's wear) and an emphasis on emerging niche markets, such as that for eco-friendly fabrics manufactured employing fair labour practices and high safety standards for the environment and catering to socially conscious customers.

A highly pathogenic strain of avian influenza could develop into a human pandemic and that could severely hamper the growth prospects of the subregion, especially for its fastest growing economy, Viet Nam; the country has already reported the highest number of human cases. Such an influenza pandemic would also slow economic growth in other countries in the subregion, with tourism likely to be affected the most severely. Containment and preventive measures need to be taken, including making widely available antiviral drugs. The formulation of a regional contingency plan for strengthening integrated health surveillance systems and for creating wider awareness of the potential severity of the problem would augment those efforts.

High oil prices pose a major risk for countries in the subregion, which import most of their energy. It there is no significant decline in energy prices, firms burdened with high fuel bills could see their profits affected as soon as the first quarter of 2006, thus indirectly having an adverse impact on national economic growth rates and raising inflationary pressure across the region. Each country's policy response will depend on the options that its macroeconomic fundamentals permit. These rarge from providing incentives to divert production from fossil fuel-intensive processes to raising taxes to discourage consumption, continuing with subsidies to avoid burdening firms with higher input costs and reducing incentives to prevent unsustainable budget deficits.

South-East Asian countries are still largely dependent for economic growth on labour-intensive, export-oriented manufacturing, something that China with its much larger labour force can do better. What can South-East Asia do under these circumstances? Some East Asian economies may be showing the way. Taiwan Province of China, for instance, has attempted to take advantage of the economic growth in China by restructuring its economy. It has transferred manufacturing units to mainland China to take advantage of cheaper labour and superior government incentives. It has also invested capital in Chinese start-up companies. For South-East Asia, restructuring by moving up the value chain domestically while shifting manufacturing to lower-cost locations within other South-East Asian countries is likely to yield economic benefits in the medium term, and Singapore has already taken important steps in this direction (see box II.4).

Box II.4. Singapore: restructuring for the future

With a per capita income of $24,220 in 2004, Singapore is the richest country in South-East Asia and the third most prosperous economy in Asia after Japan and Hong Kong, China. The remarkable success story of Singapore began in 1965, when it separated from Malaysia. Since then it has been based on a combination of sound macroeconomic fundamentals, exports (high-technology goods and services) and pragmatic policy initiatives designed to sustain the economic success of Singapore. Its strategy towards two important phenomena of current times, that is, the emergence of China and India as global economic powers and the information-technology revolution, can provide useful insights to other countries seeking innovative development strategies in an increasingly competitive, knowledge-based world.

Recognizing that labour costs and economies of scale make it difficult to out-compete the Asian giants in the production and export of manufactures, Singapore is aiming at a strategic repositioning of its economy to one that is driven by services rather than its traditional engine of growth: manufactures. An important element of this strategy is to collaborate with China and India rather than to compete with them. The recent purchase by Temasek Holdings, the Singapore Government's largest investment firm, of shares of China Construction Bank and its investments in the fast-growing cinema industry in India are part of this strategy.

The policy innovations with respect to the knowledge revolution are much more dramatic and interesting. Analysts have long been skeptical of the ability of Singapore to sustain a growth path that appeared heavily dependent on savings. In neoclassical growth economics, high savings alone help to achieve

(Continued on next page)

(Continued from preceding page)

only limited levels of economic development. Further growth requires improvements in total factor productivity or technological and organizational improvements. Singapore has immersed itself aggressively in the knowledge economy. While most countries are focusing on technology and knowledge, Singapore has placed its objectives ahead of the curve by becoming the first country to emphasize creativity through public policy. This strategy includes inviting creative people to work in Singapore, building the infrastructure for creativity, offering creative experiences at the high end of tourism and changing the education system so that creative teaching tools are used at stages of schooling even below the university level.

The initial success of the country's strategy to become a hub of technological change can be seen from the large number of information technology, financial services, pharmaceutical and food-processing multinational corporations that have set up research and development units, attracted by the world-class research facilities.[a] However, there are some doubts about the ability of Singapore to retain its acquired stock of foreign scientists, doctors, engineers and artists over the long term. Recent writings on creativity emphasize the importance of tolerance as one of three pre-requisites of a creative hub, the other two being access to technology (such as broadband) and the availability of social amenities (museums, clean air).[b] While the technological infrastructure in Singapore is one of the most advanced in the world and the cultural and ecological environments are excellent, Singapore has followed a hard-line approach towards the more open and tolerant lifestyle options found in leading creative cities in North America, Europe and Australia. Recently, the Government approved construction of two large casinos, which could signal a turn towards a less restrictive approach. A proposal to permit shows along the lines of night clubs in Paris is also receiving consideration. These are signs that official attitudes are becoming much more flexible and accommodating to the requirements of a modern creative society.

---

[a] *World Investment Report 2005: Transnational Corporations and the Internationalization of R&D* (Geneva, UNCTAD, 2005) Sales No. E.05.II.D.10.

[b] Richard, Florida, *The Rise of the Creative Class and How It Is Transforming Work Leisure, Community and Everyday Life* (Cambridge, Mass., Basic Books, 2002).

LEAST DEVELOPED COUNTRIES

Since the least developed countries in the region are relatively small and narrowly based economies, their economic growth is easily affected by subregional, regional and external developments. These factors may be natural events, such as the 2004 tsunami, or external policy developments, such as implementation of duty-free and quota-free market access for products originating from these countries.

The agricultural sector accounts for a larger share of economic output and employment in these countries than in most other developing countries in the Asian and Pacific region. As a result, weather is often a major factor determining the overall economic growth and well-being of the largely rural population in these countries. Owing to the steady growth in garment manufacturing, energy-related extractive industries and tourism, the contribution from the agricultural sector to overall economic output has generally declined.

Growth in the industrial and service sectors of the least developed countries was adversely affected by the expiration of the WTO Agreement on Textiles and Clothing, rising petroleum prices and declining tourism as a result of outbreaks of avian influenza and over-dependence on subregional markets. Since most least developed countries have limited scope for exercising an independent monetary policy, inflation is often determined largely by inflationary pressures in their major trading partners and the movement of their exchange rate. Diversification and resilience are essential if least developed countries are to overcome any adverse outcomes resulting from these possible risk factors.

A critical challenge for the least developed countries is to identify what kinds of public action can facilitate development and poverty reduction in a globalized economy, without posing barriers to international trade.

South Asia

GDP growth performance

Economic growth in Afghanistan increased owing to a rebound in agriculture

In Afghanistan, real GDP growth for 2004 was pushed up to 8 per cent as a result of the buoyant manufacturing sector (see figure II.34). The growth rate was projected to reach 13.6 per cent in 2005 as the agricultural sector rebounded following better winter and spring rainfall and the manufacturing and services sectors continued to experience strong growth. Despite the rebound in yields, the production of opium and other narcotics was projected to fall in 2005 as anti-narcotics efforts and alternative livelihood programmes intensified and low farm-gate production contributed to a decline in cultivation of the opium poppy.

With the slowdown in rent and food price increases, inflation in Afghanistan declined from 16.3 per cent in 2004 to 11.5 per cent in June 2005, and from 11.3 to 9.0 per cent, excluding rents and petroleum products. With monetary tightening, inflation was expected to decline further to 10.0 per cent by the end of the 2005. Owing to significant donor and drug-related inflows, the market-determined value of the afghani appreciated by 15 per cent in real terms in 2004. The external competitiveness of Afghanistan was expected to weaken further unless a higher level of productivity was achieved.

Bangladesh continues to experience strong industrial sector growth despite the loss of preferential treatment for apparel manufactures

Real GDP growth in Bangladesh was expected to fall from 6.3 per cent in 2004 to 5.4 per cent in 2005, owing to floods which inundated more than a third of the country's land surface at the beginning of the fiscal year. In addition to damaging crops, particularly rice, the floods destroyed housing and infrastructure. Total losses to assets and output were estimated at 3.8 per cent of GDP. Although growth in the industrial sector was initially expected to moderate with the expiration of the WTO Agreement on Textiles and Clothing, apparel exports, led by knitwear, continued to experience double-digit growth in 2005. The construction sector also grew strongly because of heavy investment by the public and private sectors. Growth in the service sector resulted from increased activity in wholesale and retail trade, transport, storage, communications and real estate. Agricultural output declined, dropping its sectoral share to slightly more than one fifth of GDP. The service sector accounted for nearly half of the total output of Bangladesh.

The impact of the floods, combined with a surge in oil and commodity prices, contributed to a rise in inflation, projected at an annual average rate of 6.5 per cent for 2005. The taka, which had generally remained stable since the adoption of the floating exchange rate regime in 2003, depreciated by 5 per cent against the dollar in early 2005.

Investment in hydropower in Bhutan led to expansion in the construction and transport sectors

In Bhutan, economic growth was projected to rise from an estimated 8.7 per cent in 2004 to about 9 per cent in 2005. Growth in 2004 was the result of expansion in transport and mining and quarrying, along with construction of the Tala hydropower project, increased government expenditure on roads and other communication facilities and a recent surge in private housing construction. The electricity-generation sector accounted for 12 per cent of GDP, and its share was expected to rise with completion of the Tala project in 2006. In addition to generating significant revenue for Bhutan through the export of electricity to India, hydropower generation is creating additional business opportunities and benefiting rural communities. The Governments of Bhutan and India signed a memorandum of understanding in 2003 for the construction of the Punatsangchhu hydroelectricity project. The tourism industry, which generates convertible currency earnings, is the most important service industry in Bhutan. Both tourist arrival and earnings increased by almost 21 per cent between 2003 and 2005.

Figure II.34. GDP and sectoral growth in selected least developed countries in South and South-West Asia, 2003-2005[a]

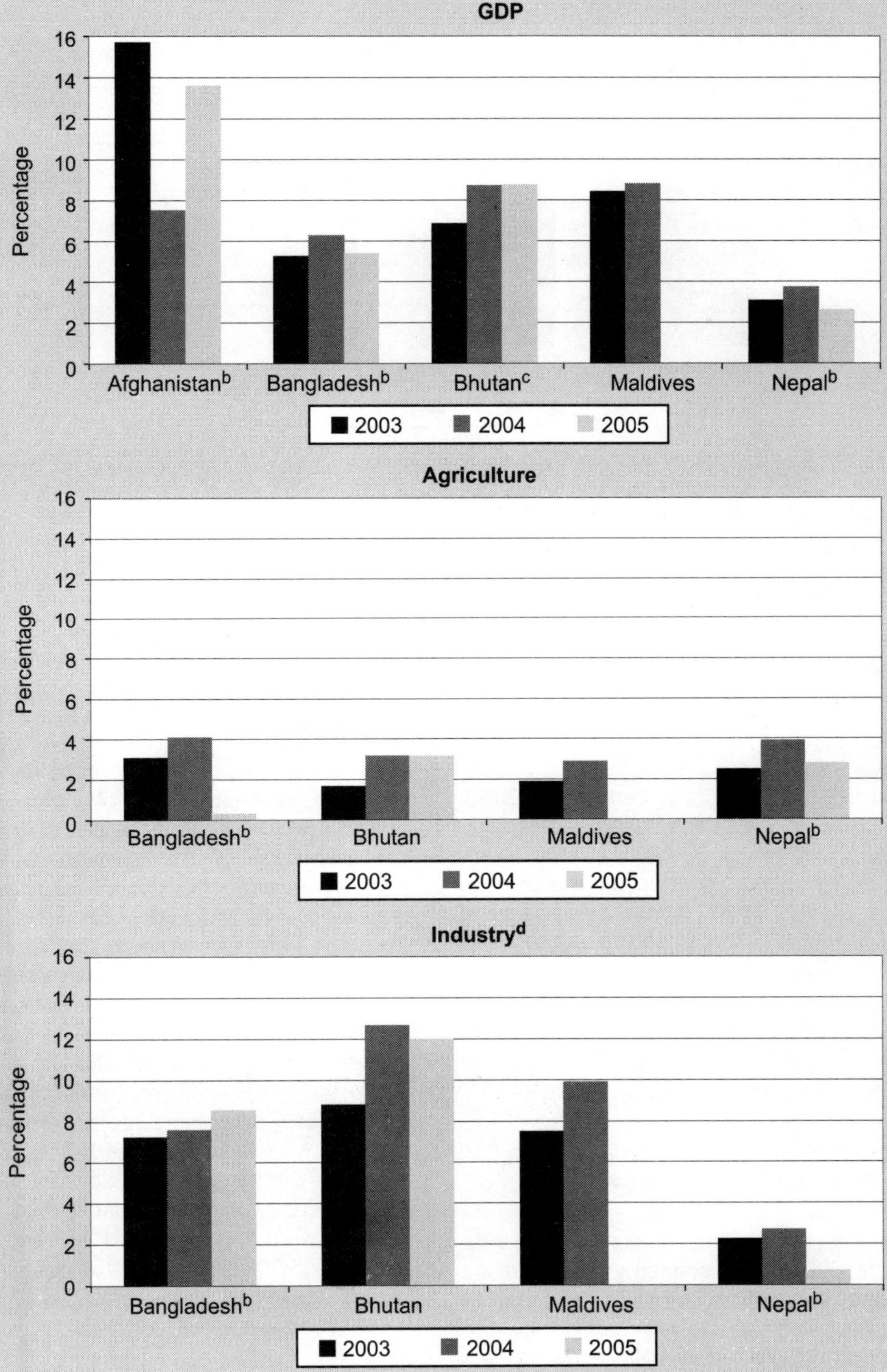

(Continued on next page)

Figure II.34 *(continued)*

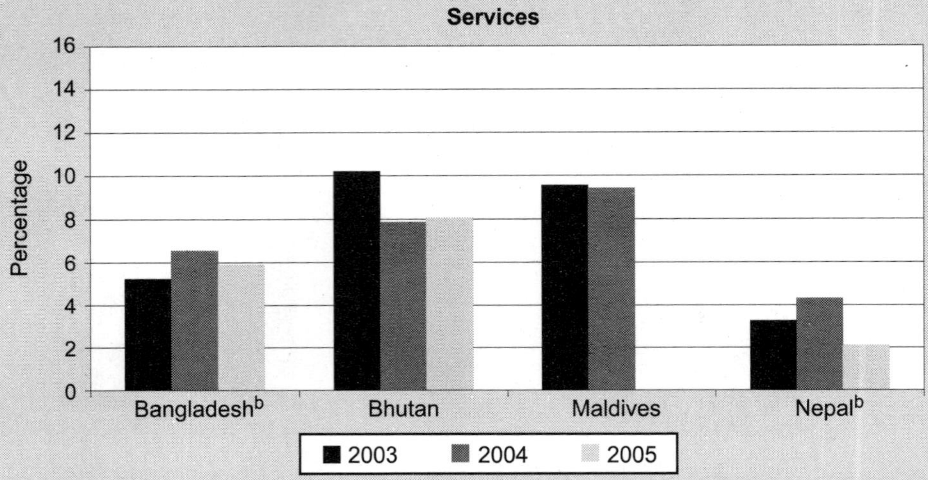

Sources: United Nations Economic and Social Commission for Asia and the Pacific, based on national sources; International Monetary Fund, *IMF Executive Board concludes 2004 Article IV Consultation with the Islamic State of Afghanistan,* Public Information Notice No. 05/9 (Washington, D.C., IMF, 2005); Bangladesh Bank website <www.bangladesh-bank.org>, accessed on 18 November 2004; Royal Monetary Authority of Bhutan, *Selected Economic Indicators* (CD-ROM) (Thimphu, 2004); and Nepal Rastra Bank, *Economic Survey 2003/04* (Kathmandu, 2004).

[a] Growth rates for 2005 are estimates.
[b] Fiscal year.
[c] GDP at factor cost.
[d] Comprising mining and quarrying; manufacturing; electricity-generation, gas and power; and construction.

Annual inflation rose from an average of 4.6 per cent in 2004 to 5.5 per cent in the 2005, owing to increasing oil prices, price movements in India and rising labour costs and local commodity prices, including construction material. In line with the strengthening Indian rupee against convertible currencies, the ngultrum appreciated 1.8 per cent in 2005. The ngultrum is pegged at parity to the Indian rupee in view of the extensive trade between the two countries and the role of India as the main source of official capital inflow.

Maldives is slowly recovering from the impact of the tsunami

In contrast to the 8.8 per cent growth rate registered in 2004, the economy of Maldives was projected to contract by 2.4 per cent in 2005, a result of the recession caused by the tsunami in late 2004 and rising oil prices. Although loss of life was limited, housing and infrastructure were damaged, the country's limited agricultural land was flooded with salt water and 5 per cent of the population lost their homes. Reconstruction of infrastructure and housing was difficult because of the geographical dispersion of the damage. Low population density outside the capital city increased the cost of service delivery as well. Tourism and fisheries normally account for 40 per cent of GDP and one third of employment; these sectors generate the bulk of foreign currency earnings. As a result of the tsunami, a quarter of the resorts were temporarily closed, resulting in a sharp fall in tourist arrivals and occupancy rates. A tenth of the fishing fleet and some processing facilities were also damaged or lost, thus affecting the fisheries sector, which accounts for most of the country's merchandise exports. These key sectors were not expected to recover until the end of 2005. The construction and transport sectors, however, were expected to benefit from reconstruction-related activities.

Despite weakening activity, inflation was projected to rise from 6.4 per cent in 2004 to 6.8 per cent in 2005, as supply constraints led to temporary price increases of construction goods and transport services. The exchange rate of the rufiyaa is pegged to the United States dollar.

Economic growth in Nepal declined as the agricultural sector was adversely affected

Economic growth in Nepal declined from a rate of 3.7 per cent in 2004 to 2.6 per cent in 2005 owing to weak performance of the agricultural sector, which accounts for 40 per cent of the country's GDP. Growth in the industrial sector also declined, as construction activity slowed. Manufacturing, primarily of vegetable ghee, jute goods, thread and zinc sheet, rose slightly with increased exports to India, but production of garments declined with the expiration of the WTO Agreement on Textiles and Clothing. Although the electricity sector grew by 8 per cent, it contributed little to industrial sector growth since its share of output remains small. Growth in trade and the restaurant and hotel sector also declined as intensified civil strife reduced tourist arrivals, adversely affecting hotel businesses and domestic trade. The transport and communication sector, however, continued to grow owing to expansion of private airlines and communication services. Non-bank financial services continued to grow, but banking services, which account for about four fifths of the formal financial sector, slowed because of low private sector demand for credit. The community and social services sector grew by 3.9 per cent, following increased compensation of public sector employees.

Despite the rise in prices of foodgrains, pulses, sugar and related products, inflation rose only slightly, from 4.0 per cent in 2004 to 4.5 per cent in 2005, moderated by relatively low inflation in India and an appreciating nominal exchange rate. The index for fuel, light and water rose by 14.7 per cent following revision of petroleum prices. The Nepalese rupee appreciated against the United States dollar in 2005 owing to appreciation of the Indian rupee against the dollar. The Nepalese rupee is pegged to the Indian rupee, which is freely convertible in Nepal.

Box II.5. The labour market in Asian least developed countries

Although detailed statistics are limited, changes in the sectoral economic output and the demographic profile of Asian least developed countries have led to shifts in the labour markets. In Bangladesh, for example, less than one seventh of the labour force is employed in the formal sector. Although the unemployment rate in 2003 was less than 5 per cent of the labour force, underemployment was estimated to be more than one third of the labour force. In such labour markets, wage levels are demand-driven rather than set by collective bargaining and they are indirectly indicative of employment trends. The rise in the fisheries and manufacturing wage indices in real terms in 2004, for example, suggested that there is demand for labour in these sectors, which could absorb new entrants into the labour force.

Since a significant share of the labour force in least developed countries is self-employed in the agricultural sector, rural unemployment and underemployment are major concerns. In Bhutan, where the agricultural sector accounts for nearly two thirds of the labour force, concerted measures are being undertaken to reduce rural poverty, including land reforms, extension of credit facilities, crop diversification and rural infrastructure development. Expansion of the industrial and service sectors in many least developed countries has led to an increase in the number of people employed in the formal sector.

In the Lao People's Democratic Republic, many people are now employed in mining, hydropower, trade and services.

An increasing number of youth are employed in the industrial and service sectors of Cambodia owing to expansion of garment manufacturing and tourism. Continued growth of these sectors is therefore critical to ensure that the labour force is fully employed.

(Continued overleaf)

(Continued from preceding page)

Shifts in the labour market are also the result of demographic changes. Since youth generally comprise a large share of the population in least developed countries, growth in the labour force is often high. The labour force in Nepal grew three times faster than domestic employment; as a result an estimated 5 per cent of the labour force was unemployed and an addition 12 per cent was underemployed in 2002. The international labour market currently accounts for one tenth of the labour force of Nepal.

Three fifths of the population of Timor-Leste is 16 years of age or younger. To generate enough jobs simply to maintain the current level of unemployment (estimated at one fifth of the labour force), the non-oil economy of Timior-Leste would have to grow 7 per cent annually. To halve unemployment in the medium term, annual non-oil economic growth in Timor-Leste would have to rise to 10 per cent. Such efforts would be complicated by the fact that wages in Timor-Leste remain significantly above those of its immediate neighbour, Indonesia.

Unemployment in least developed countries is high among youth and people with limited education. This suggests that education needs to be strengthened to ensure employability. In the Lao People's Democratic Republic, the number of years of primary education was expected to rise from five to six years, and access to tertiary and vocational education to be increased.

To reduce unemployment resulting from the mismatch between skills and job requirements, Bhutan has been strengthening its technical and vocational training to enhance skills.

Key macroeconomic policy developments

Afghanistan is expected to restructure plan of State-owned enterprises

With a budget financed from foreign grants as well as domestic revenue, Afghanistan is committed to preventing overdrafts in its fiscal budget. Owing to a significant increase in customs revenue and overflight charges, domestic revenues in the first quarter of 2005 exceeded their target, but more revenue is needed, since the ratio of savings to GDP remains low (see figure II.35). Improvements in budget preparation have reduced payment delays, notably for wages, and a supplementary development budget has been approved to incorporate additional donor-funded projects. A new public finance management law provides a transparent budget framework, a framework for internal control and audit and strict guidelines for budget formulation, execution and financing. In order to modernize the operations of Da Afghanistan Bank, the country's central bank, it is expected that its regulatory and institutional framework will be strengthened and all its commercial accounts will be transferred to commercial banks. A comprehensive restructuring plan for State-owned enterprises, with a view to eventually divesting them of commercial activities, was also expected to be instituted in 2005.

The budget deficit of Bangladesh increased owing to rural rehabilitation costs

The overall budget deficit of Bangladesh increased from 3.2 per cent of GDP in 2004 to 4.2 per cent in 2005 as funds were disbursed for rural rehabilitation following severe floods in July and August 2004 (see figure II.36). Revenue was projected to rise but would still fall short of the revised budget, owing to delays in tax administration reforms and weaknesses in audit and collection. Total spending was also expected to be lower than in the revised budget because development expenditure was lower than initially projected. With domestic financing capped at 2 per cent and external financing on concessional terms, the structure of deficit financing remains sound. Bangladesh adjusted gas, diesel and kerosene prices to reduce financial losses and improve the viability of State-owned enterprises in the energy sector. Although labour issues stalled closure of these enterprises, loss-making units were encouraged to downsize through hiring freezes and voluntary retirements.

Figure II.35. Savings and investment in selected least developed countries in South and South-West Asia, 2003-2005[a]

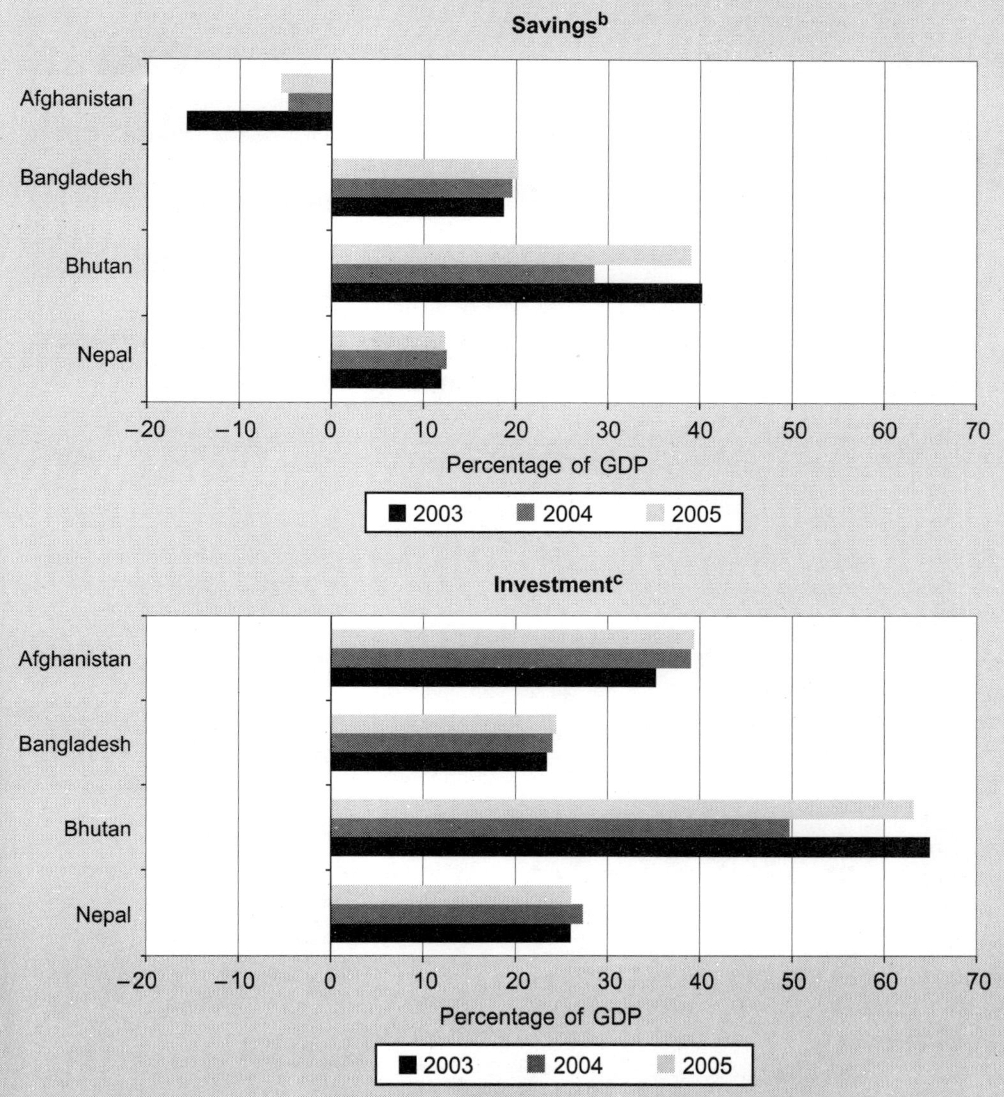

Sources: United Nations Economic and Social Commission for Asia and the Pacific, based on national sources; and Asian Development Bank, *Key Indicators of Developing Asian and Pacific Countries 2005* (Manila, ADB, 2005).

[a] Data for 2005 are estimates.
[b] Gross domestic savings.
[c] Gross domestic investment.

Growth in reserve money, private sector credit and broad money increased along with lending to the agricultural sector for flood rehabilitation and a strong demand for credit, in view of the low interest rates in Bangladesh (see figure II.37). To strengthen the banking system, Bangladesh Bank has raised minimal capital requirements, taken steps to reduce insider trading and improved the institutional framework for prudential supervision of the financial system.

Figure II.36. Budget balance in least developed countries in South and South-West Asia, 2003-2005[a]

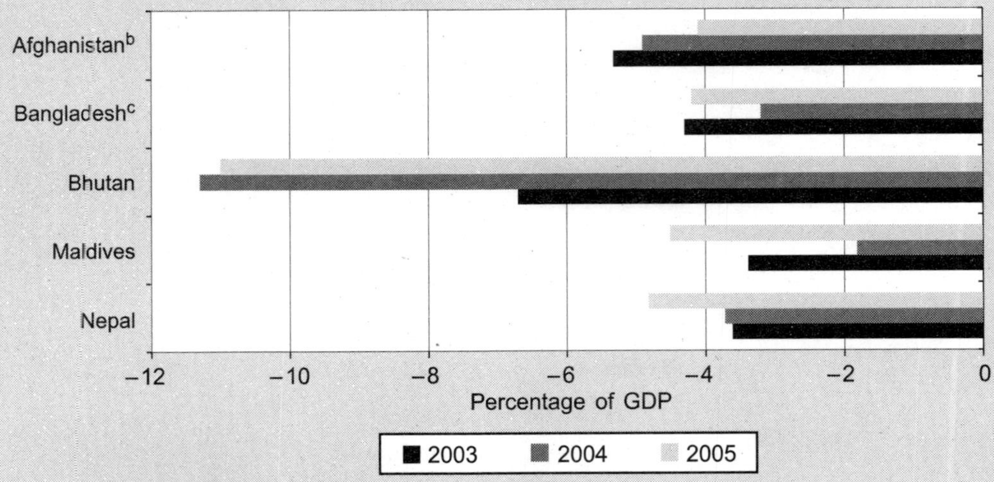

Sources: United Nations Economic and Social Commission for Asia and the Pacific, based on national sources; International Monetary Fund, *Islamic Republic of Afghanistan: Fourth Review under the Staff-monitored Program,* IMF Country Report No. 05/237 (2005); Bangladesh Bank website <www.bangladesh-bank.org>, accessed on 20 October 2005; Royal Monetary Authority of Bhutan, *Selected Economic Indicators* (CD-ROM) (Thimphu, 2005); and Asian Development Bank, *Key Indicators of Developing Asian and Pacific Countries 2005* (Manila, ADB, 2005).

[a] Data for 2005 are estimates.
[b] Operating budget balance, excluding grants.
[c] Excludes grants.

The tax system in Bhutan is being simplified and the tax base broadened

Although domestic revenue did not increase, expenditure in the revised budget of Bhutan for 2005 rose by 18 per cent to accommodate a 45 per cent increase in civil service salaries and the purchase of aircraft for the national airline. Both the overall and domestically financed government deficit for fiscal year 2005 was estimated at 11 per cent of GDP. In order to achieve the target of meeting current expenditure through domestic revenue, the tax system is being simplified by eliminating exemptions, phasing out tax holidays and broadening the tax base. The tenth five-year plan period, which will begin in July 2007, is to focus on rural electrification, construction of feeder and farm roads, education and health infrastructure and low-income housing. With its limited scope for an independent monetary policy, the Royal Monetary Authority of Bhutan has focused on indirect instruments of monetary management, such as increases in reserve requirements, the sale of central bank bills, the sale of foreign exchange to banks and the liberalization of interest rates to address the issue of excess liquidity. The central bank is also a key player in establishing a government securities market. Growth in net domestic credit, mainly in housing, contributed to growth in the money supply. Further expansion of credit by commercial banks is possible in the light of the higher liquidity and falling interest rates.

Reconstruction costs in Maldives are estimated at 50 per cent of GDP

The December 2004 tsunami resulted in the collapse of major economic activities in Maldives; reconstruction costs were estimated to be equivalent to 50 per cent of GDP, with a

Figure II.37. Inflation and money supply growth in least developed countries in South and South-West Asia, 2003-2005[a]

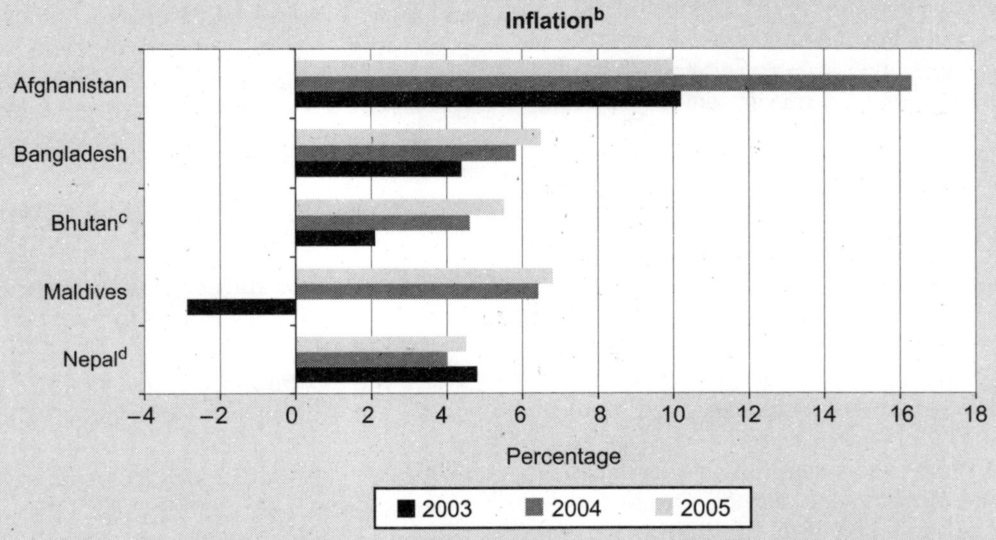

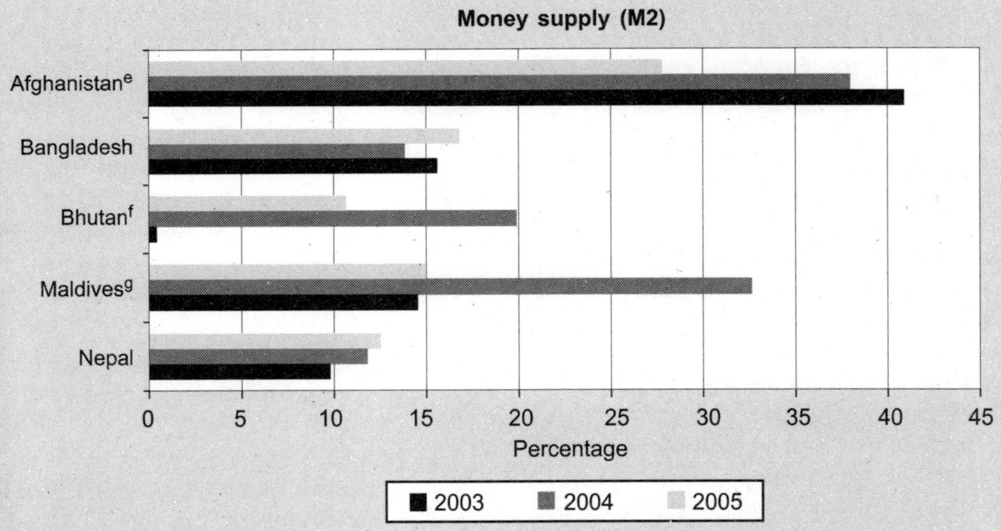

Sources: United Nations Economic and Social Commission for Asia and the Pacific, based on national sources; International Monetary Fund, *Islamic Republic of Afghanistan: Fourth Review under the Staff-monitored Program,* IMF Country Report No. 05/237 (2005); Bangladesh Bank website <www.bangladesh-bank.org>, accessed on 20 October 2005; Royal Monetary Authority of Bhutan, *Selected Economic Indicators* (CD-ROM) (Thimphu, 2005); Nepal Rastra Bank, *Economic Survey 2003/04* (Kathmandu, 2004); and Asian Development Bank, *Key Indicators of Developing Asian and Pacific Countries 2005* (Manila, ADB, 2005).

[a] Data for 2005 are estimates.
[b] Inflation rates refer to changes in the consumer price index.
[c] Inflation rates for 2004-2005 refer to the fourth quarter.
[d] Inflation rate refers to national urban consumer price index.
[e] Domestic currency in circulation.
[f] Money supply for 2005 refers to January-June.
[g] Money supply for 2005 refers to January-November.

quarter of that amount having been needed immediately to meet budgetary requirements. Budget allocations were redirected towards rehabilitation and reconstruction, and a comprehensive needs assessment was conducted in collaboration with the international community. A mechanism was also established for the spending of donor funds in a transparent and accountable manner. Greater monitoring of State-owned enterprises was expected to reduce operational expenses. A reduction in government revenue by 5 per cent of GDP was estimated owing to lower taxes on tourism. To raise the revenue, necessary for government operations, the government was expected to grant fewer import duty waivers for tourism, to reorient capital and non-wage spending towards reconstruction needs and to award no new wage increases. The bed tax increase in 2004 should have contributed to higher revenue as tourist arrivals resumed in 2005. The Government revised its budget in August 2005 and was also considering the auctioning of resorts to raise cash.

An increase in recurrent expenditure adversely affected the fiscal budget of Nepal

Despite the growth in government revenue, the fiscal budget of Nepal was adversely affected in 2005 by increased current expenditure and low capital spending. Government revenue rose from 12.6 per cent of GDP in 2004 to 13.4 per cent in 2005. A streamlined revenue structure was introduced with lower tax and tariff rates. Nepal also introduced a value added tax, consolidated tax administration and simplified tax payment procedures. The new medium-term expenditure framework has improved spending prioritization; it has also enabled consolidation of projects to avoid spreading resources too thinly and the allocation of resources to pro-poor projects. Spending on social sectors grew more quickly than spending on economic sectors. Spending on security also increased as the law and order situation deteriorated.

The industrial and commercial sectors accounted for three quarters of private sector credit in Nepal in 2005. The restructuring of two large banks, accounting for more than two fifths of commercial banking in Nepal, slowed credit expansion. The "Company act," "Insolvency act" and "Secured transaction act" were recently legislated to reduce systemic risk in the financial system. The "Central bank act" and the "Financial institutions act" were amended to make legal enforcement more effective. Despite the political instability in Nepal, stock market turnover, share prices and the market capitalization rose, and the market capitalization of listed companies grew from 8.4 per cent of GDP to 11.6 per cent during 2005.

Developments in the external sector

Re-exports constituted nearly three quarters of exports from Afghanistan

The current account deficit, excluding grants, of Afghanistan declined in 2004 owing primarily to a slowdown in imports (see figures II.38 and II.39). Imports of machinery and equipment, fabrics and clothing, and chemicals exceeded exports of dried fruits, skins and carpets, leading to an overall trade deficit. Re-exports constituted nearly three quarters of the country's projected exports. Although both FDI and concessional borrowing have increased, grants accounted for most of the overall current account surplus, equivalent to 0.7 per cent of GDP. Afghanistan is expected to rely on grants and highly concessional loans to meet its development needs for the foreseeable future. Despite a fall in bilateral debt, total external debt rose in 2003 as multilateral debt grew.

Bangladesh may eliminate quantitative restrictions on imports

Although the export earnings of Bangladesh moderated in 2005 as prices declined following the expiry of the WTO Agreement on Textiles and Clothing, preferential access to the European Union and Canada was expected to make up for any market share erosion in the United States. The value of imports rose owing to higher oil and commodity prices, increased food imports and higher demand for investment goods. The current account deficit was projected to be 1.7 per cent of GDP, with gross international reserves falling to 2.4 months of import cover. The level and dispersion of customs duty rates were reduced to three price-slabs; the quantitative restrictions were streamlined, with administrative procedures simplified and the

Figure II.38. Growth rates in merchandise export earnings and import spending in least developed countries in South and South-West Asia, 2003-2005

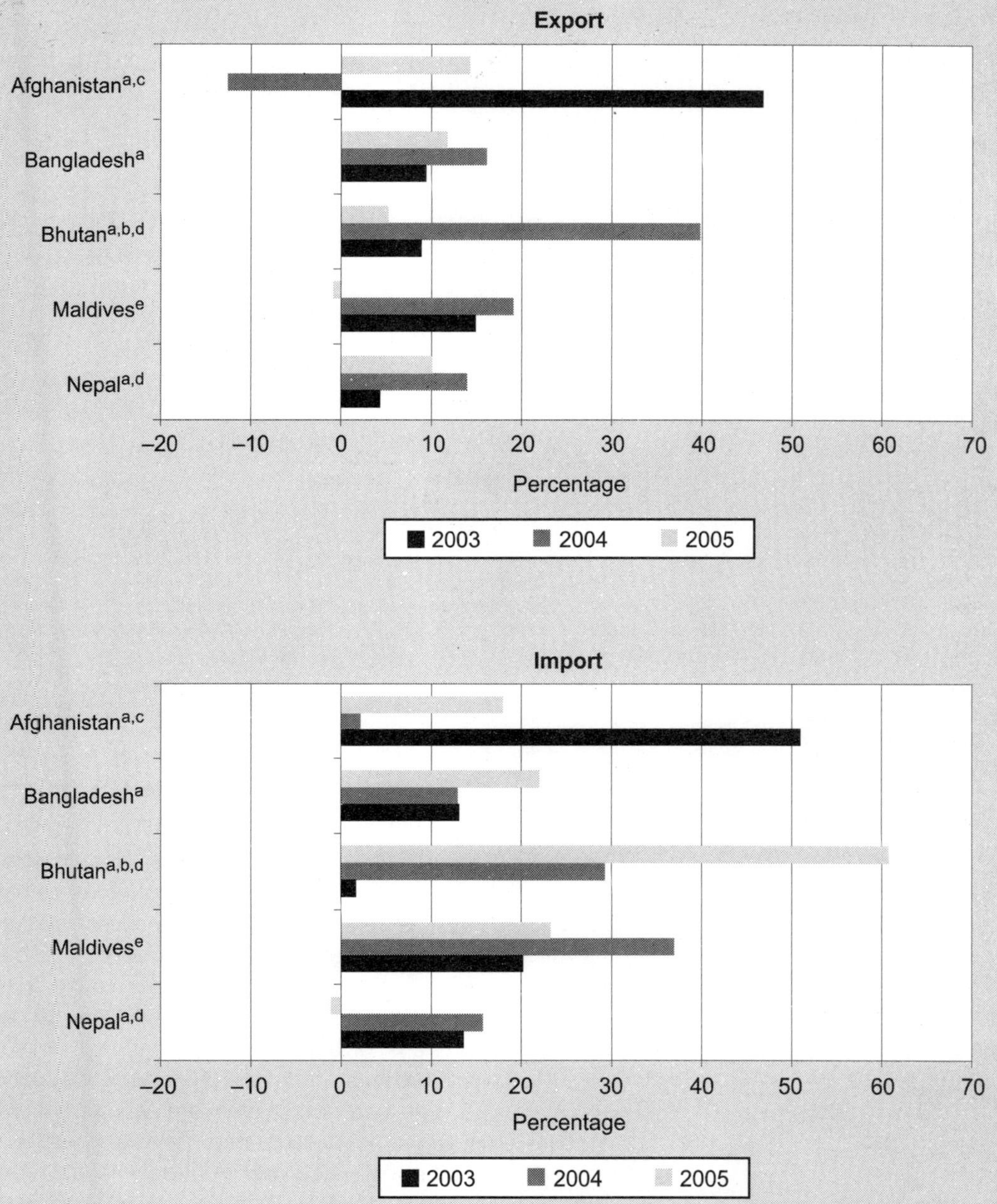

Sources: Economist Intelligence Unit, *Country Report Afghanistan* (London, EIU, 2005); Bangladesh Bank website <www.bangladesh-bank.org>, accessed on 11 November 2005; Maldives Monetary Authority website <www.mma.gov.mv>, accessed on 6 January 2006; and national sources.

[a] Fiscal years.
[b] Data for 2004 are provisional.
[c] Data for 2005 are projections.
[d] Data for 2005 are estimates.
[e] Data for 2005 are for first 6 months of the year.

Figure II.39. Current account balance in least developed countries in South and South-West Asia, 2003-2005[a]

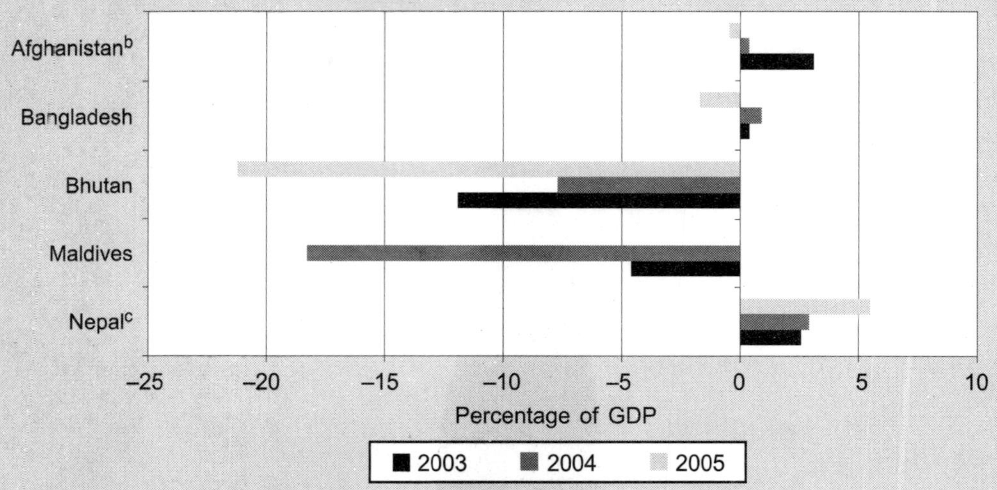

Sources: United Nations Economic and Social Commission for Asia and the Pacific, based on national sources; International Monetary Fund, *Islamic Republic of Afghanistan: Fourth Review under the Staff-monitored Program,* IMF Country Report No. 05/237 (2005); Bangladesh Bank website <www.bangladesh-bank.org>, accessed on 20 October 2005; Royal Monetary Authority of Bhutan, *Selected Economic Indicators* (CD-ROM) (Thamphu, 2005); and Asian Development Bank, *Key Indicators of Developing Asian and Pacific Countries 2005* (Manila, ADB, 2005).

[a] Data for 2005 are estimates.
[b] Includes grants.
[c] Includes official transfers.

number of restricted products halved. Restrictions were also removed on FDI in the garment sector outside of export processing zones. All trade-related quantitative restrictions on imports were expected to be eliminated and other non-tariff barriers streamlined in the 2006 budget in order to reduce the anti-export bias. The capacity of Chittagong port was also expected to be increased in order to reduce infrastructure bottlenecks.

The external debt outstanding of Bhutan rose to the equivalent of 86 per cent of GDP in 2005

Increased exports and transfer receipts narrowed the current account deficit in Bhutan to 7.7 per cent of GDP in 2004. In addition to the sale of electricity to India, which accounted for 36 per cent of the value of exports, exports included agro-based and mineral products and imports included capital equipment, food, fuel and consumer products. Countries other than India in the subregion collectively account for only 5 per cent of international trade. The trade deficit widened by 7.7 per cent owing to imports related to the Tala hydropower project and the purchase of aircraft for the national airline. Tourism receipts in convertible currency constituted 30 per cent of overall service sector receipts. However, service sector payments, such as labour remittances and debt-service payments, exceeded service receipts. Official current and capital transfers, largely in the form of grants and concessional loans and equivalent to 28 per cent of GDP, financed projects and the development of infrastructure. Commercial borrowings were negligible, and FDI, mainly in the tourism and hotel industries, was still relatively small. As a result, the balance of payments of Bhutan in 2004 recorded a surplus of 1.2 per cent of GDP, and foreign exchange reserves rose to nearly 20 months of import cover. Although external debt outstanding rose to 86 per cent of GDP in 2005, it was highly concessional and was largely the result of investment in hydropower projects. Indebtedness is not considered a serious concern; nevertheless, Bhutan welcomed the debt relief initiatives of the Group of Eight (G-8).

The loss of export receipts and tourism earnings led to a balance of payments shortfall in Maldives

The balance of payments shortfall in Maldives, owing to the loss of export receipts and tourism earnings because of the 2004 tsunami, was estimated at $160 million. Although $67 million was expected from bilateral donors and multilateral financial institutions in 2005, the shortfall could not be met by revenue measures and pledged donor grants. Since international reserves were low, donors and the International Monetary Fund were requested to provide assistance to enable the Government to leverage the balance of payments shortfall. The Paris Club was not requested to reschedule debt because most of the external debt was owed to international financial institutions and non-Paris Club countries. The debt service ratio was projected to be less than 5 per cent of the value of goods and services exports because of the highly concessional nature of the debt.

Transfer receipts in Nepal rose as pensions from abroad and remittances increased

Exports from Nepal continued to grow in 2005, but imports declined, resulting in a trade deficit equivalent to 14 per cent of GDP. More than two thirds of the exports from Nepal were imported by India. The share of petroleum products in the country's merchandise imports more than doubled between 2001 and 2005, as international oil prices rose. Service exports declined as tourism receipts fell, while service imports dropped owing to reduced travel payments to workers going abroad. Transfer receipts rose significantly, however, owing to a sharp rise in pensions from abroad, continuing growth in workers' remittances and a rise in government grant receipts. As a result, the current account surplus doubled to 5.5 per cent of GDP despite the trade deficit. The balance of payments surplus, however, declined from 3.2 per cent of GDP in 2004 to 1.8 per cent of GDP in 2005 because of a decrease in the capital account surplus.

The outstanding external debt of Nepal declined from 47.0 per cent of GDP to 44.5 per cent during 2005. Because of the concessional nature of its debt, Nepal does not qualify for debt relief under the Heavily Indebted Poor Countries Initiative and was unlikely to benefit from the G-8 debt relief package. Although the debt-servicing ratio was 9.7 per cent of exports in 2005, the burden was increasing with the maturation of old debts and the increase in outstanding debt. Foreign exchange holdings increased to 12 months of import cover by the end of 2005.

Medium-term prospects and key policy issues

Despite recent progress, poverty remains pervasive in most least developed countries. Governments need to give priority to promoting rapid and sustained economic growth. The primary goal must be to double the average household living standards as quickly as possible, since the average level of private consumption per capita currently is so low.

More than a simple expansion of GDP is required. Economic growth must be founded on the accumulation of capital, skills and productivity growth and the expansion of sustainable livelihoods and employment opportunities that increases the consumption possibilities of households and individuals.

While economic growth for poverty reduction is of paramount importance in the least developed countries, inequality and exclusion cannot be ignored. Efficiency-expanding redistribution of assets and income is important for sustained economic growth and poverty reduction in situations of generalized poverty.

Diversification is essential to ensure medium-term economic growth in Afghanistan

Economic growth in Afghanistan is projected to be at 11.2 per cent in 2006, and the agricultural sector should experience greater security and stable growth. However, to ensure growth in the medium term, greater diversification is essential. Inflation is expected to fall to 8.0 per cent by the end of 2006. Medium-term economic policies are expected to focus on facilitating the development of the private sector and on maintaining fiscal and external sustainability. Since domestic revenues cover only slightly more than half the operating revenues, a strong effort to cover operating costs with domestic revenues is needed. Strengthening the banking system is essential since a weak regulatory and institutional framework impedes the development of credit markets and the expansion of the private sector. The anti-narcotics strategy is expected to continue over the medium term but farmers need better long-term incentives to cultivate other crops to make the strategy a success.

Reconstruction costs and rising oil prices could affect growth in Bangladesh

Real GDP is expected to rise in Bangladesh to 6.5 per cent in the medium term and inflation to fall to 4.0 per cent, with increases in export diversification and private investment. Strong revenue efforts are expected to hold the budget deficit at 4 per cent of GDP. Reform of national commercial banks and State-owned enterprises is aimed at improving efficiency and fiscal sustainability. With the recovery of exports, the external current account deficit is expected to stabilize at 2 per cent of GDP, leading to a steady rise in international reserves to three months of import cover and to greater stability in the exchange rate (see figure II.40). However, growth could be adversely affected by developments in the garment sector, which accounts for a major portion of industrial production and exports; it could also be affected by higher than expected imports for flood-related reconstruction and a further rise in international oil prices. Based on this scenario, key reform measures include tax administration restructuring in order to increase revenue, divestiture of national commercial banks to contain fiscal losses, liberalization of the investment regime and reform of the energy sector to secure adequate supplies of power while ensuring fiscal sustainability.

Devolution of responsibility to local levels of administration would increase participation in Bhutan

As a landlocked country with a small domestic market, Bhutan has limited opportunities for diversified production and exports. The hydropower sector is expected to continue to play a significant economic role, with the commissioning of the Tala hydropower project in 2006, and to assist in the establishment of allied industries. The pristine environment of Bhutan and the preservation of its cultural heritage should continue to make tourism the second largest source of foreign exchange earnings after official inflows. Earnings from tourism have a broad impact, as they provide the Government with tax revenues, entrepreneurs with corporate income, enployees with wages and salaries and service providers and cottage industries with income. Bhutan has formulated regulations and prepared legislation to implement its policy on FDI. As a member of the South Asian Free Trade Area, Bhutan has agreed to lower import tariffs to between 0 and 5 per cent in 2006. Negotiations on the accession of Bhutan to WTO reached an advanced stage in September 2005. As Bhutan prepares to embrace parliamentary democracy, a draft constitution was publicly circulated in March 2005 for discussion, and a governance exercise was conducted. Emphasis is being placed on increasing participation in development decisions through the devolution of responsibility to the district and local levels of administration.

Recovery in the tourism and fisheries sectors of Maldives is expected in 2006

The tourism and fisheries sectors of Maldives are expected to recover in 2006. Rehabilitation and reconstruction of housing and infrastructure following the December 2004 tsunami are expected to take longer than previously expected and to require external financing until 2007. In view of the commitment of Maldives to maintaining the exchange rate peg, which had provided a transparent nominal anchor, the Government intends to limit borrowings or repayments to the Maldivian Monetary Authority in 2006 and to finance reconstruction from external grants and loans as well as savings in the budget. The eventual introduction of a tax on business profits is also expected to broaden the tax base.

Figure II.40. Index of exchange rates against the United States dollar in selected least developed countries in South and South-West Asia, 1996-2005[a]

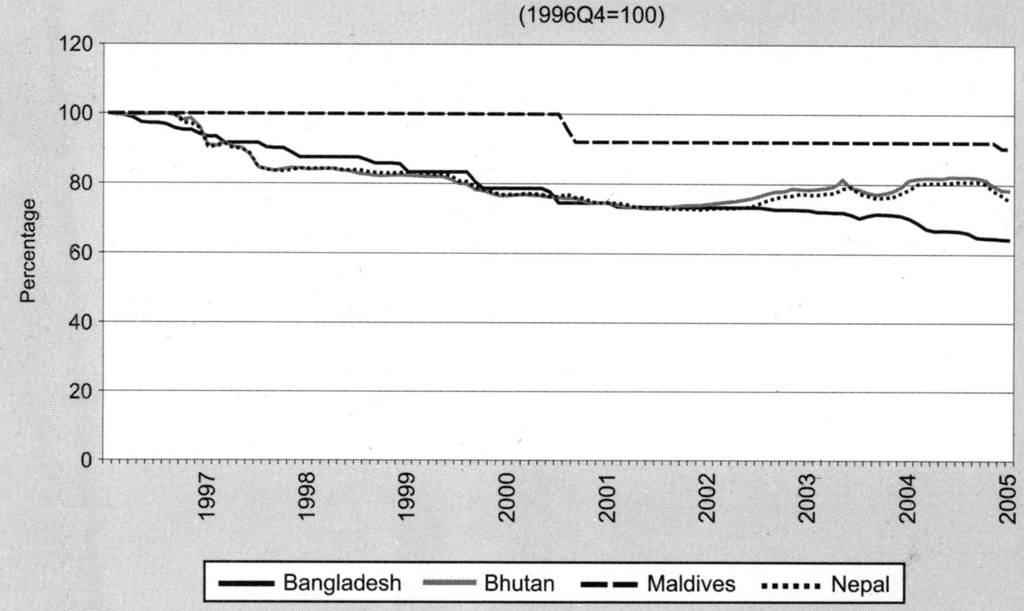

Sources: International Monetary Fund, *International Financial Statistics* (CD-ROM) (Washington, D.C., 2005); and *The Economist,* various issues.

[a] Data for 2005 are estimates.

Higher petroleum prices and expiration of the WTO Agreement on Textiles and Clothing could slow growth in Nepal

With higher petroleum prices, expiration of the WTO Agreement on Textiles and Clothing and intensification of armed conflict, GDP growth in Nepal could fall short of the 4.5 per cent rate projected for 2006. Exports to India are expected to rise, but production for the domestic market may remain suppressed owing to disruptions to domestic transport and commerce. Electricity-generation, gas and water supplies are projected to grow with the completion of new, small, power projects and better capacity utilization. With the upward adjustment of petroleum prices and increased pressure on prices in India, inflation is projected to rise by 5 per cent. Since monetary expansion has slowed and economic growth is expected to be reasonable, moderate inflation is projected in the medium term. To compensate for the investment shortfall in implementation of the Tenth Plan (Poverty Reduction Strategy Paper), the 2006 budget projects significantly higher government expenditure, revenue and grants than had been contained in the revised 2005 estimates.

The continuing conflict and economic slowdown in Nepal suggest that attaining its revenue-mobilization and capital-spending targets may be difficult. With the expiration of the WTO Agreement on Textiles and Clothing, exports from Nepal are expected to grow by 7 per cent in 2006. Higher oil prices, moderate economic growth and remittance-financed demand for consumer goods are likely to lead to import growth. Despite the increase in remittances and official grants, the current account is expected to weaken with the drop in income from services. The overall surplus in the balance of payments is projected to decline from 1.8 per cent of GDP in 2005 to 1 per cent in 2006.

South-East Asia

GDP growth performance

Garment production in Cambodia is expected to grow as safeguards are imposed

Economic growth in Cambodia was projected to fall slightly, from 7.7 per cent in 2004 to 6.3 per cent in 2005 (see figure II.41). Although growth in the agricultural sector was estimated to be higher in 2005 because of increased paddy production, growth in the industrial and service sectors was expected to be moderate. Growth in the service sector was a result of the expansion in tourism and increased domestic activities including construction. Tourism arrivals were expected to rise by one third in 2005. Growth in garment production was expected to continue as safeguards were imposed by the United States and the European Union. Forty new investment projects were approved in 2004, and garment orders increased in 2005.

Figure II.41. GDP and sectoral growth in selected least developed countries in South-East Asia, 2003-2005[a]

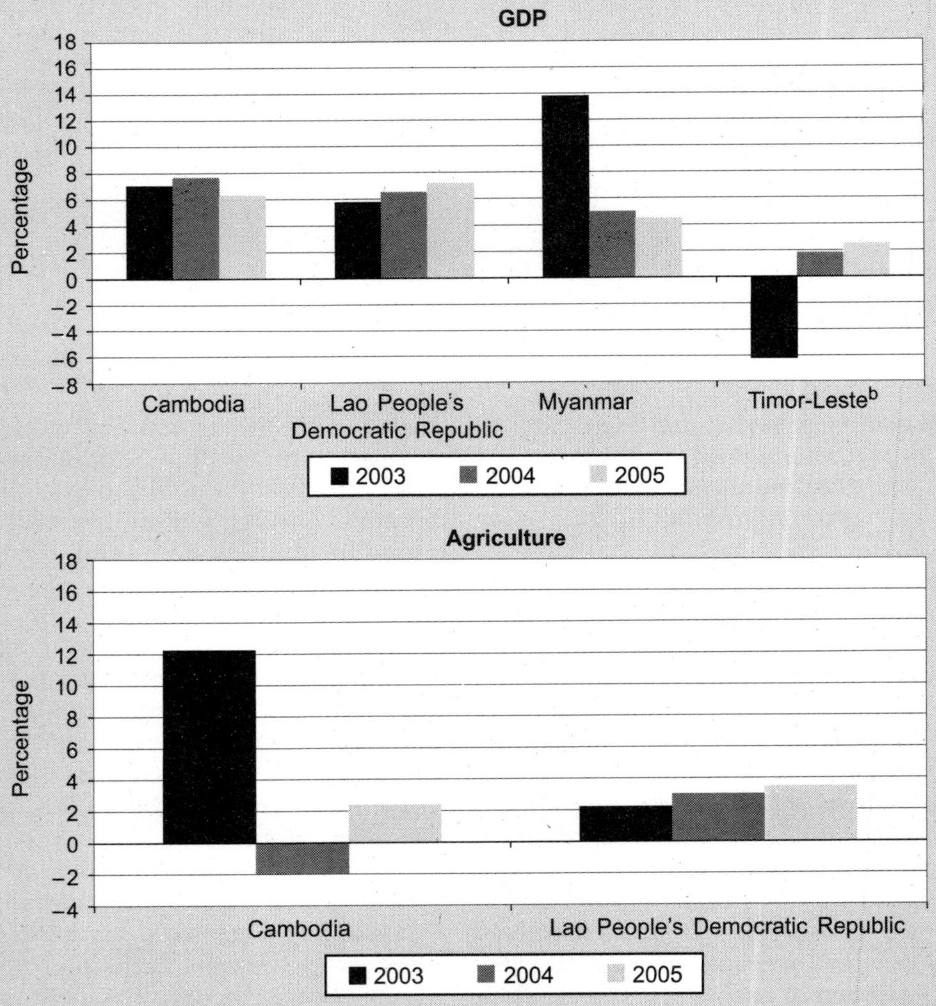

(Continued on next page)

Figure II.41 *(continued)*

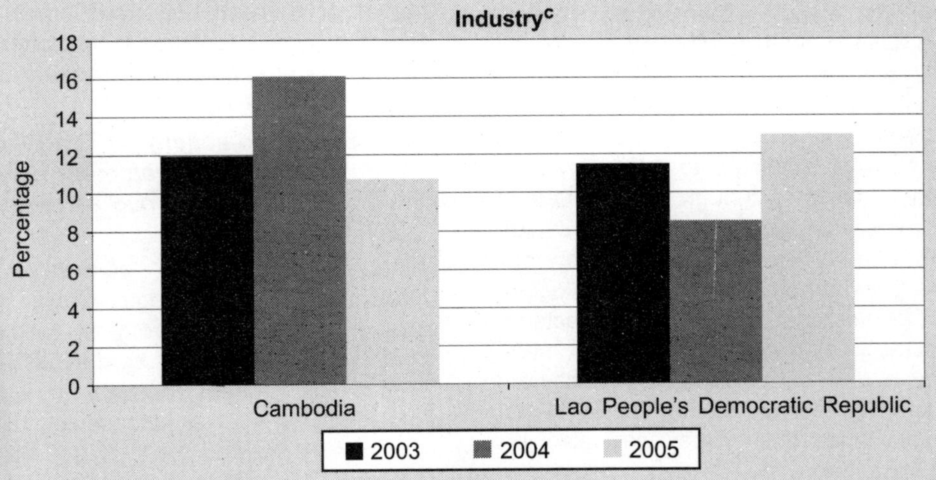

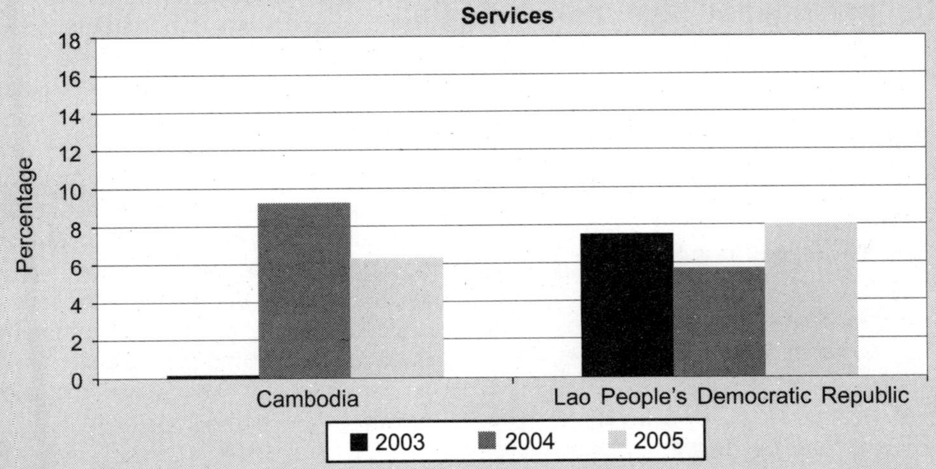

Sources: United Nations Economic and Social Commission for Asia and the Pacific, based on national sources; Asian Development Bank, *Key Indicators of Developing Asian and Pacific Countries 2005* (Manila, ADB, 2005); and International Monetary Fund, *Democratic Republic of Timor Leste: 2005 Article IV Consultation, IMF Country Report No. 05/245* (2005), "Cambodia: Statistical Appendix", IMF Country Report No. 05/245 (2005).

[a] Growth rates for 2005 are estimates.
[b] Real non-oil GDP growth.
[c] Comprising mining and quarrying; manufacturing; electricity-generation, gas and power; and construction.

Inflation in Cambodia was projected at 5.5 per cent in 2005, marginally lower than in 2004. In view of the country's large agricultural base, fluctuations in the prices of goods and services are seasonal. Drought in the first half of the year affected the production of crops and led to higher than expected food prices. Owing to the tax structure on oil imports and market oligopoly, inflation does not necessarily move in line with the prices of petrol and diesel. Because the United States dollar is widely used in the economy, domestic inflation is affected by changes in the exchange rate. In the first half of 2005, the riel depreciated against the dollar but strengthened against the baht.

Rising oil prices and declining paddy production are expected to boost consumer prices in the Lao People's Democratic Republic

In the Lao People's Democratic Republic, GDP was projected to rise from 6.5 per cent in 2004 to 7.2 per cent in 2005, led primarily by growth in mining and hydropower. Flooding in the central and southern paddy-producing areas of the country was expected to adversely affect the agricultural sector. Although growth was expected in the livestock and fisheries sectors, expansion in forestry was projected to slow as a result of the Government's policy to limit logging. Growth in the industrial sector was expected to rise considerably as production of gold nearly doubled and a new copper smelting plant came into operation. The service sector, led by tourism and wholesale and retail trade, was also projected to grow strongly.

Inflation was projected to fall from 10.5 per cent in 2004 to 8.0 per cent in 2005, but rising global oil prices and the decline in paddy production caused by flooding were expected to push consumer prices upward towards the end of the year. The exchange rate remained generally stable as the central bank maintained a spread of less than 1 per cent between the official rate and the market rate.

The informal sector remains large in Myanmar

In fiscal year 2003, GDP in Myanmar rose by 13.8 per cent, led by growth in agriculture, livestock and fisheries, manufacturing and processing, and services. In addition to increased rice production to meet domestic needs and to earn foreign exchange, the production of wheat, maize, pulses, groundnuts and sunflower seeds increased. Since the agricultural sector accounts for more than half of GDP, agricultural reform is expected to have a large impact on much of the population. The construction and transport sectors also grew substantially in fiscal year 2003 as a consequence of a significant rise in public investment in infrastructure. The informal sector remains large in Myanmar.

Central bank financing of the fiscal deficit fueled inflation in Myanmar. New administrative controls on credit creation, rice exports and increases in public and private wages, however, effectively lowered inflation from 54 per cent in fiscal year 2002 to 8 per cent in fiscal year 2003. By reducing the price of rice, however, these measures lowered agricultural income in favour of domestic rice consumers. Private investment was also curbed, and employees experienced an erosion of real wages.

Economic activity in Timor-Leste is dependent on government expenditure and subsistence agriculture

In Timor-Leste, economic growth, as measured by the change in real non-oil GDP, was projected to rise from an estimated 1.8 per cent in 2004 to 2.5 per cent in 2005, as a result of the post-drought recovery in agriculture and expansion of the banking sector. The economic structure is skewed towards government activity, including donor-funded projects, and subsistence agriculture. Social indicators are poor, and human capital remains underdeveloped, leading to inadequate administrative capacity in both the private and public sectors. Targeted public investment in infrastructure, education and health, coupled with increased private investment in labour-intensive sectors, was intended to increase productivity. Revenue from off-shore oil and gas production was expected to contribute to non-oil domestic activity and employment through the fiscal channel. Long-term economic growth may depend largely on the Government's ability to manage its oil and gas wealth and to establish an environment conducive to investment and growth in the non-oil sector.

Inflation rose from an estimated 1.8 per cent in 2004 to a projected 2.5 per cent in 2005, as the official dollar-based monetary and exchange regime reined in inflation. Both domestic demand and non-oil import prices remained stable.

Key macroeconomic policy developments

Cambodia places priority on civil service reform and an overhaul of the infrastructure

Government revenue in Cambodia was projected to reach 11.3 per cent of GDP in 2005, and expenditure to reach 16.8 per cent of GDP. As with all least developed countries, savings remain low as a ratio of GDP (see figure II.42). Tax revenue increased considerably with the implementation of the public financial management programme and increased tax compliance. Although customs and excise revenue also rose, value added tax collection on petroleum products fell one fifth in the first half of 2005 because of fuel smuggling. The government budget for 2005 has placed priority on civil service reform and overhaul of the physical infra-

Figure II.42. Savings and investment in selected least developed countries in South-East Asia, 2003-2005[a]

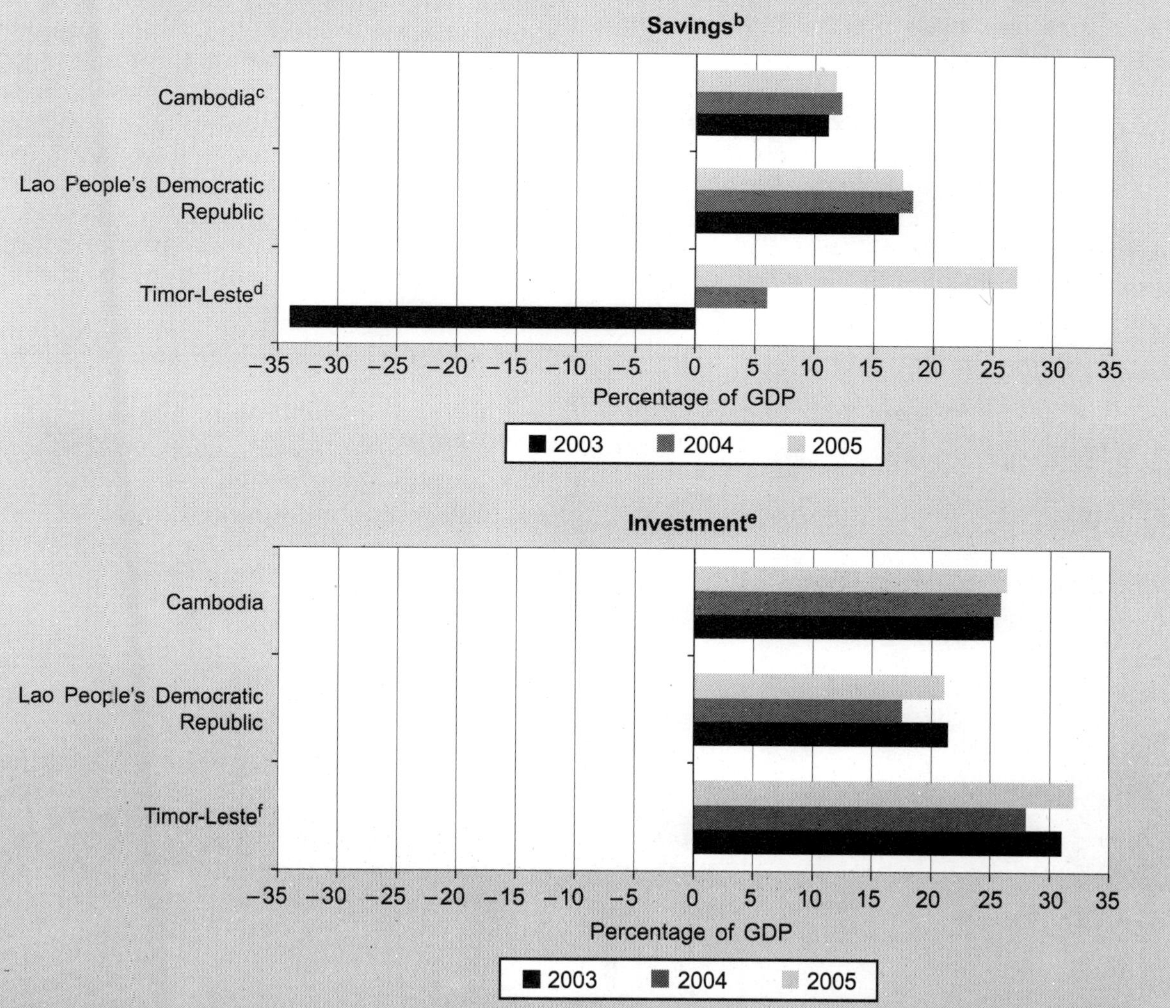

Sources: United Nations Economic and Social Commission for Asia and the Pacific, based on national sources; Asian Development Bank, *Key Indicators of Developing Asian and Pacific Countries 2005* (Manila, ADB, 2005); International Monetary Fund, *Democratic Republic of Timor-Leste: 2005 Article IV Consultation,* IMF Country Report No. 05/245 (2005).

[a] Data for 2005 are estimates.
[b] Gross domestic savings.
[c] Excluding transfers.
[d] Gross national savings.
[e] Gross domestic investment.
[f] Excludes investment relating to the oil and gas sector.

structure. Wages constitute 40 per cent of current expenditure. With completion of the bank relicensing programme in 2004, greater emphasis is being placed on strengthening the supervisory capacity of the National Bank of Cambodia and promoting a competitive banking sector. With privatization of the Foreign Trade Bank of Cambodia, the country is expected to complete its transition to a two-tier banking system in 2006. The central bank has also licensed rural finance operators as formal microfinance institutions under its legal and supervisory framework. Efforts were also made to establish an insurance sector as well as a capital market.

Stable price levels and exchange rates led to positive real interest rates in the Lao People's Democratic Republic

In the Lao People's Democratic Republic, government revenue, including grants, was estimated at 13.6 per cent of GDP in 2005, slightly less than its revised target, while expenditure was estimated to have slightly exceeded its revised target, to reach 19.9 per cent of GDP (see figure II.43). Although the fiscal deficit, including grants, was estimated to have nearly doubled during 2005, capital inflows were expected to offset most of the increase. The main sources of tax revenues were the turnover tax, excise tax and import duties, while non-tax revenues consisted mainly of overflight fees, dividends and depreciation, and administration fees. To ensure macroeconomic stability, the central bank has aimed at controlling growth in the money supply (see figure II.44). The monetary base was projected to increase by nearly one fifth between the end of 2004 and the end of 2005. As a result of the stable price level and exchange rate, interest rates at commercial banks and the real interest rate for domestic currency deposits were positive. Private savings as a share of

Figure II.43. Budget balance in least developed countries in South-East Asia, 2003-2005[a]

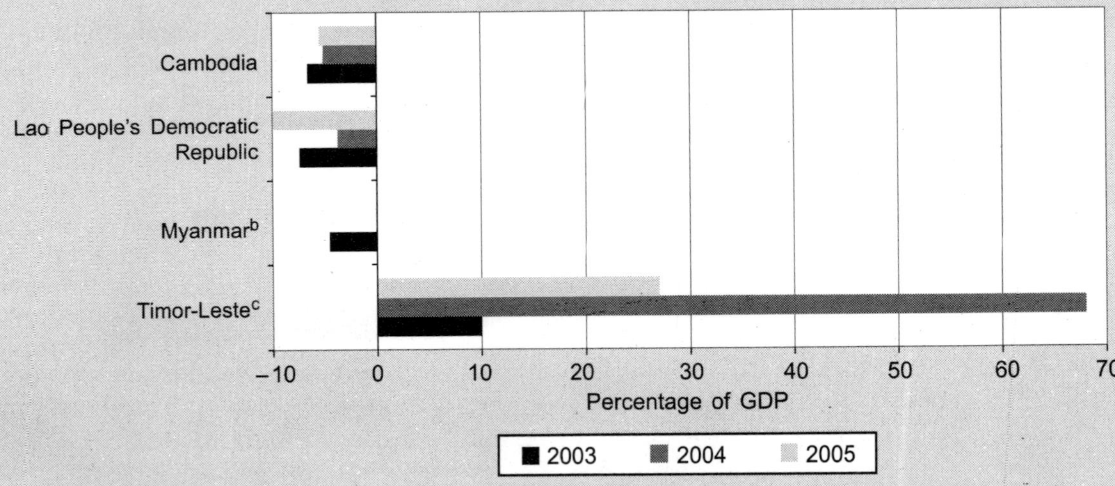

Sources: United Nations Economic and Social Commission for Asia and the Pacific, based on national sources; Asian Development Bank, *Key Indicators of Developing Asian and Pacific Countries 2005* (Manila, ADB, 2005) and *Asian Development Outlook 2005 Update* (Manila, ADB, 2005); Economist Intelligence Unit, *Country Reports* (London, EIU, 2005), various issues; and International Monetary Fund, *Democratic Republic of Timor-Leste: 2005 Article IV Consultation*, IMF Country Report No. 05/245 (2005).

[a] Data for 2005 are estimates.
[b] Includes grants.
[c] Calculated as a percentage of non-oil GDP and based on July-June fiscal year.

Figure II.44. Inflation and money supply growth in least developed countries in South-East Asia, 2003-2005[a]

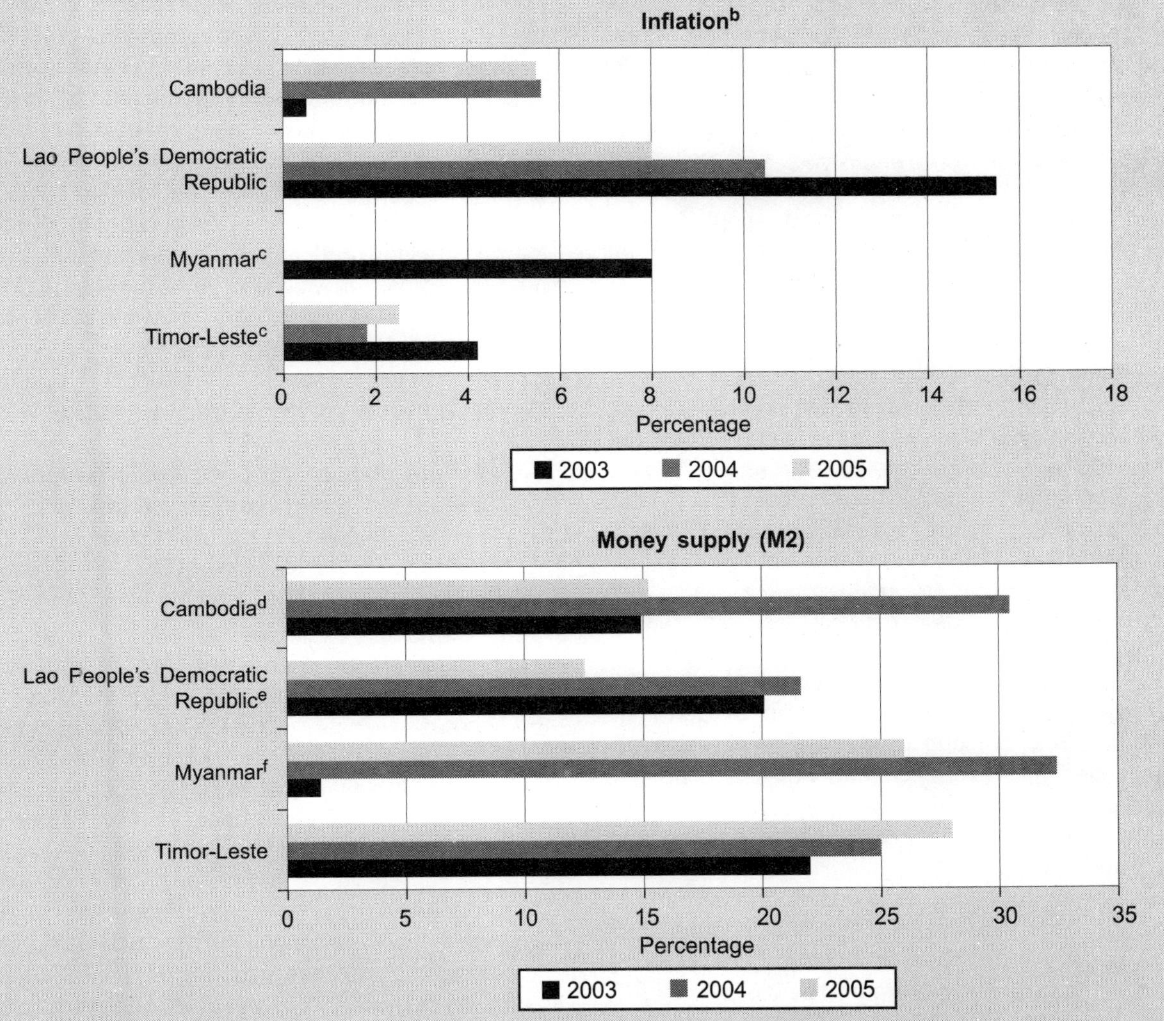

Sources: United Nations Economic and Social Commission for Asia and the Pacific, based on national sources; Asian Development Bank, *Key Indicators of Developing Asian and Pacific Countries 2005* (Manila, ADB, 2005); International Monetary Fund, *International Financial Statistics* (CD-ROM) (Washington, D.C., IMF, 2005) and *Democratic Republic of Timor Leste: Selected Issues and Statistical Appendix*, IMF Country Report No. 05/250 (2005).

[a] Data for 2005 are estimates.
[b] Inflation refers to changes in the consumer price index.
[c] Inflation rate for 2005 refers to data at the end of period.
[d] Money supply for 2005 refers to the period January-October.
[e] Money supply for 2005 refers to the period January-February.
[f] Money supply for 2005 refers to the period of January-September.

GDP were projected to rise slightly to 17.5 per cent of GDP in 2005, with foreign currency deposits constituting slightly more than three fifths of the total outstanding deposits. Total credit to the economy was expected to decrease slightly to 10.2 per cent of GDP in 2005, with industry and handicrafts taking the largest share, followed by commerce.

The official exchange rate used for tariff evaluation in Myanmar was adjusted upward

As a result of economic sanctions and a complete halt to financial assistance from multilateral institutions, Myanmar has been forced to rely largely on its own resources for more than two decades. As the country's budget deficit continued to widen in 2003, reducing its fiscal deficit through improved tax collection. Expenditure consolidation became essential in Myanmar. A motor vehicle registration fee was introduced to expand the tax base, combat tax evasion and increase tax revenues. Further improvements in tax revenues are expected based on the replacement of ad hoc exemptions with a more transparent set of rules, and the possible introduction of excise taxes on alcohol, tobacco and luxury goods as well as a value added tax. The official exchange rate used in import evaluation for tariff purposes was also recently adjusted upward. Since a large proportion of economic activities remain in the informal sector, efforts are needed to bring income from such sources into the tax net. Central government capital expenditure rose from 3.8 per cent of GDP in fiscal year 2002 to 5.8 per cent in 2003. Greater fiscal consolidation, reform of State enterprises and banking institutions, agricultural liberalization and exchange rate unification are expected to create the conditions necessary for more sustained economic growth. Confidence in the domestic financial system and the domestic currency is improving as a result of measures to enhance the liquidity and capital adequacy of the country's financial institutions. The banking sector has recovered from the crisis in 2003, and emergency liquidity supports from the central bank have been fully repaid. Earlier capital flight appears to be reversing, and the demand for domestic currency deposits are rising. Regulation and supervision of the banking sector are being strengthened to allow greater competition.

The petroleum fund of Timor-Leste is expected to be operational by early 2006

Despite large inflows of oil and gas revenues fiscal policy in Timor-Leste has remained cautious. Commencement of oil production in 2004 resulted in a large fiscal surplus, an increase in the external current account surplus and accumulation of international reserves equivalent to 15 months of imports. Efforts to ensure productive use of oil and gas revenue are needed. The petroleum fund was expected to be operational by the beginning of 2006. The rise in domestic revenue also reflects improved tax administration. Since Timor-Leste has avoided both domestic and international borrowings, it has no debt. Nevertheless, the implementation of public investment projects has been poor. Bank lending to the private sector increased threefold to 21 per cent of non-oil GDP by the end of 2004, with most funds being used for construction and small transport-related businesses. Gross investment in Timor-Leste was projected to rise to 32 per cent of GDP and gross national savings to 27 per cent.

Developments in the external sector

Under the Multilateral Debt Relief Initiative, the International Monetary Fund has extended 100 per cent debt relief to Cambodia

Cambodia registered a surplus in its balance of payments in the first half of 2005, but its current account deficit widened because of the increased costs of petroleum, which constituted a quarter of domestic imports (see figures II.45 and II.46). Garment exports under the Generalized System of Preferences, which made up more than four fifths of exports, were expected to face increasing competition in the medium term. Other exports, such as lumber and fishery products, have declined in recent years. The surplus in the services account increased significantly owing to improvements in tourism and air freight. FDI rose with the strengthening of the banking sector and expansion in the garment sector and in tourism.

Repayment of external debts incurred prior to 1993 is being negotiated with the Russian Federation and the United States. Under the terms negotiated with the Russian Federation, the debt service ratio of Cambodia is expected to be the equivalent of 2 per cent of exports over the next decade. Debt rescheduling is expected to reduce amortization payments but could increase interest obligations. Under the Multilateral Debt Relief Initiative, IMF extended 100 per cent debt relief to Cambodia in late 2005.

Figure II.45. Growth rates in merchandise export earnings and import spending in least developed countries in South-East Asia, 2003-2005

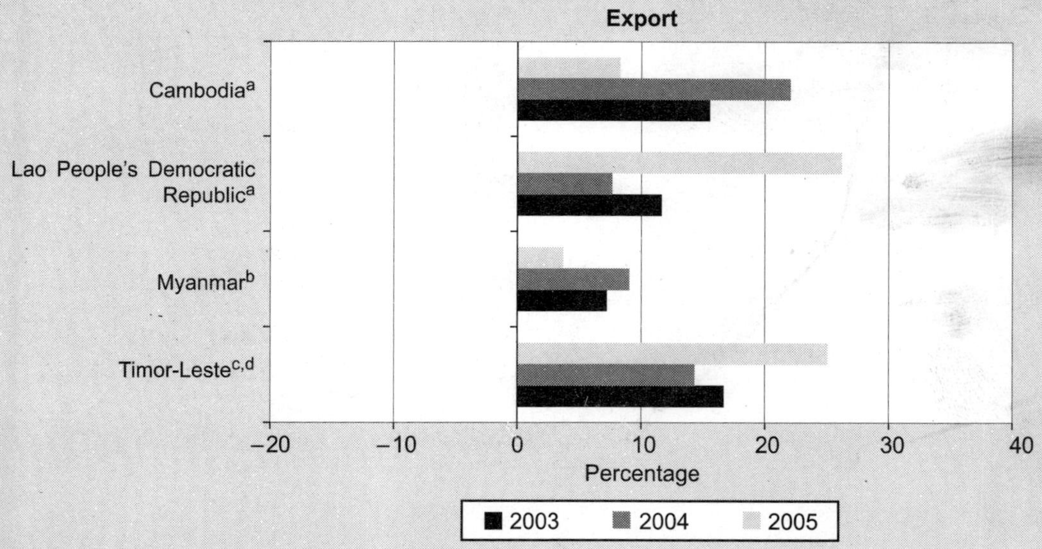

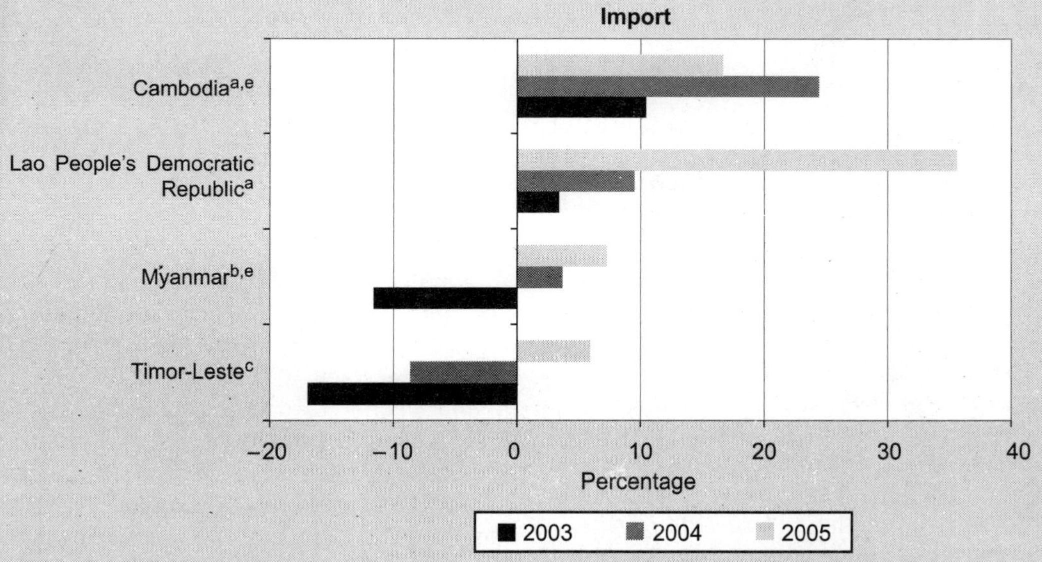

Sources: Economist Intelligence Unit, *Country Reports*, various issues; International Monetary Fund, *Country Report* No. 05/245 (2005); and national sources.

[a] Data for 2005 are estimates.
[b] Data for 2005 are Economist Intelligence Unit estimates.
[c] Data for 2004 are estimates and for 2005 are projections.
[d] Excludes oil and gas.
[e] Import value free on board (f.o.b.).

Figure II.46. Current account balance in least developed countries in South-East Asia, 2003-2005[a]

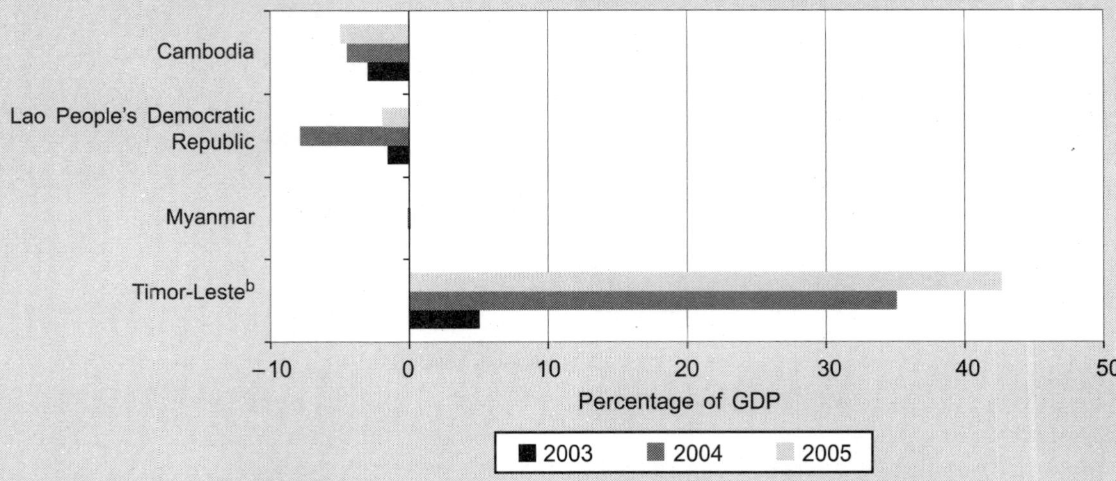

Sources: United Nations Economic and Social Commission for Asia and the Pacific, based on national sources; Asian Development Bank, *Key Indicators of Developing Asian and Pacific Countries 2005* (Manila, ADB, 2005) and *Asian Development Outlook 2005 Update* (Manila, ADB, 2005); Economist Intelligence Unit, *Country Reports* (London, EIU, 2005), various issues; and International Monetary Fund, *Democratic Republic of Timor-Leste: 2005 Article IV Consultation – Staff Report,* IMF Country Report No. 05/245 (2005).

[a] Data for 2005 are estimates.

[b] Based on percentage of non-oil GDP; includes international assistance.

Grants constitute one fifth of capital inflows to the Lao People's Democratic Republic

Exports from the Lao People's Democratic Republic, comprising textiles, electricity, wood products, gold, copper and coffee, and imports were projected to increase significantly in 2005. Although imports of consumer goods have declined in recent years, imports of capital equipment and electricity have risen; those imports are to be used in the country's gold and copper mining investments and large infrastructure projects such as the Nam Theun 2 Hydropower Project. Total capital inflows rose in 2005, with grants constituting nearly one fifth of the total. Inflows of commercial bank credits increased only marginally, however. As the country has no stock exchange, there were no portfolio investment inflows. The value of total approved FDI more than doubled, and more than a quarter of it was realized. Inflows of FDI through the banking system rose by more than 50 per cent in 2005.

Gross official foreign exchange reserves were estimated to be equivalent to 4.2 months of imports. The total external debt stock of the Lao People's Democratic Republic was estimated to have risen by more than one tenth, to 81.8 per cent of GDP in 2005. Debt stock to multilateral creditors accounted for nearly three quarters of this debt. External debt servicing was estimated to have risen to the equivalent of 10.9 per cent of exports. Although the Lao People's Democratic Republic is on the list of heavily indebted poor countries, in an effort to maintain creditworthiness for project-related external commercial loans, the Government has not submitted a request for debt forgiveness. Although no official statistical data are available on portfolio investment by nationals of the country in banks outside the country, a significant amount is believed to have been deposited in order to conduct payments for cross-border trade.

Myanmar remains committed to the Common Effective Preferential Tariff Scheme of the ASEAN Free Trade Area

Exports, especially of garments, from Myanmar have been adversely affected by international sanctions, while the services account has been eroded by larger profit repatriation and a decline in tourism receipts. In line with the commitments of the Common Effective Preferential Tariff Scheme for the ASEAN Free Trade Area, Myanmar has made progress on tariff reductions. Bilateral and regional engagements have not compromised Myanmar's commitment to multilateral trade negotiations. In 2003, the current account surplus, excluding grants, declined to nearly one fifth of the surplus in 2002. The capital account has deteriorated with higher debt service payments falling due, while disbursements have remained largely static and FDI has declined. The issue of faster accumulation of international arrears over international reserves was addressed in bilateral negotiations. The recourse to commercial loans and suppliers' credit instead of concessional assistance is expected to be temporary in view of the higher cost and shorter repayment periods for such credit. To enhance regional trade, Myanmar conducted negotiations with neighbouring countries, and this resulted in agreements on road and rail network construction.

Coffee exports from Timor-Leste rise

The external current account surplus, including international assistance, of Timor-Leste was projected to increase to 43 per cent of non-oil GDP in 2005, owing to the country's large oil and gas tax and royalty income. Merchandise imports, at 61 per cent of non-oil GDP, were projected to be significantly greater than merchandise exports, excluding oil and gas revenues, leading to a trade deficit of 58 per cent of GDP. Coffee exports, which constitute more than four fifths of all non-oil exports, rose in response to higher global prices. Since overall external price competitiveness deteriorated with the depreciation of the country's trading partners' currencies against the dollar, cautious fiscal and wage policies will be the key to preserving the competitiveness of Timor-Leste (see figure II.47).

Medium-term prospects and key policy issues

The least developed countries need to establish a sustainable growth mechanism that supports a rapid improvement in household living standards. Experience suggests that a sustainable growth process requires mutually reinforcing interactions between investment growth and export growth. Although external finance, usually aid, is vitally important in the initial stages of building an investment-export nexus, sustainability is best ensured when domestic savings start to grow along with investment and exports, and they increasingly begin to drive the process.

Sound macroeconomic policies are an essential element of long-term development strategies. However, macroeconomic objectives should be pursued through means that are consistent with long-term development objectives and that do not squeeze investment to levels that compromise future growth. A growth-oriented approach includes competitive exchange rates and the setting of low and stable interest rates in order to finance productive investment. Fiscal measures can also be used to increase corporate profitability and encourage the retention of earnings to accelerate capital accumulation.

Investment in rural roads and irrigation enables Cambodia to improve market access

Economic growth in Cambodia is expected to grow by an annual average of 6 per cent during the period 2006-2008, led largely by garment exports and oil and gas exploration. In the agricultural sector, current investment in rural roads and irrigation is expected to improve market access and productivity (see box II.6). Improved seed varieties, more diversified crops and community fisheries should also boost rural income. Growth in the garment industry is expected to be restrained, but recent reductions in operating costs should enable the industry to maintain its competitiveness. If political stability and security continue to be maintained, both construction and tourism are expected to grow. Inflation in the medium term is projected at an average annual rate of 3 per cent. Cambodia intends to reduce its primary budgetary deficit to less than 3 per cent of GDP, increase spending

Figure II.47. Index of exchange rates against the United States dollar in least developed countries in South-East Asia, 1996-2005[a]

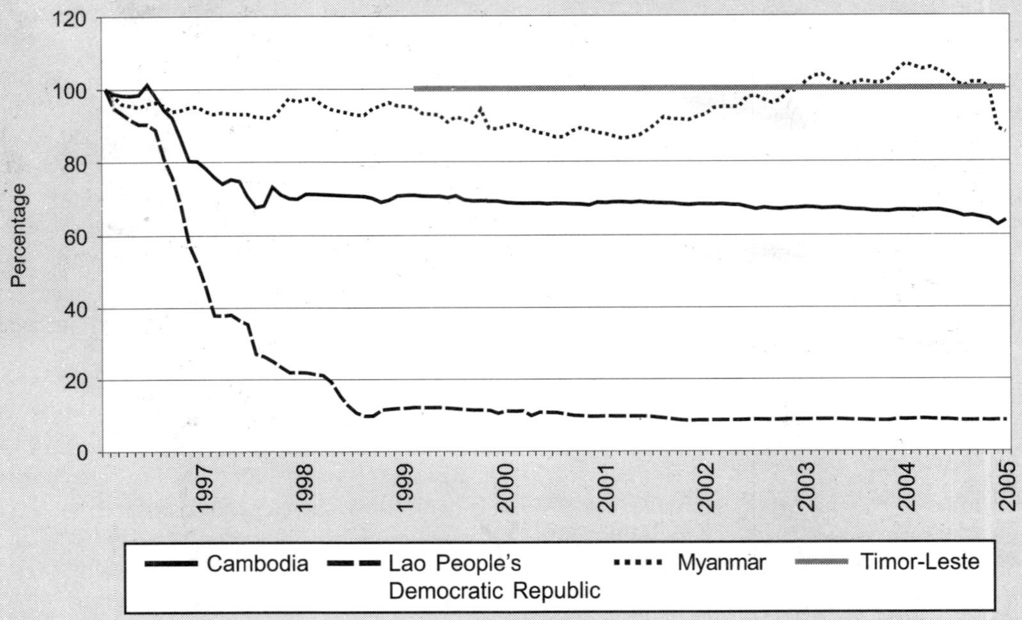

Sources: International Monetary Fund, *International Financial Statistics* (CD-ROM) (Washington, D.C., 2005); and *The Economist,* various issues.

[a] Data for 2005 are estimates.

Box II.6. Duty-free and quota-free market access for products originating from least developed countries

The Ministerial Declaration of the Sixth WTO Ministerial Conference, held in Hong Kong, China, from 13 to 18 December 2005, reaffirmed the commitment to effectively integrate the least developed countries into the multilateral trading system. Building on the commitment of the Doha Ministerial Declaration, developed and developing countries agreed to implement duty-free and quota-free market access for products originating from least developed countries by 2008. Countries also agreed to take additional measures to provide effective market access, both at the border and otherwise, including simplified and transparent rules of origin, and to give priority to sectors and modes of supply of export interest to least developed countries. Least developed countries, for their part, will be required to undertake commitments and concessions only to the extent consistent with their individual development, financial and trade needs and their administrative and institutional capabilities.

To facilitate accession of the least developed countries to WTO, priority will be given to concluding ongoing accession proceedings. To assist these countries in expanding their limited human and institutional trade-related capacities, the Declaration reaffirmed a commitment to enhance effective trade-related technical assistance and capacity-building on a priority basis. To ensure coherency, donors, multilateral agencies and international financial institutions were also requested to coordinate their work so that least developed countries are not subjected to conditionalities on loans, grants and official development assistance that are inconsistent with their rights and obligations under WTO agreements.

in the social sectors and on infrastructure development in rural areas, and raise civil service salaries by 2008. Such expenditures would require an increase in government revenues to 13.1 per cent of GDP. The current account deficit is projected to decline to 7 per cent of GDP by the end of 2008 owing to increased competitiveness and tourism. A projected external financing gap of $119 million is expected to be covered with assistance from international financial institutions.

Foreign direct investment in the Lao People's Democratic Republic will increase with the elimination of duties

In the Lao People's Democratic Republic, GDP growth is projected to range between 7.5 to 8.1 per cent during the period 2006-2008. Although growth in the agricultural sector is expected to continue, its share in GDP may decline. Both the industrial and the service sectors are projected to grow more rapidly, led by mining and quarrying and tourism. Private savings in the banking system are projected to grow, with foreign currency deposits expected to drop to half the total outstanding deposits by 2008. Private investment is forecast to rise in line with private savings. Inflation is estimated at an annual average rate of 7 per cent in the medium term. The central bank is expected to absorb any excess liquidity while the Government aims at balancing the budget. The volume to imports of capital equipment for infrastructure projects is likely to mean that imports will keep growing faster than exports. FDI is expected to increase with the elimination of import duties on production machinery, equipment and raw materials and of export duties on finished products. Other factors expected to increase FDI are the right to employ expatriates and the provision of profit tax incentives tailored to specific activities, the establishment of investment areas and the size of investments.

Myanmar recognizes need for structural reforms to promote private investment

Barring unforeseen economic shocks, Myanmar is expected to maintain its economic growth rate, given its location in one of the world's most dynamic regions and its abundant natural resources. Myanmar recognizes the need to continue making structural reforms in order to promote a more conducive environment for private investment and productivity growth. To ensure better governance and transparency, the Government has introduced measures to promote improved accounting practices and greater disclosure and to enforce financial and non-financial rules and regulations. Implementation of international best practices and recommendations is expected to require substantial resources over time.

Large fiscal surpluses averaging nearly a third of GDP are expected in Timor-Leste

The economic growth rate in Timor-Leste is expected to double to 5 per cent in 2006 as a result of increased investment spending. Assuming normal weather conditions, the expansion of technical extension services to subsistence farmers, the development of agro-businesses and the licensing of fishing are expected to accelerate growth in the agricultural sector. Higher public spending would also increase private sector activity, especially in the construction and service sectors. The higher economic growth necessary to absorb the expanding labour force requires improved budget execution and strengthening of the legislative and regulatory framework to attract private investment. Inflation is expected to be moderate in view of the current exchange and monetary regime. Based on anticipated oil and gas production, large fiscal surpluses averaging nearly a third of GDP are expected in the medium term. Enactment of pending economic legislation, finalization of bankruptcy legislation and development of a strong and independent judiciary and a comprehensive land-titling system are measures essential to ensure sustainable growth and higher employment in Timor-Leste.

DEVELOPED COUNTRIES

Australia, Japan and New Zealand

Overview

Growth slackens but remains strong in all three developed countries in the region

GDP growth in Australia and New Zealand lost some momentum in 2005. Australia and New Zealand are primarily commodity-producing and commodity-trading economies. Japan is driven more by manufacturing and relies less on trade, as measured by nearly the trade to GDP ratio. GDP growth declined by 1 percentage point in Australia but went up by 0.2 percentage point in Japan. The slowdown was much sharper in New Zealand, at more than 2 percentage points.

Domestic factors were primarily responsible for the slowdown in Australia and New Zealand. In Australia, households appear to have entered a phase of consolidation after a period of unsustainably rapid growth in borrowing and spending, and this has been accompanied by a mild downturn in housing construction. In Japan, there was a modest drop in public consumption, although private consumption and net exports maintained the relative buoyancy shown in 2004. In New Zealand, domestic demand declined considerably as interest rates rose and the contribution of net exports to GDP growth in New Zealand diminished visibly in response to an appreciating exchange rate. The current account widened further, and this holds monetary policy implications for the near term.

Prospects for 2006 are for a slight loss of momentum in Japan and New Zealand while growth should pick up in Australia. Although the external environment is expected to remain broadly stable, albeit with substantial downside risks as discussed in chapter I especially with regard to high and volatile oil prices and growing international imbalances, there is unlikely to be any noticeable change from the domestic side in the momentum for output growth. The principal components of growth, the macroeconomic background and the policy trade-offs and challenges confronting the three economies are discussed at greater length below.

GDP growth performance

Domestic factors drive output growth in the developed countries

Australia recorded its fourteenth year of continued economic growth in 2005 (see figure II.48). The 2.5 per cent growth rate in 2005 was a more sustainable pace for the Australian economy than its rapid growth in the previous few years, reflecting a significant shift in the composition of growth. Improved terms of trade and stronger business investment led the growth in domestic demand in 2005 at a time when the increased household consumption growth seen in earlier years began to decelerate. With the housing boom clearly cooling, residential investment fell for three consecutive quarters following the second half of 2004 and housing prices declined after several years of strong growth. As a result, household expenditure slowed as households attempted to reduce their increasing debt-servicing costs. Private consumption nevertheless maintained a degree of buoyancy, growing at a yearly rate of 3 per cent up to mid-2005, as employment growth and tax cuts strengthened otherwise weaker consumer confidence.

Business investment rebounded following a decline in the first quarter of 2005, owing to the continuing strong global demand and the increasing corporate profits. This virtuous combination prompted both business investment and employment demand. For instance, orders for machinery and equipment expanded by more than 18 per cent on an annual basis in the second quarter of 2005, reflecting substantial expansion of operations in the resource-processing sector.

The unemployment rate recorded a 28-year low of 5.1 per cent, with wages growing by nearly 4.5 per cent for the year to June 2005. However, towards the middle of 2005 a tightening labour market, high levels of capacity utilization and higher energy prices narrowed slightly the profitability of the business sector, thereby weakening business confidence. These constraints tended to limit the growth of production, which would otherwise have expanded vigorously in response to the more favourable external environment, in particular the solid demand for exports at a time when commodity prices were at historic highs. However, overall business investment continued to grow.

Despite the slowdown in the second half of 2004, Japan recorded significantly stronger economic growth in the year as a whole than at any time since 1997, confirming the view that Japan had finally recovered from its decade-long virtual stagnation. Growth picked up in 2005, as

Figure II.48. Economic growth and inflation in developed countries of the Asian and Pacific region, 2003-2005[a]

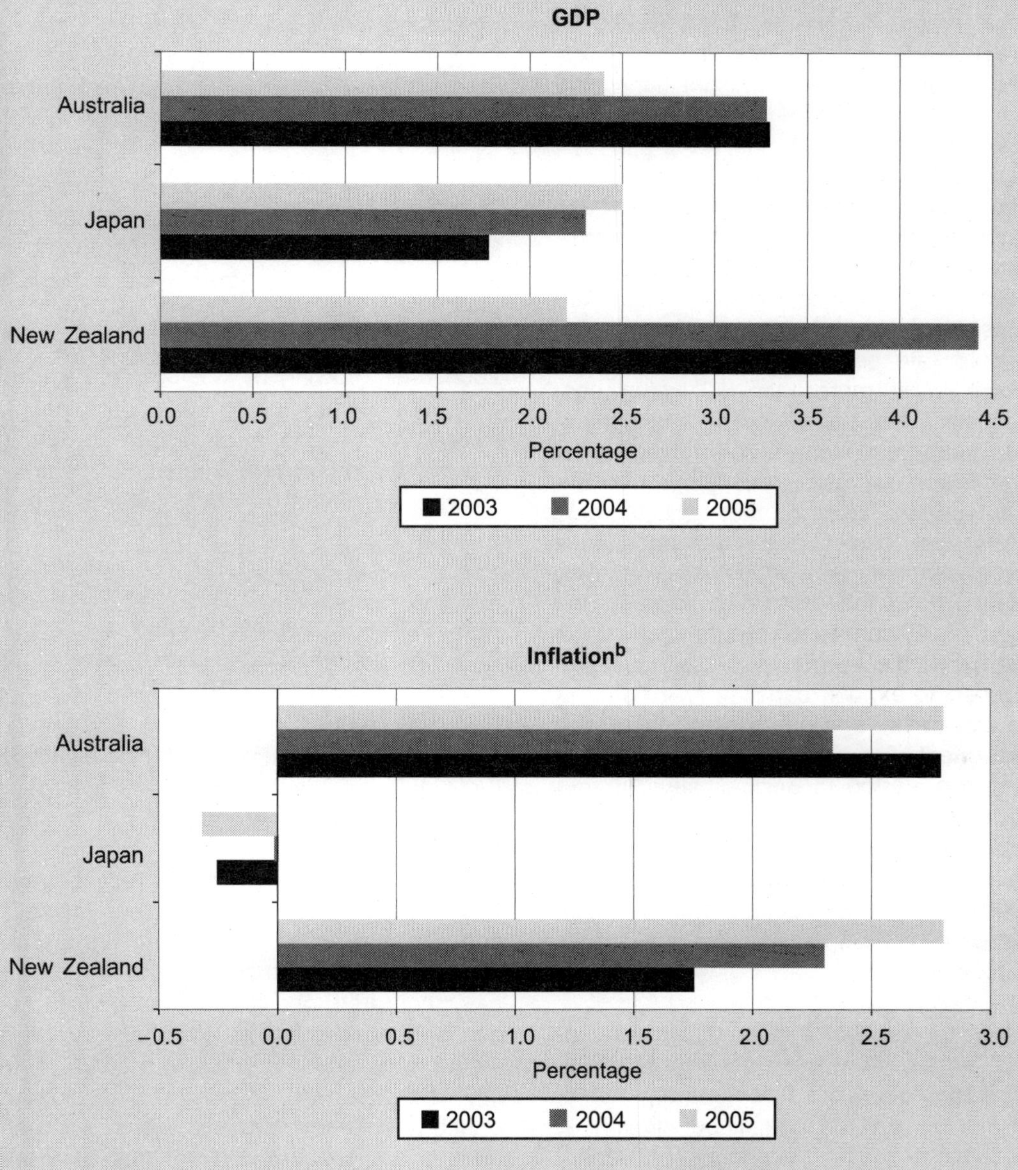

Sources: United Nations Economic and Social Commission for Asia and the Pacific, based on national sources; Japan, Statistics Bureau and Statistical Research and Training Institute, *Monthly Statistics of Japan*, January 2006; Economist Intelligence Unit, *Country Forecasts* (London, EIU, 2006), various issues; and International Monetary Fund, *International Financial Statistics* (CD-ROM) (Washington, D.C., IMF, 2006).

[a] Data for 2005 are estimates.

[b] Inflation rates refer to percentage changes in the consumer price index.

domestic investment and consumer expenditure actually appeared to have recovered, offsetting the decline in export demand in the second half of 2004. Growing optimism over the economic outlook in 2005 attracted foreign investors, as reflected in the strength of the stock market. The Nikkei stock market index reaching 15,778 in December 2005, its highest level in five years, an increase of more than 40 per cent during the year.

The strength of domestic demand in Japan can be attributed essentially to an increase in corporate profitability, following the restructuring of corporate balance sheets that began in the mid-1990s. The process has been supported by the removal of obstacles that had been undermining corporate performance since the economic bubble burst more than 10 years ago, namely, excess capacity, excess employment and excess corporate debt burden. Recent issues of the Short-term Economic Survey of Enterprises in Japan confirm that considerable progress has been achieved in reducing surplus plant and equipment and in introducing new technology in many manufacturing firms in the last few years. Encouraged by the growth of external demand, the corporate sector in Japan has now turned to expand capacity in a range of manufacturing firms and thus has increased capital investment (figure II.49). As a result, unemployment has started to decline, albeit gradually. That, in turn, has invigorated domestic demand and consumer confidence. However, slower growth of external demand and rising costs, particularly for wages and energy, might be discouraging factors for further investment growth in 2006.

Despite the recent strength of private consumption a degree of uncertainty remains. Private consumption represents more than half of GDP and is the key to sustained growth in domestic demand in the economy of Japan. While the labour market is buoyant, consumer confidence is becoming clouded by fiscal measures such as those requiring employees to increase their contributions to the public pension scheme and the planned removal of the 1999 income tax cuts in 2006. On the upside, there appears to be a longer-term shift in propensity of households to consume when income growth is low, which should soften any slowdown in domestic consumption in the near term. In view of the significant role of consumer expenditure in the growth of domestic demand in the past, the near-term growth prospects of Japan depend on whether the current momentum of household consumption can be maintained. The overall signs are positive, but longer-term trends are less sharply defined.

The economy of New Zealand weakened significantly in 2005

The economy of New Zealand experienced considerably weaker growth in 2005, following robust growth of nearly 4 per cent annually in the previous four years. Domestic demand, the primary source of strength in output growth since 2002, declined to 4.4 per cent in 2005 after growing by 3.8 per cent in the previous year, responding to the end of the property-market boom and a slowdown in employment growth. Export growth lagged far behind import growth, worsening the trade balance and making a negative contribution to GDP growth in 2005. While stronger export growth was recorded in 2004, the strength of the New Zealand dollar against the currencies of major trading partners to some degree eroded the impact of stronger external demand in 2005. The exchange rate facilitated more robust import growth in 2005, although with somewhat weaker domestic demand the pace was slower than the double-digit growth experienced in 2004.

Domestic demand in recent years has been strengthened by consistent inward migration and the ensuing increased domestic investment, such as in residential construction, which has generated jobs in sectors such as construction and allied services. With interest rates moving upward and the housing-market boom cooling when the flow of migration is slowing, residential investment showed signs of tapering off and private consumption became more subdued in 2005. Weaker consumer expenditure has reflected households' efforts to readjust their balance sheets in the wake of a cooler property market and higher interest rates. Nevertheless, the decline in housing prices has been moderate and the growth of employment has continued, both of which factors have supported consumer confidence. The expansion of business investment, on the other hand, did not fully reflect capacity constraints, as capital investment needs

Figure II.49. Consumption and investment in developed countries of the Asian and Pacific region, 2003-2005[a]

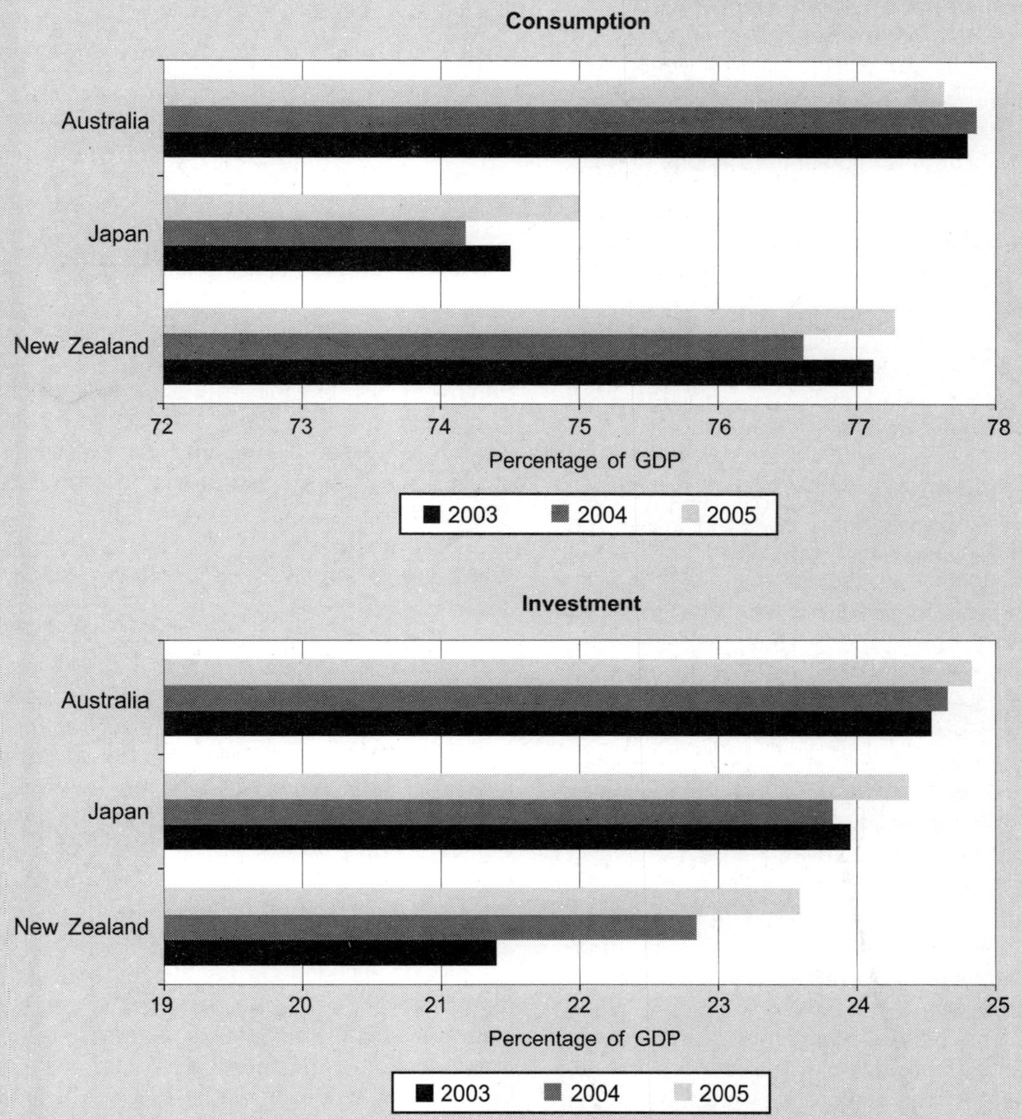

Sources: United Nations Economic and Social Commission for Asia and the Pacific, based on International Monetary Fund, *International Financial Statistics* (CD-ROM) (Washington, D.C., IMF, 2005); and Economist Intelligence Unit, *Country Forecasts* (London, EIU, 2005), various issues.

[a] Data for 2005 are estimates.

were partly satisfied by imported capital attracted by the stronger currency. The unemployment rate stood at 3.7 per cent in the second quarter of 2005, an 18-year low. The tighter labour market, however, has translated into upward pressure on wages, and employment growth slowed to 1.5 per cent in 2005 compared with 3.3 per cent in 2004, while nominal wage growth accelerated from 2.9 per cent in 2004 to 3.6 per cent in 2005.

Key macroeconomic policy developments

Inflation remained moderate and the strong Australian dollar exerted downward pressure on import prices

Inflation remained moderate in Australia at about 3 per cent, although producer prices increased, reflecting a tightening labour market and higher energy prices. Primary product prices rose by 6.5 per cent for the year to September 2005, while final producer prices rose by 3.4 per cent. The pressure on producer prices was not fully passed on to consumer prices. The consumer price index edged up from 2.4 per cent in 2004 to 2.6 per cent by the third quarter of 2005, remaining within the 2-3 per cent target band of the Reserve Bank of Australia.

Divergent trends were noted in the prices of non-tradable and tradable goods in 2004. The differences between the two types of goods narrowed in 2005, as the disinflationary effects of the stronger Australian dollar in 2002 and 2003 gradually diminished. Thus, tradables, including food and petrol, rose by 2.6 per cent for the year to September 2005 compared with a 3.4 per cent rise for non-tradables. While the stronger Australian dollar exerted downward pressure on import prices and thus on tradables inflation, strong growth in demand kept the prices of non-tradables at a high level.

The strength of domestic demand and the growing signs of capacity constraints in 2005 signalled a build-up of inflationary pressures in the economy. With the inflation rate approaching the upper limit of the policy target, the central bank increased the overnight cash rate by 25 basis points to 5.5 per cent in March 2005, the first such increase in 14 months (see figure II.50). With the boom in the property market cooling and the interest rate burden on household debt rising, there appears to be no immediate need for a further rise in interest rates, although inflationary pressure could resurface in the medium term if higher oil prices persist and the Australian dollar were to weaken significantly. Further monetary tightening would need to be carefully weighed against the impact that higher interest rates would have on highly indebted households, domestic demand and the exchange rate.

As in 2004, the fiscal position of Australia remained strong in 2005 (see figure II.51), in stark contrast to the case in Japan and other countries in the Organisation for Economic Co-operation and Development, many of which have large fiscal deficits. During 2005, the underlying cash surplus accruing to the federal Government was reported to have reached 1.3 per cent of GDP, following a 1.6 per cent surplus in 2004, despite the significant tax relief granted to individuals in 2005. The mildly expansionary fiscal policy in recent years has cushioned the slowdown in domestic demand without placing excessive stress on monetary policy or the budget. The surplus has been the result largely of higher corporate tax revenues and royalties flowing from the gain in corporate profits, in particular from the mining sector, which benefited from high export prices. The revenue increase more than offset the income tax cuts and extra spending on family assistance, health care and education.

Deflation in Japan is expected to end in 2006

Japan is still in the throes of mild deflation, although the pressure has eased considerably in recent months. The Bank of Japan has predicted that deflation is likely to end in 2006. Although Japan is a major importer of oil, recent high oil prices have not affected overall prices. Consumer prices were expected to decline by 0.3 per cent in 2005, and in terms of the GDP deflator, prices were likely to have fallen by as much as 1.2 per cent in 2005.

One explanation for the minimal impact of higher oil prices is the increase in energy efficiency in Japan. According to the Government's macroeconometric model, a 20 per cent rise in the price of crude oil would reduce GDP growth by a mere 0.1 per cent, owing largely to the steady improvement in energy efficiency per unit of nominal GDP since the oil shocks of the 1970s and 1980s. Furthermore, low import prices, particularly for imports from China, have been putting downward pressure on the overall price level, aided by ongoing deregulation of domestic markets.

With recent strong economic growth, the probable easing of deflationary pressure in 2006 and growing confidence that systemic risks in the financial sector have been largely overcome,

Figure II.50. Short-term interest rates and money supply growth in developed countries of the Asian and Pacific region, 2003-2005[a]

Short-term interest rate

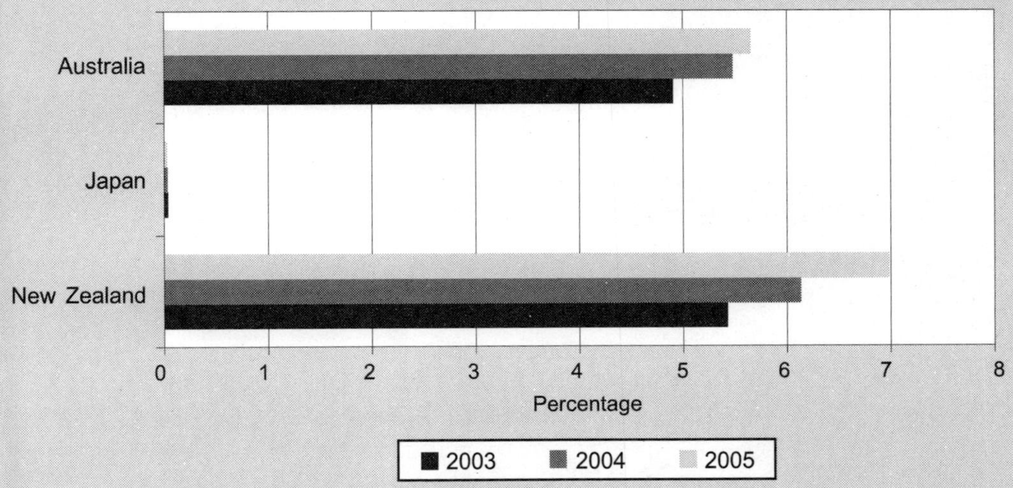

Money supply (M2)

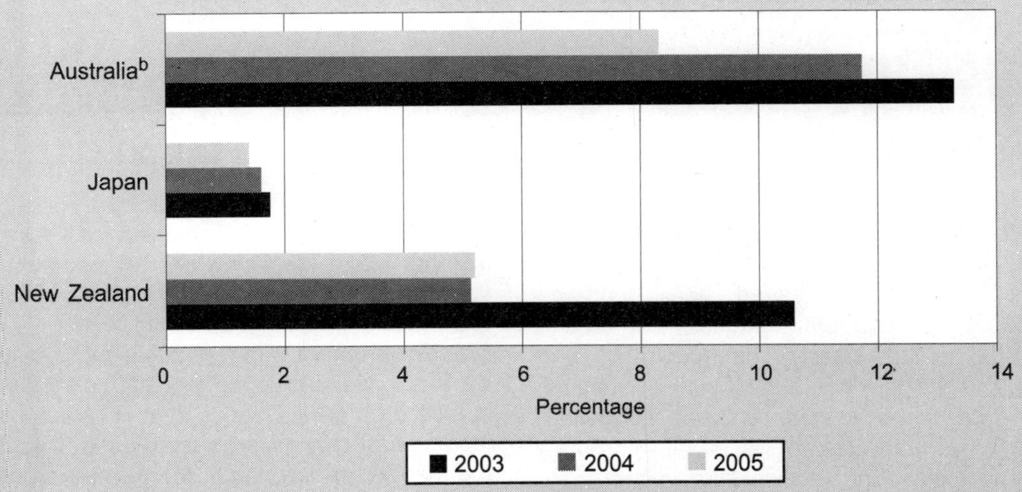

Sources: United Nations Economic and Social Commission for Asia and the Pacific, based on International Monetary Fund, *International Financial Statistics* (CD-ROM) (Washington, D.C., IMF, 2005); and Organisation for Economic Co-operation and Development, *Main Economic Indicators,* <www.oecd.org/dataoecd/>, accessed on 24 February 2006.

[a] Data for 2005 are estimates.

[b] Data refer to the period January-October.

the Bank of Japan has signaled a policy shift on deflation. Although the Bank would continue its current "easy-money" policy stance until deflation has been overcome, the zero interest rate regime is expected to end as soon as deflation is technically over. The current quantitative easing framework was intended to provide enough liquidity to counter deflationary pressure; however,

Figure II.51. Budget balance[a] in developed countries of the Asian and Pacific region, 2003-2005[b]

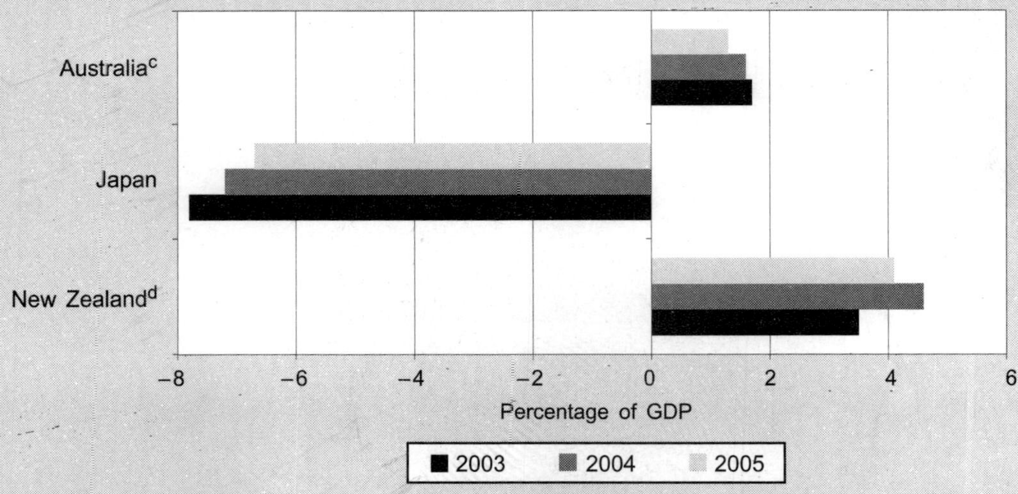

Source: United Nations Economic and Social Commission for Asia and the Pacific, based on International Monetary Fund, *World Economic Outlook, September 2005: Building Institutions* (Washington, D.C., IMF, 2005).

[a] Refers to general government fiscal balance.
[b] Data for 2005 are estimates.
[c] Data exclude net advances (primarily privatization receipts and net policy-related lending).
[d] Derived from revenue minus expenditure plus balance of State-owned enterprises, excluding privatization receipts.

its overall effectiveness has been questionable. While the intention was to encourage commercial activity through increased bank lending, banks did not expand their extension of credit, as observed in the steady contraction of loan portfolios, despite the low interest rates. There is evidence that some secular shift in borrowing preferences has been taking place, with corporations raising more bond finance than in the past. Nevertheless, the urgent need for fiscal tightening implies that any premature tightening of monetary policy could put economic growth at risk if corporate sentiments are not strong enough to absorb the interest rate rise. Moreover, a rise in long-term interest rates would increase the cost of servicing government debt; at 150 per cent of GDP, that debt is of potentially serious concern.

The public debt and the need for fiscal consolidation remain daunting challenges for the economy. While the economic recovery in Japan has contributed to an increase in tax revenues, it has not offset the rising interest payment obligations on the country's growing debt and increased expenditure, in particular rising welfare spending. The Government aims at achieving an operating balance in the budget by 2010, but its policy stance thus far has been one of gradualism and incremental change in its tax regime, thus creating the danger of slippage. More drastic measures such as a higher consumption tax have long been debated, but there are fears that such a policy could damage still-fragile consumer confidence. Consumer confidence and private consumption have improved in recent months but they could weaken again as contributions to the employee pension scheme rise and the income tax cuts of 1999 are reversed in 2006.

Incipient inflationary pressure has been evident in New Zealand for some time; the deflationary pressure from the stronger currency is fading and the impact of higher oil prices is strengthening. Despite considerable divergence among the major components of consumer price inflation, the inflation rate was well contained within the monetary authority's target range in 2004. Inflationary pressures in tradables diminished in 2005 owing to moderation of the currency's appreciation; inflation in non-tradables was higher, however, reflecting still high housing costs. Overall, producer price increases accelerated from 1.9 per cent in 2004 to 3.1 per cent in 2005, reflecting capacity constraints and a tighter labour market.

In view of the continuing strength of domestic demand and the growing evidence of capacity constraints and a tightening labour market, the Reserve Bank of New Zealand gradually raised the official cash rate from 5.0 per cent in January 2004 so that it reached 6.75 per cent in March 2005. Although high oil prices and strong wage growth suggest potential inflationary pressures, the central bank's expressed policy is that it would be guided by the likelihood of inflation over the medium term, implying that further tightening may not be imminent if current pressures prove transitory. Moreover, the possibility of further monetary tightening increases the risks of a hard landing for the economy, through a sharp fall in property prices and further appreciation of the New Zealand dollar.

The fiscal position remains strong in New Zealand. The operating budget surplus was slightly higher in 2005 than in 2004, despite a relatively expansionary fiscal policy. As in the previous year, the results for 2005 reflected higher than expected tax revenues, particularly from corporate taxes and the goods and services tax, although consumer spending was less buoyant than the previous year. So far, the Government has indicated that the surplus has been earmarked for pre-funding the pension scheme and for financing a larger capital investment programme in social infrastructure, such as health and education.

Developments in the external sector

External positions worsen in Australia and New Zealand; the current account surplus of Japan increases

In Australia, with increasing export prices, growth in the value of merchandise exports rose at a rate of 21 per cent in 2005, following similar growth in 2004, mainly on strong demand from China for minerals and fuel. The recovery of agricultural output and the increase in mining production underpinned export growth, although capacity constraints in transport and other sectors prevented the supplies from meeting the robust external demand. Export commodity prices were substantially higher than the 2001-2003 average as of June 2005. Import growth slowed, moderated by the slight depreciation of the currency and weakening domestic demand. Thus the trade deficit narrowed from 2.9 per cent of GDP in 2004 to 1.9 per cent in 2005. However, the current account deficit is estimated to have worsened to around 6.0 per cent of GDP (see figure II.52).

The narrower trade deficit was offset by a wider deficit on other current transactions and rising debt service costs. Net external debt rose from about 40 per cent of GDP in 1998 to more than 50 per cent in 2004. Although the debt is concentrated in the private sector, and the currency risk has been well managed so far, it remains a major concern. Debt denominated in foreign currencies constitutes about 65 per cent of the total and is well hedged.

A sharp slowdown in demand from China and the consequent slowdown of the economy of Japan at the end of 2004 were reminders of the growing importance of East Asian economies as trading partners for Japan in recent years. China is now second only to the United States as a destination for Japanese exports, and it is the most important source for imports, having supplied one fifth of Japanese imports in 2004 (see figure II.53).

With somewhat subdued demand from its trading partners within the Asian and Pacific region, the economy of Japan experienced modest export growth in 2005 compared with 2004. The slower export growth was the result largely of a reduction in demand for electrical machinery and slower growth in demand for non-electrical machinery from China. It is too early to say whether this represents a more generalized weakening of demand from China, which now has the capacity to produce all but the most technologically advanced manufactured goods, including capital goods, or is part of the policy-induced slowing of investment expenditures in

Figure II.52. Current account balance in developed countries of the Asian and Pacific region, 2003-2005[a]

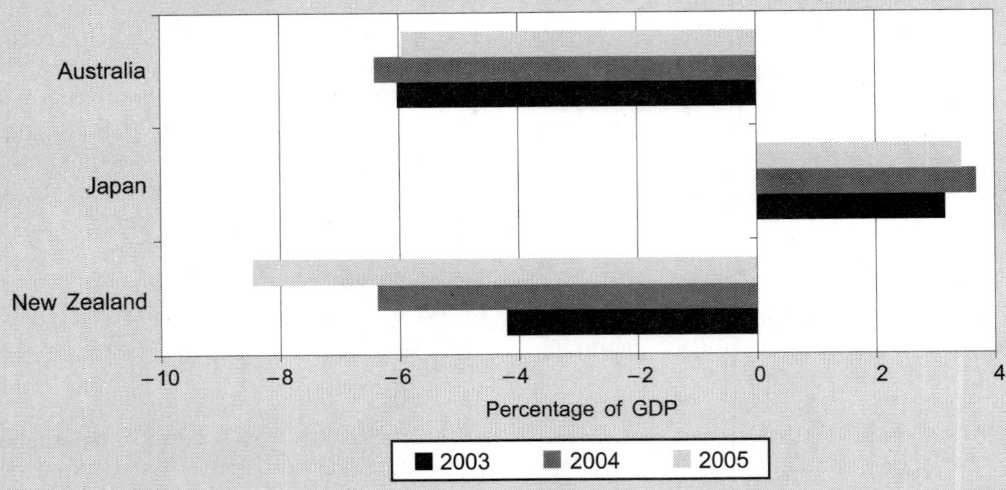

Sources: United Nations Economic and Social Commission for Asia and the Pacific, based on International Monetary Fund, *International Financial Statistics* (CD-ROM) (Washington, D.C., IMF, 2005); and Economist Intelligence Unit, *Country Forecasts* (London, EIU, 2006), various issues.

[a] Data for 2005 are estimates.

China. Whatever the case, it suggests that the current level of business investment in domestic capacity could prove unsustainable if it is predicated solely on investment demand from China.

Relatively modest export growth was exceeded by robust merchandise imports in 2005. Higher oil prices inflated the value of crude oil imports by more than 30 per cent, and imports of iron and steel soared by 60 per cent in the second quarter of 2005, on strong demand from car manufacturers and shipbuilders in Japan. The current account surplus thus narrowed from 3.7 per cent in 2004 to 3.5 per cent in 2005 as the reduction of the trade surplus partly offset the higher investment income surplus. Japan continues to attract higher flows of direct and portfolio investments from abroad, and its reserves reached $837 billion in late 2005.

The appreciation of the New Zealand dollar has started to erode the country's export performance (see figure II.54). International prices of the country's key commodities, such as meat and dairy products, have risen strongly in recent years, reflecting strong global demand and tight international supplies. The improved commodity prices are less striking when measured in New Zealand dollars, however, owing to the appreciation of the currency. In other words, improved terms of trade have been negated to some extent by exchange rate appreciation, thus lessening the impact on domestic incomes.

More alarmingly, recent robust import demand has increased the trade deficit and widened the current account deficit to 7.6 of GDP in 2005, a level not seen since the 1980s. The main reason for the growing imbalance is the shortfall in the income account caused by the repatriation of profits by foreign companies operating in New Zealand and the unpredictable changes in indirect earnings, such as tourism receipts, occasioned by changes in sentiment in countries far removed from New Zealand. Whatever the proximate cause, the current account is unsustainable at its current level, and the authorities need to develop a more robust policy approach to deal with it in the next two to three years.

Figure II.53. Growth rates in merchandise export earnings and import spending in developed countries of the Asian and Pacific region, 2003-2005[a]

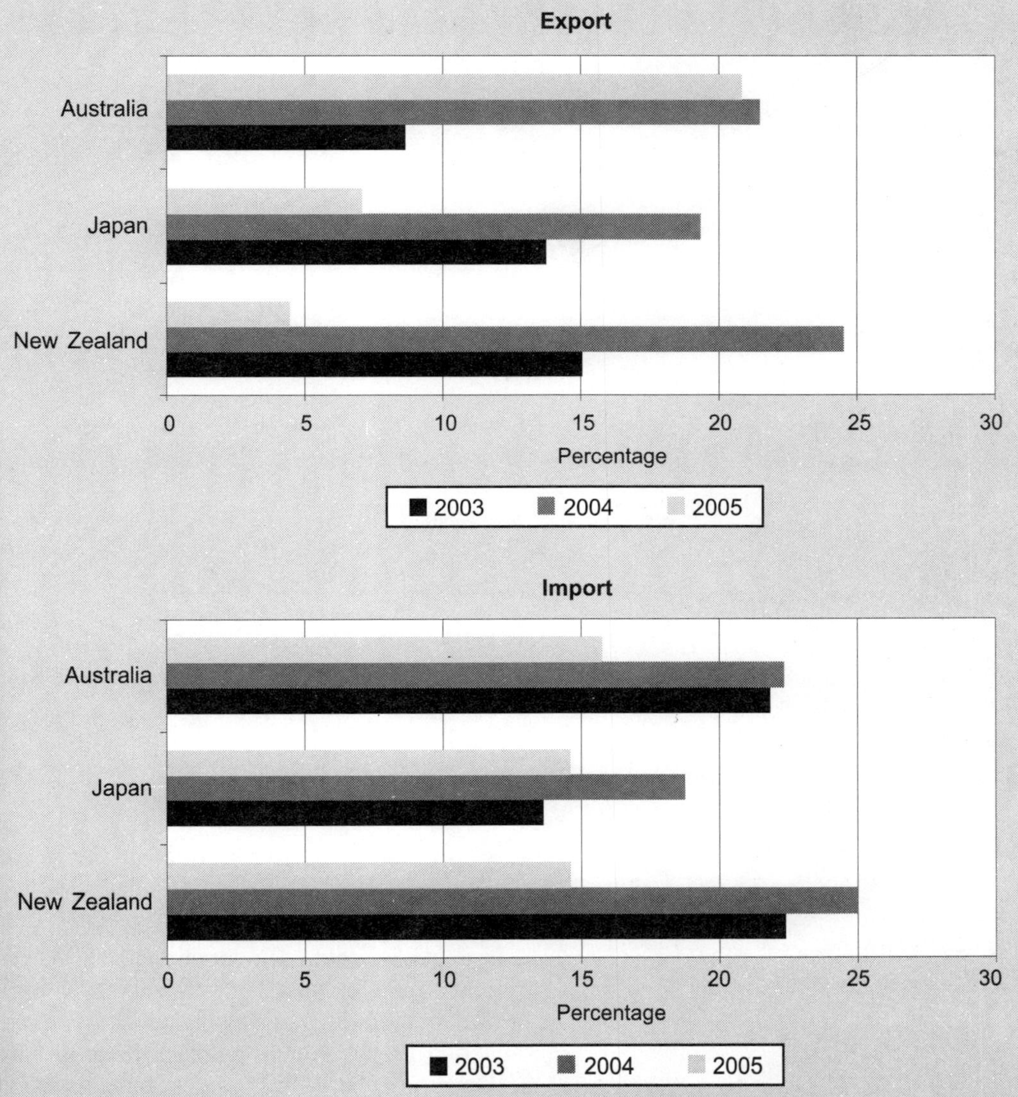

Source: International Monetary Fund, *Direction of Trade Statistics* (CD-ROM) (Washington, D.C., IMF, 2006).

[a] Growth rates for 2005 refer to January-August compared with the coresponding period of 2004.

Medium-term prospects and key policy issues

The three economies should see enhanced growth, with internal and external stability

The economies of the three developed countries are too diverse to discuss them as a group, although global developments, such as trade and rising oil prices, are likely to impinge on the three in broadly similar ways. GDP growth in Australia is expected to move back to its long-term trend in the next two to three years. Although domestic demand is likely to decline as the current increase in business investment eases and household consumption

Figure II.54. Index of exchange rates against the United States dollar in developed countries, 1996-2005[a]

(1996Q4=100)

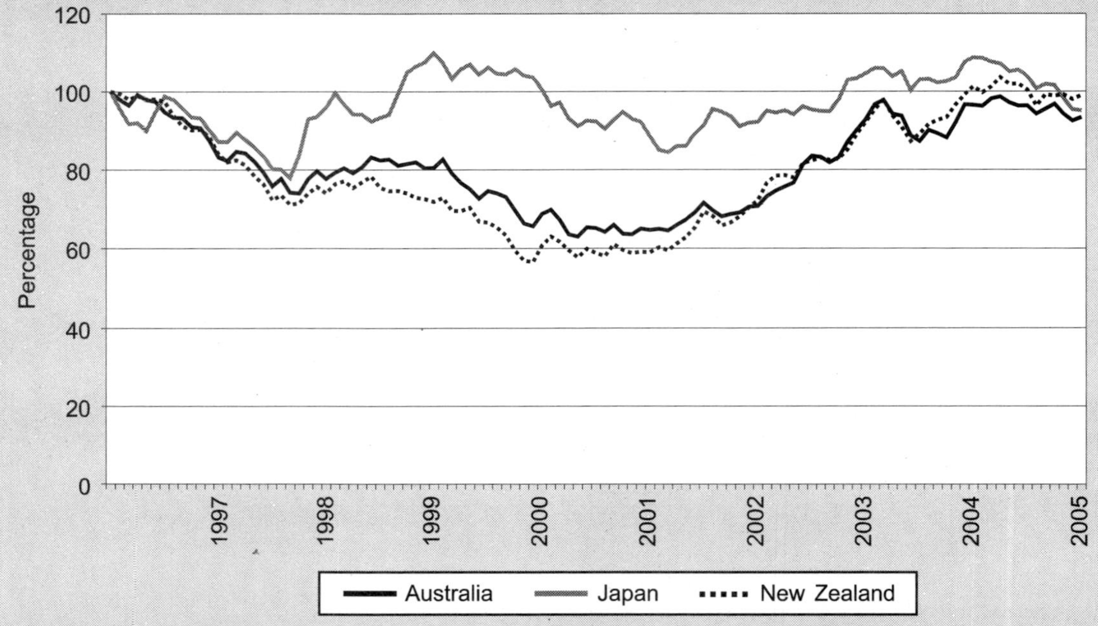

Sources: International Monetary Fund, *International Financial Statistics* (CD-ROM) (Washington, D.C., IMF, 2005); and *The Economist,* various issues.

[a] Data for 2005 are estimates.

remains subdued, export growth should retain much of its recent strength, reflecting the continuing expansion of the global economy. Domestic production should pick up as a consequence of the vigorous business investment occurring in the past two to three years and this should ease capacity constraints.

Inflation is likely to edge up as the expansion of domestic production may be accompanied by a further increase in employment and therefore in labour costs, given the low level of unemployment. Import prices might also rise, reflecting possible global inflation in raw materials and a weaker exchange rate. However, the likelihood of a general rise in raw material prices is discounted in the short term with the possible exception of new supply-side difficulties in energy markets. In addition, inflationary expectations are low, and consumers are not scrambling to ensure supplies for the future; moreover, there is little evidence of speculation in the commodity markets.

In Japan the public debt is the problem

In Japan, the critical underlying issue is the public debt. The controversial legislation to privatize the postal system, finally passed in October 2005, has significant fiscal implications. Japan Post currently holds about one fifth of the Government's outstanding bonds, a major factor contributing to the stability of the bond market and the low interest rates that have prevailed since 1999 despite the huge increase in the country's public debt. The parliamentary struggle blurred the focus of the postal reform bill and thus uncertainty remains about the process and the mechanisms of implementation as well as to what extent future public sector capital allocations might be affected. Besides the issues associated with the privatization of Japan Post, which is the world's largest deposit-taking institution and the country's largest life insurer, it remains unclear where the massive capital funds will be deployed in the future; they amount to about one quarter of total personal assets in Japan. In theory, it is possible that government bonds would no longer be absorbed by the privatized entity in the future. If so, that would create new complexities for the Government in financing its future budget deficits.

New Zealand does not appear to face major economic issues other than the current account deficit and the risks attached to funding it. In this regard, two aspects of the country's foreign debt stand out. First, foreign debt, at roughly 105 per cent of GDP, is becoming more concentrated in the banking sector and its maturity has shortened. The foreign currency composition of the debt, at just over 52 per cent, remains a large but declining share, with the currency risk substantially mitigated through hedging. Second, interest rates need to remain higher than other circumstances might demand in order to keep funding the deficit. The higher interest rates almost certainly exert some upward pressure on the exchange rate and make New Zealand exports less competitive, despite the improvement it has experienced in the terms of trade. At the same time, the higher interest rates do not appear to have succeeded in increasing domestic savings, the primary cause of the current account deficit. Reducing the current account deficit thus has major policy implications for the future that cannot be easily resolved.

Despite these risks, New Zealand remains well placed to absorb adverse shocks without undue stress. The Government's decisions in 2004 to increase international reserves and to intervene in the exchange market if the exchange rate deviates too far from its historical value are steps in the right direction. Fundamentally, the current account deficit needs to be viewed against the background of a prudently managed market environment supported by sound policies. Market participants see even major exchange rate swings as unlikely to pose a systemic risk for the economy.

III. EMERGING UNEMPLOYMENT ISSUES IN ASIA AND THE PACIFIC: RISING TO THE CHALLENGES*

INTRODUCTION

Jobless growth, the working poor and youth unemployment are becoming key concerns relating to unemployment in the region

Despite significant progress in economic growth and poverty reduction, Asia and the Pacific continues to be a region of considerable disparity, with approximately 679 million people living in poverty.

One of the main reasons behind this is the lack of adequate job creation. Labour markets in the region have hardly progressed relative to the region's economic gains. In many countries in the region, the rate of unemployment has increased although a few have witnessed some improvement in 2003. Underemployment and child labour continue to be issues of concern. The region is also confronting three specific issues: jobless growth, the working poor and youth unemployment, hence the special focus of this chapter.[1]

While the region's 5.7 per cent average annual rate of economic growth over the past 10 years has been the highest in the world and has far outpaced the global average of 2.7 per cent, employment has grown by 1.6 per cent compared with a growth rate of over 1.7 per cent annually in the labour force. As a result, increasing unemployment has sparked fears of jobless growth in some parts of the region.

The region accounts for a major share of the world's working poor, as indicated by the large share of people at the margin of the poverty line. For example, the share in total employment of those living on less than $2 a day was as high as 88 per cent in South Asia, 59 per cent in South-East Asia and 49 per cent in East Asia in 2003, although there have been significant improvements over the years.[2] This indicates that unemployment is not the only problem: equally pressing

---

* The term "unemployment" refers to all persons above a specified age who, during the reference period, were without work, currently available for work and seeking work. Persons working less than one hour per week are considered to be unemployed. It should be recognized that national definitions and coverage of unemployment can vary with regard to age limits, criteria for seeking work and treatment of persons temporarily laid off (i.e., discouraged about job prospects or seeking work for the first time).

The term "working poor" refers to the proportion of employed persons living in a household whose members are estimated to be below the poverty line.

The term "labour force" refers to the supply of labour available for the production of goods and services in an economy. It includes people who are currently employed, people who are unemployed but seeking work and first-time job-seekers but does not include unpaid workers, family workers, students and sometimes members of the military.

The term "youth unemployment" refers to the share of persons aged 15 to 24 without work but available for and seeking employment.

See International Labour Organization, *LABORSTA database on labour statistics,* <http://laborsta.ilo.org> accessed on 25 January 2006; *Key Indicators of the Labour Market,* third edition (Geneva, ILO, 2003); and ILO website <www.ilo.org> accessed on 25 January 2006; for details.

[1] International Labour Organization, *Labour and Social Trends in Asia and the Pacific 2005* (Bangkok, ILO, Regional Office for Asia and the Pacific, 2005).

[2] Ibid.

is the lack of work, particularly in the vast informal sector that is sufficiently productive to yield a decent income. Creation of decent jobs is the key to making a dent in poverty.

The region must also confront high levels of unemployment among youth and the well educated. Youth unemployment in Asia stood at 38 million in 2003, almost half the world's total. This was an increase of 36 per cent over the level a decade earlier when the global increase was only 26 per cent.[3] The gravity of the issue is reflected in a more than doubling of youth unemployment in the South-East Asian subregion. Meanwhile, many countries also face unemployment among the educated, reflecting a mismatch between supply and demand in the labour market.

Exploiting opportunities generated by globalization and the integration of markets and facing the associated challenges would be decisive in reshaping labour markets in order to generate productive and decent employment

Unemployment in all its dimensions is in part a reflection of the functioning of labour markets, themselves influenced by a host of factors. Chief among them are domestic labour-market policies, macroeconomic policies, the macroeconomic environment and the intensity of globalization. Success in addressing labour-market issues depends greatly on the ability to adapt to changing global socio-economic conditions. Exploiting opportunities presented by globalization and the integration of markets and dealing with associated issues through the introduction of appropriate policies would be decisive in reshaping labour markets in the region in order to generate productive employment.

How could the Asian and Pacific region rise to this challenge? The problem of jobless growth points to the need for a balanced approach. Labour-market policies need to go hand in hand with sound macroeconomic policies to generate employment. Appropriate social safety nets must be in place to support those adversely affected by policies and shocks, and opportunities for training must be provided to meet new demands. The region's high concentration of workers at low income levels warrants the special attention of policymakers. Increasing the productivity and income of workers requires improving their employability and opportunities for skills development. Reducing youth unemployment requires educational reforms to match the skills of new entrants to the labour market with those demanded by the market.

The purpose of this chapter is to analyse various dimensions of the unemployment problem in the Asian and Pacific region and the implications for the socio-economic well-being of its people and to recommend policy measures for addressing the challenges of unemployment. The chapter is organized as follows: it starts by giving a brief account of the unemployment situation in the region and of labour market-related issues such as underemployment and child labour. This is followed by analysis of three key issues: jobless growth, the working poor and youth unemployment. It then presents policy recommendations for addressing these issues.

UNEMPLOYMENT: DISMAL PERFORMANCE RELATIVE TO OUTSTANDING ECONOMIC ACHIEVEMENTS

The rate of unemployment increased by 20-50 per cent in the last decade, with only East Asia showing some progress recently

Unemployment trends in the Asian and Pacific region indicate rather dismal performance compared with the region's outstanding economic performance.[4] Between 1992 and 2002 the number of people unemployed rose from 4 million to 9 million in East Asia and from 5.5

3 Ibid.

4 The published unemployment rates in some countries may be underestimated as the rates are those that are officially registered. Such estimates may exclude most of the unemployed in the rural informal sector for logistical reasons. For example, in China there is a widening gap between officially registered unemployment at about 3 per cent and estimated unemployment at about 12 per cent. See Douglas Zhihua Zeng, "China's employment challenges and strategies after the WTO accession", World Bank Policy Research Paper 3522 (Washington, D.C., World Bank, 2005).

million to 14.6 million in South-East Asia and the Pacific. In South Asia total unemployment increased by 7 million during the same period. Between 1994 and 2004 the unemployment rate rose from 4.0 per cent to 4.8 per cent in South Asia, from 2.5 per cent to 3.6 per cent in East Asia and even more sharply from 4.1 to 6.4 per cent in South-East Asia and the Pacific, reflecting the effects of the Asian financial crisis in 1997, particularly in Indonesia (see table III.1).

cent a year in South-East Asia and the Pacific and by 2.2 per cent in South Asia owing to high birth rates, increasing (but still low) female participation in the labour force and extension of the working age. The population bulge created by higher fertility rates in the past is a major reason for the increasing labour supply and high unemployment in countries such as the Islamic Republic of Iran and Pakistan in Asia and most of the Melanesian countries in the Pacific.

Table III.1. Labour-market indicators

(Percentage)

	Labour-force participation rate	*Growth rate: Labour force*	*Growth rate: Employment-to-population ratio*	*Unemployment rate*	*Change in unemployment rate*	
	2004	*1994-2004*		*2004*	*1994-2004*	*1999-2004*
East Asia	75.0	1.3	−2.3	3.6	44.0	−0.2
South-East Asia and the Pacific	70.2[a]	2.4	−0.1	6.4	56.1	0.8
South Asia	60.0	2.2	−0.2	4.8	20.0	0.8
World	65.7	1.6	−1.0	6.1	10.9	0.0

Sources: International Labour Office, *Global Employment Trends January 2004* (Geneva, ILO, 2004); International Labour Organization, *Labour and Social Trends in Asia and the Pacific 2005* (Bangkok, ILO, Regional Office for Asia and the Pacific, 2005).

[a] Refers to South-East Asia only.

Performance has been no better in the more recent past. During the past five years the rate of unemployment growth has increased in South-East Asia and the Pacific and in South Asia. Only East Asia has managed to lower the unemployment rate. Meanwhile, the youth unemployment rate remained high at about 15 per cent in South-East Asia and the Pacific, twice as high as in East Asia. Natural disasters that took place in 2004 and 2005 could have further deteriorated the unemployment situation in the region.

The high rate of labour-force growth and the slow rate of job creation are behind the continued high unemployment rate

The high rate of labour-force growth and the slow rate of job creation are behind the continued high unemployment rate. During the past decade the labour force grew by 2.4 per

Low participation rates by women have historically kept labour-force participation rates low, particularly in South Asia. For example, female labour-force participation in 2000 was 22.8 per cent in Bangladesh and 16.3 per cent in Pakistan.[5] In Sri Lanka, the female participation rate was 36.5 per cent.[6] The low rates

[5] Rushidan Islam Rahman, "The dynamics of the labour market and employment in Bangladesh: a focus on gender dimensions", Employment Strategy Paper 2005/13 (Geneva, ILO, 2005). Rahman believes that the reported female unemployment rates for a country such as Bangladesh could be underestimated because women often move out of the labour force when they become unemployed for a considerable period of time, becoming "discouraged workers".

[6] The labour-force participation rate for women in Japan, a developed country, was 48.3 per cent in 2004 compared with over 60 per cent in the United States.

could be due partly to the exclusion from the labour force of women who are engaged in household economic activity. Childbearing and childcare also play a role. The increasing participation of women in the labour force could thus result in even higher rates of unemployment in the future in some parts of the region.

The second contributory factor has been the failure of job creation to keep pace with the growth in the labour force, as reflected in the declining employment-to-population ratio. Lack of formal tenure rights to land and antipathy towards open markets and private sector development in some countries, particularly in the Pacific subregion, are undermining job creation.

The demographic changes expected over the next 50 years will have important implications for labour supply and demand and could lead to a labour-market mismatch.[7] While in countries such as Japan the signs of the impact of an ageing population on the labour market are already being seen, in other countries and areas such as Armenia; Georgia; Hong Kong, China; Macao, China; the Russian Federation; Singapore; and Sri Lanka the process of population ageing is occurring rapidly and could have a major impact on the labour markets in the next half century. These countries and areas will experience acute shortages of labour. Countries with a more moderate speed of ageing, such as India and Indonesia, as well as those ageing slowly, such as Bangladesh and Pakistan, will still have an excess supply of labour. In these countries, unemployment will remain a challenge unless proper policy measures are taken to exploit the demographic dividend.

Sectoral composition of employment: agriculture is still the main provider

Agriculture and the informal economy remain the main employment providers despite an increasing trend towards services

The changing economic structure of the region has had both positive and negative impacts on employment. Over the past quarter century economies have shifted from an agricultural base towards services.[8] Reflecting this trend, the sectoral composition of employment has also changed considerably.

Agriculture's contribution to total employment in Asia declined from 82 per cent in 1950 to 62 per cent in 1990, while services and industry gained shares (see figure III.1). A similar trend is observed in the Pacific. However, in Asia agriculture still accounts for most employment. For example, despite a decline in recent years, agriculture's share in total employment, particularly in the large economies of China and India,[9] remained at more than 50 per cent (see table III.2).

High unemployment in the rural informal economy reflects a bias towards unskilled labour in the informal economy

In some countries the rural informal economy still provides the majority of employment opportunities, although it tends to employ more men than women (see table III.3). The high concentration of employment in the rural informal economy reflects a bias towards unskilled labour, abundant in most developing countries in the region, as well as imbalances in the process of structural change.

Underemployment: hidden and high

Underemployment is more widespread in the Asian and Pacific region than unemployment. Underemployment reflects voluntarily working less than full time because full-time jobs are not available, and underutilizing worker skills. Both types of underemployment directly affect the current income of workers as well as their potential future income through adverse effects on their career development prospects. In countries such

---

[7] See ESCAP, *Economic and Social Survey of Asia and the Pacific 2005* (United Nations publication, Sales No. E.05.II.F.10) for a detailed analysis of this issue.

[8] For example, the share of agriculture in GDP declined from 30 to 15 per cent in China, from 38 to 21 per cent in India, from 25 to 15 per cent in Indonesia, from 15 to 3 per cent in the Republic of Korea and from 23 to 9 per cent in Malaysia.

[9] The share of agriculture in total employment stood at 57 per cent in India in 2000.

Figure III.1. Sectoral shares of employment in Asia and the Pacific, 1950 and 1990

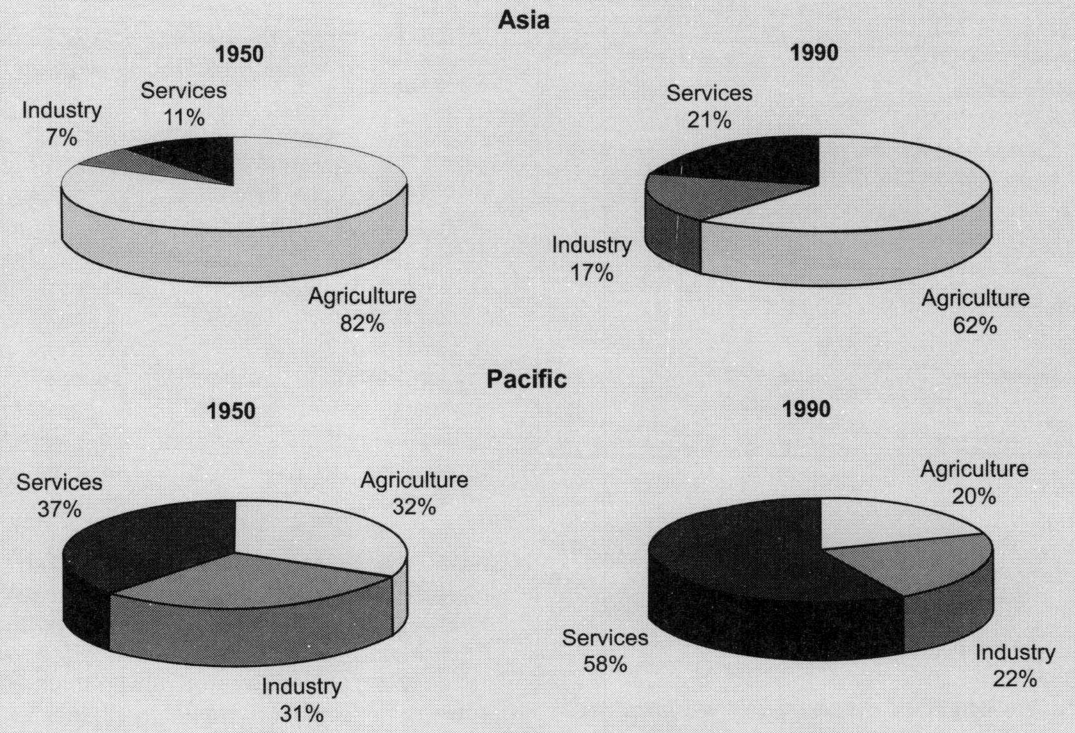

Source: International Labour Organization, *World Employment Report 2004-2005* (Geneva, ILO, 2004).

Table III.2. Employment by major economic sector in selected economies, 1990 and 2003

(Percentage)

	Agriculture		*Industry*		*Services*	
	1990	*2003*	*1990*	*2003*	*1990*	*2003*
East Asia						
China	64.9	56.6[a]	23.0	22.7[a]	12.0	20.7[a]
Republic of Korea	17.9	8.8	35.4	27.6	46.7	63.5
South-East Asia						
Indonesia	56.0	44.3[a]	13.8	18.8[a]	30.3	36.9[a]
Malaysia	26.0	14.3	27.5	32.0	46.5	53.7
Thailand	64.0	44.9	14.0	19.8	22.0	35.3
South Asia						
Pakistan	51.2	42.1[a]	19.8	20.8[a]	29.0	37.1[a]
Sri Lanka	48.6	35.6	20.9	24.3	30.5	40.1

Source: International Labour Organization, *Labour and Social Trends in Asia and the Pacific 2005* (Bangkok, ILO, Regional Office for Asia and the Pacific, 2005).

[a] Data are for 2002.

Table III.3. Employment in the rural informal economy of selected Asian countries

(Percentage)

		Total	*Male*	*Female*
India	2000	51.3	53.7	40.6
Nepal	1999	64.8	64.1	60.7
Pakistan	2000	63.8	64.1	60.7
Philippines	1995	17.3	15.8	19.4

Source: International Labour Organization, *World Employment Report 2004-2005* (Geneva, ILO, 2004).

as the Philippines significant changes in the structure of production in recent years have altered employment arrangements, accelerating growth in part-time employment.

The effect of discouraged workers on the labour force could partly explain the low official unemployment rates

Data on underemployment in the region are scant and weak. They show that underemployment is low, varying from 3 per cent of the labour force in Hong Kong, China; Pakistan; and Thailand to 10 per cent in the Philippines.[10] Those estimates appear to underestimate the unemployment in the region, however. The effect of discouraged workers, particularly women, on the labour force could partly explain the low unemployment rates. In many developing countries, such as Viet Nam, incomes are too low to enable people not to engage in work while they are searching for a better job, resulting in very low unemployment rates (2.3 per cent in Viet Nam in 2003) but high underemployment.[11]

Underemployment is especially high in rural areas and among women

Estimates of underemployment do not reflect the high level of working poverty and they also fail to correspond to the evidence. For example, according to the National Labour Force Survey of Indonesia, 40 per cent of the labour force was underemployed under the traditional standard (working fewer than 35 hours a week) in 1993 and 34 per cent in 2002. Even under a stricter standard, defined as "severe underemployment" (fewer than 25 hours per week), the survey identified 23 per cent of the workforce to be working too few hours.[12] The Asian financial crisis of 1997 forced a large movement of workers from manufacturing, construction and trade and services into agriculture and possibly informal sector employment at reduced wage rates.[13] The Sri Lanka Labour Force Survey of 2004 indicated an 18 per cent share of those currently employed worked fewer than 29 hours a week.[14] Both surveys suggest that underemployment is higher among women than men and in the agricultural, fisheries and forestry sector than in other sectors. In Bangladesh, despite a drop in total underemployment from 17.6 per cent in 1996 to 16.6 per cent in 2000, female underemployment rose from 45.5 per cent to

[10] International Labour Organization, *Key Indicators of the Labour Market* (CD-ROM), third edition (Geneva, ILO, 2003); and Ray Brooks, "Why is unemployment high in the Philippines?", IMF Working Paper 02/23 (Washington, D.C., IMF, 2002), estimates that underemployment in the Philippines is at a higher level, i.e., 17.2 per cent, for 2001.

[11] See John Luke Gallup, "The wage labor market and inequality in Viet Nam in the 1990s", World Bank Policy Research Working Paper 2896 (Washington, D.C., World Bank, 2002); and Liesbet Steer and Markus Taussig, "A little engine that could: domestic private companies and Vietnam's pressing need for wage employment", World Bank Policy Research Working Paper 2873 (Washington, D.C., World Bank, 2002).

[12] Franck Wiebe, "Income insecurity and underemployment in Indonesia's informal sector", World Bank Policy Research Working Paper 1639 (Washington, D.C., World Bank, 1996); see also International Labour Organization, *Labour and Social Trends in Asia and the Pacific 2005* (Bangkok, ILO, Regional Office for Asia and the Pacific, 2005).

[13] See, for example, International Labour Organization, "Indonesia employment strategy mission (26 April-7 May 1999) aide memoire" (Geneva, ILO, 1999), <www.ilo.org/public/english/region/asro/jakarta/publ/aide.htm>.

[14] Department of Census and Statistics Sri Lanka, *Quarterly Report of the Sri Lanka Labour Force Survey, First Quarter 2004* (Colombo, 2004).

52.8 per cent.[15] Underemployment tends to be higher in rural areas than in urban areas, reflecting the part-time nature and seasonality of work in rural areas.

Child labour: an issue of poverty

Child labour is a pervasive problem in the Asian and Pacific region, which harbours an estimated 127 million working children between the ages of 5 and 14, or 52 per cent of the world's total of 246 million.[16] Child labourers often endure dangerous and unhealthy conditions at work and are exposed to lasting physical and psychological harm. They are sometimes subject to physical and sexual abuse, particularly the girls. Child labour is bad not only because it exposes children to harsh and dangerous working conditions and deprives them of their childhood but also because of the long-term economic and social implications. Despite these negative attributes, why do children work instead of attend school? How should this issue be addressed? The answers to these two questions are as complex as the issue of child labour itself.

Poverty is the major cause of child labour

Poverty often drives parents to push their children into the workforce.[17] Negative perceptions among some parents about the contributions of schooling to employability in the formal sector are also a factor. Child labour is also influenced by adult literacy (see table III.4).[18] The lack of enforcement of labour restrictions also perpetuates child labour. Rapid rural-to-urban migration is a major cause of the

Table III.4. Child labour, level of income and adult literacy in selected Asian countries, 2003

	Economically active children, 10-14 years old (percentage)	*Annual per capita income (United States dollars)*	*Adult literacy rate, ages 15 and older (percentage)*
Afghanistan	23.5	250	–
Bangladesh	26.5	400	41.1
Cambodia	23.2	310	73.6
Lao People's Democratic Republic	24.3	320	68.7
Myanmar	22.0	220	89.7
Nepal	40.2	240	48.6
Timor-Leste	35.2	430	..

Sources: International Labour Organization, *Labour and Social Trends in Asia and the Pacific 2005* (Bangkok, ILO, Regional Office for Asia and the Pacific, 2005); United Nations Children's Fund, *The State of the World's Children 2005* (New York, UNICEF, 2004); and United Nations Development Programme, *Human Development Report 2005: International Cooperation at a Crossroads: Aid, Trade and Security in an Unequal World* (New York, Oxford University Press, 2005).

---

15 Rahman, op. cit.

16 UNICEF, Child protection website, <www.unicef.org/protection>.

17 According to K.A. Syed, A. Mirza, R. Sultana and I. Rana, "Child labour: socioeconomic consequences", *Pakistan and Gulf Economist,* vol. 10, pp. 36-39 (1991), parents represent 62 per cent of the source of child induction into employment. Also see Faraaz Siddiqi and Harry Anthony Patrinos, "Child labour: issues, causes and interventions", Human Capital Development and Operations Working Paper HCOWP56 (Washington, D.C., World Bank, 1996).

18 The intergenerational transfer of low levels of education is high in poor households. Parents with little school attainment tend to rear children who also obtain little formal schooling. See Dorte Verner and Erik Alda, "Youth at risk, social exclusion, and intergeneration poverty dynamics: a new survey instrument with application to Brazil", World Bank Policy Research Working Paper 3296 (Washington, D.C., World Bank, 2004).

increasing rate of child labour in urban areas of developing countries in the region.

Disagreements and inconsistencies in policies abound. While developing countries may consider child labour a matter of survival, developed countries tend to attach concerns about child labour to issues concerning competition from developing countries in international trade. In some countries, differences exist between the minimum working age and the ages for compulsory education, so that children can be legally employed before they complete the minimum number of years required for schooling, or are forced into an inactive period after compulsory schooling ends and before the minimum working age is reached (see table III.5). Further, in many countries children in poor families may have to work in order to attend school.[19]

Table III.5. Compulsory education and minimum working age

(Years)

	Education compulsory up to age	*Minimum working age*
Bangladesh	10	14
Iran (Islamic Republic of)	10	15
Nepal	11	14
Sri Lanka	15	14
Thailand	15	12
Turkey	14	15

Source: V. Sinclair and G. Trah, "Child labour: national legislation on the minimum age for admission to employment or work", in *Conditions of Work Digest,* vol. 10, No.1, pp. 19-146 (Geneva, ILO, 1991).

Addressing fundamental development issues is key to solving the problem of child labour

Many countries with large shares of child labour are least developed countries. The problem of child labour is unlikely to be solved without addressing fundamental development issues.

JOBLESS GROWTH: NEGLECTING THE PEOPLE

Charges of jobless growth are being heard in some countries

Concern is widespread that many countries in the region have achieved high levels of economic growth at the expense of adequate employment creation.[20] Charges of jobless growth are being heard, particularly in China and the Republic of Korea, where unemployment rates have risen recently. Does high growth lead to higher unemployment? A plot of the relationship between the average unemployment rate and GDP growth in 29 countries in the Asian and Pacific region during the period 1990-2003 shows a negative relationship, implying that economic growth leads to job creation and reduces unemployment (see figure III.2). However, further analysis indicates a weakening relationship between economic growth and employment creation.

Employment elasticities are declining, suggesting limited employment generation as a result of enhanced output growth

Globalization compels firms to be competitive and the public sector to be more efficient, leading to the diffusion of new technologies and the use of highly skilled workers. The skill bias in new production technologies and the resulting increase in productivity could induce a slowdown in job creation or even a reduction in employment, leading to jobless growth.

---

[19] For example, in Nepal 21 per cent of children 5-14 years old attend school and work outside the home.

[20] See, for example, Anushree Sinha and Christopher Adam, "Reforms and informalization: what lies behind jobless growth in India", paper presented at the Expert Group on Development Issues (EGDI) – United Nations World Institute for Development Economics Research (WIDER) Conference on Unlocking Human Potential: Linking the Informal and Formal Sectors, Helsinki (2004); B.B. Bhattacharya and S. Sakthivel, *Economic Reforms and Jobless Growth in India in the 1990s* (New Delhi, Institute of Economic Growth, 2003), <http://ieg.nic.in/worksakthi245.pdf>; and Zeng, op. cit.

Figure III.2. Relationship between average unemployment rate and GDP growth rate for 29 countries in Asia and the Pacific, 1990-2003

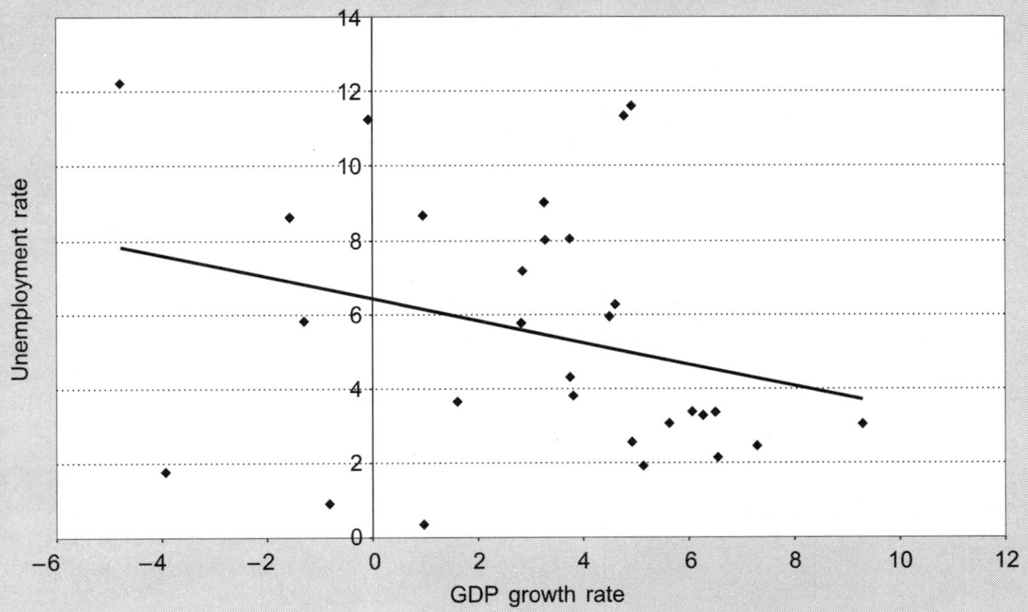

Sources: International Labour Organization, *Key Indicators of the Labour Market* (CD-ROM), third edition (Geneva, ILO, 2003); LABORSTA Internet, an International Labour Office database on labour statistics, 1998-2005, <http://laborsta.ilo.org/> accessed on 7 September 2005); and World Bank, *World Development Indicators 2005* (CD-ROM) (Washington, D.C., World Bank, 2005).

Employment elasticities declined during the 1990s in many countries in the region, indicating that growth had resulted largely from increased labour productivity (see table III.6). Declining employment elasticities are indicative of limited employment generation as a result of enhanced output growth, as in the state of Kerala in India.[21] India's organized sector reportedly may have lost approximately 1.3 million jobs during the post-reform period of 1995-2002, although such losses were not reflected in that country's Labour Bureau data.[22]

There are many underlying reasons for high growth with low employment creation, but chief among them are the absence of an appropriate policy environment and the resulting high cost for entrepreneurs. Rigidities in labour markets, particularly strict hiring and firing regulations, have driven firms to resort to hiring temporary labour and making more capital-intensive investments, while employment-protection legislation and labour-market policies, such as pension and health reform and minimum wages, have raised labour costs, thus depressing the demand for labour.[23]

The regulatory setting in labour markets in the Asian and Pacific region is quite heterogeneous (see table III.7). While Singapore has a flexible labour market with minimal regulations, China, India, Pakistan and countries in Central

21 Bhattacharya and Sakthivel, op. cit.

22 Sinha and Adam, op. cit.

23 Raquel Bernal and Mauricio Cardenas, "Determinants of labor demand in Colombia: 1976-1996", NBER Working Paper 10077 (Cambridge, Mass., National Bureau of Economic Research, 2003), <www.nber.org/papers/w10077>. Distortions have also emerged from labour-market reforms in some countries. For example, the dual minimum wage system for domestic and foreign enterprises in Viet Nam discourages labour mobility across sectors, while labour contracts introduced under the Labour Code introduced rigidities that deter job creation and reduce labour-market flexibility.

Table III.6. Employment elasticities and labour productivity in selected Asian countries, 1980s and 1990s

	Elasticity		*Productivity growth, 1980-2001 (percentage)*
	1980s	*1990s*	
Bangladesh	0.550	0.495	1.5
China	0.330	0.129	5.2
India	0.324	0.312	3.2
Indonesia	0.435	0.379	1.8
Malaysia	0.682	0.406	2.8
Thailand	0.325	0.193	3.9

Sources: Asian Development Bank, *Key Indicators of Developing Asian and Pacific Countries* (Manila, ADB, 2005); International Labour Organization, *Key Indicators of the Labour Market* (CD-ROM), third edition (Geneva, ILO, 2003).

Table III.7. Extent of employment protection in selected Asian countries

	Regular employment protection index	*Rank*
East Asia	0.57	72
China		
South-East Asia		
Cambodia	0.39	42
Indonesia	0.41	47
Malaysia	0.30	23
Philippines	0.32	27
Singapore	0.11	1
Thailand	0.30	23
Central Asia		
Armenia	0.49	64
Azerbaijan	0.47	61
Georgia	0.50	66
Kazakhstan	0.22	12
Kyrgyzstan	0.41	47
South Asia		
Bangladesh	0.38	39
Bhutan	0.35	31
India	0.51	69
Pakistan	0.57	72

Source: World Bank, Doing Business database (2005), <www.doingbusiness.org>.

Note: The rank was derived from the World Bank's Doing Business database. The index, which was also calculated from the database for 83 countries, ranges between 0, no employment protection, and 1, the highest level of employment protection.

Asia are at the other extreme, with strict employment-protection regulations, which tend to reduce employment generation (see box III.1) and lead to higher youth unemployment and self-employment.

Productivity improvement is due mainly to the substitution of capital-intensive production technologies for labour

Although improving worker productivity is a goal in all countries, most productivity improvements have come from the substitution of capital-intensive production technologies for labour. Incentives in terms of access to duty-free import of capital, provided for the purpose of attracting capital-intensive investment, explain such productivity improvement. This has led to the mass destruction of jobs in China and other countries. Trade-offs between employment and productivity growth are common in the short run as labour adjusts and responds to structural changes in the economy. However, because of friction in the market (such as skill mismatches and differences in market regulations governing labour and products) and structural changes, such adjustments take place with a lag, resulting in short-term unemployment. This underscores the need to harmonize market regulations affecting labour and products, as well as to reduce skill mismatches and improve the efficiency of the labour market through appropriate institutional arrangements.

Box III.1. The impact of employment-protection legislation on employment generation

Employment-protection legislation can affect the equilibrium of the labour market as well as the dynamics of the market vis-à-vis the business cycle. On the positive side, such legislation could reinforce job security, thereby leading to enhanced productivity and profitability. On the negative side, very strict legislation could make firms very cautious about hiring, producing an adverse impact on job creation, wages and tenure. For example, if firing costs are prohibitive, firms may resort to hiring temporary labour. The distortionary effect on the composition of employment could lead to lower wages because temporary workers have less wage-bargaining power than permanent staff. Stricter legislation could also discourage firms from expanding or drive them to use more capital-intensive production technologies. Firms may even shift operations to countries with more market-friendly labour regulations.

Source: Gaëlle Pierre and Stefano Scarpetta, "Employment regulations through the eyes of employers: do they matter and how do firms respond to them?", World Bank Policy Research Working Paper 3463 (Washington, D.C., World Bank, 2004).

Structural reforms have improved efficiency and profitability but employment has yet to recover from the negative impact

In a globalized economy, "creative destruction"[24] makes the labour market dynamic and shortens the duration of unemployment. However, the insufficient rate of new enterprise growth in the region constrains job creation and employment growth. For example, the privatization of State-owned enterprises in Cambodia and Viet Nam, while apparently improving efficiency and profitability, has led to large-scale lay-offs of labour.[25] In some countries, including China, employment has yet to recover from the negative impact of such measures.

Labour markets are an important channel for transmitting the effects of exogenous and policy-induced shocks on economic activity, employment, relative prices and resource allocation. How such shocks are absorbed depends on the flexibility of the labour market. Where labour markets are rigid and segmented, restricting the movement of labour (see box III.2), they function poorly in reallocating resources to cope with external and policy-induced shocks. The result is either firms loaded with unwanted workers, leading to inefficiency and bankruptcy, or the one-way movement of labour from the formal sector to the informal sector, often leading to unemployment and underemployment. In either case, the negative impact on employment creation could be long-lasting.

Trade liberalization: some employment opportunities with the right policies

Trade liberalization has a limited direct impact on employment but a blend of State intervention and market could create opportunities

Trade liberalization, supported by sound macroeconomic policies, has spurred much of the region's growth, but the direct effects on aggregate employment have been muted (see box III.3).[26] Trade liberalization can even have a negative impact on employment in the short run.[27] In countries with flexible labour markets, much of the impact of trade liberalization involves reallocating labour to other sectors,[28] particularly the agricultural and the informal sectors, where unemployment and underemployment

---

[24] Creative destruction denotes a "process of industrial mutation that incessantly revolutionizes the economic structure from within, incessantly destroying the old one, incessantly creating a new one". The birth of new firms is associated with the simultaneous death of old, inefficient firms in a normal and healthy process of "creative destruction" or market selection in which the fittest firms survive the test of market competition. See, for example, Jan Rutkowski, "Why is unemployment so high in Bulgaria?", World Bank Policy Research Working Paper 3017 (Washington, D.C., World Bank, 2003).

[25] International Labour Organization, *Labour and Social Trends in Asia and the Pacific 2005* (Bangkok, ILO, Regional Office for Asia and the Pacific, 2005).

[26] Bernard Hoekman and L. Alan Winters, "Trade and employment: stylized facts and research findings", World Bank Policy Research Working Paper 3676 (Washington, D.C., World Bank, 2005).

[27] Ibid.

[28] Ibid.

Box III.2. The *hukou* system and its impact on the mobility of labour in China

The central planning administrative mechanism in China required the ability to allocate human resources not only at the enterprise and sectoral levels but also across geographic locations.[a] The *hukou* system of household registration was initially implemented in 1951 in Chinese cities to maintain social peace and order, safeguard people's security and protect people's freedom of residence and movement. In 1955 it was extended to rural areas as well, and in 1958 it was tightened by restricting movement from one place to another. In addition to household registration, the expanded system also reflected government policies on administrative control over the rural influx to cities and intra-rural and intra-urban movement of the population.

Household registration under the *hukou* system defines legal residence in a village, town or city at birth and determines entitlements to local jobs, housing, schooling, health care, social security and in rural areas to farming land. Although the system had helped to ensure the country's social stability and to maintain order in cities, developments in the post-reform period would question the validity of such a rigid system.[b] Strict restrictions on migration and other constraints on mobility, such as geographically segmented systems for social insurance and the provision of public services, are prime causes of labour-market segmentation in China.[c] The *hukou* system makes unapproved migration extremely costly in terms of lost entitlements. Even approved movement can involve substantial losses, such as loss of claims on agricultural land without compensation, making the system the greatest constraint to labour mobility.[d] The *hukou* system is also considered to be a major factor contributing to rural unemployment and underemployment and to rural-urban inequality.

Despite attempts to make the *hukou* system more flexible, it continues to differentiate opportunity structures for the entire population on the basis of position within a clearly defined spatial hierarchy. Rural *hukou* holders must still pay substantially higher fees and tuition than local residents to attend schools in urban areas, while many local governments continue to encourage firms to hire local residents.[e] Improvements in labour mobility could substantially increase average marginal productivity[f] and ease the pressure on labour markets arising from the 80 million additions to the labour force projected for the next decade.

---

[a] Zhiqiang Liu, "Institution and inequity: the hukou system in China", *Journal of Comparative Economics*, vol. 33, No. 1, pp. 133-157 (2005).

[b] See, for example, Bao Xing, "Stemming the human tide", in *Chinadaily* (12 June 2003), <http://app1.chinadaily.com.cn/star/2003/0612/fo5-1.html>.

[c] L. Fox and Y. Zhao, "China's labor market reform: performance and prospects", background paper for the World Bank (Washington, D.C., World Bank, 2002).

[d] Douglas Zhihua Zeng, "China's employment challenges and strategies after the WTO accession", World Bank Policy Research Paper 3522 (Washington, D.C., World Bank, 2005).

[e] Liu, op. cit.

[f] Zeng, op. cit.

are high. In developing countries with rigid labour markets and related distortions, there is less impact on employment, as regulatory restrictions prevent labour reallocation.

Open economic policies can result in widening income disparities even though absolute income levels may rise and poverty levels may decline. For example, openness and rapid economic growth resulted in a significant reduction in poverty in China, but income equality deteriorated sharply. The ratio of urban to rural incomes rose from 2.2 per cent in 1990 to 3.1 per cent in 2002, which is extremely high by international standards.[29] Between 1990 and 2001 income inequality, as measured by Gini coefficient, rose from 0.31 to 0.36 in rural areas

---

[29] F. Zhai and T. Hertel, "Impacts of the Doha Development Agenda on China: the role of labor markets and complementary education reforms", World Bank Policy Research Working Paper 3702 (Washington, D.C., World Bank, 2005).

Box III.3. Free trade and employment

The labour impacts of free trade have long been debated. The impacts include aggregate employment, trade-related wage changes and sectoral employment. Looking at the aggregate level of employment, does freer trade destroy or create jobs? The answer starts with "it depends" both on the time dimension and the part of the economy analysed. In the neoclassical school, trade policy has little to do with long-term levels of employment, which is determined by macroeconomic variables and labour market-related institutions. In a shorter time horizon, macroeconomic policy and shocks could influence the level of employment, but these effects are considered as transitory, with equilibrium prices clearing labour markets in the long run.

Of course, trade causes changes in sectoral employment. Owing to trade-triggered structural adjustments, employment will rise in activities with a comparative advantage (this is when trade creates jobs), while employment will fall in import-substituting and contracting activities (this is when trade destroys jobs). If comparative advantage is based on relative factor endowment, this implies that a country's relatively abundant factor will generate more employment opportunities. If that factor turns out to be unskilled labour, there will be no less job creation than job destruction in the short run. However, owing to the functioning of the labour market this will push up unskilled wages relative to the rewards from other factors, and all firms will be seeking less labour until wages have adjusted with full employment and with relatively higher employment in export-related activities than previously, but with little change in the total number of jobs. In the long run, the level and sectoral composition of employment is determined by population growth, education and training, and labour market–related policies and institutions.[a]

In Thailand, for example, changes in the trade environment have been instrumental in causing job losses in textiles, clothing, food-processing and tourism and in job creation in health, business and other services, as well as in chemicals and other industries. Those who lose jobs in textile industries are unlikely to be the same people who gain jobs in fertilizer production. Thus, the existence of losers and winners is not short-lived, and the role of government in applying compensation and similar mechanisms has proven to be necessary to sustain trade reforms.

In addition to these direct effects on job creation and destruction in the short run through the opening of domestic and foreign markets, trade has indirect effects. Trade supplies cheaper and better suited inputs, thus influencing competitiveness. It also enables consumers to buy cheaper goods and services, increasing the purchasing power of their remaining income. When that income is used to buy more domestic goods and services or to finance investment, this can have a positive effect on jobs. Trade also tends to be linked with private investments. Flows of both physical and financial capital tend to affect the level of economic activity and jobs.

The recent literature provides even more support for the effect of trade on the number and composition of jobs even over the long term,[b] probably as a result of the changed character of trade. Some stylized facts on the labour implications of trade are as follows:

- The relative reward to skilled labour has increased in both developing and developed countries, accompanied by a relative increase in skilled employment in all sectors. Inequality between skilled and unskilled labour has become a global phenomenon;
- The relative prices of labour-intensive goods produced by low-skilled and unskilled workers have not fallen by much;
- Trade and trade reforms can explain only a small fraction of the wage inequality observed globally, and skill-biased technical change is still the driving force of the worsening position of low-skilled labour;
- Labour-market institutions and the efficiency of capital markets combined with social policies determine whether employment or wages will be affected more in the aftermath of changes in trade policy;
- Wage responses overshadow employment impacts in developing countries, but they are still quite small;
- The adjustment burden is felt most at the firm level: less efficient firms are forced to downsize, improve efficiency or go bankrupt. Overall, total factor productivity increases more in markets that liberalize more;
- It is difficult to identify the direct impact of trade liberalization on aggregate employment in the long run; the view of "no change" still prevails in most cases.

---

[a] Ben S. Bernanke, "Trade and jobs," remarks at the Distinguished Speaker Series, Fuqua School of Business, Duke University (Durham, N.C., 30 March 2004), <www.federalreserve.gov/boarddocs/speeches/2004/20040330/default.htm>.

[b] Bernard Hoekman and L. Alan Winters, "Trade and employment: stylized facts and research findings", World Bank Policy Research Working Paper 3676 (Washington, D.C., World Bank, 2005).

and from 0.23 to 0.32 in urban areas.[30] Employment grew just 1 per cent annually during the period, while officially registered unemployment increased from 2.5 per cent to 3.1 per cent and estimated unemployment rose from 4.2 per cent to 11.5 per cent.[31]

The story is entirely different in Malaysia. Unemployment fell sharply when trade liberalization was at its peak. How did Malaysia swim against the tide? Malaysia's success in stimulating employment growth through trade liberalization provides evidence of the importance of a balanced approach to growth and employment generation, particularly in small economies.[32] While trade liberalization together with active encouragement of foreign direct investment led to rapid employment creation, the Government also provided a supportive environment by enhancing the quality of human resources.[33] The Malaysian experience shows the success of an interaction between the State and the market in a mutually dependent and supportive environment.

Whether the Doha round brings tangible benefits to the region will depend to a large extent on how the critical issues of access to developed-country markets, rules of origin and non-tariff barriers are addressed

Trade reforms under the Doha round of trade negotiations could bring tangible benefits to the region in terms of enhanced opportunities for trade, business and employment, under the right conditions. These depend to a large extent on how the critical issues of access to developed-country markets, rules of origin and non-tariff barriers are addressed. The fact that 90 per cent of the global gains from agricultural liberalization come from improved market access highlights the importance of access to developed-country markets in reaping the benefits of trade liberalization by agriculture-dependent developing countries in the region. The above analysis indicates that the region's high growth adds little to adequate job creation. The main reason behind this appears to be the substitution of captial-intensive production technologies for labour which has been intensified by rigid labour-market regulations. While the productivity improvement and the resulting gain in income for the already employed is a welcome development, Governments need to create more jobs for the unemployed. A combination of policies including a refocus on areas where labour is concentrated, changing the incentive structure for capital and labour inputs and enhanced human resource development would be needed to address the problem of jobless growth.

THE WORKING POOR: BARELY SURVIVING

The majority of workers earn too little. Some parts of the region are no better off than sub-Saharan Africa

The most pressing labour-market issue in the region is people's inability to make a decent income from employment. Although official unemployment is relatively low and declining in some countries, a large share of the employed comprise the "working poor", defined as those earning less than $2 a day in terms of purchasing power parity (PPP). In South Asia the working poor accounted for 88 per cent of the total number of those employed in 2003, almost as high as in sub-Saharan Africa, at 89 per cent. The share was 59 per cent in the South-East Asian subregion and 49 per cent in East Asia. This is in sharp contrast to the dramatic decline in the share of the working poor earning less than $1 a day during the past two decades; in East Asia the share declined by 76 per cent from 1980 to 2003, in South-East Asia by 70 per cent and in South Asia by 41 per cent (see table III.8).

---

30 Ajit K. Ghose, "Employment in China: recent trends and future challenges", Employment Strategy Paper 2005/14 (Geneva, ILO, 2005), <www.ilo.org/public/english/employment/strat/download/esp2005-14.pdf>.

31 Zeng, op. cit.

32 R. Rasiah, "Manufactured exports, employment, skills, and wages in Malaysia", Employment Paper 2002/35 (Geneva, ILO, 2002).

33 It should be noted that Malaysia promoted foreign direct investment even though its savings rate was high enough to meet domestic investment needs.

Table III.8. Shares of the working poor in total employment

(Percentage)

	Less than $1 (PPP) a day			Less than $2 (PPP) a day		
	1980	1990	2003	1980	1990	2003
East Asia	71.1	35.9	17.0	92.0	79.1	49.2
South-East Asia	37.6	19.9	11.3	73.4	69.1	58.8
South Asia	64.7	53.0	38.1	95.5	93.1	87.5
World	40.3	27.5	19.7	59.8	57.2	49.7

Source: International Labour Organization, *Labour and Social Trends in Asia and the Pacific 2005* (Bangkok, ILO, Regional Office for Asia and the Pacific, 2005).

The likelihood that internal and external shocks will push the working poor into extreme poverty is very high

Two issues emerge from this evidence. First, despite rapid economic growth and poverty reduction, the vast majority of the employed are earning wages that are just above the $1 a day poverty line (see figure III.3). As a result, the likelihood that internal and external shocks will push the working poor into extreme poverty is very high. Second, the large employment opportunities created in the region are apparently ones of low productivity, providing low incomes and wages. Most of these low-productivity employment opportunities are in the informal sector.

Figure III.3. Income shares in total employment by Asian subregion and world in 2003

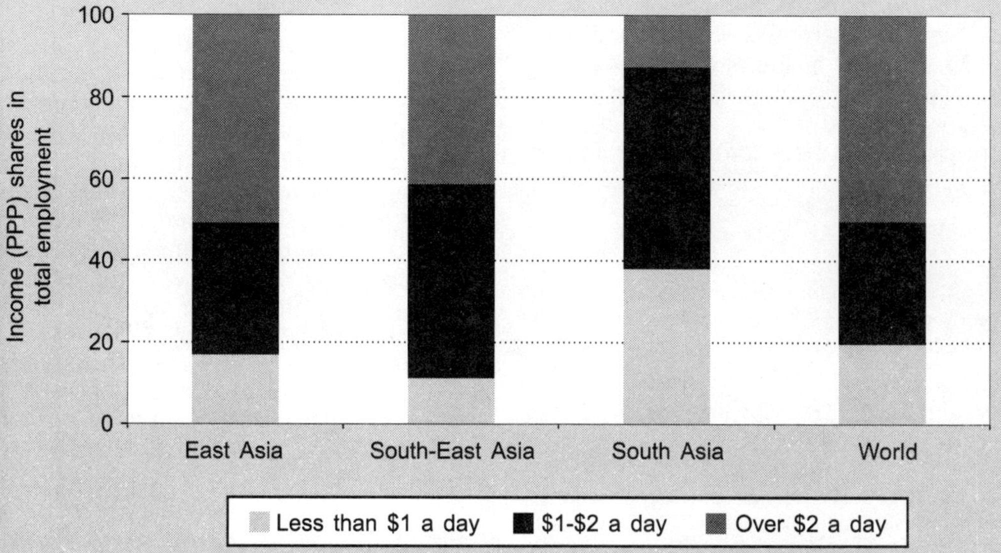

Source: Derived from International Labour Organization, *Labour and Social Trends in Asia and the Pacific 2005* (Bangkok, ILO, Regional Office for Asia and the Pacific, 2005).

In some cases such results are policy-induced. For example, labour-market reforms may entail a trade-off between unemployment and poverty through their impact on wages and labour demand. Fiscal incentives for job creation, for instance, may have a direct beneficial impact on employment but be skewed towards low-paying jobs, translating into both lower unemployment and higher poverty.[34]

Internal migration plays an important role in reshaping labour-market conditions in developing countries. Rural to urban migration is increasing in almost all countries as workers search for employment opportunities. However, such internal migration has contributed to high levels of under-employment and thus the "working poor" as a result of the limited opportunities available, and most migrants end up in low-paying jobs.

Table III.9. Share in employment and GDP of small and medium-sized enterprises in selected countries: average 1990-1999

	Share in formal sector employment (percentage)	*Share in GDP (percentage)*
Philippines	66.00	31.50
Republic of Korea	76.25	45.90
Thailand	86.70	–
Turkey	61.10	27.30
Viet Nam	74.20	24.00

Source: Meghana Ayyagari, Thorsten Beck and Asli Demirgüç-Kunt, "Small and medium enterprises across the globe", World Bank Policy Research Working Paper 3127 (Washington, D.C., World Bank, 2003).

Small and medium-sized enterprises and employment

Small and medium-sized enterprises create employment opportunities and help to reduce poverty

One particular area where the working poor are concentrated could be the small and medium-sized enterprises, particularly in the informal sector. Such firms account for more than 60 per cent of formal sector employment in most developing countries in the region (table III.9). More than 86 per cent of the labour force is employed in such enterprises in Thailand and more than 70 per cent in the Republic of Korea and in Viet Nam.[35] As such, small and medium-sized enterprises could play a critical role in employment creation in both formal and informal economies in the region.[36] Their ease of start-up and primary reliance on unskilled labour make them an ideal instrument for job creation and growth. In addition to creating jobs and reducing poverty, small and medium-sized enterprises could contribute to equitable economic growth and innovation.

The survival rate of small and medium-sized enterprises is low, as a host of factors impede their transformation into formal enterprises

Small and medium-sized enterprises are also common in the informal economy in most developing countries in the region, where employment growth often comes at the expense of productivity growth.[37] As a result, substantial underemployment is common in small and medium-sized enterprises in the informal economy, as reflected in low wages, low value added and their high "mortality" rates. For example, in Sri Lanka the value added per worker in small and medium-sized enterprises is about one third that in larger firms, and the survival rate after five years in operation is only 5 per cent.[38] A survey of small

[34] See, for example, Pierre-Richard Agénor, "Unemployment-poverty trade-offs", World Bank Policy Research Working Paper 3297 (Washington, D.C., World Bank, 2004).

[35] Meghana Ayyagari, Thorsten Beck and Asli Demirgüç-Kunt, "Small and medium enterprises across the globe: a new database", World Bank Policy Research Working Paper 3127 (Washington, D.C., World Bank, 2003).

[36] International Labour Organization, *World Employment Report 2004-2005* (Geneva, ILO, 2004); Ayyagari, Beck and Demirgüç-Kunt, op. cit., find a strong positive correlation between small and medium-sized enterprises (with a minimum of 250 employees) and employment creation for a sample of developed and developing economies.

[37] Ibid.

[38] Peter Richards in collaboration with Junko Ishikawa and Martina Lubyova, "Towards an employment strategy framework for Sri Lanka", Employment Paper (draft, EP40) (Geneva, ILO, 2002).

and medium-sized enterprises in Sri Lanka shed light on some of the factors behind their failure.[39] These include poor-quality products, lack of skill training, inappropriate government policies, lack of markets and financial facilities, difficulties in finding raw materials, high cost of finance, poor management and strong competition. Limited access to technology and services and weak entrepreneurial skills constrain the growth of small and medium-sized enterprises. In addition, the high cost of entry, the strict and time-consuming regulatory environment and rigid labour-market regulations tend to impede the transformation to formal enterprises. Providing opportunities for employment with adequate wages and income through productivity improvement and capacity-building would be key to reducing working poverty in the region. In this regard, addressing issues hampering this sector is vital for small and medium-sized enterprises to be used as a vehicle for job creation.

YOUTH UNEMPLOYMENT: BRAINS DRAINED AND WASTED

A troubling characteristic of unemployment in the region is its concentration among youth (ages 15-24). While overall unemployment in the region was about 4.4 per cent in 2004, youth unemployment ranged from 7.5 per cent in East Asia to 17.1 per cent in South-East Asia (see table III.10). South Asia has the largest population of unemployed youth, at almost 14.5 million in 2004.

The crux of youth unemployment is primarily the lack of adequate job creation to absorb the new entrants to the labour market

In most of the Pacific island countries, and Indonesia, the Philippines and Sri Lanka in particular, 25 per cent or more of the youth population is unemployed.[40] The ratio of youth to adult unemployment rates was as high as 11.9 in Bangladesh in 2000 and 6.3 in Sri Lanka in 2003. Youth account for more than half the total unemployment in Asian developing countries.[41]

Multiple causes

While demographic changes are partly responsible for the rapid increase in youth unemployment, the crux of the issue is primarily the lack of adequate job creation to absorb the new youth entrants to the labour market. This is manifested by the high proportions of young people among the unemployed in countries such as Bangladesh and Sri Lanka. The youth unemployment rate tends to be lower in countries with high average incomes. Youth unemployment also reflects a gender dimension, with women accounting for a larger share of the unemployed, except in East Asia because its dominant economy, China, enjoys greater gender equality.

Youth unemployment is affected by both demand and supply issues. Available jobs are not well paid and are unattractive, particularly for educated youth. Low levels of technology use have led to weak demand for better educated youth, resulting in unemployment in skilled categories. The type of education possessed by most youth is a poor match for most jobs.

Youth unemployment deprives young people of the opportunity to participate in the economic, social and political life of society

Youth unemployment is an enormous waste of human resources much needed for economic and social development. It deprives young people of the opportunity to participate

[39] Ibid.

[40] International Labour Organization, *Labour and Social Trends in Asia and the Pacific 2005* (Bangkok, ILO, Regional Office for Asia and the Pacific, 2005). For example, the youth unemployment rate is estimated to be 62.6 per cent for Marshall Islands (1999), 46 per cent for Solomon Islands (1999), 35.2 per cent for the Federated States of Micronesia, 31.2 per cent for Tuvalu (2002) and 30.3 per cent for Tonga (1996). In Papua New Guinea each year about 50,000 youth reach working age, but only 5,000 find jobs.

[41] International Labour Organization, *Labour and Social Trends in Asia and the Pacific 2005* (Bangkok, ILO, Regional Office for Asia and the Pacific, 2005). This is also relevant for developed countries such as Japan where the male youth unemployment rate was as high as 10.9 per cent in 2004

Table III.10. Youth unemployment by subregion and world, 2004

(Percentage)

	Youth unemployment rate		Youth to adult unemployment ratio		Youth unemployment rate by sex	
					Male	Female
	1994	*2004*	*1994*	*2004*	*2004*	*2004*
East Asia	6.5	7.5	2.8	2.7	8.1	5.8
South-East Asia and the Pacific	9.0[a]	17.1[a]	4.8	5.6[a]	13.9	15.8
South Asia	8.7	10.8	3.8	3.7	10.6	11.6
World		13.1			13.2	12.9

Sources: International Labour Organization, *Global Employment Trends for Youth 2004* (Geneva, ILO, 2004); International Labour Organization, *Labour and Social Trends in Asia and the Pacific 2005* (Bangkok, ILO, Regional Office for Asia and the Pacific, 2005).

[a] Refers to South-East Asia only.

in the economic, social and political life of society and to secure resources for a decent living and social protection, including pensions and accommodations for the establishment of families.

In countries with formal social protection systems that provide unemployment insurance or welfare assistance, youth unemployment represents an enormous burden on limited public resources. In countries without such systems, the burden is shouldered by families that have forgone income and invested in the education of their children only to find themselves continuing to provide support to their grown children.[42] Especially in families with limited resources, youth unemployment may lead to negative behaviour, marginalization and social exclusion.

Lacking opportunities in the formal labour market, young people are turning to low-paying jobs or self-employment in the informal sector, often working in hazardous conditions without proper protection and with poor prospects for the future. A combination of these factors can lead to frustration, disillusionment, marginalization and alienation. Evidence suggests that the social exclusion resulting from youth unemployment has adverse social repercussions in terms of youth violence, delinquency, substance abuse, prostitution and heightened attraction to illegal activities.[43] A poor economic and social environment provides fertile ground for recruiting youth (or forcing them) into armed conflict. The chances of unemployed youth becoming involved in violence, delinquency and substance abuse and other illegal activities are high.

Young people also make up a significant share of the 175 million global migrants, adding to the brain drain.[44] Halving the level of youth unemployment in South-East Asia and South

[42] Secretary-General of the United Nations, "Global analysis and evaluation of national action plans on youth employment: report of the Secretary-General" (A/60/133, July 2005).

[43] For example, frustration over jobs contributed to two violent uprisings by educated youth in Sri Lanka in 1971 and in the period 1987-1989; see Martin Rama, "The Sri Lankan unemployment problem revisited", World Bank Policy Research Working Paper 2227 (Washington, D.C., World Bank, 1999). Unemployed youth have been key contributors to civil unrest in Fiji and Solomon Islands and to the rising crime rate in Papua New Guinea. Teenage pregnancy and prostitution are reportedly on the rise, particularly in Fiji, Kiribati, Papua New Guinea, Solomon Islands and Vanuatu.

[44] United Nations, *World Youth Report 2005* (United Nations publication, Sales No. E.05.IV.6); United Nations, *Trends in Total Migrant Stock: The 2003 Revision* (POP/DB/MIG/Rev. 2003).

Asia could generate GDP gains of about 4-7 per cent.[45]

Unemployment among educated youth

Although unemployment usually falls, often dramatically, with the level of a person's education,[46] the relationship between the two is complex, depending on many factors including a country's level of economic development (see table III.11).

Table III.11. Share of total unemployment by education level in selected economies in 2000

(Percentage)

	Primary education	*Secondary education*	*Tertiary education*
Bangladesh	54.3	22.7	8.4
Indonesia	45.5	43.8	7.9
Macao, China	65.5	11.3	6.3
Republic of Korea	26.1	51.0	49.9
Thailand	70.6	7.2	19.2
Azerbaijan	4.8	34.2	61.1
Georgia	5.5	33.1	61.4
Sri Lanka	49.7	..[a]	49.9

Source: World Bank, *World Development Indicators 2005* (CD-ROM) (Washington, D.C., World Bank, 2005).

[a] Data for share of employment with secondary education in Sri Lanka were not available owing to inconsistencies in classification of education level.

Economic growth and education are keys to reducing youth unemployment

Countries where levels of economic development and overall human development are low seem to experience low levels of unemployment among educated youth because the demand for educated workers is high. In these countries unemployment is concentrated mostly among the abundant low-skilled and uneducated categories of the working-age population. For example, in Bangladesh and Indonesia the unemployment rate is high among youth with only a primary education. In Bhutan, unemployment is concentrated among young school drop-outs.[47] In relatively better-off and technologically more advanced economies, such as Macao, China; and Thailand, unemployment also tends to be concentrated among youth with a primary or lower level of education, as the demand is mostly for educated and skilled workers.

Unemployment among educated youth is extraordinarily high where economies are in transition or where economic development does not keep pace with rapid increases in educational attainment

In contrast, unemployment among educated youth is extraordinarily high where economies are in transition or where economic

[45] International Labour Organization, *World Employment Report 2004-2005* (Geneva, ILO, 2004).

[46] This is true for developing and developed countries; see Niall O'Higgins, "The challenge of youth unemployment", Employment and Training Papers 7 (Geneva, ILO, 1997).

[47] The mismatch between skills and job requirements is evident from the high number of foreign workers in Bhutan, estimated at about 50,000, employed largely as skilled labourers in the construction sector.

development does not keep pace with rapid increases in educational attainment. In such economies unemployment among educated youth could threaten social stability. Governments' sensitivity to that possibility is reflected in the occasional and apparently arbitrary recruitment of educated youth for public sector employment[48] Economies in transition such as Azerbaijan and Georgia have yet to exploit their educated labour force for development because of a lack of adequate demand and because of a mismatch of skills.

Unemployment among educated youth tends to reflect a search for "good" jobs and a rejection of job opportunities perceived to be "bad" according to social or cultural norms.[49] In Sri Lanka the probability of being unemployed is much higher among those with a university or post-graduate degree.[50] The share of the unemployed with 13 years or more of schooling increased from 15.4 per cent in 1990 to 29.0 per cent in 2003. In the Philippines the incidence of unemployment also tends to increase with the number of years of education.

Country experiences also show a higher concentration of unemployment among educated youth in rural areas than in urban areas. In Sri Lanka unemployment among university graduates was twice as high in rural areas (11.8 per cent) as in urban areas in 1998.[51] The problem of youth unemployment in Sri Lanka reflects the slow progress in moving to a higher growth path that demands higher levels of education and skills. While Sri Lanka's educational achievement is on a par with that in most middle-income countries, its economy is stuck in a production base with low value added, focusing mainly on primary products and low-end manufacturing.

POLICY RESPONSES: BALANCED APPROACH AND REFOCUSED ACTION

Economic growth is a necessary condition for sustainable employment generation. However, growth alone will not create employment. State interventions are also required to ensure that growth is broad based and that the benefits are passed on to the poor through employment. Governments can facilitate this process by implementing policies within a comprehensive programme of reforms. Such policy measures and reforms should target improving the macroeconomic environment, labour market-related issues and institutional development. Some policy proposals that could help to address unemployment are elaborated below.

Improving the macroeconomic environment

Sound macroeconomic policies

Unemployment has to be considered in the context of the macroeconomic environment for tangible and sustained reduction in unemployment

Unemployment has to be considered in the context of the overall macroeconomic environment if tangible and sustained reduction of unemployment is to be achieved. Labour-market policies by themselves cannot generate employment. A sufficient pull from the demand side is also necessary. Sound macroeconomic policies, a strong macroeconomic environment and a solid development agenda are imperative for the creation of adequate jobs. It is only when the government's fiscal position is strong that it can ensure the provision of basic services and safety nets to the poor and unemployed. A sound fiscal policy also stimulates private sector involvement in the development process, thereby generating employment by minimizing the crowding out of private investment. Monetary policy needs to

48 Richards in collaboration with Ishikawa and Lubyova, op. cit.

49 More than 15,000 vacancies existed in firms located in export processing zones in Sri Lanka, mainly in the garment industry, while there was excess demand for low-paying public sector employment in Sri Lanka; see Rama, op. cit.

50 Richards in collaboration with Ishikawa and Lubyova, op. cit.

51 Sri Lanka Department of National Planning, *Employment and Unemployment of Youth in Sri Lanka* (Colombo, 2002), <www.ilo.wg/public/english/region/asro/Colombo/download/ptlppro2.pdf>.

ensure low inflation, which could help to sustain real income, particularly of the poor, but also a real interest rate sufficient to induce savings. Macroeconomic policies need to accommodate wage-moderation policies to make room for private sector engagement in economic activities.

Trade liberalization

Benefiting from trade liberalization would require improving absorptive capacity and the stock of human capital

Although trade liberalization may not result in significant employment generation directly, in the long run country experiences point to the importance of trade liberalization for stimulating employment creation.[52] Specialization in areas of comparative advantage is vital for sustainability in a competitive world. Benefiting from trade liberalization requires improving absorptive capacity. The stock of human capital plays a key role. Providing a supportive environment, through domestic reforms and greater access to global markets, is also required if an economy is to benefit from trade liberalization. Adequate protection, through social safety nets, capacity-building and opportunities for training, is also needed for those who lose out because of trade liberalization.

Addressing labour-related issues

Labour-market policies need to improve flexibility and reduce costs

Improving the functioning of the labour market by increasing flexibility and reducing costs is vital for employment creation. Segmented labour markets contribute to persistent wage differentials that impede the resource allocation needed to respond to external and policy-induced shocks.

More flexible labour markets would benefit both employers and employees

Labour-market flexibility is a key determinant of the success of economic reforms.[53] Long spells of unemployment signal a stagnant labour market, with limited chances of escaping unemployment. Contributing factors are the difficulty of moving from one job to another because of firm-specific training, strict regulations controlling firing and the non-transferability of pension benefits. Firm-specific training highlights the need for minimum standards of educational attainment and technical skills. Strict firing regulations, which lead to the retention of unwanted employees, could be resolved by relaxing hiring and firing regulations, while providing relatively strong income protection for laid-off workers at the societal level. The non-transferability of pension benefits could be addressed by introducing contributory pension and retirement schemes.

High labour-market costs impede the evolution of the private sector as a major force for employment generation, and the pay-off from reducing labour costs is substantial

Reducing labour-market costs is another important reform. High labour-market costs impede the evolution of the private sector as a major force for employment generation in both the formal and informal sectors, eroding the competitive edge of developing countries and constraining businesses expansion. The pay-off from reducing labour costs could thus be substantial.[54] The main reason that so many small

[52] For example, increasing openness lay behind much of the decline in the natural rate of unemployment in Singapore; see Hiau Looi Kee and Hian Teck Hoon, "Trade, capital accumulation and structural unemployment: an empirical study of the Singapore economy", *Journal of Development Economics*, vol. 77, No. 1, pp. 125-152 (2005).

[53] Alvaro Forteza and Martin Rama, "Labour market 'rigidity' and the success of economic reforms across more than 100 countries", World Bank Policy Research Working Paper 2521 (Washington, D.C., World Bank, 2001).

[54] In Sri Lanka, for example, high labour-market costs, with no compensatory increases in labour productivity, pose a risk for loss of competitiveness to countries such as China and Viet Nam in industries with a high labour-to-capital ratio. The Termination of Employment of Workmen Act of 1971 imposes strict restrictions on firing employees. Employers are likely to try to circumvent its provisions through contracting and subcontracting and by rotating workers to keep them as probationers. High payroll taxes are another barrier to employment creation. Estimates indicate that elimination of the 9 per cent payroll tax in Colombia could result in a 13 per cent increase in employment in urban areas; see Bernal and Cardenas, op. cit.

and medium-sized enterprises remain in the informal sector is the high cost of entry and the strict regulatory environment in the formal sector. Reducing such costs is vital if the private sector is to contribute meaningfully to employment generation. Viet Nam's new law on enterprises aimed at reducing the financial and time costs of registering companies could be an example for other developing countries in the region.

Active labour-market policies

Structural issues are behind the high unemployment and underemployment rates in many developing countries in the region, primarily on the supply side. These structural problems should be addressed in the medium to long term and should focus on improving access to labour markets, job-related skills development and better functioning of labour markets. While some short-term measures may also be necessary, short-term measures such as those curtailing the labour supply, which are self-defeating in the long-term, should be avoided.

Developing human capital

Educational reforms

While low levels of education are a major cause of high unemployment in countries with low literacy rates, a mismatch between education and the skills demanded by the private sector is a concern in some countries with a higher level of educational attainment. Workers with more than a primary education appear to perform better in on-the-job training, skills-testing and evaluation; thus, they have better job prospects. Raising the age of compulsory education could provide the additional benefit of helping to reduce child labour.

It is not just the amount of education that matters but also the quality

Education and technical skills are vital to the employability of workers. While many countries in the region boast of high educational attainment, the quality of education and skills is crucial and so is the content of that learning. In many economies in transition there is a mismatch between educational content provided under planned economic systems and the skills demanded by a market economy, and those economies are lagging behind.

In a globalized economy technical knowledge needs to be adjusted to market demand and changing circumstances. Thus, while basic education remains a fundamental necessity, reforms in secondary and tertiary education to suit the changing demand would minimize the skills mismatch. The introduction of information technology and international languages for communication and technology-oriented subjects in the curricula is essential for equipping new entrants to the labour market with the necessary basic skills.

Countries where female unemployment is high or the female labour-force participation rate is low may need to take special steps to break this cycle. Education may need to provide a more conducive socio-cultural environment to encourage girls and women to attend school and to improve productivity through skills development.

Training programmes are most effective when they are tightly targeted and small-scale, with a strong on-the-job component and linked to industry

Vocational training

Many countries have vocational training programmes to enhance the employability of youth. Despite high returns to vocational training generally,[55] in many developing countries of the region vocational training does not seem to provide the required technical and practical exposure. Reasons include a lack of recent industrial exposure by trainers, lack of regular technical and pedagogical upgrading and the absence of professionalism in curriculum development. Training programmes are most effective when they are tightly targeted and small-scale, with a strong on-the-job component and linked to industry.[56]

---

[55] For example, Martina Lubyova, "Technical appendix", in Richards in collaboration with Ishikawa and Lubyova, op. cit., found that returns from a year of vocational training are substantial and nearly as high as those from a year of education at grade 10 or higher.

[56] For example, higher technical and professional education has played a significant role in economic and technical development in India by producing a good quality workforce through strong links between technical institutions and industry.

Initiatives by China, the Republic of Korea and Singapore are noteworthy. The Government of Singapore works with educational institutions to improve employment opportunities for youth through internships and apprenticeships that provide tangible work experience. Some programmes establish formal training agreements with employers while others subsidize enterprises that hire youth.

To improve the employability of migrant workers and their quality of life, the Government of China's "National migrant worker training plan" for the period 2003-2010 will offer vocational training to 60 million rural labourers who want to move into cities. Other programmes to train highly skilled labour and improve the employability and transition of the labour force include the "Programme for strengthening vocational training and improving employability" and the "National training project for highly skilled human resources", introduced in 2002, and the "Programme for training 500,000 new technicians in three years".

The Republic of Korea encourages industries and universities to work together to meet the future demand for skills. Universities that establish new departments to meet industrial needs through contracts with companies are eligible for governmental financial support for facilities and research costs. A system has been established to evaluate whether college curricula meet industrial demands. Policy measures are devised to encourage employers to expand investments in youth employment and to use human resources more effectively.

Facilitating labour-market entry

Attitudes need to be changed before they become hardened and aspirations become set

Timely intervention in enhancing the employability of youth

Interventions to enhance the employability of youth should be a key component of active labour-market policies and education reforms (see box III.4). Such programmes need to target youth early, before attitudes harden and aspirations are set.

Box III.4. Youth Employment Network

The Youth Employment Network, established in 2001 by ILO, acts as a vehicle to address the global challenge of youth employment. The initiative brings together policymakers, employers, workers and young people to pool their skills, experience and knowledge and find innovative and durable solutions to the youth employment challenge. It encourages countries to establish action plans with a priority focus on four policy areas: employability, equal opportunities, entrepreneurship and employment creation. Four countries in the Asian and Pacific region, Azerbaijan, Indonesia, the Islamic Republic of Iran and Sri Lanka, are among the 16 "lead countries" that are committed to preparing and implementing action plans for youth employment.

Several of the countries have already taken steps in that direction. The Azerbaijan National Action Plan on Youth Employment is an integral part of its overall National Action Plan on Employment. The Indonesian National Action Plan on Youth Employment develops an institutional framework for the Indonesian Youth Employment Network while raising awareness of the challenges faced by youth labour-market entrants. Sri Lanka has set up the Youth Employment Network to develop an integrated national action plan on youth employment, with a focus on reintegrating youthful former combatants into the workforce.

Career guidance and counselling

Career guidance and counselling can help to steer youth towards a career path that matches their interests and skills. This could also help to avert the anxiety and frustration that can arise from prolonged job searches and unemployment.

The provision of labour-market information could minimize the coexistence of job vacancies and skilled unemployed youth

Improving labour-market information

Timely, reliable and accurate labour-market information is essential for making policy decisions and is an integral part of corporate decision-making, particularly for business expansion. In addition, lack of access to labour-market information can lead to the coexistence of unfilled vacancies and unemployed youth with the skills needed to fill those vacancies. Improving labour-market information would not only help to fill the information gap between young job-seekers and employers but would also help in planning training systems in line with changing market demands.

Facilitating job searches

In some countries the bulk of unemployment among youth arises as a result of a prolonged search for work. This is particularly the case in countries with high levels of educational achievement, strong family structures or unemployment benefit schemes that support extended job searches. Individual job searches are less efficient and more costly than institutional arrangements organized by the State or the private sector. The Australian Job Network is a good example of institutional job-matching, job-search training and intensive assistance, reflecting individually tailored training, enterprise incentives and project-contracting.

Creating employment opportunities

Public works programmes and means-tested income transfers are the most commonly used strategies for creating employment, particularly in rural areas. However, poor targeting has made public works programmes ineffective in most cases. High opportunity costs and disruptions to traditional sources of earning are among the drawbacks of such programmes. Public works programmes could be made effective by making them self-targeting and more flexible.

Among active labour-market policies, direct subsidies for job creation appear to be the most effective in generating employment

Empirical research finds that direct subsidies for job creation are the most effective of the active labour-market policies in raising employment rates.[57] However, their cost is high and they are likely to yield diminishing returns as employment rates rise. Action is also required to ensure that such opportunities are open equally to both sexes.[58]

Country experiences provide some practical lessons. Pakistan has introduced schemes involving youth groups in labour-intensive activities. The Republic of Korea focuses on highly educated yet unemployed university graduates while recognizing that a sustainable impact must be based on an economic recovery centred on job creation. Azerbaijan identified three major strategies for job creation: providing active labour-market programmes such as public works and wage subsidies, exploiting oil sector revenues to finance employment-intensive public works and promoting a conducive environment for small and medium-sized enterprises. Indonesia seeks to exploit opportunities in emerging sectors such as tourism, mass media, health and education, environmental conservation, services and information and communications technologies. The Government also supports agro-industries to strengthen urban-rural linkages, which are critical for job creation and poverty reduction. It also seeks to mainstream youth employment issues into local economic development initiatives.

Wage and employment policy

Credible reform of public sector recruitment and wage policies could arrest high unemployment by reducing incentives for people to queue for public sector jobs

To the extent that unemployment arises from prolonged searching for "good" jobs, credible reform of public sector recruitment and wage policies could arrest high unemployment by reducing incentives for people to queue for public sector jobs. Removing the artificial benefits associated with public sector jobs and creating the conditions for sustained improvements in the quality of other jobs would help to bring about important attitudinal changes. Less stringent regulations on firing workers enforced more evenly

[57] Estevao, op. cit.

[58] The Russian Federation targets young women who are socially vulnerable and might face difficulties in the labour market; these include single mothers, women with disabilities and women released from penal institutions.

across firms and sectors would also reduce the wedge between "good" and "bad" jobs.

Unemployment benefit systems

Unemployment benefit schemes would provide a safety net for workers and facilitate flexible employment adjustment by firms in times of shock and structural change

Unemployment benefit schemes provide two important services. First, they serve as a safety net for workers during short spells of unemployment, enabling them to search for jobs or train for new ones. Second, they facilitate flexible employment adjustment by firms during times of shock and structural change. To be more effective, unemployment benefit schemes should be linked to job skills development, as in the Republic of Korea (see box III.5). Where cash transfers are involved, work instead of aid could also be considered for making efficient use of social assistance and to reduce the fiscal burden of unemployment benefit schemes.

Focus on niche industries and sectors where labour is concentrated

Developing countries in the region could benefit from the commercialization and industrialization of agriculture

In many countries in the region that experienced high economic growth but low labour absorption, skill-based technical change has become prominent in the production process while the traditional sectors have been neglected. Balancing high growth and employment creation requires improving the productivity of workers in niche industries while focusing on sectors where the majority of labour is concentrated. For example, a study by the International Center for Peace and Development indicates that the most cost-effective and affordable strategy for India is to aim for full employment through commercialization and industrialization of the agricultural sector, which has the potential to create 100 million new jobs.[59] In this regard, a reassessment of fiscal incentives for investment in capital

Box III.5. Employment insurance system in the Republic of Korea

The compulsory and contributory employment insurance system in the Republic of Korea is more than an unemployment insurance scheme. While providing the traditional cash benefits to the unemployed, the system focuses mainly on employment stabilization and job skills development aimed at preventing unemployment and promoting employment.

The employment stabilization programme is designed to harmonize efficiency and equity in the labour market through assistance with employment adjustment, regional employment stimulation and employment facilitation and the provision of labour-market information and job placement services.[a] These measures are aimed at minimizing job mismatch and encouraging employers to avoid massive layoffs, promote the employment of disadvantaged workers and create jobs in depressed regions.

The job skills development programme encourages the active participation of employees and employers in training and retraining the workforce. Employers receive subsidies for training costs and employees receive low-cost loans for skills development. The unemployed receive a job-seeking allowance and employment-promotion benefits. The system covers more than 80 per cent of workers in the Republic of Korea.

[a] Kil-Sang Yoo, *The Employment Insurance System in Korea* (Seoul, Korea Labour Institute, 1999); and Claire Harasty, ed., "Successful employment and labour market policies in Europe and Asia and the Pacific", Employment Strategy Papers 2004/4 (Geneva, ILO, 2004), <www.ilo.org/public/english/employment/strat/download/esp4.pdf>.

Well-targeted safety nets, means-tested income transfers and subsidized microcredit aimed at improving the access of the poor to financial services could also be used to help the poor to build assets.

[59] International Center for Peace and Development, "Commercial agriculture as an engine for rural development, industrialization and full employment", Prosperity 2000: A Call to the Nation, <www.icpd.org/employment/summary_of_ prosperity_2000_strategy_for_india.htm>.

as opposed to labour may be necessary. Overcrowding in the agricultural sector and the resulting low productivity could be mitigated by promoting agro-based industries.

In countries where agriculture still dominates production and employment, the emphasis should be on promoting traditional employment opportunities through accelerated growth and development in the sector. Land reform, extension services, provision of credit, crop diversification and rural infrastructure development would play a critical role in this respect. Improved marketing facilities and cooperative organizations could also be effective instruments in advancing rural employment.

Creating jobs in the informal services and agricultural sectors, with a focus on productivity improvement, is vital in providing additional employment opportunities and in narrowing the deficit in decent work (see box III.6). This process could be facilitated by measures to formalize the informal sector. Important would be a reduction in the unit labour costs prevailing in the formal sector, which act as a disincentive for informal sector enterprises to expand and make the transition to the formal sector.

Promotion of microenterprises and small and medium-sized enterprises

Microenterprises and small-scale enterprises, common in the informal sector, have substantial growth potential, but they appear to be less productive than their potential and tend to have a high "mortality" rate. To avoid such failures, these firms need a more conducive business environment, with lower entry costs, better infrastructure, more capacity-building, good governance and open-market economic settings. Improved access to credit could be a major support for microenterprises, particularly in the Pacific island countries and territories.

Entrepreneurship development

Improving the competence and aptitude to initiate, nurture and expand industrial enterprises could revitalize small and medium-sized enterprises and firmly establish them as viable options for employment in the informal sector

The development of entrepreneurship is a vital component of human resources develop-

Box III.6. Looking beyond the information technology sector in India

The global development of the information technology sector has led to a rapid expansion in information technology-enabled services in India, particularly in low-skill sectors, and an increase in the business processes outsourcing from developed countries, especially the United States.

Can the revolution in the information technology sector in India resolve India's unemployment problems and the other ills in its labour markets? Certainly not. The information technology sector accounts for less than 1 per cent of GDP in India and employs fewer than 1 million people in a total labour force of 450 million, so the sector's quantitative significance is limited.[a]

To address the unemployment issue in a broader context, particularly given its growing labour force, India would need to think beyond the information technology sector and pay attention to the needs of the non-elite strata of society, using the agricultural, manufacturing and service sectors for job creation.

---

[a] Sukti Dasgupta and Ajit Singh, "Manufacturing, services, jobless growth and informal economy: will services be the new engine of Indian economic growth?", paper presented at the United Nations University World Institute for Development Economics Research (WIDER) Jubilee Conference, 17-18 June 2005, Helsinki, <www.unu.edu/conference/conference-2005-3/conference-2005-3-papers/Dasgupta%8%20Singh.pdf>.

ment aimed at job creation. Lack of competence and the aptitude to initiate, nurture and expand industrial enterprises is a major reason why small and medium-sized enterprises and self-employment fail to become viable options for generating employment in the informal sector. Although many Governments have encouraged the development of entrepreneurship and self-employment among youth, relatively few microfinancing initiatives are specifically targeted at youth and those that are tended to be implemented by non-governmental organizations or private banks. Many initiatives are too small in scale and lacking in resources to make a substantial dent in youth unemployment. There is a need to increase national commitments to youth employment initiatives and to scale up investment in youth employment.[60]

Indonesia is fostering linkages between large and small enterprises, believing that large companies have the knowledge, expertise, resources and networks to assist small and medium-sized enterprises and start-ups in accessing the necessary support.

China's Ministry of Labour and Social Security and the All-China Youth Federation launched the "Entrepreneurship campaign for young laid-off workers" and the "China youth entrepreneurship campaign" in 1998. The former campaign was a mass experiment to support and assist young laid-off workers to achieve re-employment by enabling them to start their own businesses. It focuses on training young entrepreneurs, employment training and intermediary services. The latter campaign organizes and implements business start-up activities across the country and provides support for start-up businesses, conceptualization and intermediary services. This campaign is aimed at generating employment and re-employment through business creation. From 1998 to 2004 business start-up skill training was provided to nearly 400,000 young people, supported by nearly 90,000 enterprises that also helped directly to resettle more than 1.1 million laid-off workers.

[60] United Nations, *World Youth Report 2005* (United Nations publication, Sales No. E.05.IV.6).

Measures for labour market-related institutional development

Improving the business environment

Providing a business-friendly environment is vital for the private sector to thrive and actively engage in employment generation and fulfil its corporate responsibilities

Providing an environment that is conducive to private sector activity is a prerequisite for active private sector engagement in employment generation. In a globalized economy the ability of the State sector to generate adequate levels of employment on its own is increasingly limited.

In many developing countries in the region, however, the private sector is hampered by inconsistent policies and implementation of laws, frequent legal changes, the considerable discretionary powers of local authorities and bureaucratic harassment, complicated by the lengthy registration procedures of firms, stringent licensing and permit regimes and high taxation. Addressing such issues is vital for providing a friendly business environment. The approach adopted by the Republic of Korea could provide lessons for others. The Republic of Korea is reviewing economic and labour policies from the perspective of job creation, working to establish a business-friendly environment by stabilizing the labour market, improving the corporate investment and management environment through co-operative labour-management relationships and subsidizing small and medium-sized enterprises that create new jobs.

Corporate responsibility and social dialogue

Employers also play a role in generating employment. Corporate responsibility entails providing opportunities for training and retraining workers, establishing markets, collaborating with the public sector in providing opportunities for unemployed youth to train as interns and ensuring workplace safety and the welfare of employees.

Social dialogue requires a compromise between profit maximization by firms and optimum wages by employees

In many countries in the region, particularly those in South Asia, industrial relations have traditionally been antagonistic, characterized by mistrust between employers and unions, by a highly regulated legal framework and by an ineffective dispute-resolution system.[61] Union actions, when politically motivated and lacking law enforcement, can hurt the economy and prevent employment creation.[62] Social dialogue, involving employers, unions and even government, is a key instrument for overcoming an employment crisis. A compact between the employees and employers aimed at collectively managing labour-market outcomes could avoid such adverse effects. Such a compact could include agreements on wage moderation (to accommodate macroeconomic stability), tax cuts, employment benefits and job security. Such social dialogue entails a compromise between profit maximization by firms and optimum wages by employees through a common understanding and partnership.

Rule-based framework for the international migration of workers

International migration could help to stabilize labour markets in both labour-importing and labour-exporting countries. The migration of skilled workers from countries with excess labour could benefit labour-importing countries and help to ease the pressure on labour markets in the labour-exporting countries. A rule-based flow of people under a global framework, such as Mode 4 of the General Agreement on Trade in Services of the World Trade Organization, could produce tangible benefits for all countries.

[61] A. Sivananthiran and C.S. Venkata Ratnam, "Globalization and labour management relations in South Asia" (New Delhi, ILO, South Asia Multidisciplinary Advisory Team, 1999).

[62] In Sri Lanka, for example, a significant number of hours are lost due to union strike actions, imposing considerable costs on the economy; see Ramani Gunatilaka, "Labour legislation and female employment in Sri Lanka's manufacturing sector", Institute of Policy Studies of Sri Lanka, Labour Economics Series 14 (Colombo, 1999).

CONCLUSION

Some unemployment issues are policy-induced and others emanate from cultural and political ideologies

The changing dynamics of production in the face of globalization has sparked concerns about jobless growth in many high-growth economies in the Asian and Pacific region, leading to questions about the appropriateness of their development strategies. While a large proportion of people employed in the region are the working poor, the high rate of unemployed youth reflects a tremendous waste of human resources.

While some unemployment issues in the region are policy-induced, others are due to cultural and political ideologies inherent in some societies. Different socio-economic settings lead to different employment outcomes; thus, development policies need to be tailored to suit the circumstances in specific countries.

The problem of unemployment should be considered in the context of the overall macroeconomic and political environment

For a sustained reduction in unemployment and achieving full and productive employment, solutions have to be considered in the context of the overall macroeconomic and political environment. While economic growth is a necessary condition, growth alone cannot create sufficient employment opportunities to adequately reduce unemployment, as many economies in the region have documented. A balanced approach based on economic growth and State interventions is needed to ensure that growth is broad-based and equitable.

Foremost among the policies required are sound macroeconomic policies supported by credible labour-market policies and reforms

Foremost among the policies required for addressing unemployment are sound macroeconomic policies supported by credible labour-market policies and reforms. A distortion-free, flexible labour market would permit resources to be reallocated efficiently at times of external and policy-induced shocks. Reductions in labour costs and improvements in labour productivity are needed to sharpen the currently eroding competitive edge of developing countries in the region in a globalized setting. To bridge the gap between supply and demand while providing an enabling environment for smooth employment adjustment at times of shocks and structural change, countries need active labour-market policies, in particular policies aimed at developing human capital, facilitating labour-market entry, providing labour-market information, facilitating job searches, creating opportunities and providing targeted safety nets for the unemployed.

As Governments limit their role to that of regulators and facilitators, the role of the private sector in providing employment becomes even more vital

In increasingly open economic systems, the role of the private sector in providing employment becomes ever more vital as Governments limit their role to that of regulators and facilitators of private sector growth and employment generation. Elimination of constraints such as complex firm-registration requirements, stringent licensing and high taxation would be of paramount importance. Harmonious industrial relations through social dialogue could enhance private sector initiatives.

LIST OF TABLES

Table A.1. Population

(Thousands)

	1995	1996	1997	1998	1999	2000	2001	2002	2003	2004	2005
Developing ESCAP economies	3 387 652	3 434 879	3 481 519	3 527 432	3 572 481	3 616 661	3 659 859	3 702 223	3 743 970	3 785 437	3 826 839
East and North-East Asia	1 315 605	1 328 163	1 340 512	1 352 465	1 363 810	1 374 478	1 384 355	1 393 580	1 402 293	1 410 742	1 419 076
China	1 219 331	1 230 978	1 242 413	1 253 510	1 264 075	1 273 979	1 283 202	1 291 841	1 300 039	1 307 989	1 315 844
Hong Kong, China	6 187	6 283	6 375	6 464	6 551	6 637	6 721	6 803	6 884	6 963	7 041
Macao, China	413	420	426	433	439	444	448	451	454	457	460
Democratic People's Republic of Korea	20 918	21 134	21 336	21 525	21 700	21 862	22 011	22 147	22 271	22 384	22 488
Mongolia	2 389	2 413	2 434	2 454	2 474	2 497	2 523	2 552	2 582	2 614	2 646
Republic of Korea	45 007	45 405	45 788	46 149	46 481	46 779	47 040	47 265	47 463	47 645	47 817
Taiwan Province of China	21 360	21 530	21 740	21 930	22 090	22 280	22 410	22 520	22 600	22 690	22 781
North and Central Asia	217 575	217 730	217 846	217 921	217 934	217 875	217 751	217 586	217 407	217 245	217 125
Armenia	3 227	3 178	3 143	3 119	3 100	3 082	3 065	3 050	3 037	3 026	3 016
Azerbaijan	7 791	7 880	7 957	8 024	8 085	8 143	8 198	8 250	8 302	8 355	8 411
Georgia	5 033	4 954	4 886	4 828	4 774	4 720	4 666	4 614	4 565	4 518	4 474
Kazakhstan	15 866	15 682	15 495	15 317	15 161	15 033	14 942	14 885	14 855	14 839	14 825
Kyrgyzstan	4 588	4 648	4 720	4 799	4 878	4 952	5 020	5 084	5 144	5 204	5 264
Russian Federation	148 189	147 947	147 691	147 398	147 030	146 560	145 985	145 327	144 618	143 899	143 202
Tajikistan	5 770	5 851	5 932	6 011	6 087	6 159	6 227	6 293	6 360	6 430	6 507
Turkmenistan	4 193	4 270	4 334	4 390	4 445	4 502	4 564	4 630	4 698	4 766	4 833
Uzbekistan	22 918	23 320	23 688	24 034	24 375	24 724	25 083	25 452	25 828	26 209	26 593
Pacific island economies	7 136	7 299	7 463	7 626	7 789	7 952	8 115	8 277	8 438	8 598	8 755
Cook Islands	20	20	20	19	19	19	19	18	18	18	18
Fiji	768	777	786	794	803	811	819	826	834	841	848
French Polynesia	216	220	224	228	232	236	240	244	249	253	257
Guam	146	148	149	151	153	155	158	161	164	167	170
Kiribati	80	82	84	86	88	90	92	94	95	97	99
Marshall Islands	51	51	51	51	51	52	53	55	57	60	62
Micronesia (Federated States of)	107	108	108	108	107	107	107	108	109	110	110
New Caledonia	193	198	202	206	211	215	220	224	228	233	237
Northern Mariana Islands	57	60	62	65	67	70	72	74	77	79	81
Papua New Guinea	4 687	4 809	4 931	5 055	5 177	5 299	5 419	5 538	5 656	5 772	5 887
Samoa	168	170	172	174	176	177	179	181	182	184	185
Solomon Islands	364	374	385	396	407	419	430	442	454	466	478
Tonga	97	98	98	99	100	100	101	101	102	102	102
Tuvalu	10	10	10	10	10	10	10	10	10	10	10
Vanuatu	172	176	180	184	188	191	195	199	203	207	211

(Continued on next page)

Table A.1 *(continued)*

(Thousands)

	1995	1996	1997	1998	1999	2000	2001	2002	2003	2004	2005
South and South-West Asia	1 366 254	1 392 797	1 419 185	1 445 418	1 471 513	1 497 489	1 523 327	1 549 033	1 574 670	1 600 327	1 626 066
Afghanistan	20 669	21 471	22 031	22 476	22 999	23 735	24 724	25 912	27 231	28 574	29 863
Bangladesh	116 455	118 946	121 426	123 905	126 398	128 916	131 461	134 029	136 615	139 215	141 822
Bhutan	1 733	1 765	1 803	1 847	1 893	1 938	1 982	2 026	2 071	2 116	2 163
India	935 572	952 828	970 041	987 177	1 004 200	1 021 084	1 037 809	1 054 373	1 070 800	1 087 124	1 103 371
Iran (Islamic Republic of)	62 324	63 239	64 105	64 918	65 671	66 365	66 998	67 587	68 172	68 803	69 515
Maldives	252	259	267	275	282	290	298	306	313	321	329
Nepal	21 682	22 226	22 776	23 329	23 881	24 431	24 975	25 515	26 053	26 591	27 133
Pakistan	126 075	129 247	132 581	135 998	139 381	142 648	145 772	148 791	151 768	154 794	157 935
Sri Lanka	18 872	19 074	19 272	19 467	19 659	19 848	20 033	20 215	20 394	20 570	20 743
Turkey	62 620	63 742	64 883	66 026	67 149	68 234	69 275	70 277	71 252	72 220	73 193
South-East Asia	481 081	488 890	496 513	504 002	511 435	518 867	526 311	533 748	541 162	548 525	555 815
Brunei Darussalam	295	303	310	318	326	333	341	349	358	366	374
Cambodia	11 368	11 662	11 943	12 215	12 481	12 744	13 007	13 268	13 531	13 798	14 071
Indonesia	195 649	198 388	201 094	203 783	206 472	209 174	211 893	214 622	217 354	220 077	222 781
Lao People's Democratic Republic	4 686	4 801	4 917	5 036	5 156	5 279	5 404	5 531	5 661	5 792	5 924
Malaysia	20 362	20 892	21 427	21 961	22 486	22 997	23 492	23 971	24 437	24 894	25 347
Myanmar	44 500	45 193	45 857	46 496	47 117	47 724	48 319	48 900	49 463	50 004	50 519
Philippines	68 396	69 871	71 346	72 820	74 293	75 766	77 237	78 705	80 166	81 617	83 054
Singapore	3 478	3 588	3 703	3 817	3 923	4 017	4 097	4 163	4 220	4 273	4 326
Thailand	58 336	59 001	59 638	60 252	60 851	61 438	62 017	62 586	63 145	63 694	64 233
Timor-Leste	848	830	797	758	730	722	738	775	827	887	947
Viet Nam	73 163	74 362	75 481	76 548	77 602	78 671	79 765	80 877	82 000	83 123	84 238
Developed ESCAP economies	147 070	147 670	148 257	148 830	149 387	149 924	150 441	150 938	151 410	151 855	152 268
Australia	17 941	18 162	18 388	18 618	18 846	19 071	19 293	19 512	19 728	19 942	20 155
Japan	125 472	125 812	126 142	126 458	126 756	127 034	127 290	127 525	127 736	127 923	128 085
New Zealand	3 658	3 695	3 727	3 755	3 784	3 818	3 857	3 901	3 946	3 989	4 028

Source: ESCAP, based on United Nations, *World Population Prospects: The 2004 Revision, CD-ROM Edition, Comprehensive Dataset,* ST/ESA/SER.A/249, Sales No. 05.XIII.11.

Note: The population data represent mid-year estimates. The figures are interpolated from the medium variant of population taken from the United Nations, *World Population Prospects: The 2004 Revision*, which includes the results of three projection variants prepared for each of the economies listed above, the populations of which are projected using the cohort-component method. These variants differ from one another only on the future course of fertility, that is, they all incorporate the same assumptions about future trends in mortality and international migration. These variants are known as the low-fertility, medium-fertility and high-fertility variants, or low, medium and high for short. The low, medium and high variants constitute the core of the official estimates and projections of the United Nations. They encompass the likely future path of population growth for each country/area of the world. The low and high variants provide lower and upper bounds for that growth. The medium variant is a useful central reference for trends over the longer term.

Table A.2. Population growth rates

(Percentage)

	1995	1996	1997	1998	1999	2000	2001	2002	2003	2004	2005
Developing ESCAP economies	1.4	1.4	1.3	1.3	1.3	1.2	1.2	1.2	1.1	1.1	1.1
East and North-East Asia	1.0	0.9	0.9	0.9	0.8	0.8	0.7	0.7	0.6	0.6	0.6
China	1.0	0.9	0.9	0.9	0.8	0.8	0.7	0.7	0.6	0.6	0.6
Democratic People's Republic of Korea	1.0	1.0	0.9	0.9	0.8	0.7	0.7	0.6	0.5	0.5	0.5
Hong Kong, China	1.5	1.5	1.4	1.4	1.3	1.3	1.2	1.2	1.2	1.1	1.1
Macao, China	1.8	1.6	1.5	1.4	1.2	1.1	0.9	0.8	0.7	0.7	0.7
Mongolia	1.2	1.1	0.9	0.9	1.0	1.0	1.1	1.1	1.2	1.2	1.2
Republic of Korea	0.9	0.8	0.8	0.7	0.7	0.6	0.5	0.5	0.4	0.4	0.4
Taiwan Province of China	0.8	0.8	1.0	0.9	0.7	0.9	0.6	0.5	0.4	0.4	0.4
North and Central Asia	0.1	0.1	0.1	0.0	0.0	0.0	–0.1	–0.1	–0.1	–0.1	–0.1
Armenia	–1.4	–1.2	–1.0	–0.9	–0.8	–0.7	–0.6	–0.5	–0.4	–0.4	–0.3
Azerbaijan	1.2	1.1	0.9	0.9	0.8	0.8	0.7	0.7	0.7	0.7	0.7
Georgia	–1.5	–1.4	–1.3	–1.3	–1.2	–1.2	–1.1	–1.1	–1.0	–1.0	–0.9
Kazakhstan	–0.9	–1.0	–1.0	–1.0	–0.8	–0.7	–0.5	–0.4	–0.3	–0.2	–0.2
Kyrgyzstan	1.2	1.3	1.5	1.5	1.4	1.4	1.3	1.3	1.2	1.2	1.2
Russian Federation	–0.1	–0.2	–0.2	–0.2	–0.3	–0.3	–0.4	–0.4	–0.5	–0.5	–0.5
Tajikistan	1.5	1.4	1.3	1.3	1.2	1.2	1.2	1.1	1.1	1.2	1.3
Turkmenistan	2.0	1.8	1.5	1.4	1.4	1.4	1.4	1.4	1.4	1.4	1.4
Uzbekistan	1.9	1.7	1.6	1.5	1.5	1.5	1.5	1.5	1.5	1.5	1.4
Pacific island economies	2.3	2.3	2.2	2.2	2.1	2.1	2.0	2.0	1.9	1.9	1.8
Cook Islands	0.2	–0.3	–0.9	–1.1	–1.1	–1.1	–1.0	–1.0	–0.9	–0.8	–0.6
Fiji	1.1	1.1	1.1	1.1	1.0	1.0	0.9	0.9	0.9	0.8	0.8
French Polynesia	1.9	1.9	1.8	1.8	1.8	1.7	1.7	1.7	1.6	1.6	1.5
Guam	1.5	1.4	1.3	1.3	1.4	1.5	1.6	1.7	1.7	1.7	1.6
Kiribati	2.2	2.2	2.2	2.2	2.1	2.1	2.1	2.1	2.0	2.0	1.9
Marshall Islands	1.0	0.8	0.5	0.7	1.3	1.9	2.5	3.1	3.4	3.4	3.3
Micronesia (Federated States of)	1.1	0.6	0.2	0.0	0.2	0.3	0.4	0.6	0.6	0.6	0.6
New Caledonia	2.3	2.3	2.2	2.2	2.1	2.0	2.0	1.9	1.9	1.8	1.8
Northern Mariana Islands	4.5	4.3	4.1	3.9	3.7	3.5	3.3	3.1	2.9	2.8	2.6
Palau	2.4	2.2	2.1	1.9	1.6	1.4	1.1	0.8	0.7	0.6	0.6
Papua New Guinea	2.5	2.5	2.5	2.4	2.3	2.3	2.2	2.1	2.1	2.0	2.0
Samoa	1.0	1.0	1.0	1.0	1.0	0.9	0.9	0.9	0.8	0.7	0.6
Solomon Islands	2.8	2.8	2.8	2.8	2.8	2.7	2.7	2.7	2.6	2.6	2.5
Tonga	0.6	0.6	0.7	0.6	0.6	0.5	0.5	0.4	0.4	0.4	0.3
Tuvalu	0.8	0.8	0.8	0.7	0.7	0.6	0.6	0.5	0.5	0.5	0.5
Vanuatu	2.5	2.3	2.2	2.1	2.1	2.0	2.0	2.0	2.0	1.9	1.9

(Continued on next page)

Table A.2 *(continued)*

(Percentage)

	1995	*1996*	*1997*	*1998*	*1999*	*2000*	*2001*	*2002*	*2003*	*2004*	*2005*
South and South-West Asia	2.0	1.9	1.9	1.8	1.8	1.7	1.7	1.7	1.6	1.6	1.6
Afghanistan	4.9	4.0	3.2	2.9	3.3	3.7	4.0	4.4	4.5	4.3	4.1
Bangladesh	2.1	2.1	2.1	2.0	2.0	2.0	1.9	1.9	1.9	1.9	1.8
Bhutan	1.7	1.9	2.1	2.2	2.2	2.2	2.2	2.2	2.2	2.2	2.2
India	1.8	1.8	1.8	1.7	1.7	1.6	1.6	1.6	1.5	1.5	1.5
Iran (Islamic Republic of)	1.6	1.4	1.3	1.2	1.2	1.1	1.0	1.0	1.0	1.0	1.1
Maldives	3.0	2.9	2.9	2.8	2.7	2.7	2.6	2.6	2.5	2.5	2.5
Nepal	2.5	2.4	2.4	2.4	2.3	2.2	2.2	2.1	2.1	2.0	2.0
Pakistan	2.4	2.5	2.5	2.4	2.3	2.3	2.2	2.1	2.0	2.0	2.1
Sri Lanka	1.1	1.1	1.0	1.0	1.0	0.9	0.9	0.9	0.9	0.8	0.8
Turkey	1.7	1.7	1.7	1.7	1.6	1.6	1.5	1.4	1.4	1.4	1.3
South-East Asia	1.7	1.6	1.5	1.5	1.5	1.4	1.4	1.4	1.4	1.4	1.3
Brunei Darussalam	2.6	2.5	2.5	2.4	2.4	2.4	2.3	2.3	2.3	2.2	2.2
Cambodia	2.7	2.5	2.4	2.3	2.2	2.1	2.1	2.0	2.0	2.0	2.0
Indonesia	1.4	1.4	1.4	1.3	1.3	1.3	1.3	1.3	1.2	1.2	1.2
Lao People's Democratic Republic	2.4	2.4	2.4	2.4	2.4	2.3	2.3	2.3	2.3	2.3	2.2
Malaysia	2.5	2.5	2.5	2.4	2.3	2.2	2.1	2.0	1.9	1.9	1.8
Myanmar	1.6	1.5	1.4	1.4	1.3	1.3	1.2	1.2	1.1	1.1	1.0
Philippines	2.2	2.1	2.1	2.0	2.0	1.9	1.9	1.9	1.8	1.8	1.7
Singapore	2.9	2.9	2.9	2.7	2.5	2.2	1.9	1.6	1.4	1.4	1.3
Thailand	1.2	1.1	1.1	1.0	1.0	1.0	0.9	0.9	0.9	0.9	0.8
Timor-Leste	–0.2	–1.4	–2.6	–2.3	–0.6	1.1	2.8	4.6	5.4	5.4	5.4
Viet Nam	1.7	1.6	1.5	1.4	1.4	1.4	1.4	1.4	1.4	1.3	1.3
Developed ESCAP economies	0.4	0.4	0.4	0.4	0.4	0.4	0.3	0.3	0.3	0.3	0.3
Australia	1.2	1.2	1.2	1.2	1.2	1.2	1.1	1.1	1.1	1.1	1.1
Japan	0.3	0.3	0.3	0.2	0.2	0.2	0.2	0.2	0.2	0.1	0.1
New Zealand	1.1	1.0	0.9	0.9	0.9	1.0	1.0	1.1	1.0	1.0	0.9

Source: ESCAP, based on United Nations, *World Population Prospects: The 2004 Revision, CD-ROM Edition, Comprehensive Dataset,* ST/ESA/SER.A/249, Sales No. 05.XIII.11.

Note: Exponential growth rate, which takes into account international migration, is employed to obtain annual growth rates for the region and subregions.

Table A.3. Population projections

(Thousands)

	2005	2010	2015	2020	2025
Developing ESCAP economies	3 826 839	4 033 313	4 235 448	4 420 155	4 576 871
East and North-East Asia	1 419 076	1 459 951	1 500 326	1 532 967	1 551 826
China	1 315 844	1 354 533	1 392 980	1 423 939	1 441 426
Hong Kong, China	7 041	7 416	7 764	8 080	8 362
Macao, China	460	476	493	509	523
Democratic People's Republic of Korea	22 488	22 907	23 299	23 722	24 118
Mongolia	2 646	2 813	2 988	3 137	3 266
Republic of Korea	47 817	48 566	49 092	49 393	49 457
Taiwan Province of China	22 781	23 240	23 709	24 187	24 674
North and Central Asia	217 125	217 152	217 416	217 014	215 587
Armenia	3 016	2 981	2 970	2 952	2 908
Azerbaijan	8 411	8 741	9 083	9 384	9 596
Georgia	4 474	4 299	4 183	4 059	3 917
Kazakhstan	14 825	14 802	14 877	14 883	14 774
Kyrgyzstan	5 264	5 567	5 852	6 094	6 282
Russian Federation	143 202	140 028	136 696	133 101	129 230
Tajikistan	6 507	6 992	7 605	8 216	8 769
Turkmenistan	4 833	5 163	5 498	5 811	6 068
Uzbekistan	26 593	28 578	30 651	32 515	34 042
Pacific island economies	8 755	9 518	10 265	11 022	11 786
Cook Islands	18	18	17	17	16
Fiji	848	878	903	920	939
French Polynesia	257	274	291	307	321
Guam	170	182	194	206	217
Kiribati	99	109	118	128	138
Marshall Islands	62	73	83	94	104
Micronesia (Federated States of)	110	114	116	117	117
New Caledonia	237	257	277	296	314
Northern Mariana Islands	81	91	98	104	110
Papua New Guinea	5 887	6 450	7 013	7 602	8 205
Samoa	185	189	190	190	190
Solomon Islands	478	537	596	653	709
Tonga	102	103	104	103	101
Tuvalu	10	11	11	11	11
Vanuatu	211	232	252	273	294
South and South-West Asia	1 626 066	1 755 671	1 884 041	2 006 749	2 119 324
Afghanistan	29 863	35 642	41 401	48 032	55 443
Bangladesh	141 822	154 960	168 158	181 180	193 752
Bhutan	2 163	2 414	2 684	2 950	3 209
India	1 103 371	1 183 293	1 260 366	1 332 032	1 395 496
Iran (Islamic Republic of)	69 515	74 283	79 917	85 036	89 042
Maldives	329	371	416	461	506
Nepal	27 133	29 891	32 747	35 679	38 600
Pakistan	157 935	175 178	193 419	211 703	229 353
Sri Lanka	20 743	21 557	22 293	22 902	23 358
Turkey	73 193	78 081	82 640	86 774	90 565
South-East Asia	555 815	591 021	623 401	652 403	678 347
Brunei Darussalam	374	414	453	491	526
Cambodia	14 071	15 530	17 066	18 580	19 993
Indonesia	222 781	235 755	246 813	255 853	263 746
Lao People's Democratic Republic	5 924	6 604	7 306	8 014	8 712
Malaysia	25 347	27 532	29 558	31 474	33 223
Myanmar	50 519	52 801	54 970	57 054	59 002
Philippines	83 054	90 048	96 840	103 266	109 084
Singapore	4 326	4 590	4 815	4 986	5 144
Thailand	64 233	66 785	69 064	71 044	72 635
Timor-Leste	947	1 244	1 486	1 713	1 938
Viet Nam	84 238	89 718	95 029	99 928	104 343
Developed ESCAP economies	152 268	153 830	154 545	154 455	153 687
Australia	20 155	21 201	22 250	23 317	24 329
Japan	128 085	128 457	127 993	126 713	124 819
New Zealand	4 028	4 172	4 302	4 425	4 539

Source: ESCAP, based on United Nations, *World Population Prospects: The 2004 Revision, CD-ROM Edition, Comprehensive Dataset,* ST/ESA/SER.A/249, Sales No. 05.XIII.11.

Table B.1. GDP growth rates

(Percentage)

	1995	1996	1997	1998	1999	2000	2001	2002	2003	2004	2005[a]
Developing ESCAP economies[b]	7.1	6.7	5.7	0.4	5.8	7.3	3.9	6.1	6.5	7.4	6.6
East and North-East Asia	9.2	8.1	7.2	2.0	7.5	8.2	4.9	7.2	6.5	7.7	6.9
China	10.9	10.0	9.3	7.8	7.6	8.4	8.3	9.1	10.0	10.1	9.6
Hong Kong, China	3.9	4.3	5.0	−5.0	3.4	10.2	0.5	1.9	3.2	8.1	7.5
Mongolia	..	2.4	4.0	3.5	3.2	1.1	1.0	4.0	5.6	10.6	6.0
Republic of Korea	9.2	7.0	4.7	−6.9	9.5	8.5	3.8	7.0	3.1	4.6	3.8
Taiwan Province of China	6.4	6.1	6.4	4.3	5.3	5.8	−2.2	3.9	3.3	5.7	3.8
North and Central Asia	−4.3	−3.1	1.5	−4.2	6.3	9.8	5.9	5.2	7.5	7.4	6.9
Armenia	6.9	5.9	3.3	7.3	3.3	5.9	9.6	13.2	13.9	10.1	13.9
Azerbaijan	−11.8	1.3	5.8	10.0	7.4	11.1	9.9	10.6	11.2	10.2	26.4
Georgia	2.6	11.2	10.5	3.1	2.9	1.8	4.8	5.5	11.1	6.2	7.7[c]
Kazakhstan	−8.2	0.5	1.7	−1.9	2.7	9.8	13.5	9.8	9.3	9.6	9.2
Kyrgyzstan	−5.4	7.1	9.9	2.1	3.7	5.4	5.3	0.0	6.7	7.1	−0.6
Russian Federation	−4.1	−3.6	1.4	−5.3	6.4	10.0	5.1	4.7	7.3	7.2	6.4
Tajikistan	−12.4	−16.7	1.7	5.3	3.7	8.3	9.6	10.8	11.0	10.6	6.7
Turkmenistan	−7.2	6.7	−11.4	7.1	16.9	17.6	20.4	12.0	13.0	9.0	11.0
Uzbekistan	−0.9	1.7	5.2	4.4	4.4	3.8	4.2	4.0	4.2	7.7	7.2
Pacific island economies	−0.8	5.6	−4.3	3.5	7.1	−1.5	1.8	0.5	3.0	3.3	2.7
Cook Islands	..	−0.3	−2.3	−0.8	2.7	13.9	4.9	3.9	3.1	3.4	3.2
Fiji[d]	2.5	4.7	−2.3	1.2	9.2	−2.8	2.7	4.3	3.0	4.1	1.7
Kiribati	5.6	3.1	4.6	15.8	8.7	−0.7	2.9	−1.2	3.5	3.5	..
Papua New Guinea	−3.4	6.6	−6.3	4.7	7.6	−1.2	1.8	−1.0	2.9	2.9	3.0
Samoa	6.6	7.3	0.8	2.4	2.2	6.1	6.8	1.2	3.3	3.7	5.6
Solomon Islands	..	1.9	−0.9	1.4	−0.5	−14.3	−8.7	−2.1	5.3	5.0	2.9
Tonga	4.6	0.2	−3.0	3.6	2.3	5.6	2.5	2.6	3.1	1.6	2.8
Tuvalu	−5.0	−7.1	5.6	19.7	−0.5	13.4	5.9	1.2	2.0	3.0	..
Vanuatu	−0.03	2.5	8.6	4.3	−3.2	2.7	−2.1	−2.8	2.4	3.2	2.9
South and South-West Asia[e]	6.5	7.0	5.1	4.8	3.1	5.2	2.1	5.1	7.2	7.3	6.9
Bangladesh	4.9	4.6	5.4	5.2	4.9	5.9	5.3	4.4	5.3	6.3	5.4
Bhutan[d]	7.3	5.8	4.2	5.8	7.8	9.5	8.6	7.1	6.8	8.7	8.8
India[d]	7.3	7.8	4.8	6.5	6.1	4.4	5.8	3.8	8.5	7.5	8.1
Iran (Islamic Republic of)[d]	3.2	5.8	3.4	1.6	2.8	5.1	3.3	7.5	6.7	4.8	5.0
Maldives	7.4	9.1	10.4	9.8	7.2	4.8	3.4	6.5	8.4	8.8	..
Nepal	3.3	5.3	5.3	2.9	4.5	6.1	5.6	−0.6	3.1	3.7	2.6
Pakistan[d]	5.2	5.5	1.7	3.5	4.2	3.9	1.8	3.1	5.1	6.4	8.4
Sri Lanka	5.5	4.0	6.3	4.7	4.3	6.0	−1.5	4.0	6.0	5.4	5.5
Turkey	7.2	7.0	7.5	3.1	-4.7	7.4	−7.5	7.9	5.8	8.9	5.0

(Continued on next page)

Table B.1 *(continued)*

(Percentage)

	1995	1996	1997	1998	1999	2000	2001	2002	2003	2004	2005[a]
South-East Asia	8.3	7.6	4.5	–7.2	3.9	6.2	2.2	4.6	5.0	6.4	5.4
Brunei Darussalam	3.0	3.6	4.1	–4.0	2.5	2.8	2.9	2.8	3.1	1.7	3.6
Cambodia	6.5	5.3	5.7	5.0	12.6	8.4	5.5	5.2	7.1	7.7	6.3
Indonesia	8.2	7.8	4.7	–13.1	0.8	4.9	3.8	4.4	4.9	5.1	5.6
Lao People's Democratic Republic	7.0	6.9	6.9	4.0	7.3	5.7	5.8	5.9	5.8	6.5	7.2
Malaysia	9.8	10.0	7.3	–7.4	6.1	8.5	0.3	4.4	5.4	7.1	5.2
Myanmar	6.9	6.4	5.7	5.8	10.9	13.7	11.3	10.0	13.8	5.0	4.5
Philippines	4.7	5.8	5.2	–0.6	3.4	4.4	4.5	4.4	4.5	6.0	4.8
Singapore	8.0	8.2	8.6	–0.8	6.8	9.6	–2.0	3.2	1.4	8.4	6.4
Thailand	9.2	5.9	–1.4	–10.5	4.4	4.8	2.2	5.3	6.9	6.1	4.5
Viet Nam	9.5	9.3	8.2	5.8	4.8	6.8	6.9	7.1	7.3	7.7	8.4
Developed ESCAP economies	1.7	3.4	2.1	–0.6	0.3	2.5	0.6	0.4	1.9	2.4	2.5
Australia	3.4	4.2	3.9	5.3	4.3	3.2	2.5	4.0	3.3	3.3	2.5
Japan	2.0	3.4	1.8	–1.0	–0.2	2.9	0.4	0.1	1.8	2.3	2.5
New Zealand	3.9	3.5	2.9	0.2	4.8	3.7	2.5	4.3	3.8	4.4	2.2

Sources: ESCAP, based on national sources; International Monetary Fund, *International Financial Statistics* (CD-ROM) (Washington, D.C., IMF, December 2005); and IMF Country Reports Series; Asian Development Bank, *Key Indicators of Developing Asian and Pacific Countries 2005* (Manila, ADB, 2005); Economist Intelligence Unit, *Country Reports* and *Country Forecasts* (London, 2005 and 2006), various issues; and website of the Commonwealth of Independent States Inter-State Statistical Committee, <www.cisstat.com>, 9 January 2006 and 10 February 2006.

[a] Estimate.

[b] Based on data for 38 developing economies representing more than 95 per cent of the population of the region (including the Central Asian countries); GDP figures at market prices in United States dollars in 2000 (at 1995 prices) have been used as weights to calculate the regional and subregional growth rates.

[c] Growth rate for 2005 refers to January-September 2005 compared with corresponding period of 2004.

[d] Real GDP at factor cost.

[e] The estimates and forecasts for countries relate to fiscal years defined as follows: fiscal year 2004/05 = 2004 for India, the Islamic Republic of Iran and Myanmar; and fiscal year 2003/04 = 2004 for Bangladesh, Nepal and Pakistan.

Table B.2. Agricultural sector growth rates

(Percentage)

	1995	1996	1997	1998	1999	2000	2001	2002	2003	2004	2005[a]
Developing ESCAP economies											
East and North-East Asia											
China	5.0	5.1	3.5	3.5	2.8	2.4	2.8	2.9	2.5	6.3	4.0
Hong Kong, China	..	..	..	..	..	..	4.1	−0.7	−5.6	0.7	−2.0
Mongolia	..	4.4	4.3	6.4	4.2	−14.9	−18.5	−10.7	5.8	18.9	..
Republic of Korea	5.3	2.3	4.6	−6.4	5.9	1.2	1.1	−3.5	−5.3	7.4	2.0
Taiwan Province of China	2.7	−0.5	−1.6	−6.2	2.6	1.0	−1.9	4.5	0.2	−7.1	−3.0
North and Central Asia[b]											
Armenia	5.0	2.0	−6.0	13.0	1.0	−2.5	12.0	4.0	4.0	15.0	11.2
Azerbaijan	−7.0	3.0	−6.0	6.0	7.0	12.0	11.0	6.0	6.0	4.6	7.5
Georgia	13.0	6.0	6.5	−10.0	8.0	−15.0	8.0	−1.0	10.0	−7.0	11.9
Kazakhstan	−24.0	−5.0	−0.8	−19.0	28.0	−4.0	16.9	3.0	1.0	−0.5	6.7
Kyrgyzstan	−1.9	15.8	12.2	3.0	8.2	3.4	6.7	3.8	3.6	4.1	−4.2
Russian Federation	−8.0	−5.0	1.5	−13.0	4.0	7.7	7.5	1.5	1.5	1.6	2.0
Tajikistan	−16.0	−9.0	0.2	6.0	3.0	13.0	11.0	..	..	10.3	6.8[c]
Turkmenistan	1.0	−13.0	20.6	24.4	26.0	..	..	17.0	..	20.5	19.8
Uzbekistan	2.0	−5.7	5.8	4.1	5.5	3.2	5.0	6.1	6.8	10.0	7.3
Pacific island economies											
Cook Islands	..	12.7	4.2	33.5	9.2	0.1	−2.9	9.5	4.0	..	..
Fiji		4.7	−11.1	−6.9	13.5	−1.2	−5.8	4.3	−3.9	3.4	2.0
Kiribati	−28.9	11.6	−15.5	2.8	60.4	−20.1	13.8	4.8	33.1	11.8	..
Papua New Guinea	−0.7	7.5	−8.4	2.1	13.8	2.1	−4.7	−4.1	4.1	4.2	4.1
Samoa	12.7	3.2	−6.6	3.4	−3.1	0.1	−3.8	−6.3	−3.5	−6.5	..
Solomon Islands	..	..	3.4	−4.2	−5.6	−16.3	−4.4	5.1	..	..	..
Tonga	−1.0	−3.2	−2.0	0.8	−1.9	5.6	1.0	3.6	3.8	..	..
Tuvalu	0.6	6.1	0.0	−1.7	−1.1	−2.0	−2.6	−9.4	..	..	..
Vanuatu	2.9	4.5	9.6	8.6	−12.2	6.7	0.5	1.7	6.2	3.5	3.2
South and South-West Asia											
Bangladesh	−0.3	3.1	6.0	3.2	4.7	7.4	3.1	0.0	3.1	4.1	0.3
Bhutan	1.5	2.0	3.9	2.3	1.5	4.6	5.0	3.1	1.7	3.2	3.2
India	−0.9	9.6	−2.4	6.2	0.3	−0.1	6.2	−6.9	10.0	0.7	2.3
Iran (Islamic Republic of)	2.3	3.6	3.5	8.1	−5.6	2.9	−2.3	11.4	7.1	2.2	6.0
Maldives[d]	1.0	2.2	1.3	6.4	3.3	−0.2	5.0	15.9	1.9	2.9	..
Nepal	−0.9	3.8	4.4	0.9	2.8	4.9	5.5	2.2	2.5	3.9	2.8
Pakistan	4.9	5.4	−0.3	6.1	1.9	6.1	−2.2	0.1	4.1	2.2	7.5
Sri Lanka	3.4	−4.1	3.0	2.5	4.5	1.8	−3.4	2.5	1.6	−0.7	−0.8
Turkey	2.0	4.4	−2.3	8.4	−5.0	3.9	−6.5	6.9	−2.5	2.0	1.0

(Continued on next page)

Table B.2 *(continued)*

(Percentage)

	1995	*1996*	*1997*	*1998*	*1999*	*2000*	*2001*	*2002*	*2003*	*2004*	*2005*[a]
South-East Asia											
Brunei Darussalam	..	..	..	..	−0.1	..	..	..	..	..	..
Cambodia	3.5	1.2	5.5	5.1	3.7	−1.2	2.7	−2.8	12.2	−2.0	2.4
Indonesia	4.4	3.1	1.0	−1.3	2.2	1.9	4.1	3.2	4.3	4.1	2.5
Lao People's Democratic Republic	3.1	2.8	7.0	3.1	8.2	4.9	3.8	4.0	2.2	3.0	3.5
Malaysia	−2.5	4.5	0.7	−2.8	0.5	2.6	−0.6	2.8	5.6	5.0	4.0
Myanmar	4.8	5.0	3.7	4.5	11.5	12.4	8.7	4.2	..	..	..
Philippines	0.9	3.9	3.1	−6.4	6.5	3.4	4.7	4.0	3.2	4.9	2.0
Singapore[e]	−3.1	3.8	0.7	−7.0	−1.8	−4.9	−5.9	−5.6	−0.7	11.4	..
Thailand	4.0	4.4	−0.7	−1.5	2.2	7.2	3.2	1.0	8.7	−3.9	−3.0
Viet Nam	4.8	4.4	4.3	3.5	5.2	4.6	3.0	4.2	3.6	3.5	4.0
Developed ESCAP economies											
Australia	−6.3	23.3	−3.9	6.9	8.1	4.2	4.5	−8.2	−7.0	17.0	2.6
Japan	−6.0	2.4	−6.2	−3.1	−5.6	1.6	−4.1	4.7	−8.9	0.5	0.5
New Zealand	7.3	7.7	0.7	−5.1	6.2	2.0	2.1	0.5	−0.7	0.9	0.5

Sources: ESCAP, based on national sources; International Monetary Fund, *International Financial Statistics* (CD-ROM) (Washington, D.C., IMF, December 2005); and IMF Country Reports Series; Asian Development Bank, *Key Indicators of Developing Asian and Pacific Countries 2005* (Manila, ADB, 2005); Economist Intelligence Unit, *Country Reports* and *Country Forecasts* (London, 2005 and 2006), various issues; and website of the Commonwealth of Independent States Inter-State Statistical Committee, <www.cisstat.com>, 9 January 2006 and 10 February 2006.

a Estimate.
b Agricultural growth refers to gross agricultural output.
c Growth rate for 2005 refers to January-August.
d Including coral and sand mining.
e Agriculture also includes quarrying.

Table B.3. Industrial sector growth rates

(Percentage)

	1995	1996	1997	1998	1999	2000	2001	2002	2003	2004	2005[a]
Developing ESCAP economies											
East and North-East Asia											
China	13.9	12.1	10.5	8.9	8.1	9.4	8.4	9.8	12.7	11.1	10.1
Hong Kong, China	..	..	..	..	..	..	–3.7	–3.7	–4.8	–1.6	1.0
Mongolia	..	–3.2	–3.3	3.8	1.1	1.6	16.2	5.4	3.0	15.4	..
Republic of Korea	9.8	7.2	4.5	–8.2	12.2	11.7	3.1	6.4	6.1	9.0	5.0
Taiwan Province of China	5.0	3.1	5.8	2.7	4.5	5.9	–6.6	6.0	4.5	8.3	3.5
North and Central Asia[b]											
Armenia	2.0	1.0	1.0	–2.0	5.3	6.4	5.3	14.6	14.9	2.1	7.5
Azerbaijan	–21.0	–7.0	0.3	2.0	3.6	6.9	5.1	3.6	6.1	5.7	33.5
Georgia	–14.0	7.0	8.2	–2.0	7.4	10.8	–5.0	7.0	14.8	9.0	16.4
Kazakhstan	–8.0	0.3	4.1	–2.0	2.7	15.5	13.8	10.5	8.8	10.1	4.6
Kyrgyzstan	–18.0	4.0	39.7	5.0	–4.3	6.0	5.4	–10.9	17.0	3.7	–12.1
Russian Federation	–3.0	–4.0	2.0	–5.0	11.0	11.9	4.9	3.7	7.0	6.1	4.0
Tajikistan	–14.0	–24.0	–2.0	8.0	5.6	9.9	15.0	8.4	9.9	15.0	8.5
Turkmenistan	–9.0	20.0	–22.0	2.0	15.0	14.0	30.0	22.0	19.0	..	22.0
Uzbekistan	0.1	3.0	4.1	4.0	5.7	5.9	7.6	8.5	6.2	9.0	7.7
Pacific island economies											
Cook Islands	..	–2.0	1.2	16.3	6.6	18.2	13.3	5.0	2.7	..	..
Fiji		7.4	2.7	1.3	8.0	–7.9	9.1	2.9	3.2	3.6	-7.5
Kiribati	2.2	–4.6	9.0	101.0	18.6	–3.8	21.8	–4.9	–1.1	1.8	..
Papua New Guinea	–10.0	12.9	–15.1	11.2	8.5	–0.5	8.3	2.3	4.9	1.4	2.1
Samoa	1.8	4.6	–2.0	–9.2	2.2	13.0	12.2	0.1	5.2	5.0	..
Solomon Islands	..	..	–14.5	12.8	27.3	–31.7	–39.7	0.5	..	..	..
Tonga	21.3	5.1	–17.6	7.2	10.9	1.5	1.5	5.0	4.4	..	..
Tuvalu	–13.0	–15.4	24.4	15.3	0.8	13.2	10.3	6.5	..	..	..
Vanuatu	–2.2	–5.7	–11.1	4.3	4.7	2.1	–5.1	–6.2	–0.3	1.6	1.8
South and South-West Asia											
Bangladesh	9.9	6.9	5.8	8.3	4.9	6.2	7.4	6.5	7.3	7.6	8.5
Bhutan	13.6	5.2	–1.0	4.2	15.3	14.2	13.1	14.4	8.8	12.7	12.0
India	11.6	7.1	4.3	3.7	4.8	6.5	2.7	7.0	7.6	8.6	9.0
Iran (Islamic Republic of)	3.4	7.8	5.4	2.1	2.3	8.7	1.9	9.3	9.2	6.3	6.2
Maldives	4.7	3.3	20.3	17.1	12.1	1.2	8.0	10.4	7.5	9.9	..
Nepal	4.6	8.8	6.5	2.3	6.0	8.8	3.2	–2.8	2.3	2.7	0.7
Pakistan	4.8	4.8	3.6	1.6	4.9	1.3	3.6	5.4	5.4	13.1	10.0
Sri Lanka	8.1	6.5	7.7	5.9	4.8	7.5	–2.1	1.0	5.5	5.2	7.4
Turkey[c]	12.1	7.1	10.4	2.0	–5.0	6.7	–7.5	9.4	7.8	9.4	5.0

(Continued on next page)

Table B.3 *(continued)*

(Percentage)

	1995	1996	1997	1998	1999	2000	2001	2002	2003	2004	2005[a]
South-East Asia											
Brunei Darussalam	..	..	..	..	3.2	..	..	..	..	..	..
Cambodia	18.9	4.4	16.8	6.2	21.2	31.2	11.2	17.3	11.9	16.1	10.7
Indonesia	10.4	10.7	5.2	−14.0	2.0	5.9	2.7	4.3	4.0	3.9	4.8
Lao People's Democratic Republic	13.1	17.3	8.1	9.2	8.0	8.5	10.1	10.1	11.5	8.5	13.0
Malaysia	14.9	14.4	7.5	−10.6	8.8	13.6	−3.8	4.3	7.1	7.9	3.9
Myanmar	12.7	10.7	8.9	6.1	13.8	18.0	21.8	32.8	..	..	..
Philippines	6.7	6.4	6.2	−2.1	0.9	4.9	4.8	3.9	3.6	5.2	4.1
Singapore	9.8	7.3	7.6	0.5	6.6	11.1	−9.0	3.2	0.5	9.9	6.7
Thailand	10.9	6.9	−1.8	−13.0	9.6	5.3	1.7	6.9	9.4	8.3	5.2
Viet Nam	13.6	14.5	12.6	8.3	7.7	10.1	10.4	9.5	10.5	10.2	10.6
Developed ESCAP economies											
Australia	1.0	3.9	2.9	4.8	2.6	2.8	−0.7	6.1	2.5	1.6	1.8
Japan	0.9	3.3	2.1	−4.4	0.9	4.7	−3.2	−4.6	6.5	1.6	1.4
New Zealand	2.8	3.6	0.2	−3.3	4.9	0.1	0.3	6.1	3.7	4.3	0.0

Sources: ESCAP, based on national sources; International Monetary Fund, *International Financial Statistics* (CD-ROM) (Washington, D.C., IMF, December 2005); and IMF Country Reports Series; Asian Development Bank, *Key Indicators of Developing Asian and Pacific Countries 2005* (Manila, ADB, 2005); Economist Intelligence Unit, *Country Reports* and *Country Forecasts* (London, 2005 and 2006), various issues; and website of the Commonwealth of Independent States Inter-State Statistical Committee, <www.cisstat.com>, 9 January 2006 and 10 February 2006.

Note: Industry comprises mining and quarrying; manuafacturing; electricity-generation, gas and power; and construction.

[a] Estimate.
[b] Industrial growth refers to gross industrial output.
[c] Industry excluding construction.

Table B.4. Service sector growth rates

(Percentage)

	1995	*1996*	*1997*	*1998*	*1999*	*2000*	*2001*	*2002*	*2003*	*2004*	*2005*[a]
Developing ESCAP economies											
East and North-East Asia											
China	9.8	9.4	10.7	8.3	9.3	9.7	10.2	10.4	9.5	10.0	7.8
Hong Kong, China	..	..	..	..	..	..	1.6	3.1	4.3	8.9	8.8
Mongolia	..	4.6	9.0	0.3	3.5	18.6	8.2	12.2	7.1	4.0	..
Republic of Korea	9.1	7.2	4.8	−6.1	8.3	7.2	4.5	8.0	1.9	1.8	3.2
Taiwan Province of China	7.4	8.1	7.0	5.5	5.8	5.9	−0.1	3.0	2.9	4.8	4.1
North and Central Asia											
Armenia	..	..	..	..	..	..	..	..	..	..	..
Azerbaijan	..	..	..	..	..	..	..	..	..	..	..
Georgia	..	..	..	..	..	..	..	..	..	..	..
Kazakhstan	..	..	..	..	..	..	..	..	..	..	..
Kyrgyzstan	..	..	..	..	..	..	..	..	..	..	..
Russian Federation	..	..	..	..	..	..	..	..	..	..	..
Tajikistan	..	..	..	..	..	..	..	..	..	..	..
Turkmenistan	..	..	..	..	..	..	..	..	..	..	..
Uzbekistan	..	..	..	..	..	..	..	..	..	..	..
Pacific island											
Cook Islands	..	−1.5	−3.4	−6.5	1.1	16.2	5.4	2.9	3.1	..	..
Fiji	..	3.6	−1.3	3.9	8.5	−1.0	2.6	4.9	9.8	7.9	6.4
Kiribati	3.0	3.0	5.7	11.8	5.3	1.0	0.3	−1.1	2.1	3.0	..
Papua New Guinea	−1.0	0.0	4.1	3.1	8.4	−3.5	6.2	8.1	−0.1	2.0	2.1
Samoa	6.4	10.9	5.7	7.8	4.1	5.2	7.6	3.7	4.2	5.4	..
Solomon Islands	..	..	−1.6	4.9	−2.8	−5.8	−4.5	−9.2	..	..	..
Tonga	3.7	0.6	1.5	4.4	2.2	6.6	3.4	1.6	2.2	..	..
Tuvalu	−4.8	−9.4	3.9	27.9	−0.7	19.1	6.3	3.4	..	..	..
Vanuatu	−0.4	3.3	11.2	3.2	−1.7	1.8	−2.5	−5.1	1.8	3.3	3.0
South and South-West Asia											
Bangladesh	5.5	4.3	4.9	4.8	4.9	5.2	5.3	5.5	5.2	6.6	5.9
Bhutan	6.8	9.0	13.1	11.2	6.4	8.8	8.3	1.2	10.2	7.9	8.1
India	10.5	7.2	9.8	8.4	10.1	5.5	7.1	7.3	8.2	9.9	9.8
Iran (Islamic Republic of)	2.4	5.0	5.0	−0.9	4.5	4.0	5.7	5.5	5.1	4.8	4.0
Maldives	8.9	11.0	10.0	8.9	6.8	6.0	2.4	4.7	9.6	9.4	..
Nepal	5.9	5.9	4.8	6.7	5.4	5.7	5.3	−1.4	3.3	4.3	2.1
Pakistan	4.8	4.8	3.6	1.6	5.0	4.2	3.1	4.8	5.3	6.0	7.9
Sri Lanka	4.8	6.0	7.1	5.1	4.0	7.0	−0.5	6.1	7.9	7.6	6.7
Turkey	6.3	7.6	8.6	2.4	−1.1	5.1	−7.7	7.5	6.7	10.2	5.8

(Continued on next page)

Table B.4 *(continued)*

(Percentage)

	1995	*1996*	*1997*	*1998*	*1999*	*2000*	*2001*	*2002*	*2003*	*2004*	*2005[a]*
South-East Asia											
Brunei Darussalam	..	..	..	..	1.7	..	..	..	..	..	..
Cambodia	8.3	9.2	2.9	5.0	14.6	8.9	3.8	4.4	0.2	9.2	6.3
Indonesia	7.6	6.8	5.6	−16.5	−1.0	5.2	5.0	5.0	6.2	7.0	7.0
Lao People's Democratic Republic	10.2	8.5	7.5	5.5	6.7	4.9	5.7	5.7	7.5	5.7	8.0
Malaysia	9.6	8.9	11.1	−1.1	4.4	6.0	6.2	6.5	4.5	6.7	6.4
Myanmar	7.3	6.5	6.7	7.0	9.2	13.4	12.9	12.5	..	..	..
Philippines	5.0	6.4	5.4	3.4	4.1	4.4	4.3	5.1	5.8	7.1	6.8
Singapore	7.4	9.3	9.8	−0.2	6.3	8.0	2.4	3.1	1.3	7.5	5.2
Thailand	8.9	5.3	−1.2	−10.0	0.4	3.7	2.4	4.8	4.0	6.2	5.4
Viet Nam	9.8	8.8	7.1	5.1	2.3	5.3	6.1	6.5	6.5	7.5	8.4
Developed ESCAP economies											
Australia	5.5	3.5	4.6	4.6	5.9	3.4	3.7	4.1	3.1	4.1	2.6
Japan	2.8	3.5	2.0	0.5	−0.1	2.1	2.0	1.1	1.2	2.6	3.1
New Zealand	4.6	3.3	2.9	2.8	3.9	3.9	4.8	3.7	3.6	4.6	2.7

Sources: ESCAP, based on national sources; International Monetary Fund, *International Financial Statistics* (CD-ROM) (Washington, D.C., IMF, December 2005); and IMF Country Reports Series; Asian Development Bank, *Key Indicators of Developing Asian and Pacific Countries 2005* (Manila, ADB, 2005); Economist Intelligence Unit, *Country Reports* and *Country Forecasts* (London, 2005 and 2006), various issues; and website of the Commonwealth of Independent States Inter-State Statistical Committee, <www.cisstat.com>, 6 January 2006 and 10 February 2006.

[a] Estimate.

Table B.5. Gross domestic savings rates

(Percentage of GDP)

	1995	1996	1997	1998	1999	2000	2001	2002	2003	2004	2005[a]
Developing ESCAP economies											
East and North-East Asia											
China	42.5	41.1	41.5	40.8	39.4	39.0	39.4	40.3	42.5	44.7	47.9
Hong Kong, China	29.1	29.7	30.2	29.4	29.8	31.7	29.6	31.1	31.6	31.6	33.1
Mongolia	23.4	18.9	25.8	14.3	14.6	10.4	5.7	3.7	8.8	..	..
Republic of Korea	36.5	35.7	35.8	37.9	35.8	33.9	31.9	31.4	33.0	35.0	34.9
Taiwan Province of China	25.9	25.7	25.6	25.4	25.2	24.3	22.2	23.3	23.5	23.4	25.5
North and Central Asia											
Armenia	..	..	..	..	..	..	..	..	..	..	..
Azerbaijan	2.9	0.3	12.9	4.8	8.6	20.4	24.9	24.7	..	..	..
Georgia	–12.8	0.7	–8.5	0.4	3.1	4.9	7.5	9.6	9.7	..	..
Kazakhstan	15.3	19.8	17.1	15.9	16.1	26.4	28.7	30.1	30.8	..	..
Kyrgyzstan	9.3	3.4	14.3	–8.2	1.2	14.2	16.8	17.4	7.6	..	..
Russian Federation	28.8	27.9	24.2	21.6	31.9	38.7	34.6	30.7	32.0	..	..
Tajikistan	23.9	18.9	13.0	6.4	15.9	7.3	4.8	5.0	4.3	..	..
Turkmenistan	..	..	..	..	..	..	..	..	..	..	..
Uzbekistan	27.1	22.7	18.7	19.9	17.3	19.4	20.0	22.4	26.7	31.2	..
Pacific island economies											
Cook Islands	..	..	..	..	..	..	..	..	..	..	..
Fiji	10.1	11.8	11.5	10.9	11.1	5.1	9.7	..	..	..	..
Kiribati	..	..	..	..	..	..	..	..	..	..	..
Papua New Guinea	40.2	31.2	22.4	22.6	13.2	23.7	12.6	11.7	..	..	..
Samoa	..	..	..	..	..	..	..	..	..	..	..
Solomon Islands	..	..	..	..	..	..	..	..	..	..	..
Tonga	–26.1	–27.3	–22.1	–29.7	–18.6	–14.2	–24.9	..	..	..	..
Tuvalu	..	..	..	..	..	..	..	..	..	..	..
Vanuatu	17.0	11.8	20.3	22.4	19.2	19.3	20.6	15.6	14.9	..	..
South and South-West Asia											
Bangladesh	13.1	14.9	15.9	17.4	17.7	17.9	18.0	18.0	18.6	19.5	20.2
Bhutan	46.1	35.6	23.5	22.9	22.5	42.5	47.5	42.0	40.2	28.5	39.0
India	25.1	23.2	23.1	21.5	24.9	23.5	23.6	26.5	28.9	29.1	29.0
Iran (Islamic Republic of)	15.7	18.0	20.7	25.5	25.4	26.8	38.4	38.5	39.9	42.6	45.4
Maldives	46.8	49.2	45.9	46.7	44.2	44.2	44.9	46.3	51.4	..	
Nepal	14.8	13.8	14.0	13.8	13.6	15.2	15.1	12.1	11.9	12.5	12.3
Pakistan	15.8	12.6	13.0	16.0	12.9	17.1	17.8	18.1	17.4	17.6	13.2
Sri Lanka	14.6	15.3	17.3	19.1	19.5	17.4	15.8	14.4	15.9	15.9	16.4
Turkey	22.3	20.1	21.8	23.2	21.4	18.4	17.2	19.1	19.1	21.8	19.2

(Continued on next page)

Table B.5 *(continued)*

(Percentage of GDP)

	1995	1996	1997	1998	1999	2000	2001	2002	2003	2004	2005[a]
South-East Asia											
Cambodia	5.1	5.3	9.0	9.5	7.3	6.8	9.5	9.5	11.1	12.2	11.7
Indonesia	30.6	30.1	31.5	26.5	25.8	26.6	23.4	22.9	22.3	22.1	24.0
Lao People's Democratic Republic	11.5	12.4	9.4	14.8	16.4	15.1	15.4	17.9	17.0	18.2	17.3
Malaysia	39.7	42.9	43.9	48.7	47.4	47.3	42.3	42.1	42.3	43.8	44.5
Myanmar	13.4	11.5	11.8	11.8	13.0	12.3	11.5	10.5	..	..	..
Philippines	14.5	14.6	14.2	12.4	14.3	17.3	17.1	19.0	19.5	20.9	21.2
Singapore	50.2	51.1	52.1	53.0	49.0	47.9	44.2	44.2	46.8	48.0	49.1
Thailand	37.3	36.5	35.7	35.2	32.9	33.0	31.9	32.2	33.3	33.4	30.8
Viet Nam	18.2	17.2	20.1	21.5	24.6	27.1	28.8	28.7	27.4	28.3	29.9
Developed ESCAP economies											
Australia	21.6	22.5	22.2	21.8	22.0	21.8	22.5	22.3	..	..	..
Japan	29.6	29.6	29.8	28.7	27.6	27.7	26.4	25.2	25.6	..	..
New Zealand	23.5	22.8	21.6	19.8	20.7	22.4	24.4	22.6	..	..	..

Sources: ESCAP, based on national sources; and Asian Development Bank, *Key Indicators of Developing Asian and Pacific Countries 2005* (Manila, ADB, 2005); and World Bank, *World Development Indicators 2005* (CD-ROM) (Washington, D.C., 2005).

[a] Estimate.

Table B.6. Gross domestic investment rates

(Percentage of GDP)

	1995	1996	1997	1998	1999	2000	2001	2002	2003	2004	2005[a]
Developing ESCAP economies											
East and North-East Asia											
China	40.8	39.6	38.2	37.7	37.4	36.3	38.5	40.2	43.8	45.3	42.3
Hong Kong, China	34.7	32.1	34.5	29.2	25.3	28.1	25.9	23.4	22.8	23.0	20.6
Mongolia	31.7	29.9	28.1	35.2	37.0	36.2	36.1	32.2	29.0	36.6	..
Republic of Korea	37.7	38.9	36.0	25.0	29.1	31.0	29.3	29.1	30.0	30.2	31.2
Taiwan Province of China	25.3	23.2	24.2	24.9	23.4	22.8	17.7	16.7	16.6	20.7	20.8
North and Central Asia											
Armenia	..	..	..	..	..	..	..	..	..	..	..
Azerbaijan	23.8	29.0	34.2	33.4	26.5	20.7	20.7	34.6	53.1	54.5	..
Georgia	4.0	18.7	18.6	19.4	21.8	20.5	20.9	21.1	23.4	..	..
Kazakhstan	23.3	16.1	15.6	15.8	17.8	18.1	26.9	27.3	25.9	24.0	..
Kyrgyzstan	18.3	25.2	21.7	15.4	18.0	20.0	18.0	17.6	11.8	10.0	..
Russian Federation	21.1	20.0	18.3	16.2	14.4	16.9	18.9	17.9	18.2	17.9	17.5
Tajikistan	21.3	13.3	17.7	13.4	16.6	9.4	9.2	10.8	10.8	..	..
Turkmenistan	..	..	38.7	45.5	4.0	35.4	32.6	26.7	25.5	..	..
Uzbekistan	24.2	23.0	18.9	20.9	17.1	19.6	21.1	21.2	20.8	23.9	..
Pacific island economies											
Cook Islands	..	..	..	..	..	..	..	..	..	..	..
Fiji	13.6	11.4	11.5	13.4	14.9	12.6	14.8	13.8	14.2	13.5	..
Kiribati	..	..	..	..	..	..	..	..	..	..	..
Papua New Guinea	21.9	22.7	21.1	17.9	16.1	21.3	21.8	19.8	..	..	..
Samoa	..	..	..	..	..	..	..	..	..	..	..
Solomon Islands	..	..	..	..	..	..	..	..	..	..	..
Tonga	22.1	21.5	17.3	18.3	20.7	20.7	19.0	..	..	..	..
Tuvalu	..	..	..	..	..	..	..	..	..	..	..
Vanuatu	23.2	20.2	18.8	17.7	20.8	22.1	20.0	21.2	19.8	..	..
South and South-West Asia											
Bangladesh	19.1	20.0	20.7	21.6	22.2	23.0	23.1	23.2	23.4	24.0	24.4
Bhutan	46.7	43.0	33.0	35.7	39.7	60.5	65.1	66.2	64.9	49.7	63.1
India	26.9	24.5	24.6	22.6	26.0	24.2	23.0	25.3	27.2	30.1	30.3
Iran (Islamic Republic of)	14.9	15.3	16.2	24.7	26.0	27.1	32.6	33.9	34.9	35.2	35.5
Maldives	31.5	30.5	33.2	30.1	33.6	26.3	28.1	25.5	32.3	..	..
Nepal	25.2	27.3	25.3	24.8	20.5	24.3	24.1	24.1	26.0	27.3	26.1
Pakistan	19.1	19.0	17.9	17.7	15.6	17.4	17.2	16.8	16.7	17.3	16.8
Sri Lanka	24.2	24.2	24.4	25.1	27.3	28.0	22.0	21.2	22.1	25.0	26.6
Turkey	25.6	25.0	25.6	24.3	24.0	25.0	15.9	21.4	23.3	27.1	25.5

(Continued on next page)

Table B.6 *(continued)*

(Percentage of GDP)

	1995	*1996*	*1997*	*1998*	*1999*	*2000*	*2001*	*2002*	*2003*	*2004*	*2005*[a]
South-East Asia											
Cambodia	12.8	15.2	14.4	12.0	17.0	17.3	21.2	20.1	25.2	25.8	26.3
Indonesia	31.9	30.7	31.8	25.4	21.8	21.1	19.2	19.0	18.9	21.0	21.7
Lao People's Democratic Republic	24.5	29.0	26.2	24.9	22.7	20.5	21.0	24.0	21.4	17.5	21.1
Malaysia	43.6	41.5	43.0	26.7	22.4	27.3	23.9	23.8	21.4	22.5	21.5
Myanmar	14.2	12.3	12.5	12.4	13.4	12.4	11.6	10.4	..	..	..
Philippines	22.5	24.0	24.8	20.3	18.8	21.2	19.0	17.6	16.6	17.0	17.2
Singapore	34.2	35.8	39.2	32.3	32.0	32.5	26.0	22.8	14.8	18.3	18.3
Thailand	42.1	41.8	33.7	20.4	20.5	22.8	24.1	23.9	25.0	27.1	30.9
Viet Nam	27.1	28.1	28.3	29.0	27.6	29.6	31.2	33.2	35.4	35.5	38.5
Developed ESCAP economies											
Australia	22.2	22.2	23.1	23.5	24.1	21.7	22.5	24.7	25.1	25.4	25.7
Japan	27.8	28.4	28.1	26.9	26.3	26.3	25.8	24.2	23.9	23.8	24.4
New Zealand	21.5	21.5	20.5	19.2	20.1	19.5	19.8	20.5	22.1	23.5	24.3

Sources: ESCAP, based on national sources; and Asian Development Bank, *Key Indicators of Developing Asian and Pacific Countries 2005* (Manila, ADB, 2005); and World Bank, *World Development Indicators 2005* (CD-ROM) (Washington, D.C., 2005).

[a] Estimate.

Table B.7. Inflation rates

(Percentage)

	1995	1996	1997	1998	1999	2000	2001	2002	2003	2004	2005[a]
Developing ESCAP economies[b]	34.9	16.5	9.9	13.8	12.8	6.3	7.2	5.5	4.8	4.7	4.8
East and North-East Asia	10.9	6.4	3.2	2.3	−0.7	0.8	1.4	0.1	1.4	3.2	2.2
China	17.1	8.3	2.8	−0.8	−1.4	0.4	0.7	−0.8	1.2	3.9	1.9
Hong Kong, China	9.0	6.4	5.8	2.8	−4.0	−3.8	−1.6	−3.1	−2.5	−0.4	1.1
Mongolia	56.7	46.9	36.6	9.4	7.5	11.8	8.2	1.5	4.6	11.0	10.0
Republic of Korea	4.4	5.0	4.4	7.5	0.8	2.2	4.1	2.7	3.6	3.6	2.8
Taiwan Province of China	3.7	3.1	0.9	1.6	0.2	1.2	0.0	−0.2	−0.3	1.6	2.3
North and Central Asia	215.9	64.3	17.6	25.7	76.3	19.9	20.4	15.0	12.9	10.2	12.0
Armenia	176.0	19.0	13.8	9.0	0.6	−0.8	3.1	1.1	4.8	6.9	0.6
Azerbaijan	412.0	20.0	3.7	−1.0	−8.6	1.8	1.6	2.8	2.2	6.7	9.6
Georgia	163.0	39.0	7.1	4.0	19.2	4.1	4.7	5.6	4.8	5.7	8.2
Kazakhstan	176.0	39.0	17.4	7.0	8.4	13.2	8.3	5.8	6.4	6.9	7.6
Kyrgyzstan	43.0	32.0	23.0	10.0	35.9	18.7	7.0	2.1	3.1	4.1	4.3
Russian Federation	197.5	47.7	14.8	27.7	85.7	20.8	21.5	15.8	13.7	10.9	12.7
Tajikistan	443.0	270.0	72.0	43.0	26.0	24.0	36.5	10.2	17.1	6.8	7.8
Turkmenistan	1 005.3	992.4	83.4	17.2	24.1	7.2	11.6	8.7	6.5	10.0	10.5
Uzbekistan	304.6	54.0	58.8	17.8	29.0	24.9	27.2	24.2	13.1	1.7	7.1
Pacific island economies	11.4	8.1	3.8	11.1	9.5	10.7	7.0	8.4	10.7	3.0	2.0
Cook Islands	0.9	−0.6	−0.4	0.8	1.3	3.2	8.7	3.4	2.0	0.9	..
Fiji	2.2	2.4	2.9	8.1	0.2	3.0	2.3	1.6	4.2	3.3	3.0
Kiribati	4.1	−1.8	2.6	4.3	0.6	0.9	7.0	1.6	2.6	−1.9	..
Papua New Guinea	17.3	11.6	4.0	13.6	14.9	15.6	9.3	11.8	14.7	2.1	1.0
Samoa	−2.9	5.4	6.9	2.2	0.3	1.0	3.8	8.0	0.1	11.7	7.8
Solomon Islands	9.6	11.7	8.1	12.3	8.0	7.1	7.7	9.4	10.0	7.1	6.2
Tonga	1.5	3.0	2.1	3.3	4.5	6.3	8.3	10.4	11.6	11.0	9.6
Tuvalu	5.6	0.0	1.6	0.6	4.0	3.9	1.4	5.0	3.3	2.8	..
Vanuatu	2.2	0.9	2.8	3.3	2.0	2.5	3.7	2.0	3.0	1.4	2.5
South and South-West Asia[c]	31.7	26.7	26.1	29.2	19.5	16.2	16.3	14.5	10.0	6.4	6.9
Bangladesh	8.9	7.0	3.7	9.0	7.0	2.8	1.9	2.8	4.4	5.8	6.5
Bhutan	9.5	8.8	6.5	10.6	6.8	4.0	3.4	2.5	2.1	4.6	5.5
India[d]	10.2	9.4	6.8	13.1	3.4	3.8	4.3	4.0	3.9	3.8	4.5
Iran (Islamic Republic of)	49.4	23.2	17.3	18.1	20.1	12.6	11.4	15.8	15.6	15.2	14.5
Maldives	5.5	6.3	7.5	−1.4	3.0	−1.2	0.7	0.9	-2.9	6.4	6.8
Nepal[e]	7.6	7.2	8.1	8.3	11.4	3.5	2.4	2.9	4.8	4.0	4.5
Pakistan	12.3	10.7	11.8	7.8	5.7	3.6	4.4	3.5	3.1	4.6	9.3
Sri Lanka[f]	7.7	15.9	9.6	9.4	4.7	6.2	14.2	9.6	6.3	7.6	11.6
Turkey	88.1	80.3	85.7	84.6	64.9	54.9	54.4	45.0	25.3	8.6	7.7

(Continued on next page)

Table B.7 *(continued)*

(Percentage)

	1995	1996	1997	1998	1999	2000	2001	2002	2003	2004	2005[a]
South-East Asia	6.1	5.6	4.8	21.3	7.7	2.3	4.9	4.5	3.3	4.0	5.9
Cambodia	1.1	10.0	9.2	13.3	−0.5	−0.8	0.7	3.7	0.5	5.6	5.5
Indonesia	9.4	7.9	6.2	58.5	20.3	3.6	11.5	11.9	6.6	6.1	10.5
Lao People's Democratic Republic	19.7	13.0	27.6	90.9	128.4	25.1	7.8	10.6	15.5	10.5	8.0
Malaysia	4.0	3.4	2.8	5.2	2.8	1.5	1.4	1.8	1.2	1.4	2.9
Myanmar	25.2	16.3	29.7	51.5	18.4	−0.1	21.1	54.0	8.0	..	..
Philippines	6.7	7.5	5.6	9.3	5.9	4.0	6.8	3.0	3.5	6.0	7.6
Singapore	1.8	1.4	2.0	−0.3	0.1	1.3	1.0	−0.4	0.5	1.7	0.4
Thailand	5.7	5.9	5.6	8.1	0.2	1.7	1.6	0.6	1.8	2.8	4.5
Viet Nam	16.8	5.7	3.2	7.3	4.1	−1.7	−0.4	3.8	3.1	7.8	8.4
Developed ESCAP economies	0.3	0.3	1.7	0.6	−0.2	−0.3	−0.3	−0.6	−0.1	0.2	0.0
Australia	4.6	2.6	0.3	0.8	1.5	4.5	4.4	3.0	2.8	2.3	2.8
Japan	−0.1	0.1	1.7	0.6	−0.3	−0.7	−0.7	−0.9	−0.3	0.0	−0.3
New Zealand	3.7	2.3	1.2	1.2	−0.1	2.6	2.6	2.7	1.8	2.3	2.8

Sources: ESCAP, based on national sources; International Monetary Fund, *International Financial Statistics* (CD-ROM) (Washington, D.C., IMF, December 2005); and IMF Country Reports Series; Asian Development Bank, *Key Indicators of Developing Asian and Pacific Countries 2005* (Manila, ADB, 2005); Economist Intelligence Unit, *Country Reports* and *Country Forecasts* (London, 2005 and 2006), various issues; and website of the Commonwealth of Independent States Inter-State Statistical Committee, <www.cisstat.com>, 9 January 2006 and 10 February 2006.

Note: Rates of inflation refer to percentage changes in the consumer price index.

a Estimate.
b Based on data for 38 developing economies representing more than 95 per cent of the population of the region (including the Central Asian countries); GDP figures at market prices in United States dollars in 2000 (at 1995 prices) have been used as weights to calculate the regional and subregional growth rates.
c The estimates and forecasts for countries refer to fiscal years defined as follows: fiscal year 2004/05 = 2004 for India, the Islamic Republic of Iran and Myanmar; and fiscal year 2003/04 = 2004 for Bangladesh, Nepal and Pakistan.
d Data refer to consumer price index for industrial workers.
e Data refer to national urban consumer price index.
f For Colombo only.

Table B.8. Budget balances

(Percentage of GDP)

	1995	*1996*	*1997*	*1998*	*1999*	*2000*	*2001*	*2002*	*2003*	*2004*	*2005*[a]
Developing ESCAP economies											
East and North-East Asia											
China	–1.0	–1.9	–2.0	–2.6	–3.2	–3.1	–2.8	–3.2	–2.7	–1.5	–1.7
Hong Kong, China	0.3	2.1	6.5	–1.8	0.8	–0.6	–5.0	–4.9	–3.3	–0.4	–0.4
Mongolia[b]	–1.5	–2.6	–9.1	–14.3	–11.6	–7.7	–4.5	–5.8	–4.2	–2.2	–3.3
Republic of Korea	0.3	0.2	–1.4	–3.9	–2.5	1.1	1.2	3.3	1.1	0.7	–0.4
Taiwan Province of China	–1.1	–1.4	–1.7	0.2	–1.3	–4.8	–6.6	–3.0	–2.5	–2.5	–2.5
North and Central Asia											
Armenia	..	..	–4.7	–3.7	–7.4	–6.3	–3.8	–2.4	–3.2	–2.3	–2.9
Azerbaijan	..	..	–2.8	–2.0	–2.8	–1.9	–2.0	–1.2	–1.2	0.8	0.7
Georgia	..	..	..	..	–6.7	–4.7	–2.0	–2.2	–1.3	–1.3	–3.5
Kazakhstan[b]	–2.4	–4.4	–4.0	–4.4	–3.3	–0.1	–0.4	–0.4	–1.0	–0.3	–0.5
Kyrgyzstan[b]	–11.5	–5.4	–5.2	–3.0	–2.5	–1.9	0.4	–1.1	–0.8	–0.5	–0.9
Russian Federation	–4.9	–7.4	–6.4	–4.8	–1.2	2.4	3.1	1.7	2.4	4.9	6.3
Tajikistan	..	..	–4.1	–2.7	–2.4	–0.6	–0.6	–2.4	–1.8	–2.7	–4.3
Turkmenistan	..	..	–0.2	–2.6	0.0	–0.3	0.9	–2.7	–1.8	–2.2	–3.2
Uzbekistan	..	..	–2.5	–2.3	–3.2	–3.9	–3.6	–0.8	–0.4	–0.4	–0.7
Pacific island economies											
Cook Islands[b]	–2.8	–7.8	1.1	–2.5	–2.4	–1.8	1.3	0.2	–0.8	..	..
Fiji[b]	–0.2	–4.7	–6.5	5.0	–0.3	–3.2	–6.5	–5.6	–6.0	–3.2	–4.3
Kiribati[b]	16.2	–11.0	25.7	40.9	17.1	18.7	..	..	..	..	..
Papua New Guinea[b]	–0.5	0.5	0.2	–1.8	–2.6	–2.0	–3.5	–3.9	–0.8	1.5	–0.6
Samoa[b]	–7.0	1.4	2.2	2.0	0.3	–0.7	–2.3	–2.1	–0.6	–0.9	–0.9
Solomon Islands[b]	..	..	..	–0.3	–3.7	–7.8	–12.7	–11.0	–1.9	8.3	–0.5
Tonga	1.2	0.8	–1.2	–2.5	–0.2	0.8	–0.2	1.2	–3.8	–0.7	..
Tuvalu[b]	..	..	–31.8	19.1	–3.5	–2.2	–45.7	33.7	..	..	..
Vanuatu[b]	–2.7	–1.7	–0.5	–9.4	–1.6	–7.0	–3.7	–1.5	–1.8	0.4	–0.2
South and South-West Asia											
Bangladesh	–4.6	–4.7	–3.7	–3.4	–4.6	–6.1	–5.2	–4.7	–4.3	–3.2	–4.2
Bhutan[b]	0.1	2.2	–2.3	0.9	–1.7	–3.8	–10.5	–11.6	–6.7	–11.3	–11.0
India[b]	–4.2	–4.1	–4.8	–5.1	–5.4	–5.7	–6.2	–5.9	–4.5	–4.5	–4.3
Iran (Islamic Republic of)	–0.2	–0.2	–1.0	–2.2	–0.2	–0.2[c]	–0.4	–4.1	–2.9	–3.0	–4.3
Maldives[b]	–6.4	–2.5	–1.3	–1.9	–4.1	–4.4	–4.7	–4.9	–3.4	–1.8	–4.5
Nepal[b]	–4.8	–5.6	–5.1	–5.9	–5.3	–4.7	–5.9	–5.4	–3.6	–3.7	–4.8
Pakistan	–5.6	–6.5	–6.4	–7.6	–6.1	–5.4	–4.3	–4.3	–3.7	–3.0	–3.3
Sri Lanka	–10.1	–9.4	–7.9	–9.1	–7.5	–9.9	–10.8	–8.9	–8.0	–8.2	–8.2
Turkey[b]	–4.1	–8.4	–7.8	–7.1	–11.7	–10.3	–16.0	–14.4	–11.2	–7.0	–3.0

(Continued on next page)

Table B.8 *(continued)*

(Percentage of GDP)

	1995	*1996*	*1997*	*1998*	*1999*	*2000*	*2001*	*2002*	*2003*	*2004*	*2005[a]*
South-East Asia											
Cambodia	–7.3	–6.3	–3.8	–5.4	–3.9	–4.9	–6.8	–6.5	–6.6	–5.1	–5.5
Indonesia	2.2	1.0	0.5	–1.7	–2.5	–1.1	–2.4	–1.3	–1.7	–1.2	–0.8
Lao People's Democratic Republic	–9.0	–9.1	–8.4	–11.1	–7.6	–6.0	–7.6	–4.9	–7.4	–3.7	–9.9
Malaysia	0.8	0.7	2.4	–1.8	–3.2	–5.7	–5.5	–5.6	–5.3	–4.3	–4.0
Myanmar[d]	–3.2	–2.2	–0.9	–5.7	–4.5	–8.4	–5.9	–4.1	–4.5	–5.9	..
Philippines[b]	0.6	0.3	0.1	–1.9	–3.8	–4.0	–4.0	–5.3	–4.6	–3.9	–3.4
Singapore[e]	7.8	6.9	3.4	2.5	0.5	2.0	1.6	–1.1	–1.6	–1.1	0.4
Thailand[f]	3.0	0.9	–1.5	–2.8	–3.3	–2.2	–2.4	–1.4	0.4	0.1	–0.1
Viet Nam[g]	..	..	–4.8	–2.6	–1.4	–2.4	–4.7	–4.5	–3.3	–4.9	–4.9
Developed ESCAP economies[h]											
Australia[i]	–2.1	–0.9	0.1	0.4	1.4	1.8	0.9	1.1	1.7	1.6	1.3
Japan	–4.7	–5.1	–3.8	–5.5	–7.2	–7.5	–6.1	–7.9	–7.8	–7.2	–6.7
New Zealand[j]	3.3	2.7	2.2	2.1	1.5	1.3	1.6	1.7	3.5	4.6	4.1

Sources: ESCAP, based on national sources; International Monetary Fund, *International Financial Statistics* (CD-ROM) (Washington, D.C., IMF, December 2005); and IMF Country Reports Series; and *World Economic Outlook Database* (Washington, D.C., IMF, 2005); Asian Development Bank, *Key Indicators of Developing Asian and Pacific Countries 2005* (Manila, ADB, 2005); and Economist Intelligence Unit, *Country Reports* and *Country Forecasts* (London, 2005 and 2006), various issues.

a Estimate.
b Including grants.
c If the Oil Stabilization Fund had been taken into account as government revenue, there would have been a surplus of 8.6 per cent of GDP.
d Including grants since 1998.
e Budget surplus/deficit is computed from government operating revenue minus government operating expenditure minus government development expenditure.
f Data refer to a government cash balance comprising the budgetary balance and non-budgetary balance.
g Excluding grants and including on lending.
h Data refer to general government fiscal balance.
i Data exclude net advances (primarily privatization receipts and net policy-related lending).
j Government balance is revenue minus expenditure plus balance of State-owned enterprises, excluding privatization receipts.

Table B.9. Current account balances

(Percentage of GDP)

	1995	1996	1997	1998	1999	2000	2001	2002	2003	2004	2005[a]
Developing ESCAP economies											
East and North-East Asia											
China	0.2	0.9	4.1	3.3	2.1	1.9	1.5	2.8	3.2	4.2	6.7
Hong Kong, China	..	..	–4.5	1.5	6.4	4.2	6.0	7.8	10.6	10.0	12.1
Mongolia[b]	–5.5	–10.0	1.3	–7.8	–6.7	–5.7	–7.6	–9.6	–7.7	1.2	2.2
Republic of Korea	–1.7	–4.1	–1.6	11.7	5.5	2.4	1.7	1.0	2.0	4.1	2.3
Taiwan Province of China	2.1	3.9	2.4	1.3	2.8	2.9	6.5	9.1	10.2	6.2	4.6
North and Central Asia											
Armenia	–17.0	–18.2	–18.7	–22.1	–16.6	–14.6	–9.4	–6.2	–6.7	–4.5	–4.9
Azerbaijan	–16.6	–29.3	–23.1	–30.7	–13.1	–3.2	–0.9	–12.3	–27.8	–30.4	–12.9
Georgia	–19.1	–18.7	–14.4	–7.6	–7.1	–8.8	–6.6	–6.5	–9.4	–8.3	–10.4
Kazakhstan	–1.2	–3.7	–3.8	–5.8	–1.0	2.0	–6.4	–4.2	–0.9	1.3	6.4
Kyrgyzstan	–15.7	–23.3	–7.8	–25.1	–20.2	–9.1	–3.7	–5.0	–5.2	–4.6	–4.0
Russian Federation	2.2	2.8	0.0	0.1	12.6	18.0	11.0	8.4	8.2	10.3	11.9
Tajikistan	–16.9	–7.2	–5.4	–9.1	–3.1	–7.1	–6.9	–1.4	–0.3	–2.7	–4.0
Turkmenistan[c]	0.2	0.1	–21.6	–34.5	–20.5	6.4	0.2	1.9	0.9	–2.8	–0.1
Uzbekistan	–0.2	–7.0	–3.9	0.3	–0.8	1.6	–1.0	1.2	8.9	0.8	4.5
Pacific island economies											
Cook Islands	..	..	..	..	..	..	..	..	..	..	..
Fiji	–1.0	3.1	1.5	–0.3	–3.8	–6.3	–7.2	–3.0	–7.2	–16.4	..
Kiribati	–6.1	–19.9	20.3	30.4	3.3	3.9	17.0	–1.5	–17.2	–14.2	..
Papua New Guinea	13.9	6.0	–2.4	1.6	4.2	10.0	9.1	–4.3	3.9	2.9	2.5
Samoa	..	..	3.9	6.6	2.4	4.8	–11.9	–7.3	–0.5	–8.9	–14.4[d]
Solomon Islands	2.5	4.0	–10.1	2.7	6.6	–10.6	–12.8	–7.2	1.4	1.1	–7.9
Tonga	–13.3	–5.8	–0.9	–11.5	–0.9	–6.4	–10.1	5.0	–3.0	3.8	–2.2
Tuvalu	..	..	39.0	20.7	..	..	..	..	..	..	..
Vanuatu	..	..	–1.1	2.7	–5.4	2.1	0.8	–7.9	–10.6	–8.0	–6.1
South and South-West Asia											
Bangladesh	..	..	–1.3	–0.6	–0.9	0.0	–1.7	0.5	0.4	0.9	–1.7
Bhutan	..	14.6	5.2	10.2	2.3	5.4	1.5	–10.9	–11.9	–7.7	–21.2
India	–1.7	–1.2	–1.4	–1.0	–1.0	–0.6	0.7	1.3	1.8	–0.9	–1.3
Iran (Islamic Republic of)	..	3.9	1.4	–1.1	12.0	17.5	7.1	3.1	0.6	2.4	5.7
Maldives	–4.6	–1.6	–6.8	–4.1	–13.4	–8.2	–9.4	–5.6	–4.6	–18.3	..
Nepal[e]	..	–8.7	–8.0	–1.5	0.1	4.5	4.9	4.3	2.6	2.9	5.5
Pakistan	–3.7	–7.4	–6.0	–2.9	–3.1	–0.3	0.5	3.7	4.9	1.9	–1.4
Sri Lanka	–6.1	–4.9	–2.6	–1.4	–3.6	–6.5	–1.4	–1.4	–0.4	–3.2	–4.5
Turkey	–1.4	–1.3	–1.4	1.0	–0.7	–4.9	2.3	–0.8	–3.4	–5.2	–5.9

(Continued on next page)

Table B.9 *(continued)*

(Percentage of GDP)

	1995	1996	1997	1998	1999	2000	2001	2002	2003	2004	2005[a]
South-East Asia											
Cambodia	−3.2	−3.1	0.6	−5.8	−5.1	−2.8	−1.1	−1.5	−2.9	−4.4	−4.9
Indonesia	−3.2	−3.4	−2.4	4.3	4.1	4.8	4.2	3.9	3.4	1.1	0.9
Lao People's Democratic Republic	−19.5	−18.5	−17.5	−11.7	−8.3	−0.5	−4.7	0.3	−1.5	−7.8	−1.9
Malaysia	−9.8	−4.4	−5.9	13.2	15.9	9.4	8.3	8.4	12.9	12.6	11.6
Myanmar[c]	−0.2	−0.2	0.0	−0.2	−0.1	−0.1	−0.1	0.04	−0.02	−0.02	..
Philippines	−4.4	−4.8	−5.3	2.4	9.5	8.2	1.9	5.5	4.4	2.4	3.6
Singapore	17.5	15.0	15.6	22.3	17.9	12.9	16.8	17.7	29.2	26.1	24.0
Thailand	−7.9	−7.9	−2.1	12.8	10.2	7.6	5.4	5.5	5.6	4.5	−1.4
Viet Nam	−9.0	−8.2	−5.7	−3.9	4.1	3.6	2.1	−1.7	−4.9	−2.0	−0.9
Developed ESCAP economies											
Australia	−5.4	−3.9	−3.1	−5.0	−5.7	−4.1	−2.4	−4.3	−6.0	−6.4	−5.9
Japan	2.1	1.4	2.2	3.0	2.6	2.5	2.1	2.8	3.2	3.7	3.5
New Zealand	−4.9	−5.8	−6.5	−3.9	−6.1	−4.7	−2.4	−3.7	−4.2	−6.4	−8.5

Sources: ESCAP, based on national sources; International Monetary Fund, *International Financial Statistics* (CD-ROM) (Washington, D.C., IMF, December 2005); and IMF Country Reports Series; Asian Development Bank, *Key Indicators of Developing Asian and Pacific Countries 2005* (Manila, ADB, 2005); and Economist Intelligence Unit, *Country Reports* and *Country Forecasts* (London, 2005), various issues.

a Estimate.
b Including official transfers since 1998.
c At official exchange rates.
d Refers to data up to second quarter.
e Including official transfers.

Table B.10. Change in money supply

(Percentage)

	1995	1996	1997	1998	1999	2000	2001	2002	2003	2004	2005[a]
Developing ESCAP economies											
East and North-East Asia											
China	29.5	25.3	20.7	14.9	14.7	12.3	15.0	19.4	19.7	14.8	18.4
Hong Kong, China	10.6	12.5	8.7	11.1	8.3	9.3	−0.3	0.5	6.3	7.3	8.2
Mongolia	32.6	25.8	32.5	−1.7	31.6	17.6	27.9	42.0	49.6	20.4	34.3[b]
Republic of Korea	15.6	15.8	14.1	27.0	27.4	25.4	13.2	11.0	6.7	−0.6	5.0
Taiwan Province of China	9.4	9.1	8.0	8.6	8.3	6.5	4.4	2.6	5.8	7.4	6.3
North and Central Asia											
Armenia	64.3	35.1	29.2	36.7	14.0	38.6	4.3	34.0	10.4	22.3	31.2[c]
Azerbaijan	25.4	17.1	41.4	−15.2	20.1	73.4	−10.5	14.6	30.8	46.1	25.2[d]
Georgia	..	41.4	44.0	−1.1	21.1	39.4	18.5	17.9	22.8	42.4	39.1[d]
Kazakhstan	108.2	20.9	24.1	−14.1	84.4	45.0	40.2	30.1	29.5	69.3	46.9[c]
Kyrgyzstan	..	14.8	32.2	17.5	33.7	11.7	11.3	33.9	33.4	32.1	19.0[c]
Russian Federation	112.6	29.6	28.8	37.6	56.7	58.0	36.3	33.8	38.5	33.7	37.0[c]
Tajikistan	..	78.7	105.1	28.2	37.3	57.2	68.0	11.7	50.4	5.8	..
Turkmenistan	567.8	247.8	107.2	67.7	75.7	83.3	23.8	..	..	..	..
Uzbekistan	151.9	119.0	45.6	27.5	32.7	37.1	54.3	29.7	27.1	47.8	..
Pacific island economies											
Cook Islands	..	10.9	15.7	23.6	−0.8	..	14.4	3.2	9.9	9.6	..
Fiji	4.5	0.9	−8.7	−0.5	13.6	−1.5	−3.1	7.8	25.0	10.5	18.8[b]
Papua New Guinea	13.7	30.7	7.7	2.5	9.2	5.0	1.6	4.0	−0.4	12.4	32.2[c]
Samoa	24.4	6.3	15.2	2.5	15.7	16.3	6.1	10.2	14.0	8.3	11.4[e]
Solomon Islands	9.2	15.3	6.7	2.5	7.0	0.6	−13.6	6.0	25.4	17.5	21.6[b]
Tonga	0.7	5.3	7.8	14.7	11.9	18.8	14.9	7.8	14.4	13.2	17.9[c]
Vanuatu	13.3	10.1	−0.4	12.6	−9.2	5.5	5.7	−1.7	−0.8	9.9	12.6[c]
South and South-West Asia											
Bangladesh	16.1	8.3	10.8	10.2	12.8	18.6	16.6	13.1	15.6	13.8	16.8
Bhutan	36.0	9.4	58.6	16.4	31.4	16.1	7.6	28.5	0.4	19.9	10.7[f]
India	11.0	18.7	17.7	18.2	17.1	15.2	14.3	16.8	13.0	16.7	17.1[b]
Iran (Islamic Republic of)	30.1	32.5	23.7	20.4	21.5	22.4	27.6	24.9	24.5	23.0	19.0[f]
Maldives	15.6	26.0	23.1	22.8	3.6	4.1	9.0	19.3	14.6	32.6	15.0[d]
Nepal	16.1	14.4	11.9	21.9	20.8	21.8	15.3	4.4	9.8	11.8	12.5
Pakistan	13.8	20.1	19.9	7.9	4.3	12.1	11.7	16.8	17.5	20.5	15.5[c]
Sri Lanka	35.8	11.3	15.6	13.2	13.4	12.9	13.6	13.4	15.3	19.6	15.0[g]
Turkey	103.6	117.3	97.5	89.7	100.3	40.5	86.2	29.1	14.6	22.1	21.8[b]

(Continued on next page)

Table B.10 *(continued)*

(Percentage)

	1995	1996	1997	1998	1999	2000	2001	2002	2003	2004	2005[a]
South-East Asia											
Cambodia	44.3	40.4	16.6	15.7	17.3	26.9	20.4	31.1	14.9	30.4	15.2[c]
Indonesia	27.6	29.6	23.2	62.3	11.9	15.6	13.0	4.7	8.1	8.1	19.0
Lao People's Democratic Republic	16.4	26.7	65.8	113.3	78.4	46.0	13.7	37.6	20.1	21.6	12.5[h]
Malaysia	24.0	19.8	22.7	1.5	13.7	5.2	2.2	5.8	11.1	25.4	24.2[b]
Myanmar	36.5	38.9	28.8	34.2	29.7	42.4	43.9	34.7	1.4	32.4	26.0[b]
Philippines	23.9	23.7	23.1	8.6	16.9	8.1	3.6	10.4	3.6	9.9	15.4
Singapore	8.5	9.8	10.3	30.2	8.5	–2.0	5.9	–0.3	8.1	6.2	6.5
Thailand	17.0	12.6	16.4	9.5	2.1	3.7	4.2	2.6	4.9	5.4	9.6
Viet Nam	22.6	25.7	24.3	23.5	66.5	35.4	27.3	13.3	33.1	31.0	29.1
Developed ESCAP economies											
Australia	8.5	10.6	7.3	8.4	11.7	3.7	13.2	5.6	13.3	11.7	8.3[c]
Japan	2.7	2.3	3.1	4.1	3.4	1.1	2.2	3.4	1.8	1.6	1.4
New Zealand	9.3	16.1	5.2	1.8	5.0	2.3	6.8	7.7	10.6	5.1	5.2

Sources: ESCAP, based on national sources; International Monetary Fund, *International Financial Statistics* (CD-ROM) (Washington, D.C., IMF, December 2005); and IMF Country Reports Series; and Asian Development Bank, *Key Indicators of Developing Asian and Pacific Countries 2005* (Manila, ADB, 2005).

Note: Changes in money supply refer to the annual percentage change in the broad money supply as represented by M2. M2 is defined as the sum of M1 and quasi-money, where M1 denotes currency in circulation plus demand deposits, and quasi-money consists of time and savings deposits plus foreign currency deposits.

a Estimate.
b Refers to September 2005 compared with the corresponding period of 2004.
c Refers to October 2005 compared with the corresponding period of 2004.
d Refers to November 2005 compared with the corresponding period of 2004.
e Refers to August 2005 compared with the corresponding period of 2004.
f Refers to June 2005 compared with the corresponding period of 2004.
g Refers to May 2005 compared with the corresponding period of 2004.
h Refers to February 2005 compared with the corresponding period of 2004.

Table B.11. Merchandise export growth rates

(Percentage)

	1995	1996	1997	1998	1999	2000	2001	2002	2003	2004	2005
Developing ESCAP economies											
East and North-East Asia											
China	22.9	1.5	21.0	0.5	6.1	27.8	6.8	22.4	34.6	35.4	31.1[a]
Hong Kong, China	14.8	4.0	4.0	−7.5	−0.1	16.1	−5.9	5.4	11.8	15.9	12.1[b]
Macao, China	7.2	−0.1	7.6	−0.3	2.7	15.4	−9.4	2.5	9.5	9.0	−14.3[b]
Mongolia	32.3	−13.0	34.5	−18.8	−1.7	18.1	−2.4	0.2	19.7	39.1[c]	4.8[d]
Republic of Korea	30.3	3.7	5.0	−2.8	8.6	19.9	−12.7	8.0	19.3	31.0	12.3[a]
North and Central Asia											
Armenia	25.5	7.0	−19.7	−5.2	5.0	29.7	13.6	47.7	35.8	4.2	34.0[b]
Azerbaijan	−2.5	−0.9	23.8	−22.4	53.3	87.8	32.6	−6.3	19.6	39.4	37.0[b]
Georgia	−1.3	29.2	20.6	−19.6	23.3	38.7	−3.0	8.8	33.6	39.6	33.0[b]
Kazakhstan	62.5	12.6	9.9	−16.3	2.9	63.2	−5.3	11.9	33.7	55.5	40.0[b]
Kyrgyzstan	20.3	23.5	19.6	−14.9	−11.7	11.2	−5.7	2.1	19.8	23.5	−6.0[b]
Russian Federation[f]	21.6	9.9	−4.1	−14.3	1.5	39.0	−3.0	5.3	26.7	33.6	34.0[b]
Tajikistan	52.2	2.8	−3.1	−20.0	15.4	13.8	−16.8	13.0	8.1	14.8	−3.0[b]
Turkmenistan	−12.3	−10.6	−55.4	−20.9	100.3	110.1	4.8	9.0	27.2	6.6	21.4[c]
Uzbekistan	10.7	49.3	−4.4	−20.1	−0.6	0.9	−16.3	−7.1	26.9	32.4	26.3[c]
Pacific island economies											
Fiji	3.6	24.1	−23.9	−11.6	19.4	−6.8	−4.7	1.2	34.6	−3.3	19.4[g]
Papua New Guinea	13.4	−2.4	−14.8	−16.1	9.1	7.3	−13.7	−9.5	34.4	15.6	25.5[e]
Samoa[h]	151.4	14.8	45.5	30.5	103.8	8.2	−15.7	−0.7	−10.4	9.3	−9.9[d]
Solomon Islands	17.1	−3.5	7.5	−27.6	−3.6	−46.5	−27.6	22.7	28.4	30.3[c]	3.6[d]
Tonga[i]	6.2	−24.8	0.4	−17.8	12.6	−11.6	2.1	66.8	−0.2	−21.3	14.2
Vanuatu	13.2	6.7	16.9	−4.0	−24.2	5.8	−26.8	1.0	32.3	28.6[c]	14.3[d]
South and South-West Asia											
Afghanistan[j]	..	..	..	..	..	..	−37.7	82.1	46.7	−12.6	14.3[d]
Bangladesh[i]	..	11.8	13.8	16.8	2.9	8.3	12.4	−7.4	9.4	16.1	11.8
Bhutan[j]	10.2	39.7	1.7	12.1	−5.9	9.1	−12.9	4.1	8.9	39.7[k]	5.2[c]
India[i]	20.3	5.6	4.5	−3.9	9.5	21.1	−1.6	20.3	20.4	24.9[c]	26.0[d]
Iran (Islamic Republic of)[i]	−5.5	22.0	−17.9	−28.6	60.3	35.3	−16.0	18.1	20.4	30.6	37.1[g]
Maldives	12.7	−6.0	12.3	6.6	−4.3	18.8	1.4	20.1	14.9	19.1	−0.8[g]
Nepal[i]	−9.8	2.3	9.8	12.7	17.4	37.6	4.6	−18.8	4.3	14.0	10.1[c]
Pakistan[i]	19.4	7.0	−4.4	3.7	−9.8	10.1	7.4	−0.7	22.2	10.3	17.0
Sri Lanka	18.6	7.8	13.3	1.9	−2.6	19.8	−12.8	−2.4	9.2	12.2	10.6[d]
Turkey	19.5	7.3	13.1	2.7	−1.4	4.5	12.8	15.1	31.0	33.6	16.9[a]

(Continued on next page)

Table B.11 *(continued)*

(Percentage)

	1995	1996	1997	1998	1999	2000	2001	2002	2003	2004	2005
South-East Asia											
Brunei Darussalam	3.0	8.3	8.3	−50.2	28.9	23.9	5.5	3.1	28.6	2.1	6.4[l]
Cambodia	74.3	−24.6	33.9	4.4	41.1	24.1	12.1	11.8	15.5	22.0	8.3[c]
Indonesia	..	5.8	12.2	−10.5	1.7	27.6	−12.3	3.1	8.4	12.6	21.6[e]
Lao People's Democratic Republic	..	..	−1.4	7.7	−10.5	9.5	−3.3	−5.9	11.6	7.6	26.2[c]
Malaysia	21.0	7.0	−27.1	32.7	12.1	16.2	−10.4	6.0	12.5	20.5	11.2[b]
Myanmar	..	..	3.9	9.3	7.0	44.3	48.3	3.5	7.2	9.0	3.7[c]
Philippines	29.4	17.7	22.8	16.9	18.8	8.7	−15.6	9.5	2.9	9.5	2.9[a]
Singapore	22.5	5.8	0.0	−12.2	4.4	20.3	−11.8	2.8	15.3	24.6	14.3[e]
Thailand	24.8	−1.9	3.8	−6.8	7.4	19.5	−7.1	4.8	18.2	21.6	15.4[b]
Timor-Leste	..	..	..	..	..	..	−20.0	50.0	16.7	14.3[c]	25.0[d]
Viet Nam	34.4	33.2	26.6	1.9	23.3	25.5	3.8	11.2	20.6	31.5[m]	20.0[d]
Developed ESCAP economies											
Australia	11.7	13.7	4.7	−11.3	0.1	12.7	0.4	2.8	8.6	21.5	20.8[l]
Japan	12.1	−7.2	2.4	−7.9	8.1	14.1	−15.6	3.3	13.7	19.3	7.1[l]
New Zealand	14.2	5.0	−2.5	−18.0	6.6	4.0	5.8	5.2	15.1	24.5	4.5[l]

Sources: ESCAP, calculated from national sources; International Monetary Fund, IMF Direction of Trade Statistics Database; and Country Reports Series; Economist Intelligence Unit, *Country Reports*; United Nations Economic Commission for Europe, *Economic Survey of Europe, 2005 No.1* (United Nations publication, Sales No. E.05.II.E.7); World Bank, *East Asia Update, November 2005: Countering Global Shocks* (Wahsington, D.C., IMF, 2005); ASEAN website <http://www.aseansec.org>; and website of the Commonwealth of Independent States Inter-State Statistical Committee <www.cisstat.com>.

a Refers to first 10 months of 2005.
b Refers to first 11 months of 2005.
c Estimate.
d Projection.
e Refers to first 9 months of 2005.
f Federal State Statistics Service (Rosstat) data including trade flows not crossing the Russian borders such as off-board fish sales and estimates of the value of goods exported or imported by individuals within an approved duty-free quota.
g Refers to first 6 months of 2005.
h Fiscal year data from 1999 to 2005.
i Fiscal year data.
j Fiscal year data from 2002 to 2005.
k Provisional.
l Refers to first 8 months of 2005.
m Preliminary.

Table B.12. Merchandise import growth rates

(Percentage)

	1995	1996	1997	1998	1999	2000	2001	2002	2003	2004	2005
Developing ESCAP economies											
East and North-East Asia											
China	14.2	5.1	2.5	–1.5	18.2	35.8	8.2	21.2	39.9	36.0	16.7[a]
Hong Kong, China	19.1	3.0	5.1	–11.6	–2.7	18.5	–5.5	3.3	11.7	16.9	10.6[b]
Macao, China	–3.8	–2.1	4.1	–6.1	4.3	10.6	5.8	6.0	8.9	26.3	11.7[b]
Mongolia	32.0	4.5	5.3	8.2	–2.6	19.2	2.5	8.7	9.8	23.5[c]	9.7[d]
Republic of Korea	32.0	11.3	–3.8	–35.5	28.4	34.0	–12.1	7.8	17.6	25.5	16.2[a]
North and Central Asia											
Armenia	71.1	27.0	4.2	1.1	–10.1	9.1	–0.9	12.5	29.6	5.6	30.0[b]
Azerbaijan	–14.1	43.9	–17.4	35.6	–3.8	13.1	22.1	16.4	57.6	33.4	21.0[b]
Georgia	13.9	78.4	37.4	–6.4	–31.9	8.1	5.2	6.7	56.1	61.9	37.0[b]
Kazakhstan	6.9	11.4	1.4	1.1	–15.2	37.0	27.6	2.1	27.7	52.0	37.0[b]
Kyrgyzstan	64.7	60.5	–15.4	18.8	–28.7	–7.7	–15.7	25.7	22.1	31.2	16.0[b]
Russian Federation[f]	24.0	8.6	5.9	–19.4	–31.9	13.5	19.8	13.5	23.6	31.8	31.0[b]
Tajikistan	48.1	–17.5	12.3	–5.2	–6.8	1.8	1.9	4.8	22.2	56.1	4.0[b]
Turkmenistan	–7.1	–25.9	17.0	–14.8	48.8	18.7	32.0	–9.8	18.5	32.2	13.0[c,g]
Uzbekistan	5.6	71.5	–11.2	–25.3	–4.0	–5.0	–1.3	–13.8	9.8	27.2[g]	35.3[c,g]
Pacific island											
Fiji	0.6	14.0	–10.1	–19.7	25.3	–7.9	4.8	9.2	39.1	14.6	13.7[h]
Papua New Guinea	7.8	23.3	–1.6	–27.0	–0.1	–7.0	–6.4	14.6	10.3	22.4	0.4[e]
Samoa[i]	15.1	7.4	1.2	–1.9	26.5	–12.6	19.2	11.5	–1.0	12.5	16.9[d]
Solomon Islands	8.6	–1.9	42.4	–40.8	–12.9	–11.9	–7.6	–31.2	36.8	15.8[c]	42.1[d]
Tonga[g, j]	35.4	–8.6	–12.9	18.6	–21.2	10.2	–8.3	11.6	22.3	11.4	25.5
Vanuatu	6.4	5.5	–3.5	–5.6	9.3	–7.2	0.8	–4.5	16.4	6.0[c]	14.1[d]
South and South-West Asia											
Afghanistan[k]	..	..	..	..	..	..	–8.9	52.5	50.9	2.1	17.9[d]
Bangladesh[j]	..	18.8	3.2	5.1	6.5	4.6	11.5[g]	–8.5	13.1	12.9	22.0
Bhutan[k]	4.6	14.1	18.4	3.7	19.2	14.0	–8.3	9.9	1.7	29.2[l]	60.8[c]
India[j]	21.6	12.1	4.6	–7.1	16.5	4.6	–2.8	14.5	24.4	48.4[c]	28.0[d]
Iran (Islamic Republic of)[g,j]	1.2	17.3	–5.8	1.2	–6.0	12.3	20.2	21.6	34.1	23.9	12.5[h]
Maldives[g]	20.9	12.6	15.6	1.5	13.6	–3.4	1.3	–0.5	20.2	36.9	23.2[h]
Nepal[j]	21.9	6.1	21.2	–11.8	–11.0	22.1	–0.2	–10.6	13.6	15.7	–1.1[c]
Pakistan[j]	21.4	13.6	0.8	–14.9	–6.8	9.3	4.1	–3.6	18.2	27.6	32.3
Sri Lanka	11.4	2.4	7.8	0.4	1.5	22.4	–18.4	2.2	9.3	19.9	14.7[d]
Turkey	53.5	22.2	11.3	–5.4	–11.4	34.0	–24.0	24.5	34.5	40.7	21.0[a]

(Continued on next page)

Table B.12 *(continued)*

(Percentage)

	1995	1996	1997	1998	1999	2000	2001	2002	2003	2004	2005
South-East Asia											
Brunei Darussalam	7.2	18.8	−10.3	−26.0	−43.1	7.5	−7.9	23.9	−17.7	22.4	6.0[m]
Cambodia[g]	59.5	−9.7	1.9	−1.7	36.5	21.9	8.0	10.6	10.4	24.4	16.7[c]
Indonesia[g]	..	8.1	4.5	−30.9	−4.2	31.9	−14.1	2.8	10.9	28.0	32.1[e]
Lao People's Democratic Republic	..	..	−6.0	−14.7	0.3	−3.4	−4.7	−12.4	3.4	9.5	35.6[c]
Malaysia	25.5	2.0	−27.2	5.7	9.1	25.1	−10.0	8.3	4.7	25.9	8.9[b]
Myanmar	..	..	12.7	16.4	−10.7	−0.9	9.9	−9.9	−11.6	3.7	7.3[c,g]
Philippines[g]	24.4	22.2	10.8	−17.5	3.6	12.2	−4.2	7.2	14.2	8.8	0.3[a]
Singapore	21.5	5.6	0.8	−23.3	9.4	21.3	−13.9	0.4	9.9	28.1	14.7[e]
Thailand	31.9	0.6	−13.4	−33.8	16.9	31.3	−3.0	4.6	17.4	25.7	26.0[b]
Timor-Leste	..	..	..	..	..	..	17.4	−6.3	−16.9	−8.6[c]	5.9[d]
Viet Nam	40.0	36.6	4.0	−0.8	2.1	33.2	3.7	21.8	27.9	26.5[n]	22.5[d]
Developed ESCAP economies											
Australia	14.8	7.1	0.4	−1.7	7.6	3.3	−10.0	14.4	21.8	22.3	15.7[m]
Japan	22.6	4.0	−3.1	−17.1	10.7	22.1	−8.0	−3.4	13.6	18.7	14.6[m]
New Zealand	15.6	7.0	−1.4	−13.6	14.3	−2.9	−4.3	13.0	22.4	25.0	14.6[m]

Sources: ESCAP, calculated from national sources; International Monetary Fund, IMF Direction of Trade Statistics Database; and Country Reports Series; Economist Intelligence Unit, *Country Reports*; United Nations Economic Commission for Europe, *Economic Survey of Europe, 2005 No.1* (United Nations publication, Sales No. E.05.II.E.7); World Bank, *East Asia Update, November 2005: Countering Global Shocks* (Wahsington, D.C., IMF, 2005); ASEAN website <http://www.aseansec.org>; and website of the Commonwealth of Independent States Inter-State Statistical Committee <www.cisstat.com>.

[a] Refers to first 10 months of 2005.
[b] Refers to first 11 months of 2005.
[c] Estimate.
[d] Projection.
[e] Refers to first 9 months of 2005.
[f] Federal State Statistics Service (Rosstat) data including trade flows not crossing the Russian borders such as off-board fish sales and estimates of the value of goods exported or imported by individuals within an approved duty-free quota.
[g] f.o.b. value(s).
[h] Refers to first 6 months of 2005.
[i] Fiscal year data from 1999 to 2005.
[j] Fiscal year data.
[k] Fiscal year data from 2002 to 2005.
[l] Provisional.
[m] Refers to first 8 months of 2005.
[n] Preliminary.

Table B.13. Annual average exchange rates

(Local currency per United States dollar)

	Currency	1995	1996	1997	1998	1999	2000	2001	2002	2003	2004	2005[a]
Developing ESCAP economies												
East and North-East Asia												
China	yuan renminbi (Y)	8.3514	8.3142	8.2898	8.2790	8.2783	8.2785	8.2771	8.2770	8.2770	8.2781	8.1962
Hong Kong, China	Hong Kong dollar (HK$)	7.7400	7.7343	7.7421	7.7453	7.7575	7.7912	7.7990	7.7990	7.7870	7.7882	7.7781
Mongolia	tugrik (Tug)	448.61	548.40	789.99	840.83	1 021.87	1 076.67	1097.70	1 110.31	1 146.54	1 185.28	1 142.09
Republic of Korea	won (W)	771.27	804.45	951.29	1 401.44	1 188.82	1 130.96	1 290.99	1 251.09	1 191.61	1 145.32	1 026.05
Taiwan Province of China	new Taiwan dollar (NTD)	26.486	27.458	28.703	33.445	32.266	31.225	33.800	34.575	34.418	33.422	32.200
North and Central Asia												
Armenia	dram (dram)	405.91	414.04	490.85	504.92	535.06	539.53	555.08	573.35	578.76	533.45	457.79
Azerbaijan	Azeri manat (M)	4 413.54	4 301.26	3 985.38	3 869.00	4 120.17	4 474.15	4 656.58	4 860.82	4 910.73	4 913.48	4 726.64
Georgia	lari (L)	..	1.2628	1.2975	1.3898	2.0245	1.9762	2.0730	2.1957	2.1457	1.9167	1.8147
Kazakhstan	tenge (T)	60.95	67.30	75.44	78.30	119.52	142.13	146.74	153.28	149.58	137.16	132.91
Kyrgyzstan	som (som)	10.820	12.810	17.362	20.838	39.008	47.704	48.378	46.937	43.648	42.650	40.990
Russian Federation	ruble (R)	4.5592	5.1208	5.7848	9.7051	24.6199	28.1292	29.1685	31.3485	30.6920	28.9260	28.2789
Tajikistan	somoni	0.12	0.30	0.56	0.78	1.24	2.08	2.37	2.76	3.06	2.97	3.12
Turkmenistan	Turkmen manat (M)	111.9	3 257.7	4 143.4	4 890.2	5 200.0	5 200.0	5 200.0	5 200.0	5 200.0	5 200.0	..
Uzbekistan	som (som)	29.78	40.07	62.92	94.49	124.63	236.61	423.31	769.50	971.30	1 020.00	..
Pacific island economies												
Cook Islands	New Zealand dollar ($NZ)	1.5152	1.4543	1.5083	1.8632	1.8886	2.1863	2.3776	2.1542	1.7182	1.5152	1.4085
Fiji	Fiji dollar (F$)	1.4100	1.4033	1.4437	1.9868	1.9696	2.1286	2.2766	2.1869	1.8958	1.7300	1.6901
Kiribati	Australian dollar ($A)	1.3514	1.2773	1.3439	1.5888	1.5497	1.7173	1.9320	1.8386	1.5340	1.3514	1.3158
Papua New Guinea	kina (K)	1.2821	1.3179	1.4337	2.0580	2.5387	2.7647	3.3738	3.8865	3.5537	3.2258	3.1250
Samoa	tala (WS$)	2.4722	2.4618	2.5562	2.9429	3.0120	3.2712	3.4722	3.3750	2.9976	2.7778	2.7027
Solomon Islands	Solomon Islands dollar (SI$)	3.4100	3.5664	3.7169	4.8156	4.8381	5.0889	5.2780	6.7488	7.5059	7.4800	7.5424
Tonga	pa'anga (T$)	1.2700	1.2323	1.2635	1.4921	1.5991	1.7585	2.1236	2.1952	2.1420	1.9700	1.9506
Tuvalu	Australian dollar ($A)	1.3514	1.2773	1.3439	1.5888	1.5497	1.7173	1.9320	1.8386	1.5340	1.3514	1.3158
Vanuatu	vatu (VT)	112.11	111.72	115.87	127.52	129.08	137.64	145.31	139.20	122.19	111.79	109.82
South and South-West Asia												
Afghanistan	afghani (Af)	..	18.10	25.10	37.48	48.86	67.31	55.73	44.78	49.19	47.79	..
Bangladesh	taka (TK)	40.280	41.794	43.892	46.906	49.085	52.142	55.807	57.888	58.150	59.510	64.341
Bhutan	ngultrum (Nu)	32.430	35.433	36.313	41.259	43.055	44.942	47.186	48.610	46.581	45.320	44.078
India	Indian rupee (Rs)	32.43	35.43	36.31	41.26	43.05	44.94	47.19	48.61	46.58	45.32	44.10
Iran (Islamic Republic of)	rial (Rls)	1 747.93	1 750.76	1 752.92	1 751.86	1 752.93	1 764.43	1 753.56	6 906.96	8 193.89	8 613.99	8 967.63
Maldives	rufiyaa (Rf)	11.77	11.77	11.77	11.77	11.77	11.77	12.24	12.80	12.80	12.80	12.84
Nepal	Nepalese rupee (NRs)	51.890	56.692	58.010	65.976	68.239	71.094	74.949	77.877	76.141	73.670	71.698

(Continued on next page)

Table B.13 *(continued)*

(Local currency per United States dollar)

	Currency	*1995*	*1996*	*1997*	*1998*	*1999*	*2000*	*2001*	*2002*	*2003*	*2004*	*2005[a]*
Pakistan	Pakistan rupee (PRs)	31.640	36.080	41.110	45.050	49.500	53.648	61.927	59.724	57.752	58.260	59.524
Sri Lanka	Sri Lanka rupee (SLRs)	51.250	55.271	58.995	64.450	70.635	77.005	89.383	95.662	96.521	101.190	100.523
Turkey	Turkish lira (LT)	0.05	0.08	0.15	0.26	0.42	0.63	1.23	1.51	1.50	1.43	1.35
South-East Asia												
Cambodia	riel (CR)	2 450.83	2 624.08	2 946.25	3 744.42	3 807.83	3 840.75	3 916.33	3 912.08	3 973.33	4 016.25	4 109.72
Indonesia	rupiah (Rp)	2 248.61	2 342.30	2 909.40	10 013.60	7 855.20	8 421.78	10 260.19	9 311.19	8 577.13	8 938.85	9 710.36
Lao People's Democratic Republic	new kip (NK)	804.69	921.02	1 259.98	3 298.33	7 102.03	7 887.64	8 954.58	10 056.33	10 569.04	10 585.50	10 655.25
Malaysia	ringgit (M$)	2.500	2.516	2.813	3.924	3.800	3.800	3.800	3.800	3.800	3.800	3.788
Myanmar	kyat (K)	5.6100	5.8609	6.1838	6.2738	6.2233	6.4257	6.6841	6.5734	6.0764	5.7500	5.9188
Philippines	Philippine peso (P)	25.710	26.216	29.471	40.893	39.089	44.192	50.993	51.604	54.203	56.040	55.105
Singapore	Singapore dollar (S$)	1.4200	1.4100	1.4848	1.6736	1.6950	1.7240	1.7917	1.7906	1.7422	1.6900	1.6641
Thailand	baht (B)	24.920	25.343	31.364	41.359	37.814	40.112	44.432	42.960	41.485	40.220	40.249
Viet Nam	dong (D)	11 038.3	11 032.6	11 683.3	13 268.0	13 943.2	14 167.7	14 725.2	15 279.5	15 509.6	15 827.1	15 873.9
Developed ESCAP economies												
Australia	Australian dollar ($A)	1.3486	1.2773	1.3439	1.5888	1.5497	1.7173	1.9320	1.8386	1.5340	1.3576	1.3158
Japan	yen (¥)	94.06	108.78	120.99	130.91	113.91	107.77	121.53	125.39	115.93	108.19	110.20
New Zealand	New Zealand dollar ($NZ)	1.5235	1.4543	1.5083	1.8632	1.8886	2.1863	2.3776	2.1542	1.7173	1.5060	1.4085

Sources: ESCAP, based on International Monetary Fund, *International Financial Statistics* (CD-ROM) (Washington, D.C., IMF, January 2006); and *The Economist*, various issues.

[a] Estimate.

Since the 1957 issue, the *Economic and Social Survey of Asia and the Pacific* has, in addition to a review of the current situation of the region, contained a study or studies of some major aspect or problem of the economies of the Asian and Pacific region, as specified below:

1957: Postwar problems of economic development
1958: Review of postwar industrialization
1959: Foreign trade of ECAFE primary exporting countries
1960: Public finance in the postwar period
1961: Economic growth of ECAFE countries
1962: Asia's trade with western Europe
1963: Imports substitution and export diversification
1964: Economic development and the role of the agricultural sector
1965: Economic development and human resources
1966: Aspects of the finance of development
1967: Policies and planning for export
1968: Economic problems of export-dependent countries. Implications of economic controls and liberalization
1969: Strategies for agricultural development. Intraregional trade as a growth strategy
1970: The role of foreign private investment in economic development and cooperation in the ECAFE region. Problems and prospects of the ECAFE region in the Second Development Decade
1971: Economic growth and social justice. Economic growth and employment. Economic growth and income distribution
1972: First biennial review of social and economic developments in ECAFE developing countries during the Second United Nations Development Decade
1973: Education and employment
1974: Mid-term review and appraisal of the International Development Strategy for the Second United Nations Development Decade in the ESCAP region, 1974
1975: Rural development, the small farmer and institutional reform
1976: Biennial review and appraisal of the International Development Strategy at the regional level for the Second United Nations Development Decade in the ESCAP region, 1976
1977: The international economic crises and developing Asia and the Pacific
1978: Biennial review and appraisal at the regional level of the International Development Strategy for the Second United Nations Development Decade
1979: Regional development strategy for the 1980s
1980: Short-term economic policy aspects of the energy situation in the ESCAP region
1981: Recent economic developments in major subregions of the ESCAP region
1982: Fiscal policy for development in the ESCAP region
1983: Implementing the International Development Strategy: major issues facing the developing ESCAP region
1984: Financing development
1985: Trade, trade policies and development
1986: Human resources development in Asia and the Pacific: problems, policies and perspectives
1987: International trade in primary commodities
1988: Recent economic and social developments
1989: Patterns of economic growth and structural transformation in the least developed and Pacific island countries of the ESCAP region: implications for development policy and planning for the 1990s
1990: Infrastructure development in the developing ESCAP region: needs, issues and policy options
1991: Challenges of macroeconomic management in the developing ESCAP region
1992: Expansion of investment and intraregional trade as a vehicle for enhancing regional economic cooperation and development in Asia and the Pacific
1993: Fiscal reform. Economic transformation and social development. Population dynamics: implications for development
1995: Reform and liberalization of the financial sector. Social security
1996: Enhancing the role of the private sector in development. The role of public expenditure in the provision of social services
1997: External financial and investment flows. Transport and communications
1998: Managing the external sector. Growth and equity
1999: Social impact of the economic crisis. Information technology, globalization, economic security and development
2000: Social security and safety nets. Economic and financial monitoring and surveillance
2001: Socio-economic implications of demographic dynamics. Financing for development
2002: The feasibility of achieving the millennium development goals in Asia and the Pacific. Regional development cooperation in Asia and the Pacific
2003: The role of public expenditure in the provision of education and health. Environment-poverty nexus revisited: linkages and policy options
2004: Poverty reduction strategies: tackling the multidimensional nature of poverty
2005: Dynamics of population ageing: how can Asia and the pacific respond?

READERSHIP SURVEY

The Poverty and Development Division of ESCAP is undertaking an evaluation of this publication, ***Economic and Social Survey of Asia and the Pacific 2006,*** with a view to making future issues more useful for our readers. We would appreciate it if you could complete this questionnaire and return it, at your earliest convenience, to:

Chief
Poverty and Development Division
ESCAP, United Nations Building
Rajadamnern Nok Avenue
Bangkok 10200, THAILAND

QUESTIONNAIRE

	Excellent	***Very good***	***Average***	***Poor***
1. Please indicate your assessment of the *quality* of the publication on:				
• Presentation/format	4	3	2	1
• Readability	4	3	2	1
• Timeliness of information	4	3	2	1
• Coverage of subject matter	4	3	2	1
• Analytical rigour	4	3	2	1
• Overall quality	4	3	2	1
2. How *useful* is the publication for your work?				
• Provision of information	4	3	2	1
• Clarification of issues	4	3	2	1
• Its findings	4	3	2	1
• Policy suggestions	4	3	2	1
• Overall usefulness	4	3	2	1

3. Please give examples of how this publication has contributed to your work:

....

....

....

....

4. **Suggestions for improving the publication:**

....

....

....

....

5. **Your background information, please:**

Name: ....

Title/position: ....

Institution: ....

Office address: ....

....

Please use additional sheets of paper, if required, to answer the questions.
Thank you for your kind cooperation in completing this questionnaire.